AF844905

# Legislating International Organization

# Legislating International Organization:

## THE US CONGRESS, THE IMF, AND THE WORLD BANK

Kathryn C. Lavelle

OXFORD
UNIVERSITY PRESS

OXFORD
UNIVERSITY PRESS

Oxford University Press, Inc., publishes works that further
Oxford University's objective of excellence
in research, scholarship, and education.

Oxford New York
Auckland Cape Town Dar es Salaam Hong Kong Karachi
Kuala Lumpur Madrid Melbourne Mexico City Nairobi
New Delhi Shanghai Taipei Toronto

With offices in
Argentina Austria Brazil Chile Czech Republic France Greece
Guatemala Hungary Italy Japan Poland Portugal Singapore
South Korea Switzerland Thailand Turkey Ukraine Vietnam

Copyright © 2011 by Oxford University Press

Published by Oxford University Press, Inc.
198 Madison Avenue, New York, New York 10016

www.oup.com

Oxford is a registered trademark of Oxford University Press

All rights reserved. No part of this publication may be reproduced,
stored in a retrieval system, or transmitted, in any form or by any means,
electronic, mechanical, photocopying, recording, or otherwise,
without the prior permission of Oxford University Press.

Library of Congress Cataloging-in-Publication Data
Lavelle, Kathryn C.
Legislating international organization : the US Congress, the IMF, and the World Bank / Kathryn C. Lavelle.
p. cm.
Includes bibliographical references and index.
ISBN 978-0-19-976534-8 1. International Monetary Fund.
2. World Bank. 3. United States. Congress. 4. Monetary policy. I. Title.
HG3881.5.I58L38 2011
332.1′52—dc22 2011006171

To Mom, who taught me to love teaching, and

To Dad, who taught me to love the study of politics

# CONTENTS

# PREFACE

This is a book about the politics behind the IMF and World Bank in the United States Congress. It is a historical study that draws upon mid–twentieth century pluralist and realist traditions to understand how policy is formulated. Yet it is also methodologically innovative. To analyze the relationship among national and international institutions, I spent nine months as an American Political Science Association Congressional Fellow, working on the staff of the House Committee on Financial Services. While I knew from previous research that interest groups play a role in the relationship, I wanted an assignment in Congress where I could observe them firsthand in an area that had not been previously studied. On interviews with multiple personal and committee offices during the placement period, staffers assured me that interest groups are impossible to miss no matter where I worked because, in the words of one, "they are here every day." Extending the insights of that experience to the academic discipline of political science forced me to confront the deep divide in the discipline between the study of interest groups in American politics, and the study of nongovernmental organizations (NGOs) and transnational advocacy movements in international relations. The two subfields rarely speak directly to each other and frequently employ research methodologies that analyze power and outcomes differently across time. The task of bringing them together has left me obligated to individuals and organizations as wide-ranging as the topic itself.

My first debt is to those individuals who were willing to "think outside the box" and support this project before it took the shape that it did. Jeff Biggs and Veronica Jones at the American Political Science Association, and Chairman Barney Frank, Jeanne Roslanowick, Scott Morris, and Daniel McGlinchey of the House Committee on Financial Services taught me everything I know about Congress with their unfailing wit, good humor, and inordinate patience in explaining "how a bill becomes a law." Maria Giesta, Peter Kovar, Patty Lord, Michael Paese, Jim Segel, Dennis Shaul, and Dave Smith furthered my education in the practice of politics on a daily basis when I was working on the Hill. My cohort of political scientists in the 2006–2007 fellowship year, including Michelle Chin, Brendan Doherty, and Jessica Gerrity, were similarly invaluable in helping me to understand the academic literature on Congress. Not least, my former colleague Frances Lee impressed me with the opportunities the fellowship could provide, based on her own experience, and offered important scholarly input into the project. While fellows are prohibited from gathering data for publication during the year, an insider's knowledge of the process and wide range of contacts gained from the program were invaluable in assembling materials available in the public domain related to my own experience.

After a year back in Cleveland, I was fortunate to receive a residential fellowship from the Woodrow Wilson International Center for Scholars in Washington, DC. The center provided an unparalleled environment to complete the research and writing of an interdisciplinary book that takes history and the world of practical politics seriously. I was able to attend the annual meetings of the IMF and World Bank in fall 2008 and spring 2009 as well as attend additional NGO coalition meetings connected to IMF and World Bank appropriations. While I was at the center, numerous individuals offered their own understandings of the policy process inside Congress, the executive branch, and the advocacy community. In particular, I appreciate the help of David Biette, John Dysland, Dagne Gizaw, Lee Hamilton, Kent Hughes, Michelle Kamalich, David Klaus, Bill Krist, John Sewell, Janet Spikes, Philippa Strum Mike Van Dusen, and Don Wolfensberger. While I was in Washington, many individuals outside the Wilson Center generously extended their time and insights, which helped to fill in the gaps between the archival record, congressional testimony, and official media. I thank Ray Ahearn, Farrah Barrios, James Boughton, Thomas Dawson, John Donaldson, William Frenzel, James Galbraith, Jo Marie Griesgraber, Barry Hager, Jerome Levinson, Karin Lissakers, Barbara Matthews, Allan Meltzer, Jim Orr, Sergio Pombo, Susan Rzemien, Jonathan Sanford, Micaela Schrader, Ted Truman, Marc Uzan, Samy Watson, Marty Weiss, and others who asked to remain anonymous.

During the course of drafting the manuscript, useful discussions on the topic and theoretical orientation were provided by the Institute for Global and International Studies at The George Washington University, and the School of International Studies at American University. Other fellows at the Wilson Center in my cohort likewise advanced the theoretical component with their numerous discussions during the course of the year. Special thanks go to Nitsan Chorev, Bettye Collier-Thomas, David Edelstein, Rich Friman, Deirdre LePan, Jennifer Mittelstadt, Kimberly Morgan, Liselotte Odegaard, Gul Berna Ozcan, George Shambaugh, Samer Shehata, and Jodi White.

Once a draft of the manuscript was complete, I benefited enormously from extensive discussions of the subject in Canada, where I could consider the politics of my own country outside of it. Eric Helleiner and Jonathan Kirschner generously organized a manuscript workshop at the University of Waterloo. The participants in the workshop, Randy Germain, Randy Henning, Devesh Kapur, Bessma Momani, Mike Tierney, and Kate Weaver, contributed such insightful commentary that it was necessary to revise the entire project.

The penultimate draft profited from a semester at the Munk Centre at the University of Toronto, where I had time, peace, and quiet to redraft it. I am particularly grateful to Louis Pauly for making this opportunity possible and adding his own insights to the project. Tina Lagopoulos worked constantly to make my stay at the Centre pleasant. Special thanks go to those who offered comments while I was there, including Steven Bernstein, Al Berry, Ian Clark, Stephen Clarkson, Joelle Dumouchel, Jennifer Jeffs, Renan Levine, Troy Lundblad, Sylvia Ostry, and Joe Wong.

The unsung heroes of academic research are archivists around the world who make the right information available to the people who need it. Premala Isaac at the IMF archives in Washington, Ansoumane Diara and Bernhardine Pejovic at the League of Nations Archives in Geneva, Erica Mosner at the archives of the Institute for Advanced Study in Princeton, and Kenneth Rose at the Rockefeller Archive Center in Tarrytown all provided a good deal of assistance and input. Although not himself an archivist, Dr. Roger Horowitz at the archives of the Center for the History of Business, Technology and Society in Hagley, Delaware, provided valuable commentary and advice on the Bretton Woods section of the book. I was able to use the archival resources of the Hagley Museum and Library, having received generous research support. Special thanks also go to Carol Lockman for making my stay there so pleasant.

It would have been impossible to obtain the necessary fellowships, funding, and momentum for this book without the selfless contribution of academic colleagues who were willing to discuss it informally and write letters of support. None of this would have been possible without Phil Cerny, Jerry Cohen, Leslie Elliot-Armijo, John Echeverri-Gent, Randall Germain, Randy Henning, Pete Moore, Lou Pauly, Tony Porter, Elliot Posner, Herman Schwartz, Tim Sinclair, Mireya Solis, and Joseph White.

Additional funding was provided by the Long Chair in World Affairs at Case Western Reserve University. My colleagues have graciously accommodated my numerous absences from campus. I am particularly grateful to Alec Lamis, my ACES mentors Dave Hammack and Vincent McHale, and my writing coach Mary Murray. I also appreciate the efforts of Jenny Ross and Julia Smearman, my research assistants at the Wilson Center, Emily Moorman, and Ali Hasanali, my research assistant at Case. Final thanks go to Dave McBride and the anonymous reviewers at Oxford University Press who helped me pull the final book together.

# Legislating International Organization

# Introduction

This study investigates Congress as an institution that operates in the international struggle for power and resources. Whereas studies of Congress in the field of American politics understand it to be a formal political structure that favors some efforts and hinders others within the governmental process, I understand it to be a political institution both within the American system of checks and balances, as well as within formal and informal processes of *global* governance.[1] In the US system, its chief institutional lever is the act of legislating. In the international system, the act of introducing a bill, holding hearings on it, and drafting correspondence to leaders on related policy issues likewise prompts political responses in multilateral institutions, subsequently shaping their roles and operations, whether or not the individual bill actually becomes a law. Members of Congress who hope to influence policy direct the lever of legislation by working with domestic constituencies.

Over time, these domestic constituencies have been affected by changes in the structure of the international political economy, chiefly the trajectory of the Cold War and the rise of transnational capital markets, which compels some interest groups to become active on an issue and others to stay out of it. In the course of their development, they have become enmeshed in the activities of international networks. The literature on transnational activist movements in international relations misses the domestic political institutional dimension of the story because it is focused on the transnational nature of the movements.[2] The literature on domestic political institutions in American politics misses the international dimension.[3] In connecting the two literatures, this study reveals how multilateralism has been grounded in distinct domestic constituencies in American politics, as well as the problems that have occurred when it has not.

My specific focus is on the legislation concerning the activities of the two international financial institutions (IFIs) established at the end of the Second World War: the International Monetary Fund (IMF), which was created to stabilize the international payments system, and the World Bank, which was created to generate long-term lending for recovery and development.[4] The role of Congress with respect to these international organizations (IOs) is unique among the world's democratic donor states, because it is the "indispensable legislature."

US membership was a key factor that allowed them to begin operations after the war. Both the IMF and the World Bank are headquartered in Washington, DC, and the US has appropriated the largest sums to them. Both require 85% of their total voting power to amend articles, change quotas, or make other significant changes. With the US share above 15% of the total votes, this requirement effectively gives it a veto over major decisions. Since Congress makes policy and does not ratify it in the Parliamentary tradition, the executive branch, interest groups, representatives of the US Treasury Department, and other interested constituencies must consult with Congress each time key decisions take place.

Most of these actors do not welcome the congressional role. The legislature appears to be an obstacle course through which they must navigate to secure funds. Most members do not devote a great deal of attention to IMF and World Bank issues on an ongoing basis, which complicates the process. Yet other members *do* devote attention to these issues. While they are small in number, they have worked with allies in the executive branch, private-sector interest groups, nongovernmental organizations (NGOs), and even those inside the IFIs, to champion dramatic change on the orientation of the IMF and World Bank toward human rights, poverty alleviation, women, organized labor, debt relief, transparency, and the environment by using bills to effect cooperation and compliance. Moreover, while the IFIs are not high priorities on the congressional agenda, the results of legislative involvement matter greatly to millions of those people living in poverty who are the subjects of the lending programs and projects the IFIs seek to address.

Given the impediments in domestic politics, how is it that the IFIs receive funding through Congress at all? And in the international sphere, how is the US legislature able to exert policy influence greater than, and different from, the legislatures in other advanced, industrial democracies? This inquiry reveals that contrary to conventional understandings that the US opposes multilateral solutions to the world's problems, Congress has provided consistent support for the IFIs, although successful collaboration depends on the policies that the Bank and Fund follow. The reliance on procedure, however, means that concerned members of Congress play a role in influencing policy toward multilateralism that is often overlooked. To begin to understand the nature of Congress as an international, as well as a domestic, political institution, I detail how members of Congress, acting with their allies in the interest group and NGO community, use the institutional levers of legislating, such as letters, hearings, and amendments to bills, to advocate for policy change in IOs. Whereas studies of American politics commonly understand legislative advocacy to be lobbying activities seeking to shape an individual bill within the institution, I use the term *congressional advocacy* to refer to the process wherein American legislators use the institutional mechanisms of Congress to influence public policy and resource-allocation decisions outside of formal American institutions of rule and within international organizations.

In my view, the story of congressional advocacy toward the IFIs is one where domestic banking interests become increasingly entangled in international concerns. The formal legislative process acts as a filter for the broader American political system, itself operating through the work of interest groups that help shape legislators' preferences while working on issues. Interest groups are an important part of the process because as allies they provide information, help to craft bills, attract wider attention to causes, and offer expert testimony as legislation moves along on Capitol Hill. As Congress has become increasingly enmeshed in the international political system, the legislative process also attracts the efforts of advocacy groups that work in transnational networks on behalf of the global community. In addition, foreign governments can, and do, work with lobbyists as long as they meet certain reporting standards, although foreign governments cannot donate money to legislators. The upshot is that multilateralism in the American political system has been driven from the bottom up, as well as from the top down, by constituencies for international organizations in the US system.

An exogenous crisis, advocacy campaign, or interbranch dispute over legislative powers within the American government prompts congressional advocacy. Outcomes vary because the US legislature is a collective body and not a monolithic institution. Different external interests, including the international organizations themselves, may try to use alternative tools to block policy changes others may promote. Since it is a forum as well as an actor, it can frequently appear as if the institution advocates on both sides of an issue. Nonetheless, history shows that congressional advocacy is the most supportive of the work of IFIs, in terms of providing funding and making minimal policy requests, when bipartisan, domestic constituencies whose work resonates with their missions are mobilized on the IMF and World Bank's behalf. It is the most adversarial when a crisis or campaign prompts members to call for change, and the IMF or World Bank lacks defenders. Particularly in these moments of crisis, members of Congress and their allies in civil society have shaped the contours of the multilateral form in a manner that is sporadic but potent.

Therefore, to understand the relationship between Congress and the Bretton Woods financial institutions, it is necessary to investigate this formal political institution as well as the broader configuration of domestic American politics with respect to their work in international finance. When formal processes are taken into consideration, it becomes apparent that the separation of powers inherent in the structure of the American political system affects the functioning and operations of the World Bank and IMF, unlike other parliaments in industrial democracies, for two main reasons: First of all, Congress is more open to group interests than they are, making it an avenue through which national and international interest groups can pursue their goals in concert with sympathetic members. Second, Congress is an agent in its own right, with its own stake in the outcome of the Madisonian checks-and-balances system outlined by the framers of the Constitution. The tension between the legislature and executive is not constant and reflects myriad circumstances.[5] Yet even in periods where Congress is relatively less assertive vis-à-vis the executive, it tends to protect its budgetary discretion.

## The Problem Relationship

The problem examined in this book is a relationship. Thus, it is not a conventional inquiry in international relations because it does not investigate the problem of relations among states. Rather, it examines the relationship between a legislature and two international organizations in order to understand the domestic institutional bases of support for economic multilateralism in their most powerful, democratic, member. Within the legislature, the relationship might not appear to be a problem at all. Congress tends to be a reactive body, particularly in US foreign policy. Most members do not devote a great deal of time to IMF and World Bank issues, because the geographic allocation of seats in both the House and Senate makes district and state concerns much higher priorities.[6] Financial politics do not operate like trade politics, because in the trade area the costs and benefits of a given measure accrue to specific firms and sectors that organize and take their concerns to individual members of Congress for action. In the multilateral financial area, the benefits of systemic financial stability are distributed so widely across the US population, and the time lag between action on a legislative measure and its policy outcome is so long, that societal groups lack incentives to organize support for the international organizations that promote stability: the IMF and World Bank.

However, actors outside the institution do view the US Congress as a considerable problem. Representatives to the IMF and World Bank from other countries often view Congress as another sign of the intrusive, arbitrary exercise of American power that stalls budgetary outlays and compels the IFIs to adopt policies they would not otherwise choose to. Adherents to the unitary executive model of government in studies of US Constitutional law subscribe to the view that the president controls the entire executive branch of government. Those favoring a strongly unitary executive would advocate for the strongest possible role for the president in foreign policy, with minimal congressional involvement.[7] Americans' rating of their own legislature is almost always lower than their rating of the sitting president.[8] Scholars in international political economy have pointed out that the separation of powers in the US system poses a direct challenge to its global leadership because the coalition-building practices of domestic political parties obstruct the formation of consistent policies.[9] These coalitions comprise domestic political interests that are deeply entrenched in American society.

Therefore, congressional advocacy is a problem for international organizations; yet an understanding of the advocacy of the institution toward an IO is critical to understanding their operations because it provides the missing link among the literatures on domestic interest groups, transnational advocacy networks, and the formal operations of an American political institution that is necessary to permit and facilitate the functioning of effective global arrangements. History provides the best window for analysis because the institutions of Congress, the IMF, and World Bank have all been subject to dramatic changes driven by the international political economy.

Admittedly, relationships run in two directions. In focusing on the objective of Congress to influence an IO, this study systematically emphasizes the legislature-to-IO direction. Nonetheless, implicit in the explanation for policy outcomes in the IMF and World Bank is their own agency, or ability to operate through the same channels themselves to generate support and seek to influence Congress. Thus, the study details the IMF, World Bank, and US Treasury Department's repeated success in gaining funding—notwithstanding that it is frequently delayed and comes with undesirable (from some participants' perspectives) conditions attached. Rather than ignoring the agency of the IMF and World Bank, I show how, despite official restrictions on formal lobbying activity, a part of the unfolding of this narrative involves the actions of the IFIs themselves that have become increasingly adept at navigating the same congressional channels to present their interests to members of Congress, albeit in concert with the US Treasury. Traditionally, the World Bank has been the more effective of the two in this regard because the president has been an American national. However, in recent times the IMF has also fostered a network of contacts on Capitol Hill through which to provide information and work with organized interests to promote mutual goals.

## The Institution of Congress as an Advocate in International Politics

This book questions both international relations and legislative studies alike: How has the US legislature provided so much financial support for economic multilateralism in the face of significant apathy and outright opposition to it from various interests in domestic American politics, and at the same time influenced policy outcomes in the IMF and World Bank? I argue that the complexities of the appropriations process present opportunities for members to provide the requisite material support, yet they also shape US policy toward the IFIs because members of Congress active on these issues must create compromise legislation that will generate sufficient support to make it through. The history demonstrates surprisingly consistent support for multilateralism, albeit support with strings attached. The "strings" are derived from groups pursuing policy goals through sympathetic channels. The groups themselves are formed and re-formed in response to broader shifts in the structure of international lending activity.

Thus, since most of the policy changes originate elsewhere, Congress serves as a transnational conduit for reform. Nonetheless, there are instances when initiatives for change *do* originate in the legislature. They do so because Congress is seeking to preserve its role as an institution within the branches of the US government, and not advocating specific policy measures toward the IFIs. Chiefly, members have inserted provisions into IFI legislation that preserve the legislature's budgetary discretion and other authority in relation to the executive branch. The dual dimensions of policy conduit and institutional assertion tend to be lost in studies that focus exclusively on either the international relations aspects of accountability mechanisms of Congress in relation to the IFIs, or on American politics analyses of roll-call votes on the floor of the House of Representatives.[10] Overlooking one side or the other tends to mischaracterize the relationship as overly anti-multilateral, isolationist, or internationally uncooperative.[11]

To understand how this support has been configured and reconfigured across time, I examine stages of the legislative process that require broad constituencies for passage, particularly those involving funding and that have contained significant policy initiatives for the Bank and the Fund. Because these processes are handled by a relatively few members who devote resources to their involvement in these issues and know how to maneuver within the system, an understanding of legislative procedure is essential. As the IMF's importance has waxed and waned, and the World Bank has increasingly relied on funding that must be resupplied every three years, Congress has been able to exert influence through a variety of formal and informal channels that have evolved during the same years. Such legislative involvement reinforces US influence on the organizations overall, and it also opens new avenues for a range of national and international interest groups to press for their interests outside the confines of formal party organization or national representation. Therefore, the distinctive features of each stage of the relationship result from a combination of exogenous changes in the international political economy and endogenous institutional change in Congress.

The most significant exogenous changes from the international political economy have resulted from the buildup, progression, and end of the Cold War, as well as the restoration of international lending after World War II. At first, large international banks borrowed from depositors in one country and then lent that money to other borrowers in the same or other countries. Thus, banks were the traditional intermediaries. Over time, borrowers entered lending markets directly by issuing their own bonds or by using increasingly sophisticated instruments, like asset-backed securities. Depositors and borrowers from banks have similar interests insofar as the time frame of the arrangement, its terms, and its risks can be constructed in a more systematic fashion. Those who participate directly in securities markets may do so for a variety of reasons and seek a variety of risk profiles handled through even more sophisticated derivative products. They may seek short-term profit or long-term appreciation of assets. They may benefit from cooperating with other market participants to preserve the value of the assets, or they may benefit from their default if they took that side of a bet through a credit-default swap. Hence, the disintermediation of credit transition transferred the business of banking from traditional banks to investment banks, with a different domestic regulatory structure in the US and vastly different political interests.

Foremost among the endogenous changes to Congress has been the move from a strong committee system to a stronger party system; its shifting relationship to the executive branch; and its shifting relationship to organized interests in all areas, which has altered how policy is shaped between the state and civil society.[12] One of the most significant effects of this institutional change within Congress has been that ever-larger omnibus packages preserve a role for congressional agency through individual members in negotiating with the executive, yet allow for legislative initiatives on many items to pass outside the deliberative committee hearing framework. In a large package, attention is deflected from the IFIs and focused on the nucleus of the legislation. Within Congress, the increasing use of omnibus legislation has helped maintain funding for the IFIs despite opposition, because skilled members and their staffs who support international organizations, together with the executive branch, can negotiate with party leadership to include them in a manner that satisfies all interested parties.[13] These inside deals are fragile, however, and support for the IFIs is constantly subject to the variable political terrain in domestic US politics that can alter the coalition in the next legislative sequence. The result for the Congress-IFI relationship is that Congress acts; yet members almost never take public positions on the IMF and World Bank through the recorded vote.

The congressional advocacy devices that result from the internal and external causes intend to change policy in a target IO. Therefore, success is not necessarily measured by whether or not an individual bill or amendment passes. Rather, advocacy is successful when policies change in the IOs themselves. A high degree of bargaining and personal relationships forged through informal networks play a significant role in influencing the policy agenda at very high levels, and, given the rise of omnibus legislation, bypass the formal deliberative processes on the floors of the House and Senate. To be successful in episodes of "divided government," when the president is from one party and Congress controlled by the other, supporters of the IFIs must either agree on specific policies or be willing to compromise with their opposition. The risk is that the wider the number of groups in the coalition, the more vulnerable it becomes to breaking up in the next legislative struggle.

The predictive value of this model of congressional behavior is in the long run, where the exogenous changes of the end of the Cold War and changes in the structure of international lending have created some new organized interests, while others have dropped off. Congress has been the most supportive of the IFIs in stages when their work advances that of the US banking and corporate communities, evidenced by a clear stake that banks and corporations have in the work of the IFIs, and the legislature's subsequent funding of the budgetary commitments of the executive branch with few or no calls for policy changes. Congress has been the least supportive of the IFIs in the absence of any domestic constituency working on their behalf. In these stages, it delays funding requests; and when it does eventually provide resources, it attaches the most onerous policy prescriptions. As this history has progressed, the collapse of support from traditional corporate and financial constituencies has posed a distinct challenge to the future of economic multilateralism.

Why study congressional advocacy and not parliamentary advocacy elsewhere? The position of the US at the center of the international political economy, together with the structure of its domestic political institutions, confers a unique role on the US Congress in the international system. First of all, the structure of the world political economy generates new interest groups and erodes the connection of others to the work of the Bretton Woods financial institutions. These groups operate in coalitions that form and re-form as they are concerned with specific policy issues in US and international politics. Although they also approach Treasury and the IMF and World Bank, they approach Congress as a part of this process because it is the endpoint for many policy debates that are waged elsewhere. The Bank and the Fund respond by instituting reform connected to legislation, preempting legislation with incremental policy change, or resisting the reforms and working with defensive coalitions. Second, the other major shareholders of the IMF and World Bank do not have coequal branches of government that control revenue in the same manner as Congress. Of the largest five shareholders of the IFIs, only France has a system that is quasi-presidential. In states with stronger traditions of civil service, IMF and World Bank issues are left to ministries with a great deal of financial and development expertise.

## The Plan of the Book

To provide evidence for these assertions, I rely on primary historical research on the relationship drawn from archives, interviews, congressional testimony, and board minutes from the international financial institutions where available. Much of the interaction that occurs between Congress and the IMF and World Bank occurs at the highest level of political parties—that is, committee chairs, ranking members, majority and minority leaders, and Speaker. It is not easy to reconstruct the actions of many of these individuals, because they are not eager to publicize them, particularly when supporting the IFIs could be construed in a politically harmful light. Interviews and archival documentation, and preferably a combination of the two, reveal how the relationship unfolds and can include, or exclude, the management boards of the IFIs. While the boards are far from irrelevant, a good deal of work on the IMF and World Bank that emphasizes the internal relationship between management and staff misses the external pressure on boards to change broader programmatic goals from a higher political level.[14]

While history fails the test of parsimony in social scientific analysis, it does reveal demonstrable patterns that lead to policy change in IFIs as a result of congressional processes. These patterns mirror others in US politics, yet they contain transnational elements. Hence, congressional networks operate locally with respect to the agencies and executive branch in Washington, DC, and are at the same time nested within larger transnational networks of the world system. History is best able to investigate the institutional base because multilateralism and Congress have both changed dramatically since 1945 and complicate the gathering of systematic data on the phenomenon. Rather than theorizing the two levels, national and international, as distinct fields of political activity, I draw on Chorev's analysis of trade policy and Cerny's conceptualization of the state as being enmeshed in an expanding and increasingly complex web of political, social, and economic relationships, both of which demonstrate a more fluid divide between different levels on a unified field of action.[15]

Each empirical chapter of the book contains a thick description of a stage in the chronology of the relationship between congressional politics and the workings of IOs, and world politics more generally. In each, congressional advocacy resulted from a combination of endogenous institutional change in Congress and exogenous shocks from changes in the international political economy. The first chapter sets forth the concept of congressional advocacy as a heuristic model to provide insight into the relationship between the legislature and Bretton Woods financial institutions. It then connects the model to the fields of US foreign policy, international relations, and American politics. The chapter subsequently details the formal and informal levers pulled by members of Congress seeking to influence policy outcomes in the IFIs. With these procedures in mind, it then moves to an exploration of the theoretical contribution an understanding of congressional advocacy makes to studies of American politics and international relations.

The second chapter begins the empirical investigation and explores the politics of what I term the *enactment stage* in the relationship, which accompanied the passage of the Bretton Woods Agreement Act. The Treasury Department's legislative strategy was a response to the previous failure to gain ratification of the Treaty of Versailles, ending World War I, in the Senate. The Roosevelt administration's Treasury learned from that experience, however. Promoters of the agreement focused on their opposition and attempted to broaden the circle of support through a massive education campaign in civil society extolling the benefits of economic multilateralism. When the Bretton Woods agreements moved through the legislature, they brokered a compromise to garner the acquiescence of the financial community in the form of an interagency committee that would report to Congress every six months on US participation in the IMF and World Bank. The result was that the US joined, but domestic constituencies were not immediately connected to the work of the IFIs.

The third chapter explores what I refer to as the *building stage* of the relationship, when the IFIs came into being, and the compromises reached during the enactment of the Bretton Woods Agreement Act took effect. The initial support for membership had been widened by Treasury. But remaining societal resistance to their operations challenged any substantive involvement of the financial community in their work. During this stage, Congress was largely dormant on IMF and World Bank issues, unless the IOs needed legislation to create new agencies under the umbrella of the World Bank group. The stage is nonetheless important for the exogenous changes in the international political economy that occurred therein. The world economy recovered from the war during these years, and the Cold War intensified. The IFIs began to draw new constituencies into their operations when international lending resumed, and they came to embody an alternative model of capitalist economic development to communist ones. The World Bank created constituencies in the banking and corporate worlds as part of a process of changing the required securities regulations and offering bonds to expand its lending capabilities. However, when the International Finance Corporation (IFC) and International Development Association (IDA) were created under the umbrella of the World Bank, their activities were curtailed by compromises over their charters in Congress.

The *development stage*, examined in the fourth chapter, was triggered by the exogenous shock of the end of the fixed-parity system in the IMF and the rise of lending to aid economic development. In this stage, the constituencies for the IMF and World Bank were able to become more assertive in the US political system because the international changes were accompanied by endogenous changes in procedure that opened the institution to the influence of interest groups in a new way. The Legislative Reorganization Act of 1970 recommended the opening of congressional committee hearings to the public. Later reforms included publication of roll-call votes in open reports, increases in committee staff resources, and an expansion of the Congressional Research Service. Eventually, the US Congress floor proceedings were televised. As a result of the bipartisan "sunshine coalition," information that was available to the public about Congress grew exponentially, while committee chairs became more responsive to their members and less dominant.[16] These domestic reforms crossed over into IFI activity when congressional staff and others began to ask the IMF and World Bank for information about lending and project arrangements that enhanced the debate both inside and outside the formal organizations.

As a result, members of Congress, working with interest group allies, were able to become more aggressive concerning their opposition to specific loans and arrangements by the World Bank to countries that violated human rights. These efforts were not successful. Supporters of the IFIs in the banking community, at Treasury, and on the Banking Committees were able to strip human rights amendments in conference committees on bills, and provide funding for the unpopular Witteveen Facility by arguing against the need for a formal appropriation. Nonetheless, the wider involvement of groups in the activities of the IMF and World Bank exposed a need for new legislative maneuvers to ensure their funding. Moreover, legislation connected to the end of fixed parity and the devaluation of the dollar contained the mandate that Congress approve future gold sales, thus involving Congress in later activities of the IMF.

Chapter 5 considers what I term the *debt stage* in the relationship that followed the exogenous shock of the debt crisis of the 1980s and the later changes resulting from the end of the Cold War in the international political economy. During this stage, the IMF, and to a lesser degree the World Bank, became fully and directly engaged with the money-center banks, themselves international players. "Bailouts" of money-center banks through the Fund were politically unpopular, yet the banks were powerful allies. Endogenous changes in congressional procedure concerning budgetary legislation accommodated the needs of the new era. Members supporting IFI funding began to include the measures in large appropriations bills so that they could provide the larger amounts necessary but avoid public criticism from those who opposed the banks and the IFIs. As international activism and interest in poverty alleviation grew, members also sought to influence the direction of lending toward Africa. In one instance, Congress provided an appropriation for a fund that was not requested by the executive branch.

With a powerful and wide circle of supporters in domestic and international politics for their work during the debt stage, Congress funded budgetary requests with minimal policy intervention. Eventually, the resolution to the debt crisis of the 1980s altered the structure of the international banking community yet again, and some groups' interest began to taper off in the new environment that did not rely so heavily on the money-center banks. Also, toward the end of this stage the Cold War ended. The creation of the World Bank inspection panel marked the clear end of the debt stage, when World Bank supporters were able to apply pressure through the budget process to compel substantive policy changes in the Bank over the objections of some member states.

Chapter 6 explores what I refer to as the *moral hazard stage* in the Congress-IFI relationship. The exogenous shock from the international political economy was the 1997 Asian financial crisis. By the late 1990s, the money-center banks controlled a smaller percentage of global capital flows, and new interest groups associated with disintermediated forms of international capital entered the debate.[17] A greater number of NGOs became involved. Individual members saw IFI funding as a vehicle through which they could advance their opposition to abortion. The endogenous institutional change in Congress was provided by the Republican takeover of the House in 1994. This combination of internal and external causes stalled congressional advocacy efforts toward the IFIs as so many different groups attempted to attach policy prescriptions from different ideological perspectives.

The sense that the IMF contributed to the problem of moral hazard became more prominent in policy circles, as some on the left and right began to argue that public bailouts insulated private investors and banks from the downside of their overseas risks. As the number of organized groups widened, the range of policy issues where an agreement could be reached narrowed. When the IMF went to Congress for additional resources during the 1997 crisis, the compromise reached to obtain funding mandated an advisory commission on the IFIs that would evaluate their role in the world economy. Without the unified money-center banking and corporate bedrock of support, the reforms that followed included debt relief and a plan to change the future composition of IDA loans to grants. By the end of the moral hazard stage, international finance operated within a growing patchwork of formal and informal governance arrangements. The IMF and World Bank searched for roles to remain relevant.

The seventh chapter considers what I consider to be the current, *revived stage.* It was triggered by the exogenous shock of the international dimensions of the 2008 financial crisis combined with the endogenous change of a Democratic Congress working with a Democratic presidential administration for the first time in over a decade. For some observers, the crisis pointed to the dramatic failure of the Fund to accomplish what it was established to do in the first of its Articles: "to promote international monetary cooperation . . . [by providing] the machinery for consultation and collaboration on international monetary problems."[18] For other observers, it pointed to a need for a new Bretton Woods arrangement altogether. The IMF and World Bank each received a round of funding. Yet, in the absence of the traditional constituency of support in the banking community that was cut down by the crisis, even a popular, new Democratic president and Democratic Congress had difficulty in attaching IMF provisions to a supplemental appropriations bill. Congress passed the fifteenth replenishment of IDA but included labor provisions in the legislation that were not popular with the World Bank. The IMF's involvement in the Greek and Irish bailouts of 2010 may secure its role in relation to the European Union, but it poses serious challenges to future quota increases in the 212th Republican Congress should the Fund play too overt a role as a bailout mechanism for European banks. Hence, the questions, For how long will the IMF be revived? and What role will the World Bank play? remain unanswered.

The eighth, concluding, chapter uses the past to provide clues to the future. It is apparent that members of Congress do not act alone. They work with allies on initiatives in the Treasury, interest groups, and even the IMF and

World Bank. Congressional procedural maneuvers can prove to be the endpoint for many decisions about the broad policy orientations of the IFIs that take place elsewhere. Initiatives for dramatic change are best when there is the widest possible involvement in a specific proposal and a specific piece of legislation. Nonetheless, the wide base necessary, and the growing involvement of actors that are both critics and constituencies for the IFIs, makes these coalitions much more fragile with respect to the next round of debate. Thus, economic multilateralism requires a popular base of support among individuals and groups that understand the benefits that result from transnational cooperation and the work of the IOs. While this support does not necessarily need to come from a constituency in the financial, corporate, or NGO community, it needs to come from some constituency in American politics, and industrial democracies more generally. Otherwise, the IMF and World Bank will easily become marginalized and inconsequential to the global political economy, rather than central to it.

1

# Congressional Advocacy Toward International Organizations

> He [McNamara] did not like people who made speeches that were going to cause trouble with Congress, because getting either replenishments or what have you through Congress was a continual topic. From the day that I arrived in the Bank until the day I left, there was never a period while Congress was in session without some Bank legislation in committee, on the floor, et cetera. We were always living under the scrutiny of Congress.
>
> —William Clark, Vice President for External Relations, The World Bank[1]

The American Congress is a domestic political institution. Yet the checks and balances among the branches of the United States government ensure that it plays a role in world politics, both as an actor that provides funds and as a forum where a range of interests assemble, deliberate, and influence policy across a range of global issues. The international role of Congress is not always apparent. In classic accounts of the history of multilateralism, its geographic orientation and nationalist politics have appeared to pose obstacles to multilateral cooperation, particularly when members disagree with various aspects of the operations of international organizations (IOs). Yet despite problems in the relationship between the legislature and IOs, individual members of Congress have also championed multilateralism. Moreover, the legislature has eventually provided the bulk of the material resources necessary to finance executive branch commitments for multilateral activities.

The field of international relations understands the multilateral form to coordinate behaviors among three or more states on the basis of generalized principles of conduct, rather than exclusively through private banks or bilateral treaties.[2] The creation of the International Monetary Fund (IMF) and World Bank at Bretton Woods was thus a watershed for the multilateral form in the area of money and credit, because these IOs form the core formal structure for international economic relations in the postwar world system. The multilateral form, however, sits awkwardly among the three branches of

American government. The Bretton Woods Agreement Act does not provide for any official legislative role in the functioning of the IMF and World Bank. Nonetheless, long-standing *political* relationships exist among them in the absence of formal-legal ones. They are a by-product of the routine legislative advocacy efforts that operate in American politics among firms, business groups, trade associations, nongovernmental organizations (NGOs), and political parties seeking to influence domestic legislative outcomes. In this book, I explore the advocacy of members of the legislature in promoting specific policy goals, which I term "congressional advocacy." It is "congressional" because the actions of the institution are unique to the structure and functioning of a bicameral American legislature with an independently elected president, situated within the US system of checks and balances. It is "advocacy" because like-minded legislators work with their allies in the broader community to try to change policy outcomes in IOs and not just to promote multilateralism as an abstract goal.

How does the institution of Congress advocate toward IOs in the face of inner conflict and apathy, as well as in an absence of any prescribed channel through which to influence their activities? Members of Congress advocate by using the procedural levers at their disposal within their own institution. These levers have changed as the institution of Congress has changed internally. Since IOs lack geographic constituencies and present both political opportunities and challenges to political parties, IOs and their supporters must cultivate relationships with legislators who are willing to spend time and political capital on their issue. The constituencies for the IFIs in American politics have changed as the international political economy has evolved. Critics of IOs use the same levers and react to the same international forces. Since the legislature is a collective body, congressional advocacy efforts can, and frequently do, operate on more than one side of a policy issue.

Therefore, unlike studies that perceive the US Congress to be fundamentally at odds with multilateralism as an institutional form, this history depicts Congress as a global forum enmeshed in transnational business, banking, and advocacy communities. Some members of Congress have been stalwart advocates of IOs, particularly when backed by strong organized domestic constituencies providing information and support. However, these groups shift according to the backdrop of the international political and financial system that generates new interests and erodes others. The end of the Cold War and the disintermediation of credit have proved to be the two major structural political and economic developments, respectively, that have spun off new interest groups and reconfigured the others. Those concerned with the US Cold War competition with communism, international banks, and multinational corporations have constituted the core constituencies of the IMF and World Bank in the past. As the global political economy has evolved in the postwar era, their defection has exposed the vulnerabilities of the IFIs in the US political system.

## The Argument of the Book

I argue that exogenous shocks from the international political economy prompt congressional advocacy toward the IFIs in the pursuit of specific goals. Societal groups, both national and transnational, approach like-minded members who, in turn, work through the legislative procedures to obtain results in the IO. Thus, support for the IMF and World Bank is never in the abstract. When legislation involving the IFIs moves through each chamber, the process of attaching policy prescriptions builds support for the bill and draws groups into the system as constituencies for the IFIs. While the natural constituencies of international organizations in international relations are member states and their designated representatives, I use the term "constituencies" to depict these groups in the American political process in the sense that they are involved in, or served by, the work of the IFIs. They promote the policies of the IFIs, seek to change them, or end them. The domestic supporters for multilateralism in the US work with their opposition in other parties, or those advancing different policy prescriptions, to achieve their goals through a complicated process mostly connected to budgetary negotiations.

Given the distribution of outcomes when members of Congress use a variety of institutional levers to advocate for change, together with the possibility for diverging factions to advocate in an opposing direction, the outcomes of any *one* vote on a bill or amendment cannot be predicted with precision. However, an examination of the connection between the work of the IFIs to the structure of international lending and the global distribution of power allows us to predict certain aspects of congressional behavior in the long run. In sum, the undulation of the US business community's need for, and involvement with, the IMF and World Bank, particularly the banking sector, explains a good deal about the centrality of the IFI's role, or lack thereof, in the international economy.

When studies of international relations theory are crossed with studies of interest group operations in American politics, the result reveals that domestic constituencies in advanced, industrial democracies complicate the operations of IOs but are necessary for their successful functioning. Over time, the domestic constituencies' work has connected with that of transnational societal groups. IOs need American constituencies to work with members of Congress who are willing to champion requisite budgetary and other legislation. Moreover, constituents in domestic politics with their own resources can generate support through private donations to IOs and tacit cooperation.[3] Conversely, angry constituencies generate reform proposals with policy contradictions that will be attached to the funding. Nonetheless, economic multilateralism flourishes in the American political system when it connects with the broadest possible base of open domestic support or, at a minimum, when it connects with powerful allies, such as banks and financial services firms, that can work behind the scenes to advance goals. In the absence of either, economic multilateralism flounders, and the missions of IOs flounder along with it.

Hence, congressional advocacy efforts toward the IFIs are the most supportive when groups working on their behalf marshal bipartisan support and can make a case to the legislature for the work IOs do that benefits the US economy. Congressional advocacy efforts are the most adversarial in terms of demanding unpopular (from the viewpoint of the IFI) policy changes, or denying funding in the face of an exogenous crisis where there is little apparent need for their work, or it appears to harm the US economy. Thus, the composition of the coalition of their promoters provides insight into the future prospects of the IFIs.

All of the strategic decisions made by participants in the process mean that campaign contributions and party affiliation no doubt play a role in shaping a member of Congress's orientation on issues, and in the access of organized groups to the member to present their case. Yet the large amount of scholarly literature on the importance of campaign contributions, lobbying, and roll-call voting on the floors of the House and Senate has produced few conclusive results. Part of the problem lies with the analytical difficulty of separating different sources of money in politics from results that can vary from electoral results, to individual bill sponsorship, to individual votes. Money is only one of the many resources available in a campaign.[4] With respect to congressional advocacy toward the IFIs, contributions do not determine individual policy outcomes, because a member makes numerous decisions in the course of a piece of legislation's history. The IO must respond with respect to policy. The extension of the chain of events allows for other resources, such as time, media attention, public relations efforts, and information provided by actors to sway the result. Moreover, many individuals and groups have come and gone in the course of an issue's history. Hence lobbyists and other organized interests must continuously seek out new support in a shifting context, and they do so from both political parties.

I contend that political parties matter in episodes of congressional advocacy because majority parties determine the procedures in the House and to a lesser degree the Senate. As major scholars of Congress have noted, parties control committee assignments and structure many legislative alliances.[5] In the House, minority party leaders are severely handicapped by House rules, which empower a reasonably cohesive majority to control the legislative process and prevail without consultation.[6] In the more collegial Senate, party plays less of a role because the minority retains the ability to offer amendments and conduct extended debate on the floor. The process can be frequently hijacked by senators seeking their individual policy and electoral goals to the extent possible, given the rules that limit the extent to which policy making can be pushed off of the floor to committees or leadership.[7] Nonetheless, parties in both chambers are groupings with members who have common political interests in winning elections and wielding power, and not just individuals who share ideological preferences. As Lee argues, "Votes do not break along party lines only because individual members have preexisting ideological preferences that range along a continuum with Republicans clustered on the right and Democrats on the left. Instead, party structure can derive from members' explicitly political calculations about their collective interests as fellow partisans."[8]

Therefore, on issues where a member is apathetic, he or she may vote a certain way to advance the broader goals of the party as a team. Particularly in the House of Representatives, the team helps individual members with an interest in IFIs as long as the party leadership is on board with a strategy for handling the issue. Partly leadership can make sure that the issues are packaged into larger bills, coordinated with Senate versions, and brought before the Rules Committee (in the House).[9] Members are willing to delegate some power and resources to committees and party leaders because it helps to overcome the collective-action problems inherent in lawmaking. Leaders, in turn, can facilitate the passage of legislation that furthers the members' policy goals by providing coordination services, facilitating log rolls, and using leadership power aggressively to enhance the party's image.

The president matters because the degree to which his party, policy preferences, and electoral goals coincide with, or conflict with, those of the majority party in either chamber determines the context within which the legislative process operates.[10] Teamwork and execution of the specifics can determine the ultimate success or failure of an initiative; hence personal relationships and networks account for many results. These relationships and networks overlap with party affiliation but are not exclusively determined by them. Given the range of ideologies operating on IFI issues and frequency of divided government, support in getting issues included in legislative packages and keeping them there when they go to the floor has cut across party lines. Moreover, the ability to work with the opposition on measures to promote policy goals can determine the success or outcome of a piece of legislation.

Therefore, congressional advocacy efforts ultimately rest upon the actions of individual members of Congress who promote the IFIs, despite the necessity of coordinating with political parties that can structure alliances across chambers and the executive branch. Classical theorists of American politics such as Robert Dahl depicted politicians to be complicated human beings with a number of motives.[11] One of these is certainly a desire for power or influence. But a politician wants power for a reason. And each member of Congress has a unique set of private preferences that are inner, highly subjective feelings concerning what they regard as desirable for themselves and others. Their private preferences can be distinguished from their publicly articulated and discussed ones. The two do not necessarily coincide. A member of Congress's preferences are shaped by his or her loyalties, attitudes of deference and respect, view of a desired future for him- or herself, religion, as well as his or her constituency, society, country, the world, or posterity. Their motives could be as altruistic as wanting to fight global poverty, or as idiosyncratic as having a desire to travel to the foreign countries where development projects are located. The significance of these private preferences are magnified when the other influences of constituency, party, and interest groups are weak.[12]

The empirical evidence offered here provides support for Dahl's and other pluralist theorists' insight that when interest groups are active, they can be effective.[13] But in many areas of foreign policy, such as the IMF and World Bank, the limited engagement of party and nearly nonexistent mass geographic constituencies mean that the private preference of the legislator influences his or her *choice* of the group to which he or she defers for information, advice, and plan of action.[14] Many groups are not mobilized on IMF and World Bank issues, or when they are, they cancel each other out. This allows a greater range of policy latitude for members. The persistency, consistency, and sharing of attitudes about a narrow issue-area can create clusters of members that are more inclusive than just one individual acting alone, yet less inclusive than political parties.[15]

Of course, writing about aspects of the political world that are so personal, and frequently meant to be concealed to outsiders, poses a unique methodological problem. Some information may simply not be available. Other information may be difficult to verify. Admittedly, the problem with using history, and case studies in particular, to learn from the past is that there tends to be an overreliance on events that are dramatic and highly visual, accompanied by an ignorance about crises that were averted.[16] Outcomes tend to be dichotomized into success or failure, and there is a general unwillingness to admit that success may have been unattainable at all. There will not necessarily be more of the same. Nonetheless, the benefits in taking the long view outweigh many of the risks.

## Institutional Mechanisms of Advocacy

The IMF and World Bank's Articles of Agreement stipulate that the only interaction between members and the two institutions shall be through their treasury, central bank, stabilization fund, or other fiscal agency. Under these terms, how can Congress advocate toward the Bretton Woods institutions at all? Congress holds the most influence when the IMF and World Bank need money. Therefore, congressional leverage chiefly derives from the power of the purse and operates according to the multiple specific mechanisms devised for funding the constituent units of the Bank and the Fund. Firms, business groups, trade associations, and NGOs, either individually or through activist networks of like-minded firms and groups, regularly seek to introduce, enact, or modify necessary legislation through direct lobbying, by providing information, and by educating legislators. Commonly referred to as "legislative advocacy," these activities are well documented in the interest-group literature in American politics and the activist network literature in international relations.[17]

Less studied, yet just as significant, are efforts made by legislators on behalf of these same groups to use elements of the legislative process to change public policy and resource-allocation decisions within international organizations. As discussed earlier, I refer to such activity as "congressional advocacy" in order to differentiate it from customary legislative advocacy conducted by interest groups. The mechanisms available to members of Congress in advocating for policy change in IOs are unique to the structure and functioning of the bicameral American legislature that operates with an independently elected president who may not be from the same political party that controls one or the other chamber. Members advocate for policy change with their allies in the broader interest-group community. A consideration of congressional advocacy for a certain course of action in the IMF or World Bank illuminates what happens in formal political institutions where the ideas about policy that humans hold meet stark material considerations and the specifics of legislation, which in turn drive legislative coalition-building.

Despite the complexity of the game, certain similarities in the process have remained across time. A high degree of sophistication is required to navigate this process. It occurs at the top levels of congressional leadership, the executive branch, and the management of the Bank and the Fund. Hence, any IMF or World Bank legislative issue is generally a game of "inside baseball" where insiders use the details or minutiae of the congressional process in a strategic way to gain the requisite authorization, funding, or approval.[18] The goal of the game is to eliminate opposition, and not to win everyone over to the ideological underpinnings of economic multilateralism. If opposition appears, members of Congress, organized interest groups, and officials at the IMF and World Bank work to find acceptable compromises. If a full-blown legislative fight develops, each side will attempt to bring other organized interests to join their efforts.

To continue the "inside baseball" metaphor, a manager's tactics vary from pitch to pitch. Teams do not always comprise the same players. The outside actors that provided the large campaign contributions and funding in support of IFIs at different points in their histories likewise shift. While leadership, particularly the majority party, has mechanisms for keeping members in line, they do not choose to employ them on each issue in the same way. Thus, a particular configuration of party support and campaign contributions on one roll-call vote does not guarantee a similar configuration on later votes, or support when the measure is reconfigured into a larger package. It is useful, therefore, to have legislative allies who are from the other party or who have a different base of political support and work with different groups, because the rationales for agreement can shift from version to version.

As the number of participants widens and includes more international advocacy efforts, societal actors and members of Congress calculate whether or not it is worth the effort to pursue a goal, and whether or not to engage the issue publicly or seek to resolve it privately through sympathetic, high-level government officials. These officials may respond in order to preempt further action, or they may choose to work with opponents to it to prevent it from coming into effect. As the process unfolds, either side constantly assesses the degree of opposition to their activity. The outcome of any one effort of elements within Congress to use institutional mechanisms to advocate for change in an IO is such that the policy initiative may become US law (and thus impose conditions on an IO), it may fail, or elements of it may be adopted by the IO to preempt legislation. The ability of groups and individuals to navigate the system, together with the size of the coalition they can construct, explains the variation in congressional outcomes demanding policy reforms.

In the US system, the executive branch negotiates agreements among states and designates representatives to international organizations, whereas Congress is the branch of the US government that writes the laws. Hence, formal mechanisms derive from the legislature's lawmaking activities and result in a concrete budgetary appropriation, directive to the US representative, or legal sanction. The informal mechanisms are part and parcel of the broader policy process in Washington, DC, among congressional staffs, bureaucrats at the relevant agencies, interest groups, media in a given issue area, and prominent academics. This congressional role in the policy process influences far more sweeping changes in IOs than the more circumscribed legislative role would imply, in terms of their programmatic agendas, level of resources, and ability to play a role in resolving the critical issues of the day.

Congress exerts a great deal of influence over the IFIs because it invites broad participation by design and because it is so intensely enmeshed in Washington, DC, policy networks. The density of issue networks surrounding Capitol Hill is significant because individuals move along similar career trajectories in Washington, with similar stopping points along the way. Therefore, there is not one manner in which the networks form. For example, it is common for an official to work on the Hill on a congressional staff for one of the relevant committees, then in the Treasury's Office of International Affairs, possibly serve as the US executive director to either the Bank or the Fund, and eventually "burrow in" to a permanent position in the civil service, Bank, or Fund staff.[19] Even at the highest levels many individuals, such as Secretary of the Treasury Timothy Geithner and former Treasury Secretary Lawrence Summers, worked at the IMF and World Bank earlier in their careers. These career paths generally necessitate Senate confirmation that can be stalled or complicated by bad feelings or unpleasant histories at earlier stages. Many individuals will thus avoid confronting individual members of Congress who may reappear in another role in the course of a political career in Washington, DC.[20]

While Congress may not have the deep resources other individuals, think tanks, NGOs, and business organizations in these networks can access to develop policy proposals, it is the venue where *final* action is generally achieved, because the body actually allocates funds, approves treaties, writes authorizing legislation, and retains the power to declare war.[21] Moreover, Washington draws lobbyists from all over the world, as well as globally organized pressure groups.[22] Even when Congress plays an essentially passive role in acting as a forum for others' disputes, the potential for struggle will compel financial interests to seek to steer clear of solutions that *do* require congressional action. Finally, proposals not originating with interest groups—i.e., those originating with a member or staff—arise because multilateralism comes into conflict with the separation of powers in the US system.

## PULLING FORMAL LEVERS IN THE LEGISLATURE

Congress must pass laws concerning participation in the IFIs in three general areas: changes to the Articles of Agreement; IDA replenishments; and IMF, International Bank for Reconstruction and Development (IBRD), or IFC quota increases. The arrangement of committee jurisdiction in Congress complicates legislative activity because the House and Senate handle the issues differently. Moreover, the type of appropriation sought calls for different types of action that is the province of budget experts and "insiders."

Changes to the articles are relatively rare. IMF, IBRD, or IFC quota increases occur intermittently and require an appropriation. A consistent determination of the budgetary consequences of quota increases, however, has never been clearly established because it could be argued that the money remains available to the US government.[23] A provision in the IMF's Articles of Agreement requires member countries to maintain the value of their subscriptions in terms of a common denominator—gold. After the 1967 Commission on Budget Concepts, initial questions about the budgetary consequences arose. In the 1970s, the US sought to devalue its currency and was obligated to pay currency into the Fund in order to maintain the same gold value. However, payments, subscriptions, drawings, and other transactions are treated as monetary exchanges of assets. That is, the United States' Fund subscription works like a deposit in a bank that can be used by the bank for lending to others and also to establish a line of credit for the depositor—in this case the US. The liability is essentially offset by the increased asset value of the subscription and thus is not the same as other budgetary expenditures that are no longer available for use.[24] In fact, it was not until the late 1970s that some members of Congress insisted that the IMF obtain an appropriation through the formal process.

IDA replenishments are far more regular congressional activities than changes to articles or quota increases and must pass through the regular congressional budgeting process.[25] Figure 1.1 depicts the budgeting system associated with the IFIs and demonstrates that decisions are made in a piecemeal and inconsistent manner. Budget scholars concur that the structure does not fit easily with the necessities of drawing up and maintaining a disciplined budget in most areas of US politics, let alone the IFIs.[26] The complexity of Figure 1.1 is significant, because it depicts the dispersion of authority over the IFIs across the institution. It likewise shows how key

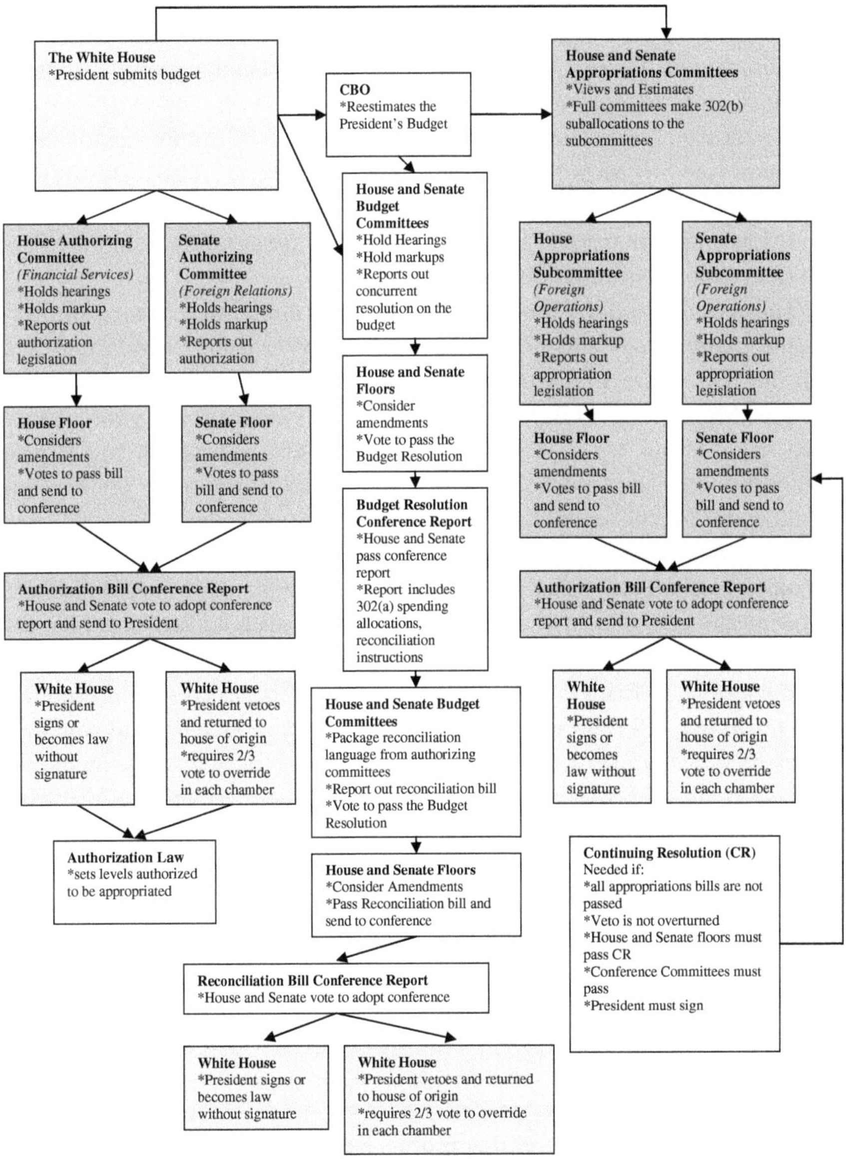


FIGURE 1.1 The Appropriations and Budget System for Multilateral Development Finance.

decisions are made by a very small number of representatives, senators, and staff within the broader process, and few pieces of legislation follow this path precisely.

Since IDA depends on an annual appropriation, authorization and appropriations hearings and legislation are relatively regular. The initial step in securing funding of any kind is the passage of authorizing legislation for the program. An authorization bill authorizes a program, specifies its aim, and establishes a ceiling of money that Congress can use to finance it within a set period of time. In the case of IDA, authorizations are generally for a three-year period that coincides with a replenishment round. The second step is inclusion of the expenditure in the Foreign Operations appropriations bill that grants the actual budgetary authority, or authorization for the outlay itself, approved by Congress under the ceiling established by the authorizing bill. Appropriations bills are "must pass" legislation that originate in the House.[27] There are thirteen annual appropriations bills that together fund the entire federal government. The IFI appropriations (and IDA is one of them) are grouped within the Foreign Operations appropriations bill.

The types of activity conducted by the four committees (two authorizing and two appropriating in each chamber) foster different relationships with the IFIs. Since the authorizing committee has legislative jurisdiction over the IMF and World Bank, and authorizations are held every three years when negotiations for a replenishment round are completed, the House Committee on Financial Services and the Senate Committee on Foreign Relations follow the activities of the IFIs carefully. Members and staff consult with Bank officials on policy matters and follow the ongoing IDA negotiations, as well as any other current matters that may require legislation. In following the activities of the IFIs, these committees hold hearings on matters of interest or concern to members, staff, and the general public. Although officials from the IMF and World Bank themselves are prohibited from testifying, US representatives from the Treasury Department can, and do, testify on behalf of the relevant IO. In some instances, arrangements can be made in an ad hoc manner for officials to participate in meetings with multilateral parliamentarians.[28]

The dynamics of appropriations committees are somewhat different from those of other committees, because either side of any dispute knows that the these bills must pass. Appropriations hearings are held annually in conjunction with the president's budget request. Thus, individuals who testify are almost always US government officials from the Department of the Treasury, or former US World Bank officials. Studies of the foreign-aid appropriations process conclude that there are more continuities than change each year in the foreign-aid area.[29] Nonetheless, the appropriations committees operate within the budgeting system in Congress, and that process has undergone substantive change since the IFIs were established.

One of the most significant changes is that appropriations bills attract riders—i.e., attempts to change policy that go beyond simple funding of agencies—despite congressional rules that prohibit changes to authorizations.[30] The necessity of passing appropriations bills results in their use within the congressional machinery as a strategic means of including measures that might otherwise be vetoed by the president. That is, appropriators can insert policy changes into bills that have a greater chance of passage because the bill must be passed, although the provisions should apply only for the term of the fiscal year. In recent years, the insertion of these provisions became possible because the Republican House leadership pressured committee leadership to include them, and the Rules Committee waived points of order against them. On the Senate side, leadership did not enforce its rule against legislation in appropriations bills between 1995 and 1999.[31] Many provisions were removed in conference committees; nonetheless, the IFIs have not escaped the practice of inserting legislation into appropriations bills. For example, the budget for FY 2009 stipulates that the secretary of the treasury should instruct the US executive directors of the international financial institutions to use their voice and vote to support projects in Tibet under certain circumstances.[32]

In addition to passing laws, Congress interacts with the IMF on a regular basis through annual hearings. The secretary of the treasury is obligated by US law to submit a report to Congress each year on the progress, if any, in the US executive director's efforts to influence reform in the IMF. After submitting the report, he or she must appear before the House Committee on Financial Services and the Senate Committee on Foreign Relations to present testimony on progress made in reforming the IMF, status of efforts to reform the international financial system, compliance of countries with any conditions attached to assistance from the Fund, and the status of international anti–money laundering and counterterrorist financing standards by the IMF.[33] In recent years, this testimony has ranged beyond the activities of the Fund.

Finally, Congress can insert directives to the US executive directors in other legislation. When executive directors are directed to conduct certain activities, these provisions may be virtually impossible to enforce, or be simply ineffective, as is the case when the executive director is the only one to vote "no" on a loan and is easily outvoted by the rest of the board. Furthermore, many such provisions are stripped in conference committees from the bills that contain them. However, they are significant political vehicles, because members can then point to having taken a public stand on issues ranging from abortion, to opposing aid to a hated enemy state via the IFIs, without its having had any real policy effect.

Therefore, the different types of legislation that can affect the IFIs directly come from widely different sources because power is fragmented in the congressional system. Since the Senate Banking Committee does not have jurisdiction over the IFIs, the differing jurisdictions between the House (financial services) and Senate (foreign relations) further "orphan" the legislation because it does not fall within the regular purview of committee chairs who may meet regularly to discuss other items on both of their (either banking or foreign affairs) agendas.[34]

Despite its cumbersome nature, the budgeting system must produce results. Since budget committees must continually interact with the tax committees (House Ways and Means, and Senate Finance), House and Senate appropriations committees, and their authorizing committees in each chamber, the pressure to pass a bill requires a great deal of alliance building that may be fleeting and directed at very specific issues.[35] At a minimum, building a successful bipartisan coalition for any piece of legislation requires a strategy for cutting down the size and intensity of opposition to it.[36]

## PULLING INFORMAL LEVERS IN THE LEGISLATURE

Martin demonstrates that when the executive branch negotiates a treaty, it must anticipate reaction in the legislature or the agreement will not be ratified.[37] Yet the need for ratification of formal agreements is only the beginning of the political story. IOs need to raise money to finance their day-to-day operations. While the IMF need only approach Congress when it seeks to expand its resources or change its Articles of Agreement, the World Bank requires an annual appropriation for IDA. Therefore, the exchanges between the IOs and Congress are more numerous than would be immediately apparent, and are more acute in a crisis. The president and Treasury must work constantly with members of Congress who craft compromise legislation that will generate sufficient support to make it through the appropriations process. Compromises provoke reform in the IOs.

The president plays a role in the process because he is the leader of his party and the executive branch is no doubt preeminent in the conduct of US foreign policy. His presidential administration plays a major role in initially selecting the top Treasury officials who will interact with the Bank and Fund, and negotiate for the United States in these forums. The administration likewise participates in the annual budget process and in negotiations on omnibus bill packages with the legislature. It must calculate how much political capital it will spend on a given policy initiative. The Treasury must manage the administration's agenda on the Hill, which can be helped when his party is in the majority or hindered when it is not. Yet the president does not work in a vacuum. In their study of treaty politics and the rise of executive agreements, Krutz and Peake argue that were a president to exercise unilateral authority on every international agreement, it would have negative repercussions in many other areas of activity in which they are reliant on Congress, such as budgeting, confirmations to the executive branch and judiciary, and policy making. Therefore, congressional constraints matter when considering mechanisms of shared power.[38] Although congressional involvement may not always be legally mandated, it may well be politically efficacious.

Given the fluid nature of the budgetary alliances in Congress, the broad dispersion of individuals connected to the IFIs, and the relative lack of importance of these issues to many constituents, there exist many informal mechanisms that grow out of the formal processes which can be even more influential. Much of this influence is personal and involves the exchange of political favors. Although IFI officials cannot testify before Congress, there are no prohibitions on office meetings between members and administrators. Contact between the chair of a committee, his or her staff, and the relevant agency—in this case the Department of the Treasury—is ongoing. Congressional staffs request briefings on issues of concern to interest groups and constituents, and particularly with respect to ongoing negotiations such as IDA that will result in a request for funding. At times, members and staff have been invited to attend negotiations as observers. Members of Congress frequently write letters to appropriate heads of IOs on issues of concern that can be instigated by news coverage, NGO, or constituent pressure. These letters can also be directed to the secretary of the treasury for his or her input in the process.

While bills rightfully receive the most scholarly attention in legislative studies, a great deal of congressional influence over IFIs derives from the institution's ability to threaten, refuse, or fail to legislate. Hence, a great deal of the political activity inside and surrounding Capitol Hill lies with threatened or failed bills. While the likelihood of a specific provision making it into law might be slim, individuals will nonetheless work to preempt it if minor accommodations can be made. For example, the chair of a committee may refuse to move a piece of legislation out of the committee until certain provisions are met. Of course, opponents could gain the necessary votes to release it;[39] however, this maneuver would likewise involve a political calculation involving the strength of their conviction in favor of, or opposed to, a provision against the degree of effort it would take to fight for, or against, it. Likewise, a threat to mandate formal reporting requirements on a specific issue by the Treasury to Congress may never become a law; the threat, however, may trigger informal agreements among the Treasury, World Bank, and IMF to share information informally on a regular basis to avoid the formal requirement.

Figure 1.2 depicts congressional advocacy designed to influence the IMF and World Bank that highlights the three main mechanisms Congress uses to influence outcomes: letters, hearings, and legislation. As part of the informal process, Treasury, the IMF, or World Bank may respond to prevent further legislative action. However, other groups within the interest community may form to take the other side. If the legislation continues to move, groups may mobilize against it or in favor if it. Thus, the legislative outcome may be written into law or not. Nonetheless, it is not the only policy outcome in the IO.

The growth and quality of Capitol Hill staff since the IFIs were created have increased the possibility for congressional oversight beyond legally mandated hearings or legislative mark-up sessions. The Legislative Reorganization

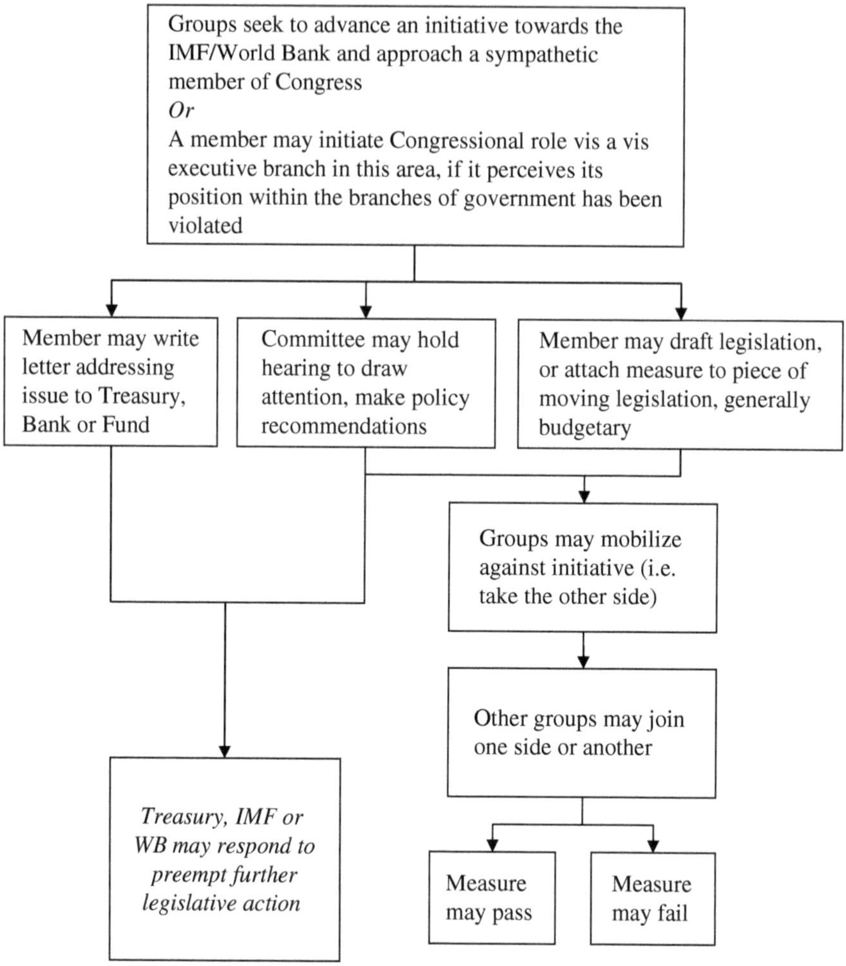


FIGURE 1.2 Congressional Advocacy Toward the IMF and World Bank.

Act of 1946 prompted considerable change for congressional staffing because it allowed for a more professional, specialized system. The conditions of employment on the Hill, such as lack of tenure or clearly defined career patterns, result in a proliferation of young and short-term aides. Personal relationships among staff members are significant in this environment and change according to the interests and style of the member.[40] Staff members can attend meetings and effectively act as surrogates for members, thus allowing them to take on a role in many more issues than they could alone. Congress as an institution has been able to initiate more federal policy for this reason, and its expansion of influence extends to the IFIs because specialized staff can likewise meet with groups, follow policy issues, and contact relevant authorities on behalf of their members.

Nonetheless, staff is a necessary but not sufficient condition for action on an issue. Committee chairs and individual members must consider the efforts of staff to be worthwhile in order for them to be effective.[41] Hence, the degree to which a committee or subcommittee takes an interest in the IFIs rests ultimately with the chair. Committees may go through a period of benign neglect for a time when the issues are not considered because it is not of interest to the chair, or committee chairs may agree that one chamber will take the lead on an issue if the other chooses to make a different issue a priority. This division of attention may reflect different party majorities in each chamber, preferences of the chairs, or the appearance of more important issues, such as war.

## Theoretical Implications of Congressional Advocacy

A study of the relationship between Congress and the IFIs through the history of their repetitive, sequential interactions has implications for the fields of international relations as well as American politics that cannot be understood when either is considered in isolation or from disconnected case studies. Classic treatments of US foreign policy present the US as oscillating between two international policy poles of isolationist and internationalist sentiments, with each dominating different epochs of US history.[42] When Congress is included in these conceptualizations, it is generally considered a holdout of isolationist sentiment, reluctant to support multilateral impulses in order to serve parochial interests.[43] Within literature on international political economy, Susan Strange argued that there has always been an inherent conflict in US foreign policy between goals of liberalism for the pursuit of commercial and financial interests, and realism for the pursuit of political and military ones.[44]

Yet the reality of the institution is far more nuanced. As a collective body, Congress does not exclusively hold one sentiment or another at any given point in time. Rather, the institution is a forum for conflict itself. Considerations of congressional advocacy reveal that different elements within the institution can use its levers to promote policy goals in IOs that are at odds with one another. When it acts on its own (and not interest group–inspired) impulses, it acts to preserve its budgetary role within the structure of American political institutions. Therefore, an examination of the internal operations of Congress in this area contributes to studies of American politics because it reveals how members use procedure and the budget lever, among other devices, to influence policy in an area of low mass constituent interest. The success of these efforts by members of Congress with their allies in US and international civil society contributes to studies of international relations because it reveals the limits of endogenous explanations of policy change in international organizations, divorced from their context in the formal political institutions of the hegemonic state where ideas must be translated into concrete political action. First, I turn to the contribution a consideration of congressional advocacy makes to studies of US politics.

## US POLITICS: MEMBERS OF CONGRESS AS POLICY MAKERS

No doubt, the IMF and World Bank are areas of low interest in Congress. Even when categorized as having any ideological content and grouped with the United Nations, International Criminal Court, and International Arms Control Treaties into a conflict between "multilateralism vs. unilateralism," they constitute the smallest proportion of the roll-call agenda.[45] Scholarship on Congress pays scant attention to the institution's relationship to international organizations, aside from studies of trade politics, because it is not the primary concern of most legislators and holds almost no value in reelection.[46]

Mayhew's study of American government implies that a member has more policy latitude when the issue is of less concern to constituents in his or her district.[47] Arnold theorizes that members may attempt to anticipate and respond to citizens' *potential* preferences, even if their constituents have no established opinions.[48] I do not deny that members of Congress take public positions on issues that please their constituencies; yet they also desire to form and implement public policy over the longer term through both formal and informal patterns of influence. Few existing studies in either American politics or international relations explore how or why members of Congress exert policy influence in areas of low mass constituent interest because their nature as low-interest areas does not attract the attention of researchers. Such an investigation therefore reveals a good deal about how legislators actually go about influencing policy when constituent interest is low.

Moreover, a good deal of the existing literature on Congress does not lend itself to investigating both formal and informal patterns of influence. For example, Epstein and O'Halloran's work on congressional oversight of domestic agencies models interest-group input wherein agencies make proposals, interest groups have an opportunity to lobby Congress, and then Congress decides whether to accept or reject the proposal.[49] Yet by the researchers' own admission they abstract away much of the institutional structure of Congress, deliberately leaving vague whether their "median congressional voter" is on the floor, in a committee or subcommittee, or is the median member of a legislative coalition that is interested in the relevant policy area.[50] Therefore, their model is not a useful representation to investigate oversight of international organizations, where so much influence is exerted through informal channels and procedural levers.

Other existing work on the Congress-IFI relationship relies on roll-call votes as standardized data with which to measure support or opposition to the IFIs. Along these lines, Broz and Hawes's work rests on four individual roll-call votes connected to IMF quota increases—three that occurred as a part of the Latin American debt crisis and one as part of the Asian currency crisis.[51] In a later piece, Broz isolates five roll-call votes on funding the IFIs and conflates bills with amendments and nonbinding motions to instruct conferees.[52] With respect to ideology, Broz argues that conservatives see international organizations like the IMF as particularly prone to waste and inefficiency, whereas liberals tend to be more optimistic. Ideology provides the foundation upon which legislators evaluate the IFIs.[53] Senate deliberations are curiously absent these analyses.

The problem with this work is that in relying on so few instances where votes are recorded, it ignores the broader process and actions in the Senate, thus leading to gross generalizations and incorrect findings about the connections among party, ideology, and policy proposals. Broz never seriously questions whether some members might not have policy preferences on the IFIs at all, but go along with a vote for other reasons, such as wanting to make the other team "look bad." Nor does he question why so few votes are taken and how they are kept off of the floor of the House. The analysis of an individual vote may not be incorrect, but it is frozen in the moment it was taken. For example, money-center banks certainly lobbied members of Congress on the IFIs during the Latin American debt crisis and, to a lesser extent, the Asian financial crisis; yet the structure of the banking system has changed since these crises. Few of the money-center banks have survived, whereas hedge funds, private equity funds, and disintermediated bond markets have proliferated. These new groups have not always supported the growth of the IFI programs, depending on the issue. Finally, the Senate plays a role, if not a more important one, in US foreign policy as well as the budget deliberations. Leaving it out of the analysis, as this work does, omits an important component of the process.

As Redman demonstrates in his classic *Dance of Legislation,*[54] the legislative process involves a back-and-forth flow of attached, and removed, policy provisions between the House and Senate as a bill proceeds from committee, to floor, to conference, and back in each. When observed repeatedly over time, the process reveals that the bundling of a measure related to the IFIs into the larger package is a great part of the political story itself. Therefore, the recorded vote is no doubt the single most visible and standard indicator of what individuals have contributed to a congressional decision. However, a roll-call vote does not reveal anything about the earlier phases of lawmaking where policy considerations played the major role, such as drafting a bill, conducting hearings, guiding it in committee, and building a political coalition. Moreover, Arnold reminds us that the powerful, ambitious, and eloquent members play the same role in casting a vote that the weak, lazy and inarticulate do.[55]

Hall asserts that members must decide what position to take on a bill, as well as how active to be on it.[56] Lawmakers are never equally involved in the process, and they are also not merely gatekeepers. Those who are active in the network propose legislation, work with interest groups and staff on other committees to develop it, and interface with the relevant agencies on issues known to be of concern to them. The picture of the "dance" of legislation is that the crucial vote on many bills is often not the final one on ratification but an earlier one, such as a procedural vote that determined whether amendments would be allowed, or a vote on an amendment that would have made it unacceptable to a majority of representatives or the president.[57]

In addition, the roll-call vote is not an effective way to designate responsibility for *inaction.* Congressional inaction rarely results from a floor vote that was rejected. It usually occurs because no legislator would introduce a bill, the committee never acted, the Senate objected, a conference committee failed to resolve differences between House and Senate, the president vetoed it, or time ran out. Inaction is particularly important for the IMF and World Bank, given the degree of apathy with respect to their activity in both chambers.

A longer-term, transnational view shows that since few geographic constituencies organize on behalf of, or in opposition to, the IMF and World Bank, interested members willing to work inside the congressional machinery on these issues have wide latitude to shape policy. To do so, they work with increasingly international advocacy groups. Whereas in the 1950s and 1960s organized interests were not as diverse, the iron triangles that Lowi warned signaled the "end of liberalism" grew more internally conflicted.[58] In the 1970s, the committee structure in Congress became less powerful and the political activity of groups expanded to the degree that theorists termed "hyperpluralism."[59] Jeffrey Berry pointed out that the interest-group explosion in those years added a degree of complexity in which the likelihood of conflict among competing coalitions increases.[60] For Berry, citizen groups that mobilize members, donors, or activists around interests other than their vocation or profession allow individuals the choice to support issues they care most about, as opposed to having them packaged by a political party. These groups' legislative success upsets traditional policy-making networks because they increase the number of participants who need to be satisfied.

This study adds a layer to the earlier analyses. When members seek to influence policy in the IMF and World Bank, the inclusion of the considerations of international interest groups that contact influential members increases the number of interests that must be satisfied and that complicate the formation of any stable coalition. Indeed, NGOs such as those in the debt-relief network that are domiciled outside the US rarely approach Congress directly, but they do contribute to issue networks by introducing policy proposals their US affiliates bring to members. Likewise, international think tanks generally do not work with Congress directly, but do provide briefings to finance ministries that contribute to international policy debates. Their reports are read by congressional staff regardless of whether or not that was the intent of the publication. This layer successfully fosters a global community concerned with the operations of the IFIs. Nonetheless, it complicates the domestic US process even beyond what Berry proposes, because international politics on IFI issues have a tendency to further deconstruct any notions of the "national interest."

The operational difference between national and transnational involvement is that domestic interest groups, such as banks and trade associations, approach members on many issues in the course of a two-year Congress. The likelihood of having to work with a member again soon means that these groups have high incentives to compromise and work within the system. Conversely, single-issue groups participating in transnational issue-advocacy networks such as environmental networks, debt relief networks, and IFI watchdog groups answer to international constituencies and may approach members only once in a two-year Congress, or not at all. Therefore, their incentives to compromise (and preserve the working relationship for the near future) are dramatically different. When the traditional domestic business groups and transnational issue-advocacy groups are mixed in a coalition, it can achieve impressive results; yet the different incentives to compromise in the future also make any contemporary IFI coalition even less stable than before.[61]

## INTERNATIONAL RELATIONS: THE ROLE OF CONGRESSIONAL ADVOCACY IN STUDIES OF ECONOMIC MULTILATERALISM

What does an understanding of congressional advocacy tell us about the international organization side of the relationship? A growing literature in the study of international organizations questions whether change in their operations derives from internal or external causes. Whereas the traditional realist approaches minimized the significance of IOs as actors independent of powerful nation-states,[62] contemporary approaches see a role for them as more autonomous bureaucracies with considerable latitude to generate norms. For Barnett and Finnemore, the rational-legal authority inherent in IOs gives them the power to act independent of the states that created them when they create categories, create interests, and transfer models of policy organization around the world.[63] They argue that the nature of change in IOs is highly path dependent on existing rules and culture inside the organization.[64] The principal-agent (PA) model posits that groups of member governments may empower IOs as agents with real decision-making authority.[65] Specific work on the IMF and World Bank develops these themes. For example, Chwieroth's work on the IMF argues that preference formation takes place within IOs despite conflict over how norms should be interpreted and applied.[66]

The problem with these internal investigations of the Bretton Woods institutions is that they miss the external levers powerful states and private actors retain in creating norms and institutional agendas.[67] Without incorporating notions of congressional advocacy efforts into the theoretical understanding, work focusing on the internal operations of the IOs has a naïve quality with respect to the rich political context within which the US exercises power. Congressional advocacy efforts operate among the heads of the IOs, finance ministries, foreign affairs ministries, and congressional leadership—thus at a higher level than the executive board of the IMF or World Bank. Internal operations and staff culture at the IMF and World Bank no doubt determine specific lending arrangements; however, many of the broad policy orientations of the IFIs are the subject of political struggles among politicians, private-sector interest groups, and NGOs waged elsewhere. The US Congress is certainly not the only such forum, but it is a significant one. Hence, while existing work does what it sets out to do—explain the lending agreements and projects with each country—it misses the congressional dimension because Congress has never been very successful in influencing specific loan arrangements.

Conversely, other work on the IOs emphasizes the exogenous contexts within which the IFIs operate. In the sociological literature, Babb understands frames as interpretive devices that function to organize experiences and guide action.[68] The Treasury Department of a given presidential administration provides a frame to mobilize support for the multilateral development banks in Congress and elsewhere. Within constructivist literature on international relations, Weaver argues that the "organized hypocrisy" of the World Bank results from the contradiction between the demands of its external environment, Congress included, and the theories, goals, and best practices it claims to uphold.[69] In more rationalist work on the IMF, Gould presents compelling empirical evidence that supplementary financiers have leverage over the design of the Fund's programs because they provide external resources to augment those provided by the Fund itself. Hence they seek to influence the programs' design to ensure that borrowers will use the money in the way they prefer.[70] Woods's study of the IMF and World Bank begins with the premise that powerful governments set the bottom line for their operations and that competing interests in the US lead them in contradictory directions.[71]Finally, journalist accounts such as Mallaby's study of the World Bank and Blustein's examination of the 1997 Asian financial crisis incorporate both internal and external factors into their analyses.[72]

Despite the mix of internal and external influences, these examinations do not go inside the legislature to uncover patterns in the procedural relationship among external groups, Congress, its members, and outcomes in IOs. Bauer, Pool, and Dexter's insight from the study of US interest groups is that political outputs can be something very different from what any of the interested parties wanted or sought. The *process* matters because the structural parameters in part determine how people see their interests, to which ones they attended, and therefore how they behaved.[73] In legislative campaigns, groups can define the interests of their partisans, not just based on ideas and framing, but according to the parameters of the coalition and specific requests of their components. Differently constructed, the same groups might choose the other side, depending on who is on it, and what they seek.

Therefore, this study of the relationship between the legislature and IFIs demonstrates a deep degree of ideological and normative conflict within advocacy coalitions that is not apparent because many actors are actively seeking to keep some issues off the public agenda. When working on real legislation, coalitions on IFI issues demonstrate the adage that "politics make strange bedfellows." Literature on lobbying finds that lobbyists tend to make and maintain contact with those members who already agree, or with those whose views they least need to change. To put it another way, legislators tend to listen to lobbyists who tell them what they want to hear.[74] A lobbyist or NGO only rarely seeks to persuade a member, but is an important source of information for those members already well-disposed toward the interest group who provide costly policy information, political intelligence, and labor in exchange for the member's constitutional access to the process, political capital with their colleagues, and effort.[75] The work of business pressure groups is directed at persuading *industry executives* to write or talk to their member; and into general public relations and education. In order to reach members who disagree and bring them into the coalition, interest groups do not try to convince others, but would much rather work with *other* interest groups that have the requisite connections to coordinate a legislative strategy.

Since coalitions of support "float" from one piece of legislation to another, the rationales and information used to generate support float as well. A new issue, such as debt relief, might bring new interests, such as the Christian right, into the coalition. Nonetheless, previous rationales survive. Christian groups approach members with whom they have connections, and groups with other rationales—such as fiscal conservatives who see the IFIs as financially irresponsible—approach those with whom *they* have connections. Other groups take sides depending on how the issue is aligned, who else is in a coalition, and what they are seeking.

Thus, when interest groups work through Congress they have the effect of augmenting state power, because they make the legislature with its budget-denying capacity a locus of activity through which to influence IOs. Nonetheless, the activity that operates within the congressional arena is far from exclusively American in scope. While US-based advocacy groups, businesses, and business associations predominate, they work within transnational coalitions where local branches may or may not agree with the interests of the transnational agent.

## Conclusion: The Congressional Role

While this book focuses on congressional advocacy toward the Bretton Woods institutions, it is applicable to other international organizations. The ultimate congressional sanction is to deny a funding request. To prevent this outcome,

IOs need advocates on Capitol Hill and hence broad domestic constituencies of support. Without anyone willing to expand political capital on their behalf, and without securing funding through the budget process, they will not be able to perform their functions adequately in the global political system. The history of the IMF and World Bank reveals that the legislature has eventually provided funding for these organizations at critical moments in their development. The problem is that the funding generally comes with demands for policy change emanating from these same political constituencies.

On high-profile international negotiations, policy makers must choose among bargaining tactics to secure domestic ratification of agreements and economic cooperation, as international relations literature has previously explored.[76] However, where media attention is sporadic, the nature of the financial issues complicates wide-scale participation, and few members have an active interest in the issue, a great deal of influence can be—and has been—exerted outside the domain of formal negotiations. Therefore, when Congress intervenes in an issue, the US, and even individual legislators, can be perceived to assert inordinate control over international organizations. Yet without the congressional lever in the international system, there would be no other entity so open to the efforts of interest groups and NGOs that could possibly alter their course of action.[77]

# 2

# Enacting a Multilateral Framework for Finance

## TREASURY AND CONGRESSIONAL COMPROMISE

> I might say that if there is one thing that stands out in my mind in regard to Bretton Woods, it is the care, the serious regard, of your American delegation to secure a document that would protect American interests, and to avoid issues that might be hurtful to its passage in the Congress.[1]
>
> —Frederick M. Vinson, Secretary of the Treasury

Although the multilateral form existed prior to the twentieth century,[2] the failure of the US to join the League of Nations after the Senate did not ratify the Treaty of Versailles was the first major episode of congressional assertion into the formal operations of an international organization. Nonetheless, I argue that the origins of congressional advocacy toward the IMF and World Bank are to be found in this episode. To demonstrate this claim, this chapter compares the legislative paths of the Treaty of Versailles and the Bretton Woods Agreement Act to demonstrate how the institution of Congress was initially able to guide the earliest orientation of the Bretton Woods institutions, given what had happened with the League earlier. This chapter therefore compares the legislative trajectories of the Treaty of Versailles and the Bretton Woods Agreement Act to demonstrate how the institution of Congress was initially able to shape the contours of economic multilateralism in what I refer to as the "enactment stage."

The exogenous shocks that triggered both of these legislative struggles were the two hegemonic wars of the twentieth century and the breakdown in trade and financial relations that accompanied them. The recurrence of European conflict and the Great Depression led many policy makers to connect notions of American security to a stable global economy. The chapter shows that the Treaty of Versailles did not lack for domestic constituents. In fact, societal groups worked to promote the League in the US throughout its twenty-odd-year history. It failed because President Woodrow Wilson included the

Covenant of the League with the legislation for the Treaty of Versailles, resisted any alterations to it, could not work with the opposition to it, and never resolved the Constitutional questions connected to the role of Congress in the conduct of US foreign policy. Conversely, President Franklin D. Roosevelt's Treasury Department perceived opposition to the Bretton Woods Agreement Act in the New York banking community, and Congress addressed it from the start and worked to compromise as the legislation moved through the House and Senate.

Therefore, on the domestic side of the equation, specific provisions in both pieces of legislation brought some groups into the coalition of support and left others out. The political outputs became something different from what many of the interested parties wanted or sought. In both legislative campaigns, groups helped to define the interests of partisans according to the demands of components of the coalitions. If the coalitions had been differently constructed, the same groups might have chosen the other side.

The result of the combination of internal and external inputs was that in the enactment stage explored here, the US Treasury led the coalition of support for the Bretton Woods Agreement, which sought to expand the IFI's constituencies in civil society beyond the New York banking community, and thus break its hold on the banking committees in Congress. Compromises reached during the course of the bill's passage altered the manner in which the US would participate in the IMF and were inserted at decisive moments in the House and Senate deliberations when the legislation would have otherwise died. The maneuvers and circle of support were intended to gain passage of the legislation, however, and not to turn the banking community into supporters.

Thus the chapter demonstrates the connection among groups, the legislature, and the IOs that commenced with the enactment of the legislation required to join. Congressional influence on the IFIs is episodic but powerful. Individual members such as Henry Cabot Lodge (R-MA), Robert Taft (R-OH), Robert F. Wagner (D-NY), Charles W. Tobey (R-NH), and Brent Spence (D-KY) either prevented the US from joining earlier IOs and/or shaped the mechanisms of participation that were established when it did. The involvement of groups concerned with the legislation led to compromises and specific outcomes. Specifically, the version of the bill that passed provided that the new IOs would be managed not by neutral experts but by government representatives. The US representative would have to report to a cabinet-level committee and would have to obtain its approval before voting on any matter that required his approval under the Articles of Agreement. He or she would need to have the committee's agreement on specific matters, such as a waiver of the conditions on Fund lending or a declaration that the dollar was a scarce currency.[3] Congressional approval would be required to change the gold content of the dollar. These provisions would provide an opportunity for the same domestic organized groups that had pressed for their inclusion to filter their interests through Congress to influence outcomes in later IFI policies and programs.

Thus, the legislation established political channels through which the institution of Congress could advocate for policy changes in the IFIs, even if a formal role for the legislature did not exist in the Bretton Woods agreement itself. However, these constituencies were mobilized for enactment and not for the work of the IFIs. The next chapter will show that once the IOs were established, Congress largely stepped back. It did not engage in any serious efforts to direct specific loans or projects in the early years.

## Congress and the Failure of the Treaty of Versailles

Anti-multilateral sentiment in Congress is generally traced to the failure of the Senate to ratify the Treaty of Versailles, and thus the failure of the US to join the League of Nations as part of the package. The episode loomed large in the minds of policy makers and societal groups who later fought for passage of the Bretton Woods Agreement Act in Congress. However, often overlooked is the fact that the treaty itself had a high degree of popularity in the Senate and in US society as a whole. Its opponents were able to defeat it by attaching amendments that were unacceptable to its supporters. After two votes where it was defeated as amended, it was eventually dropped from the Senate's agenda.

The problem of American participation in multilateral institutions appeared to be a problem of Congress. When decision making is shifted from the domestic US political system to an international body, the action threatens the delicate checks and balances set forth in the Constitution with respect to the assignment of specific roles and responsibilities to the legislature. Hence, American support for multilateralism has been challenged by a hesitation to situate decision making in international bodies from this earliest episode. In the case of the Treaty of Versailles, the provisions for a League of Nations triggered a partisan, interbranch struggle not only over the US's international commitments but over the institutional power to declare war between the president and Congress. The institution of Congress thus advocated on behalf of itself to preserve its ability to make international policy with respect to war. Those supporting the League were unable to allay these interbranch concerns, but they did learn from them in the next episode.

### WOODROW WILSON AND THE LEAGUE OF NATIONS

American participation in the League of Nations poses a fascinating paradox: The organization owed its existence to the perseverance of an American president during the negotiations for the Treaty of Versailles, yet the US never joined it. While historians debate the role of Woodrow Wilson in negotiating the Treaty of Versailles, as well as his role in its defeat in the US Senate, none deny his personal commitment to the centrality of the League in the peace negotiations at the end of the Great War. One observer at the conference wrote: "There is no doubt that President Wilson considered the League of Nations project his particular idea."[4] Yet the defeat of the treaty resulted from several of Wilson's decisions concerning its negotiation and packaging in the Senate, which is surprising since he had so many early legislative victories, such as the Federal Reserve Act and the Clayton Antitrust Act.

Initially elected president in 1912, Wilson had benefited from a split in the Republican Party between Theodore Roosevelt and William Howard Taft. He won a very narrow reelection in 1916, and the US entered the war shortly thereafter. As it wore on, Wilson amassed a degree of power that antagonized a Republican Congress already marginalized and ineffective. Moreover, Wilson's personal manner was aloof. Many viewed his extended trips overseas and personal connection to the negotiations as a lack of attention to US interests and overcommitment of American resources to Europe.[5] His own secretary of state, Robert Lansing, warned him of the complications that would arise from his personal involvement in the treaty negotiations, not least the need for his participation in the domestic aspects of the legislation.

During the congressional race of 1918, Wilson made an unsuccessful plea to the American people to elect a Democratic Congress as a matter of national security. Sentiment against him hardened among those who already disliked him, because this request implied that Republicans could not guard the best interests of the country. After the election in that year, Republicans held a narrow Senate majority and the members of the foreign relations committee were overwhelmingly Republicans opposed to the idea of a League. Thus, William H. Taft warned Wilson to consult the Senate Foreign Relations Committee in negotiating a peace. He had specifically suggested appointing senators as negotiators.[6] The practice of sending senators to negotiate treaties was not unknown, although it was controversial. Previously, William McKinley had sent senators to at least five commissions to negotiate treaties.[7] Yet at the end of World War I, Harry White was the sole Republican on the delegation and a friend of both Theodore Roosevelt and Henry Cabot Lodge. Unsurprisingly, he did not support the League. Other prominent Republicans, such as William Taft or Elihu Root, might have helped with the sentiment in the Senate because they were perceived to be more accepting of notions of a League.

When the negotiations finished, the armistice was concluded on the basis of Wilson's Fourteen Points. His chief contribution was in securing the decision to set up a League that all states could all accept.[8] When Wilson returned home, he knew that the Senate would oppose the League. Therefore, he tied the Treaty of Versailles to the League of Nations in one legislative proposal that would have to be accepted as a whole. When the struggle in the Senate turned to questions of the provisions in the treaty, Wilson famously made his appeal directly to the American people for the package and ruined his health.

The Senate as a whole voted on the treaty two times. During the first vote November 19, 1919, forty-two Democrats and thirteen Republicans voted to defeat it as amended with reservations. During the second vote, on March 19, 1920, twenty-three Democrats and twelve Republicans again voted to defeat it as amended. Therefore, Democrats actually voted against the treaty as amended by Republicans. Lodge argued that Wilson had taken away any Democratic support for his "League with reservations" because he would not comprise. Thus, Wilson destroyed the organization.[9] Lodge had voted for it twice. Conversely, Wilson blamed Lodge and the Republicans for their objections to the treaty as negotiated.

## THE INTERBRANCH STRUGGLE AND THE LEAGUE

Beneath the bitter personal and partisan disputes that emerged over the ratification in the Senate was a serious interbranch dispute over the executive power of the president vis-à- vis Congress. As a scholar of Congress, Wilson was well aware of the implications of the treaty that did challenge the separation of powers in the US political system. Lodge and others quoted sections of his work *Constitutional Government* during the course of the struggle, and specifically asserted the right of the Senate to advise concerning treaties.[10] While Lodge was an openly partisan senator and friend of Wilson's rival Theodore Roosevelt, his actions also resulted from his alarm at the president's efforts to override and disregard the checks-and-balances system in the US Constitution.[11] Lodge had likewise insisted on the prerogative of the Senate in making treaties under Republican administrations.

As discussed, the debate came to an impasse in the Senate because Republicans sought four reservations to the treaty that would be included in the ratification. Democrats refused the Lodge reservations on the grounds that they would invalidate the best points of the negotiated agreement. One of the most contentious issues was Article X of the Covenant, which contained the essence of the collective-action mechanism. Some senators sought to add reservations to Article X that would more clearly articulate when the US was obligated to engage in acts of war, a power they argued was reserved by Congress under the US Constitution. Wilson countered that the US representative on the Council of the League held the power to veto any action, and thus an international body would not be making that ultimate decision. However, Wilson's argument begs the question of congressional involvement because the veto would then be held by an appointee of the executive branch and not Congress.[12] Additional reservations sought guarantees that US appointees to the League would require Senate confirmation and special provisions for the Monroe Doctrine. While the senators no doubt had a variety of reasons for pursuing the course of action they did in blocking the treaty, they were nonetheless defending their prerogative, and Congress's, to make war.

## PARTISANSHIP AND THE LEAGUE

The intensely partisan nature of the struggle over the Treaty of Versailles speaks to the issue of ideology and international organization that persists to the present day. As discussed in Chapter 1, many issues of policy design exist separate from strict ideological concerns. The preexisting ideological preferences of either Democrats or Republicans are not the only determinant of party-line votes. The members may be making explicit political calculations about their collective interests as a party.[13] At first glance, the two votes on the Treaty of Versailles appear to be quite ideological and partisan. Yet both parties had, at times, supported internationalist notions of a collective-action mechanism to keep the peace. Within the United States, a group of distinguished Americans formed the League to Enforce Peace on June 17, 1917, to work toward the specific goals of a League of Nations and World Court. Bipartisan from its inception, the group elected Republican William Howard Taft as its president. At one time Henry Cabot Lodge was a member of the organization. Pacifists opposed the group because they viewed its "win the war" platform as a coercive means of promoting peace. Eventually, Wilson joined it and incorporated the idea of a League constitution and a mechanism for organizing the peace into his broader crusade for the law of nations over the tyranny of war.[14]

When the treaty was moving through the Senate, many organized groups on the right and the left actively supported the League and the treaty. The American Federation of Labor, the Church Peace Union, the National Grange, and many colleges and universities had gone on the record in favor of ratification of the treaty and membership in the League.[15] American corporate leaders such as John J. Raskob (then of General Motors) appealed to senators that they pass the League treaty.[16] Throughout the debate in the Senate, moderate pro-League Republicans were in the awkward position of negotiating with the Republican majority *without* any hope that the Democrats would support the moderate reservations they sought.[17]

The way the treaty and the League were bundled also created opponents who were not necessarily antagonistic to the idea of multilateralism. For example, many liberal internationalists, such as Herbert Croly, Walter Lippmann, William Bullitt, and Oswald Garrison Villard, opposed the treaty and therefore opposed the League as a component of it. After the peace conference ended in Europe, John Maynard Keynes proposed that the US guarantee the payment of German reparations. When Wilson refused, Keynes referred to him as "the greatest fraud on earth." He went on to write his critical assessment of the Versailles Treaty, *The Economic Consequences of the Peace.* James A. Salter, who was an economist on the British delegation and later head of the Reparations Commission, asked Keynes to moderate his position on Wilson, if for no other reason than the effect it would have on the ratification of the treaty in the US.[18]

Far from being on the right side of the political spectrum, or an enemy of economic multilateralism when designing the Bretton Woods institutions, Keynes published his book, which is considered to have influenced American public opinion against membership as the debate heated up in the Senate.[19]

The contradictions over membership in the League did not end with the final vote on the Treaty of Versailles March 19, 1920. The two elements of the legislation, the treaty and the League, were ultimately handled individually. The US Congress ended the war with a joint resolution. Wilson vetoed it but was overridden by a substantial majority. The next year, the US concluded a separate treaty with Germany on August 21, 1921, that contained some of the harshest clauses of the Versailles Treaty. The League, however, did come into operation and Americans were employed there at its highest levels. Since the debate had been so bitter and outwardly partisan, the State Department in the subsequent Republican administration initially declined to answer invitations to League-sponsored conferences. However, the informal relationship changed rapidly. Republican Charles Evans Hughes began a State Department tradition of refusing to comment on League activities by responding to any questioner that the US was not a member. Nonetheless, he did quietly endorse cooperation with the technical and humanitarian work of the organization's agencies early in its history.[20]

By 1928, much of the public controversy over US membership had dissipated. The Democratic Party ended its open support for membership, and the Republican Party endorsed the idea of nonpolitical cooperation. Herbert Hoover never articulated a clear League policy as president, despite his support for Wilson at the time of the treaty debate. While Roosevelt had likewise supported membership for the US during those years, his administration failed to articulate a clear League policy and placed it low on his overall list of international priorities.[21] Generally, the US would send observers to meetings who were essentially US representatives without voting rights. Financial support came from the State Department's emergency fund and not congressional appropriations. In an early effort to keep a sensitive issue off of the public agenda, any public debate that would have halted payments was prevented. One League staffer's recollection was that it was a "well-known secret" in Geneva that the office of the US permanent advisor to the League at its headquarters "hummed" with activity in the late 1930s.[22]

Therefore, in the first episode of congressional advocacy toward an IO, the opponents of multilateralism in Congress were successful in preventing the US from joining the League. But contradictions in policy had been apparent from the start as well. The failure of the Senate to ratify the treaty did not end societal support for the work of the League in the United States or in Congress. Those members of Congress and presidential administrations willing to participate in the League's activities used private arrangements to promote policies aligned with their personal preferences, regardless of party. Individual

American philanthropies also supported the work of the League through private contributions. The magnitude of the Rockefeller library gift was so large that the League had to find a new site for its headquarters to accommodate it.[23]

While any American influence over policy outcomes was vehemently denied within and outside the League, this collaboration had some results, particularly in the work of the social and humanitarian section. Moreover, the experience of the first episode enabled the passage of the Bretton Woods Agreement Act because supporters of economic multilateralism learned from their experiences.

## Congress and the Passage of the Bretton Woods Agreement

The US experience with negotiating and ratifying the Bretton Woods agreements was nearly a mirror opposite that of the League of Nations. With the League, a majority of members supported the Treaty of Versailles but could not agree on the amendments attached. In the years that followed, a substantial degree of tacit cooperation ensued with the transnational business community, philanthropies, and individuals in the work of the economic section.[24] Conversely, when the Treasury Department sought passage of the Bretton Woods agreement, it addressed the problem of Congress and any interbranch rivalry head-on. The agreement passed, and the US joined the newly created international organizations. Nonetheless, international organizations do not flourish in the absence of a domestic political base in the US. In the next episode, the same domestic political opponents to the New Deal and Bretton Woods agreement were able to shape the operations of the early IFIs to make them more amenable to the banking community that had sought to prevent passage. Thus, in the negotiation of modifications during the ratification process and in the early, precedent-setting meetings, the IMF that emerged was shaped by the outcomes of these congressional compromises.

One of the first efforts Treasury made with respect to economic multilateralism after the war was to integrate a strategy for congressional approval by circulating plans for a stabilization fund and reconstruction bank among prominent business organizations, academics, and the media who were likewise concerned with the problems of postwar currency stabilization, its desirability, and means of effectuation. Thus, they sought to expand the circle of support into the broader business community through a massive education effort. In addition, they approached individuals who would present opposition to the measure, such as Randolph Burgess. Working with Treasury, the State Department advocated Bretton Woods as an integral part of its broader plan for a network of peace organizations and stressed the importance of the monetary agreements as essential to the working of the peace in every speech, article, and pamphlet on international cooperation.[25] Treasury and State identified key members of Congress for the treaty's passage and invited them to attend as US delegates when the forty-four countries met at Bretton Woods, New Hampshire, July 1–22, 1944, to approve the recommendations for an International Monetary Fund and World Bank.

Hence, supporters from the executive branch, legislative branch, and civil society worked to eliminate opposition to multilateralism directly by segmenting the banking community over the issue of the membership in the Fund, then pointing to these differences in relevant congressional testimony. While the San Francisco conference on the United Nations was being held, they presented the Bretton Woods agreement as a unique opportunity that, when accepted, would unify the postwar world behind US leadership. This section argues that as a result of this formidable "sales project" by the Treasury and State Departments to avoid the failures of the past, a policy network of supporters of multilateral cooperation began to construct constituencies for the nascent IMF and World Bank that would be deepened in later years as they found their footing.

## NEGOTIATING THE BRETTON WOODS AGREEMENT

The Bretton Woods agreements emerged from a set of proposals circulated among the US and British finance ministries, key groups in civil society known to support multilateral efforts, and those known to pose obstacles to them. Unlike the negotiations for the League of Nations, members of Congress were included in the Bretton Woods meetings. The design of the Bretton Woods agreement is also uniquely linked to the Roosevelt presidency and the structure of the international system at the end of World War II. Franklin Roosevelt entered his presidency predisposed toward multilateralism. As assistant secretary of the navy in the Wilson administration, he had supported US membership in the League. Nonetheless, Roosevelt downplayed open discussions of his postwar plans, multilateral or otherwise, even after the US entered the war because tensions among allies existed over the Bolshevik revolution and the nature of British imperialism. The Council on Foreign Relations offered to study postwar issues, including multilateralism, secretly and report on its findings to the State Department. Secretary of State Cordell Hull accepted the offer and the Council created four committees in the area of postwar armaments, economic relations, colonial territories, and cross-border aggression. The Rockefeller Foundation provided financial support for the project, and Norman Davis was responsible for coordinating the studies and presenting them to the State Department. The private nature of the Council facilitated these arrangements and allowed them to remain secret.[26]

More specific proposals for the financial institutions commenced with the circulation of various memorandums by Harry Dexter White and John Maynard Keynes as early as 1941.[27] Both Keynes and White sought to facilitate balance-of-payments equilibrium in an international environment of multilateral trade and in domestic conditions of full employment. White devised the US plan for financial collaboration and had the advantage of working through the Treasury Department headed by Henry Morgenthau, Jr., who enjoyed better relations with Franklin Roosevelt than Cordell Hull at the State Department did. The Fund and the Bank would be principal agencies for postwar international finance, designed as true institutions of international government. Keynes's plan for an International Clearing Union was similar to those of White's Stabilization Fund. A Clearing Union would make large overdraft facilities available to its members. When the plans were published in April 1943, both received opposition even within their own countries.[28] Keynes, together with White and others, did not want a later US revision published. They feared that the drafting committee's work would then become the proposal and that "Congress etc., would start taking the draft to pieces."[29] Rather, they advocated publishing the revised plan after the conference was concluded.

However, even before the plans were published, they were widely discussed. The White plan was circulated among the major business associations in the US and they, in turn, began to prepare generally supportive positions on it. The Chamber of Commerce, National Association of Manufacturers (NAM), National Foreign Trade Council (NFTC), and American Bankers Association (ABA) shared and discussed views among themselves, as well as with their respective memberships. NAM, the NFTC, the US Chamber of Commerce, the American section of the International Chamber of Commerce, and the National Foreign Trade Council organized an international businessmen's conference in 1944 where they affirmed their support for a postwar order underpinned with free trade and some currency-stabilization mechanism. The US Chamber of Commerce voted in favor of forming a United Nations organization at its first meeting after the war.[30]

The serious divisions that emerged within the major business associations over the proposals concerned the type of economic organizations that would form after the war ended. The most serious occurred over the proposals for a stabilization fund. For example, the Los Angeles Chamber of Commerce supported the early Bretton Woods proposals, whereas the main organization did not. Likewise, academics discussed the proposals, mostly along the lines of their support or opposition to the New Deal.[31] Other critics objected to any international organization wherein the US possessed only minority control, particularly when resources would be freely available without regard to the creditworthiness or economic policies of borrowing countries.[32]

Eventually held in July of 1944, the United Nations Monetary and Financial Conference sought to fix currency rates to facilitate and expand international trade following the war along the lines of Keynes's and White's plans. Nineteen of the forty-four states invited to the Bretton Woods Conference were from Latin America. Constituting the largest regional bloc and not having been included in the US civil society exchanges, they sought to address the role of economic development in the Bank's charter by encouraging equal weight for development assistance to be given both to areas affected and not affected by the war.[33] Specifically, Mexico sought to have the term "development" included in the initial title of the World Bank: the International Bank for Reconstruction and Development (IBRD).[34] Despite additional differences over relative quota positions, the role of silver, and commodity-price stabilization, they became strong supporters of the Bretton Woods negotiations.

The US delegation to the Bretton Woods Conference comprised twelve members. Six were from the executive branch and four from the legislature: the chair and ranking member of the House Banking and Currency, and Senate Banking Committees. Two were private citizens: Edward E. Brown, chair of the First National Bank of Chicago and president of the Federal Advisory Committee of the Federal Reserve System; and Mabel Newcomer, chair of the Department of Economics and Sociology at Vassar College. With four members of Congress present, one was able to attend every meeting of the conference. Moreover, Secretary Morgenthau was accompanied to New Hampshire by four government press relations officers, as well as Mr. Frederick Smith, the Treasury Secretary's special public relations counselor, and Mr. Arthur Sweetser of the Office of War Information (formerly of the League of Nations secretariat), who prepared propaganda for foreign as well as domestic dissemination. Morgenthau also hired public relations consultant Randolph Feltus to coordinate the bill's passage in Congress.[35] Thus, he had publicity advisors at nearly every step of the process.

Concerns about alienating the support of prominent members of the banking community were evident during the negotiations. For example, Leon Fraser, a former president of the Bank for International Settlements (BIS), had proposed that the BIS might be a suitable instrument for performing the functions contemplated for the IMF. White, commenting on Fraser's remark, responded that the BIS had become German-controlled during the war. Despite its location in neutral Switzerland, fourteen of the sixteen BIS directors had come under German control. This situation left only the Swiss and Swedish directors as possible free agents, and an American president. Morgenthau supported the proposal that the BIS be terminated, as the action would be useful for overseas anti-Nazi propaganda. Hull disagreed, and Edward Brown from the First National Bank of Chicago sought a compromise. These men were concerned that if the BIS termination were included in the Bretton Woods agreement, it would stir up further opposition from men such as Thomas Lamont of Morgan Stanley, Leon Fraser, and others who were identified with it.[36] Although the BIS termination was included, the organization survived after the war. The next step after the agreements were finalized was to work within the congressional machinery for ratification.

## SECURING PASSAGE OF THE BRETTON WOODS AGREEMENT IN CONGRESS

Having laid the groundwork well in advance, the community of support for the Bretton Woods community expanded their efforts. The victory was important not only for the immediate purposes of establishing an IMF and World Bank, but for the broader message it would send to the world concerning the sincerity of US efforts to forge multilateralism in other areas, chiefly the United Nations. Led by the Treasury Department, the supporters worked with sympathetic members of the same business associations, academics, and members of the media as before. Having had members of Congress present in New Hampshire had not guaranteed the support of these men; for example, Jesse Wolcott, the ranking member from the House, chose to reserve his support until the conclusion of the hearings when he sponsored a compromise that incorporated some of the criticisms of the bill. However, it did mean that the chair and ranking member of each committee was aware of the difficulties that existed in creating an agreement among forty-four states. They made multiple references to their attendance and the importance of preserving the "spirit" of the conference in future US economic relations during the hearings.

### Preliminary Strategies of the Treasury together with the National Foreign Trade Council

The strategy of the Treasury Department was to work through business associations such as the NFTC to mitigate known opposition to the Bretton Woods agreement. Thus, the month after the conference concluded, two representatives of the Treasury, Edward Bernstein, the assistant director of monetary research, and Ansel Luxford, met with C. E. Hunter, who was the chair of the NFTC Committee on Monetary Policy and Exchange Stabilization, Eugene Thomas, and William Swingle of the NFTC to discuss the ideas that the Treasury Department had with respect to how to present the proposals to exporters and importers. One observer from the council remarked after the meeting:

> The Treasury officials indicated that they were definitely engaged in an international selling program, to present the Bretton Woods proposals in a favorable light to the country, and that they looked upon the Council as the medium through which such a program could be carried to foreign traders, outside of any consideration which may be given by bankers' groups and associations.[37]

Treasury argued that the council should not just consider the proposals in the NFTC Committee on Monetary Policy and Exchange Stabilization, which mostly comprised bankers. The NFTC countered that while the consideration of the Bretton Woods matter would go first to that committee, the banking session at NFTC meetings would not be limited to bankers. In fact, bankers were generally not a large percentage of the attendance, and any proposal made at the convention as a whole would not simply represent bankers' opinions but would be a cross section of all foreign trade interests.[38] Dr. Bernstein and Mr. Luxford agreed that Treasury would attend the upcoming NFTC convention and have a full discussion of the proposals, particularly at the banking session. The secretary of the treasury or undersecretary would present the proposals at the bankers' luncheon and then Mr. Hunter would lead a no-holds-barred discussion session that afternoon with other representatives of the Treasury Department.[39]

The officials from Treasury sought a favorable declaration on the Bretton Woods proposals from the convention, arguing that not to approve them would throw private enterprise in international trade into jeopardy. To pursue this goal, they requested a meeting in Washington or New York, where representatives of the Final Declaration Committee of the Convention would meet for a full day if necessary—to have the Treasury and other Washington departments give officials full information on the proposals before any resolution was adopted. The NFTC advised that this was not possible because the Final Declaration Committee was selected on the opening day of the convention and would not be able to meet in advance. Rather, the NFTC would consider the possibility of meeting with a group of bankers and industrialists who would discuss it with the Treasury, and they would be the largest percentage that might eventually be represented on the Final Declaration Committee.[40] Alternately, a subcommittee could be appointed from the Final Declaration Committee to meet with the subcommittee on monetary policy and exchange stabilization with power to draft the final declaration paragraph on this subject. The group could meet with representatives of the Treasury who would presumably be at the convention.[41] Treasury would send 1,000 copies of the Articles publication to council members with no endorsement. The Treasury would also prepare a summary with questions and answers that would be made ready for the convention and used as background information for the banking session. No definite agreement on these matters was reached.[42]

To extend the discussion beyond the convention, the Treasury officials requested the NFTC arrange for group meetings throughout the US with industrialists and foreign traders in leading cities to hear explanations of the Bretton Woods agreements from the Treasury and US delegates to the conference. The NFTC declined to sponsor such meetings in its own name, but agreed that after the convention it would assemble foreign trade clubs and Chambers of Commerce with whom there were already close connections and offer the opportunity to hear from Treasury officials. Hence, these meetings would be called in various cities by individual groups and not by the NFTC officially, although they would be based on a proposed itinerary throughout all parts of the country to be checked with Treasury.[43]

As scheduled, the 31st National Foreign Trade Convention referred the Bretton Woods final act to a committee of industrialists, bankers, and others interested in foreign trade for study and recommendations. It was agreed that the committee would then make a report to the NFTC directors that would be the basis for their position on the final act. Specifically, the committee would question whether and when Congress should ratify participation in these two organizations and whether the capital of the Export-Import bank should be increased. Dr. Percey Bidwell, director of studies at the Council on Foreign Relations, was selected to work as the economist and secretary of the committee.

A serious debate within this committee followed in the months leading up to the congressional hearings, with overt attention paid to generating support for the legislation. For example, Alfred Mallon, a vice president and treasurer of the Pillsbury Flour Mills Company, approved of the Bank and thought most foreign traders knew there was a need to stabilize foreign exchange. He wrote to Clarence Hunter, the chair of the committee and a vice president of the New York Trust Company:

> My own position is that the Committee should favor the Bretton Woods' proposals very substantially, but given the setting in which this proposal is coming up, I would be prepared to accept modifications in the spirit in which I have discussed them above. . . . I think the important thing to judge is whether or not a reasonable set of modifications can command a wider support in Congress (the place where the plans must have the support) and at the same time still preserve the fundamental objectives of the original draft proposals.[44]

When the committee assembled on December 20 to develop its recommendations to the board, it divided into majority and minority opinions on the matter. The majority, formed among the industrial members and one banker, favored outright approval of the proposals without major modifications, although they were willing to accept minor ones. The minority view, formed exclusively among banking members, favored granting the IBRD the ability to make stabilization loans within a stabilization department. They would abolish quotas and the right to devalue arbitrarily. In their view, states would need to negotiate the assistance required to maintain its exchange after a stabilization loan. The committee agreed that the majority would write a report and recommend ratification of the Bretton Woods Final Act to the board, and the minority would supplement this report with comments outlining their proposed changes. The directors would then determine how to use the report.[45]

In January of the New Year, members wrote to the chair, with their views on the NFTC majority report, as well as the minority and the American Bankers Association (ABA) views, which were well known among the men. As before, the bankers mostly supported the views of the ABA. Among those bankers who did not, such as H. Salinger of the First National Bank of Chicago, there was agreement as to the thrust of the ABA proposals. However,

Salinger argued that the US needed immediate tools to prevent a German collapse in the spring; therefore, he supported the proposals as they were drafted.[46]

The Finance Committee of the NFTC remained divided over the proposal. Some members felt that it should be modified per the ABA modifications. Specifically, they wanted to eliminate features of the Fund and replace it with a department in the Bank that could negotiate currency-stabilization agreements as needed. They did not want to give stabilization credits to members, nor allow for the 10% adjustment in par value automatically, as they felt this would lead to chaos.[47] However, the US should participate in permanent international institution where heads of central banks and treasuries may meet regularly for consultation and collaboration on international monetary problems. They expressed unqualified support for the IBRD to aid in reconstructing the war-devastated nations and development of economically undeveloped countries.[48] Nonetheless, they recognized that these purposes could be achieved through two methods and mechanisms—as proposed, or as modified by the ABA proposal.

Therefore, the International Finance Committee of the NFTC concluded that they represented only one part of a complex pattern, many elements of which have not been explained by the government. Such a comprehensive program would include the World War I debts, Lend-Lease settlements, the Johnson Act, Export-Import Bank, policy on cartels, subsidies, tariffs, government bulk purposes, government foreign relief, and government foreign credit operations.[49] The key prerequisite to a monetary agreement was the establishment of an understanding between the US and Great Britain, open to other members of the Commonwealth, with respect to future financial and commercial policies.[50]

The efforts of the supporters of the agreement, led by the Treasury and the NFTC, detailed the planning and organization of a legislative strategy that took the concerns of civil society seriously. When disagreement persisted in the NFTC finance committee, Treasury officials continued to work toward a compromise. The details of the episode also show that groups were fully aware of the positions of related groups on this legislation, as well as their efforts to incorporate ideas of others' proposals into their own, in this case those of the ABA. Therefore, the support came from groups that cut across party lines.

### The American Bankers Association and Objections to the Proposals

The societal groups opposing the Bretton Woods proposals were led by the ABA. As had been the case with opposition to the Treaty of Versailles, their opposition was not necessarily ideological. Many bankers, such as Thomas Lamont, had been strong advocates for the treaty and the economic work of the League of Nations. However, many bankers outside of the New York community supported the act. Opposition stemmed from the specific mechanisms that would cut into the international operations of some banks and the manner the legislation was bundled with the IMF and World Bank into one legislative proposal. The opposition of the ABA was not a surprise. Representatives of the Treasury had approached the ABA prior to the Bretton Woods Conference, yet had not invited representatives of the association to attend as delegates. At that time, the ABA filed an initial statement with the Treasury stating that they did not approve of certain specifics of the plan.[51]

The immediate objection of the ABA to the proposals had to do with placing lending authority in the hands of an international agency, as opposed to a national one such as the Export-Import Bank. The US would have a minority of votes in the IMF and World Bank, despite having provided the largest share of hard currency. In the Bank there would be a veto power over loans floated in dollars, but not in the Fund. Therefore, the organization viewed the Fund in particular as "handing over to an international body the power to determine the place and kind of use of our money."[52] They argued that the plans as drafted would encourage inflation, delay economic adjustments, and fail to protect the principles and interests of the US. Nonetheless, the bankers retained their internationalist outlook as demonstrated during the League period. They drew a clear connection between economic disturbances as an underlying cause of war. The ABA wrote: "To avoid war the nations must learn to work together in economic matters as well as political. The more we do business with the citizens of other countries to our mutual advantage, the less likely we are to find ourselves forced into war with them."[53]

The views of individual members of the ABA were not uniform. Similar to the NFTC, the ABA delegated a committee to state its position at its annual convention. This "administrative committee" was chaired by W. Randolph Burgess, the vice chair of the board of National City Bank of New York and president of the ABA. Most members of this committee were representatives of large New York banks, including those engaged in international finance. They initially approved of the proposal, then reversed themselves. However, as with the NFTC, other bankers approved of the agreements in their entirety, including the southern and western ones. The Independent Bankers Association of 2,000 country banks supported it. Individual bankers supported it, such as Edward Brown of Chicago. The perception at the time was that the strategy of those bankers opposed was to amend, make reservations, stall, and kill the institution with indirection.[54]

### The Proposals in Congress

The manner in which the proposals passed through each chamber, then were reconciled through compromise with the most recalcitrant opposition in the ABA, shaped the form of the American participation that followed and thus the contours of the organizations themselves. At every step, Treasury worked with groups supporting and opposing the legislation to ensure its passage. On January 9, President Roosevelt gave his annual budgetary message and recommended immediate establishment of the Bank and Fund. He had delayed the introduction of the Bretton Woods results until after the election in order that his administration could build bridges to Republican internationalists and undercut what influence the more isolationist wing of the Republican Party might have had before it.[55]

Robert F. Wagner (D-NY) and Charles W. Tobey (R-NH) introduced "A Bill to Provide for the Participation of the United States in the International Monetary Fund and the International Bank for Reconstruction and Development" into the Senate February 15, 1945, as S. 540. Brent Spence (KY, chair) introduced H. R. 2211 with exactly the same wording into the House. Public hearings on 2211 began on March 7 in the House and ended March 23, 1945. In a nod to the importance of having attended the conference in New Hampshire, Treasury Secretary Henry Morgenthau, Jr., began his testimony by thanking the chairman of the committee (Brent Spence), Mr. Wolcott, Senator Tobey, and Senator Wagner for keeping his feet on the ground at all times. He said: "You gentlemen kept reminding us of what was practical from the point of view of Congress, what we could or could not pass."[56] Frederick Vinson, then director of economic stabilization, also testified that:

> Secretary Morgenthau was always anxious and desirous of securing the viewpoint of the Members of the House and Senate on the delegation as to what they thought about the alternatives that were being discussed. And if I may say it, I will admit, if pressed, that I endeavored to use all my experience on the Hill in thinking what Congressmen and Senators would think about different issues.[57]

These men communicated the sense that the US had not cooperated prior to the war and had paid a high price. Were a Bretton Woods–type agreement to have been in place, World War II could have been prevented. The chief opponents to the bill, Senator Robert Taft (R-OH) and Representative Frederick Smith (R-OH), took the view that the IFIs would constitute Keynesian economic planning on an international scale. Thus, the congressional struggle became one between those who preferred to place monetary and exchange-rate governance in the hands of civil servants, and those who preferred it in the hands of the private New York and London international banking communities.[58]

Throughout the congressional hearings, the Treasury Department continued to work with the business community and allies on the Hill to ensure passage. On February 17, 1945. Morgenthau and officials of the State Department agreed to an off-the-record discussion with a question-and-answer session on the agreement and its relation to plans for world organizations with representatives from leading national organizations. An all-day conference was held in Washington at the Commerce Department auditorium on February 28.[59] Following that meeting, a women's action committee that attended held an evening session on Bretton Woods and passed a resolution in favor of the program. The organization proceeded to write members of Congress, urging its adoption promptly and without amendment.[60] Staff at the Treasury Department prepared speeches for Senator Wagner, Representative Spence, and others in support of the proposals. In addition, they compiled replies to anti–Bretton Woods testimony of individuals such as Edwin Kemmerer. They provided copies of charts that had been used in House hearings for the floor debate.[61]

Morgenthau and White argued their plan formally, informally, and quietly before other groups and individual members of Congress. In March, when Morgenthau feared that information on Bretton Woods was lagging, he invited a group of columnists and radio commentators to lunch at the Treasury Department. Critics of Morgenthau's tactics from Senator Robert Taft's staff complained that "the guests got chicken a la king (now quite scarce in Washington), salad, rolls, cheese, ice cream and a beverage. The Treasury got some mighty fine publicity for Bretton Woods."[62] In some cases, Harry White collaborated with groups to the extent that he was viewed as the author of their final report, such as with the Independent Bankers Association's positive report on Bretton Woods.[63]

## The House Debate

The first step in the bill's enactment was in the House of Representatives. Organized labor emerged as a key supporter of the bill and the weekly Congress of Industrial Organizations (CIO) newsletter urged its readers to pressure Congress to adopt the program without amendment on the premise that the availability of jobs was connected to exports through loans. Formal representatives of labor groups visited members of Congress who opposed the bill to persuade them to change their views.[64] The president of the American Federation of Labor, William Green, testified that the chief source of prosperity would come from productive employment, which would support enlarged markets for our home use. In addition, smaller states would benefit from the opportunity to satisfy their economic needs through international agencies, as opposed to bilateral agreements with a dominant power.[65] Byrl Whitney of the Brotherhood of Railroad Trainmen and James Carey of the Congress of Industrial Organizations also testified in favor of the act insofar as it would promote exports.[66] Similarly, the National Grange and National Farmers Union sought ratification for the expansion of trade and gains to employment.[67]

While the bill was being debated in the House, the NFTC council board of directors finally adopted a resolution on March 20 stating that they would like to see a comprehensive economic policy, but even without it, they favored the adoption of the Bretton Woods agreement substantially as drafted. They immediately forwarded this official position to Wagner in the Senate. Individual NFTC members also directed their positions toward members of Congress.

Many staunchly pro–Bretton Woods NFTC members, such as Carl Wynne, the managing director of Overseas Industries in Chicago, were annoyed that the Council had been so timid in its final resolution because at a later date it would not get the credit it deserved for support of international organizations.[68]

The split in the NFTC reflected the broader split in the business community. Whereas a small group of powerful bankers in New York opposed ratification because they believed they could profit from a continuation of the practices of the past by earning fees on foreign-exchange trading, other members of the business community recognized that stability in exchange markets would expand the volume of trade. At the NFTC, Wynne pointed out that while some banks would lose a small amount of business, most banks would gain handsomely from the growth that would follow.[69] Internal communications indicate that the business groups continued to communicate among themselves with respect to what the other business associations' positions were. The Independent Bankers Association, a group of small banks organized in Nebraska in 1942 with no large city banks among its members, came out in favor. Also in favor was the Pennsylvania Bankers Association and presidents of the eleven leading banks of Philadelphia, which was an important group at the time.[70]

Also in March, the president of the Chamber of Commerce asked its Finance Department Committee to make recommendations to the board of directors on the Bretton Woods proposals. The president of the Chamber also requested that they consult with representatives of the Foreign Commerce Department Committee and the Committee on International Postwar Problems. They did so March 2 and 3. Prior to the conference, they read all of the materials circulating. At the conference, they listened to officials from the Treasury.[71] The Finance Department Committee concluded that the Bretton Woods proposals were consistent with policies of the Chamber. "The Committee is of the opinion that these commitments of the Chamber justify and require a most sympathetic attitude toward proposals for international collaboration to promote stabilization of currencies and to facilitate the extension on a sound basis of credits for reconstruction and development."[72] While the Chamber took the position that the IBRD should be established immediately, it was closer to the ABA position on the Fund, calling for further study and alternative methods of currency stabilization.

Despite the number of groups eventually expressing open support for the bill, Brent Spence informed Morgenthau that the bill would most likely be voted down in committee because of the pressure from the ABA as late as March 22. Burgess then approached Edward Bernstein, White's assistant, about the ABA's position. The organization would be willing to support the proposals with the right modifications. From the Treasury's perspective, major modifications would require the convening of a new conference. However, representatives would be willing to talk to the ABA, and they met with Burgess in New York to lay the groundwork. As a result of the discussion, which lasted the better part of a day, they developed a compromise position that would allow for the appointment of the same executive director for the Bank and the Fund. To meet the major objection of the bankers concerning Fund management, they would coordinate American policy on a board wherein the bankers would be represented by the president of the Federal Reserve Bank of New York. The legislation would require congressional reports from the American representatives. After the initial meeting, Burgess met with several individuals in New York individually, then in a group with Treasury. Were some common ground to exist, representatives of the two groups would then approach Spence and Wolcott.[73]

Despite some differences that remained, the bankers tentatively agreed to oversight by the US government and the New York financial community of the activities of the Bank and the Fund. The act would thus create a cabinet-level, interdepartmental council that would be chaired by the secretary of the treasury to formulate US policy. Rather than vote an amended bill, the committee drafted a new one (H. R. 3314) with the compromise language and voted it out with a 23–3 vote on May 24. On June 7, 1945, H. R. 3314 passed the House floor 345–18 with the compromise language. The compromise therefore created the National Advisory Council (NAC), which would report to Congress every six months on US participation in the IMF and World Bank.[74]

## The Senate Debate

On June 1, 1945, a committee of businessmen and bankers formed to support Bretton Woods for the final push. As in the contemporary Congress, interest groups provided members with information. Similarly, the Business and Industry Committee for Bretton Woods made public a series of reports on how international monetary agreements would affect specific industries, including cotton, tobacco, petroleum, automotive, motion picture, electronic, shipping, and machine tool plants. It sent copies to the members of the Senate Banking and Currency Committee as well as to the NFTC. The result was that a wider swath of individual senators could see how the agreement would affect key geographical constituencies in their home states. While this information did not necessarily change their minds, it did offer some a rationale for support.

When the amended bill moved to the Senate, Senator Robert A. Taft, who had objected to aspects of the program the previous year, led the opposition. Taft had predicted that Congress would approve the aspects of the Bretton Woods agreement that allowed for continuous consultation with other nations, and would authorize the secretary to participate in the stabilization fund. However, he did not believe that Congress would approve any plan that placed US money into a fund with an international board in which the US had a minority voice. Moreover, he did not believe Congress would approve any plan that required the government to restrict or regulate foreign-exchange transactions in the US, yet impose complete government control of all international transfers of funds. Finally, he did not think that Congress would place power in the hands of a representative of the president without the approval of Congress, who would have the ability to change the gold value of the dollar.[75] Thus, in the Senate, Taft argued that the US should initially make an agreement with Great Britain and stabilize the pound. As drafted, the US would contribute "real money," whereas others would not.[76]

As literature on interest groups predicts, the groups that opposed the agreement gravitated to sympathetic members like Taft and Wolcott and sent them information about the opposition.[77] For example, they wrote Taft to inform him of television shows that had aired in support of Bretton Woods and suggested that he appear on the same shows to explain the other side. Burgess of the ABA wrote Jesse Wolcott with advice about editorials and included those supporting the ABA position for his use as well.[78] However, the Business and Industry Committee for Bretton Woods also wrote Taft to try to persuade him to their point of view. Taft's opposition provoked anxiety on the part of supporters of the bill because they feared that others would follow him.[79]

As detailed in the previous section, when the bill moved to the Senate, the ABA had already modified its view in a compromise. The organization acknowledged that discussions before Congress had resulted in general acceptance of the plan for the Bank, but it had pointed out dangers in the Fund. Whereas the ABA had originally sought to merge the functions of the two, its strategy now shifted from seeking a merger of the two institutions to "safeguarding" the operations of the Fund. In this way, a more harmonious agreement on the legislation could be reached, provided the safeguards for the Fund would be adequate. Toward this end, the ABA outlined four recommendations that should be made conditions for the acceptance of the US of membership in the Bank and the Fund, and sent them to Senator Taft in late June. The Bank should have the power to make loans for financial and monetary rehabilitation and for exchange stabilization; the short-term character of advances by the Fund should be clarified; the same directors and alternates should be designated for the Bank and the Fund; and further consideration of Article VII with respect to scarce currency should be deferred.[80]

Burgess acknowledged that the banking community was split on the issue and testified to the Senate that "I was just commenting, I think, as we recessed, on methods that might suggest themselves for safeguarding the operations of the Fund as an alternative to a more drastic revision of the whole plan."[81] These changes could be grouped in two main categories: who would run the Fund, and creating a structure that would support the management. Burgess sought reassurance that the Fund would actually have the authority to raise objections as to the way its money would be used.[82] At the conclusion of the Senate hearings, Burgess issued a statement that while the Senate committee had further strengthened the proposals with its amendments, the Senate committee did not adopt a few recommendations that had been advocated with respect to assuring the short-term use of the Fund, providing for the same directors for both Fund and Bank, and safeguarding the "scarce currency" provision. In his view, the most important related to protecting the Fund from abuse by specifying clearly that the revolving fund would revolve. If the Fund were to become frozen, the "scarce currency" provision would go into effect and the whole program could break down.[83]

Despite these reservations, by late June Burgess testified that Congress could go ahead with the Fund due to amendments that had passed the House previously. Mr. Burgess agreed under questioning by Senator Robert A. Taft that he still had a personal dislike for some phases of the fund, particularly that the Bank and the Fund did not share a board of directors. Nonetheless, he saw that public sentiment ran strongly in favor of the Fund's establishment. So many groups had been drawn into the debate that even he could see that it was going to happen in some form, regardless of his objections.[84] A representative from the NFTC did not testify because they felt their opinion was in the report. However, their support was evident as well insofar as Secretary Morgenthau testified in the Senate and mentioned Carl Wynne by name in arguing that Bretton Woods would lower the risk to exporters. It would thus work to their benefit, as well as the benefit of increased employment in sectors that supplied these exports.

Thus, when passed, the Bretton Woods Agreement Act departed from the original conceptions of a Bank and a Fund. Rather than being managed by impartial financial experts as these plans had envisioned, they would be managed by representatives of national governments. The act further subordinated the US executive director to the NAC, the cabinet-level committee created in the compromise language of the House version. The US executive director would have to have the Council's approval before voting on any matter on which his approval was necessary under the Fund articles. He or she would also need to have the Council's approval before voting for a waiver of the conditions on Fund lending, or a declaration that the dollar was a scarce currency.[85] Finally, he or she would need congressional approval to change the gold content of the dollar.

Ultimately, the argument that carried the day was the sense that the US must take a chance on the institutions at a time when the San Francisco conference on international organizations was being held. It divided the Republicans against themselves—winning over traditional isolationists like Senator Tobey and leaving the fight to hard-liners like Senator Taft. By mid-July, Senator Taft was isolated from a majority of his own party. In addition, the Treasury Department advanced the argument that international monetary cooperation was a national security concern.[86] The act passed the House by an overwhelming majority. A last-minute effort to postpone the Fund was defeated by a vote of

52–31. Therefore, on July 18, 1945, the Senate passed the legislation authorizing US participation in both the Bank and the Fund.[87]

The legislative fight had been difficult, but it was successful because the Treasury sought to widen the base of support for the organizations from the beginning by reaching out to sympathetic groups in civil society and working to eliminate resistance from those opposed through compromise. Pressure from the ABA had persisted well into the struggle and could have prevented the bill from moving out of the House committee. Major modifications would have required a new international conference, but minor ones would not. In meeting with Burgess in New York, Treasury's compromise attempted to allow for enough domestic participation through the National Advisory Council. Thus, Congress and the banking community were successful in securing a hook into the operations of the stabilization fund, and issues lingered from the ratification struggle once the Fund commenced operations.

## Conclusion: The Enactment Stage

In the enactment stage of the Congress-IFI relationship, Treasury mobilized the support of the widest possible swath of civil society to secure passage of the Bretton Woods Agreement Act through a massive education campaign extolling the benefits of membership in the new organizations. The business community participated in drafting plans for the organizations and crafting legislative compromises that allowed for future influence. Section 5 of the Bretton Woods Agreement Act ensures a formal role for the legislature. It stipulates that the president must seek the formal permission of Congress before s(he) can change the par value of the dollar in the IMF. Moreover, the National Advisory Committee provided for a statutory role in the operations of the IOs.

In this manner, supporters of multilateralism overcame the obstacle of Congress that had blocked membership in the League when the Treaty of Versailles failed to gain ratification in the Senate. However, the Bretton Woods constituencies were mobilized to pass the bill and not on behalf of the work of the organizations when established. The banks that opposed passage were the most immediately and directly involved in the latter project. Therefore, the compromises that had been reached with the ABA when the bill moved through each chamber had a direct effect on their setup and initial operations. The next chapter will show that for multilateralism to flourish with the US as a member, the work of IOs must connect with the work of relevant groups in the American political economy.

3

# Building Constituencies for the Bretton Woods Framework

## BANKS, BIG BUSINESS, AND THE COLD WAR COALITION

> I was one who had as much doubt about the Monetary Fund as anybody in this room. I was President of the A.B.A. when that was discussed and lead the group that gave battle on the Monetary Fund. We did not think that was just the way to do it. I must say that sitting there and watching its operation, day by day, you are impressed with the fact that country by country, they are exerting steady pressure on those countries to do what they ought to do with respect to their currencies.[1]
>
> —W. Randolph Burgess, Deputy to the Secretary of the Treasury

In the years following the enactment of the Bretton Woods Agreement Act through the 1960s, the IFIs did not need annual appropriations as they would in later stages. Congressional advocacy operated when bills were needed to create new agencies under their auspices, and members amended the Articles of Agreement of the IFIs to secure passage. For example, the National Advisory Council (NAC), established during the passage of the Bretton Woods Agreement Act, influenced the profiles of the young IMF and World Bank when it sought to conserve the Fund's monies until the Western European countries had completely recovered from the war. Hence, in the "building stage" of the Congress-IFI relationship covered in this chapter, Congress mostly stood outside the operations of the young IMF and World Bank. Nonetheless, I argue that this building stage is significant because during these years significant exogenous changes occurred as the world economy recovered from the war. Foremost, as international lending resumed, the IFIs began to evolve and draw new constituencies in through their lending operations and projects. By the end of the stage, banks, big business, and strongly anti-communist members of Congress were firmly aligned in their political favor.

The external backdrop for this chapter is a world economy recovering from the devastation of World War II. The IMF and World Bank commenced operations with the US as a member, but in an economic setting that appeared to have either little need for them, or a need that was so great as to overwhelm them relative to the resources they were allocated. As the large money-center banks eventually resumed their international lending by building their branch banking operations to service multinational corporate clients, the contours of the recovery took shape.

The institution of Congress remained relatively closed during the 1950s and 1960s. The committees and their chairs directed a good deal of the powers and resources in the House of Representatives, whereas party leaders played a much more circumscribed role. After the Reorganization Act of 1946, rules determining committee jurisdictions allowed little leeway. Thus, committee chairs commanded the committee's agenda, organization, budget, and staff. The chair decided which bills would be considered and in what order. Neither the party leaders nor members had any practical means for removing the chair. Hence, he or she did not need to be responsive to any internal party constituency in order to retain his or her position. The rules augmented their power because votes were not recorded when bills were amended. Since the chair knew how a member voted and could retaliate, challenges to the committee were rarely issued.[2] These arrangements prevented any serious public discussion of policy issues in the IFIs. Few, if any, oversight hearings were held, and appropriations were neither sought nor granted.

The result of this combination of internal and external circumstances meant that congressional efforts shaped the profiles of the IMF and World Bank in episodic but powerful ways. This chapter details how the early leadership crisis at the IBRD and the need for securities legislation to expand the lending base of the World Bank meant that a more powerful executive team, tightly connected to Wall Street, eventually shaped it into a conservative lending institution. Rather than financing postwar European reconstruction, it channeled the flow of private investment dollars from the US to international reconstruction and development projects with an international guarantee.[3] While the overt objective of working with Wall Street was not to turn it into a constituency for the IFIs, the investment banks that managed the World Bank's issues eventually became powerful political allies of the institution and leadership moved freely among them.

In other examples, congressional advocacy operated when new entities were created. Longtime supporters of multilateralism, such as Nelson Rockefeller, worked to create an International Finance Corporation (IFC) under the World Bank's umbrella. The IFC proposal met with opposition from the business community. The legislation providing for US membership and an initial subscription passed, but it barred the new agency from investing in equity stocks or participating in the management of the firms in which it invested. Agricultural interests worked with senators to create a soft-loan facility for developing countries, the International Development Association (IDA), under the World Bank umbrella, whereas developing countries had made an earlier proposal under the auspices of the United Nations. The IDA legislation passed. But in the absence of some way to replenish the money it lent, IDA required an annual appropriation to replenish its lending capacity. The replenishment later became the annual mechanism for Congress to transmit policy proposals to the World Bank.

The domestic constituencies that were built during this stage would prove invaluable in the legislative struggles of the next one. When IDA would later encounter difficulties in securing its appropriation, supporters such as David Rockefeller testified in Congress on behalf of the organization. When the debt crisis of the 1980s threatened the banking system, the IFIs' connection to Chase, Citibank, and Bank of America would help to move legislation in a hostile political climate.

## The Young IMF and World Bank: State and Nonstate Actors Forge the Multilateral Form

Once the IFIs were established, the dynamic among management, key individuals in the advocacy community, and key members of Congress meant that the IMF commenced its work in an environment that had never wanted it to exist. Moreover, the Bank needed the participation of the financial community in an uncertain legal environment for its securities. Both the Bank and the Fund thus worked to involve these same groups in their early operations. The IMF and World Bank did not need to approach Congress directly in the early years, because the IMF did not request a quota increase in its first decade, and the IBRD was preoccupied with internal dynamics attached to its management. Therefore, the policy community took on the outward appearance of consensus and equilibrium; yet serious contradictions within this community persisted and prevented the IOs from playing a central role in the global economy as intended.

### UNRESOLVED PROBLEMS IN THE INTERNATIONAL MONETARY FUND

Tension between the New York banking community and the IMF did not end with the establishment of the organization. A loan to Great Britain for reconstruction came before Congress the next year and challenged multilateral sentiments yet again. When the Marshall Plan began operations, it provided an alternate source of monies and deflected European drawings from the Fund. Thus, there was very little lending in the organization's early years. In fact, private international lending after the war remained stagnant through much of the 1950s. Figure 3.1 shows that foreign borrowing in the US dropped off after the reconstruction loans in the 1947–1948 period and remained flat until the 1960s.

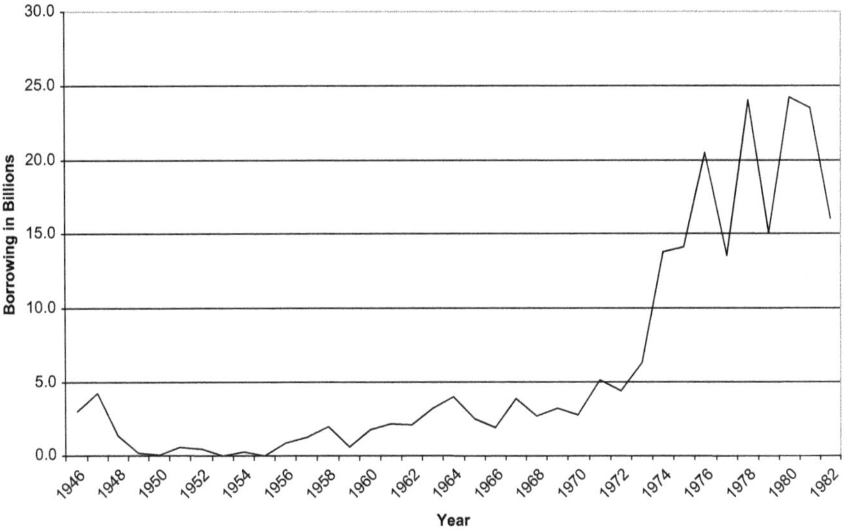


FIGURE 3.1 Foreign Borrowing in the US 1946–1982.

*Source:* Data from Federal Reserve Statistical Account *Flow of Funds Accounts of the United States.*

At the inaugural meeting of the Bank and the Fund in Savannah, Georgia, in March 1946, what participants termed a "bad spirit" developed between the US delegation and practically each of the other delegations.[4] The Europeans and Canadians were particularly disturbed that the IMF headquarters would be located in Washington, DC. To these delegations, the Americans appeared to consider every technical question with reference to US politics. Hence, the Fund had to be located in Washington near the Federal Reserve Board and the US Treasury.[5] In a separate debate, the UK sought an IMF that would preserve sovereignty of borrowers in financial affairs, and the US wanted a more interventionist IMF.[6] As the debate progressed, the US maintained its position along the lines of the ABA's earlier insistence that there should be some check on the right of a Fund member to draw—that is, conditionality. Borrower countries did not want to see each Fund transaction regarded as an application to the Board. Moreover, the US sought full-time executive directors and alternates who would devote themselves full-time to the business of the Fund so that it would retain a powerful voice in its day-to-day operations.[7] Keynes had wanted an international secretariat with an executive board meeting only occasionally. The articles are unclear on this point.[8]

The National Advisory Council (NAC), created by the Bretton Woods Agreement Act, issued early instructions to the US executive director of the IMF to conserve the resources of the Fund for use after the Western European recovery was complete. There were no drawings from the Fund in 1950 at all. In emphasizing the surveillance role for the Fund, the NAC reshaped the role of the organization during the transition from its founding to its operations into a far more advisory one of monitoring exchange rates and enforcing exchange stability.[9]

When Per Jacobsson addressed the fifth International Banking Summer School in Oxford in 1952, it appeared that little progress had occurred toward multilateralism. The IMF was still not conducting many transactions and the Bank was making most of its loans outside Europe, in small amounts. It had made none of the type of reconstruction loans that the Financial Committee of the League of Nations had organized.[10] When the executive board agreed to adopt the concept of conditionality, the members sought to reinvigorate the IMF and accommodate the US. By the mid-1950s, it had adopted a policy of differentiating between drawings in the successive credit tranches and in relation to the size of the member's quota.[11] It would not be until the 1960s that the Fund's liquidity greatly increased, and ten central banks supplemented their quota subscriptions to the Fund with the capacity to borrow among themselves.[12]

## WORKING WITH WALL STREET: STATES, BANKS, AND THE IBRD

The early operations of the World Bank progressed somewhat differently. Problems with raising capital and stabilizing its management tied the World Bank closely to financial interests on Wall Street that would develop into a political constituency able to assist in the American political process for many years to come. President Harry Truman initially found it difficult to fill the position of president of the nascent IBRD and eventually persuaded Eugene Meyer to get it started. Meyer commanded the respect of the financial services community because he had spent a considerable portion of his career in it, where he had moved from a position at Lazard Freres to serving as a governor of the Federal Reserve Board, head of the War Finance Corporation and the Farm Loan Board, and later to publishing the *Washington Post.* He maintained an impressive network of friendship with the heads of the major investment banks from these experiences, such as Russell Leffingwell of J. P. Morgan and Co.

As with the IMF, the resources of the Bank were actually quite small. It was organized in such a way that members would pay subscriptions to its capital fund in accordance with their economic capacities in three parts: 2% in gold or US dollars, 18% in local currency, and the remaining 80% in a guarantee fund. The Articles of Agreement emphasized the facilitation of investment by others, and not on investment by the Bank itself. Hence, for the Bank to raise money in private capital markets, it would have to win the confidence of the investing community and sell its own bonds so that it could devote the proceeds to development projects. This was a problem, because the Bank's founders had underestimated the magnitude of European reconstruction as well as the degree of damage that depression and war had left on the psychology of private investors. That damage meant that the Bank could not sell Asian, Latin American, or European bonds.

Meyer immediately met with representatives of investment banks, commercial banks, savings banks, and insurance companies to establish contact between the Bank and the market. One of the primary concerns of the market representatives was the relaxation of state laws restricting investments by insurance companies, savings banks, and trustees in International Bank securities. The insurance company representatives informed Meyer that they would prefer that the Bank or the federal government attempt to secure the relaxation of these laws, since their own efforts could be interpreted as prejudging those securities as investments. Their sense was that issues guaranteed by the Bank would be more difficult to market than the Bank's own direct obligations. Moreover, they were very interested in what experience and qualifications the executive directors of the Bank and members of the staff would have, once appointed.[13]

When the first loans were discussed, Meyer met with the representatives of the government, investment banks, and individuals from the Bank. The old questions concerning the role of Bank lending surfaced immediately insofar as the investment banks were primarily concerned with the specifics of the issue, whereas the loan committees' primary concern had to do with the effect of the projects on the balance-of- payment situation in the country, and thus whether or not the loan would be repaid. The question of who would staff the Bank was also an immediate concern for Meyer. This task was complicated by the requirements that certain positions be filled by nationals of certain countries. As a part of working to create any new institution, Meyer had to determine the boundaries between the president and the executive directors in the overall management of the organization.

As he outlined the shape of the Bank through his choices for department heads, Meyer came to realize that he wanted these men to organize the departments as if they were their own, and to set appropriate policies accordingly. Moreover, the individual who succeeded him in six months or a year would be asked to take over a project that he had created. Therefore, he came to the conclusion that these responsibilities should be for a younger man who could follow through on the policies over the long term. He resigned quite suddenly, six months into his first term, and prior to any of the Bank's lending or first bond issue.[14] Thus, the Bank's prestige fell to an all-time low.[15]

Meyer's resignation and the division among its top officials exposed the problems of marketing the Bank's bonds to the general public. One group sought to go ahead with the Bank's first issue, handling market issues as they arose. The other group sought to gain the assurance of the market prior to the first issue. The Wisconsin State Banking Commission was an early detractor from IBRD securities, arguing that the guarantee of European countries on foreign securities after World War I had not prevented most losses. Approximately a third of the US$11 billion US investors had purchased in foreign government securities in the 1920s remained in default when the IBRD opened.

Therefore, the job of the Bank was to convince the investing public that it could make good on its obligations even in the event of a world depression.[16]

Like the Fund, the Bank directed itself at European reconstruction in its early years. In the first two years, the Bank spent approximately US$500 million for reconstruction and US$16 million for development. Less developed countries (LDCs) could not prepare applications, so the Bank had to send technical assistance teams to help them. When Marshall Plan aid eventually came, its (European) recipients were excluded from Bank financing. Therefore in the Bank's first ten years overall, 43% of its monies were directed to industrial countries in Europe for reconstruction and program loans for Australia, New Zealand, South Africa, and Japan. Of the monies used for developing countries in the Bank's first twenty years, approximately 75% was spent on infrastructure projects.[17] As with the Fund, the sums directed at redevelopment were inadequate to meet the needs of the economic crisis that threatened Western Europe after the war. Hence, the massive transfer through the Marshall Plan overshadowed both of the Bretton Woods institutions, and in the immediate postwar years they were mostly bypassed.[18]

Eventually, John J. McCloy emerged as a successor to Meyer. McCloy had been a Wall Street lawyer active in government. However, his Wall Street colleagues saw his appointment as an opportunity to take control of the Bank from the New Deal influence of Morgenthau. Thus, the presidents of Morgan Stanley, Chemical Bank, National City Bank, and J. P. Morgan all encouraged him to take the position. He was reluctant to do so insofar as he did not want to encounter the same differences with the US executive director, Emilio "Pete" Collado, as Meyer had. Therefore, as part of his negotiations for the position, he traveled from New York to Washington for a meeting with the non-American board directors and presented them with an ultimatum of sorts. Eugene Black would replace Collado as US executive director, and Robert L. Garner would become the Bank's vice president.[19] In addition, he insisted on the primacy of his authority over the executive directors in setting policy. Loan initiatives would come from the management and not from the executive directors.

Although not as the framers had intended at Bretton Woods, McCloy, Black, and Garner worked to organize the World Bank along commercial lines. Nelson Rockefeller loaned the men his house in Washington, and for three months they worked to create a market for securities, set up a loan apparatus, and run the operation on a conservative basis with respect to loan conditions.[20] Given US state securities law at the time, which did not have a category for the IBRD's securities that would make them eligible for institutional investors to purchase, Bank officials embarked on an initial tour with an accompanying public relations campaign in order to obtain legislation and rulings in various states that would qualify bonds of the Bank as appropriate investments for national banks, commercial and savings banks, and insurance companies.[21]

Other problems blocked private-sector participation as well. Private enterprise would not seek Bank financing for fear that the government guarantee required by the Bank would subject them to closer government scrutiny and interference. Governments were likewise skeptical, because giving a guarantee also gave the appearance that they were playing favorites. They also wanted to be free to submit their own proposals, because government-owned facilities would enhance their own prestige. Later, these problems would result in proposals for an IFC. Currency was also a problem in that repayment was required in the currency borrowed.

To change the image of the Bank, McCloy, Garner, and Black decided to issue securities in April of 1947. Initially, they spoke to bank and insurance conventions to solicit support. E. Fleetwood Dunstan, who had been vice president for investment portfolio at the Bankers Trust Company, became the new marketing director for the IBRD. His office was located in New York in the building of the Federal Reserve Bank. His staff, together with volunteers from a number of investment banking and brokerage houses, worked for approximately five weeks using the telephone to urge the purchase of World Bank Bonds. Hence, the efforts resulted in a changed attitude in a remarkably short period of time, despite the small size of the first issues.[22] In addition, a partner of Morgan Stanley & Co., Francis T. Ward, became associated with the IBRD to assist in marketing the bank's initial bond issue on what was to have been a temporary basis.

As individuals moved in and out of public service, the Bank continued to pull talent from Wall Street firms with connections that extended as far back as the 1920s and well before J. P. Morgan, Morgan Stanley, or the IBRD came into being. John J. McCloy had consulted the chairman of J. P. Morgan about Morgan's interwar experience when he became head of the IBRD.[23] The J. P. Morgan chairman, Russell C. Leffingwell, critiqued sovereign lending to McCloy, arguing that politics had been confused with finance and foreign aid had been disguised as loans.[24] Leffingwell was particularly wary of Latin American loans and argued that if the IBRD made such loans, they would tarnish the organization's image. McCloy did not share Leffingwell's feelings for Latin Americans, arguing that bankers had played a role in tempting the region into overborrowing. Although the World Bank did eventually make Latin American loans, it insisted that Peru, Chile, and other nations first settle outstanding debt with private bondholders. Hence, Latin American debt did not shape the bank's own credit.[25] McCloy was succeeded by Eugene Black, formerly a senior vice president at Chase. Upon leaving the World Bank, McCloy became president of the Chase Bank.[26]

In 1951, the Bank offered its first issue through the method of underwriting on the basis of a negotiated price. Morgan Stanley and First Boston comanaged the issue: Morgan Stanley was the most prestigious investment banking house in the country at the time, and First Boston was rapidly expanding and subsequently became the largest investment bank in the world.[27] In 1952, the Bank turned to a negotiated underwriting that would be comanaged by Morgan Stanley and First Boston, and underwritten by a nationwide syndicate of about a hundred investment houses, most of them headquartered in New York.[28] Large institutional investors, particularly insurance companies, subscribed to this offering. Attempting to source lending from outside the United States, the Bank issued the first major distribution of government-guaranteed securities in 1953 in six major financial centers. The underwriters of this issue included fourteen Dutch financial institutions, and its distributors included banking houses in London, Basel, Zurich, Brussels, and Stockholm. The issue was significant because it was the first major distribution of government-guaranteed securities on an international scale since the League's Austrian conversion loan in 1934. Therefore, despite its initial reluctance to comanage issues, Morgan Stanley comanaged three World Bank issues with First Boston between the founding of the World Bank and 1953. These three bond issues totaled US$185 million.[29]

Even closer collaboration with private capital markets occurred in December of 1954 when the Bank and Morgan Stanley arranged for the Belgian government to borrow $30 million from private investors and $20 million from the Bank to finance a Belgian port and waterway installation. Moving beyond selling loans from its portfolio to underwriting a public bond sale, the Bank was able to expand its activities.[30] Joint financing allowed the Bank to support direct borrowing from private investors by member governments without actually issuing a guarantee. Fourteen additional combined operations with the market occurred between 1954 and 1960, when most of the borrowers no longer needed to rely on Bank assistance.[31] By 1958, the Bank's private offerings were quickly oversubscribed. During its first decade, it had sold three issues denominated in Canadian dollars, two in florins (Netherlands), two in pounds (UK), six in Swiss francs, and an initial two in Germany.

Connections between the IBRD and Wall Street affected the types of loans that were made. In the early years, a sound loan meant that the project would produce earnings that would contribute to repayment. Thus, the early lending in developing countries was overwhelmingly directed toward capital infrastructure such as railways, communication facilities, power plants, and port facilities. A deeper examination of development needs might have produced a wider range of lending, such as education and urban development; however, some Bank officials felt that to lend in the social field would hurt the Bank's position in the financial community.[32]

Thus, once the US joined the World Bank, the banking community was able to shape its direction from outside. Direct congressional involvement was low because the IBRD worked to raise money privately and did not seek capital subscription increases that would have required an appropriation in these early years. Moreover, information on bank loans was not readily available to the

American public. Yet the ties fostered between Wall Street and the Word Bank would prove to be beneficial when later appropriations were needed and information about lending would become available.

## The Changing Relationship between the IMF and the Banking Community in the 1960s and 1970s

As the world economy recovered from the ravages of World War II and currencies gradually returned to convertibility, the environment for banking changed and the role of the IMF along with it. These changes in the relationship between banks and the IMF would eventually lead to their support for quota increases in congressional appropriations where they had once resisted it and, like the World Bank, create a powerful constituency for the IMF in domestic American politics in the money-center banks.

### THE GROWTH OF INTERNATIONAL MONEY-CENTER BANKING

As of 1950, opportunities for cross-national investment had been limited. A non–US citizen wishing to borrow US dollars privately could issue New York dollar bonds but would then assume dollar risk. Generally, a foreign country would not allow the citizen to service the bond in dollars without finance from the World Bank or Export-Import Bank, making the London market virtually inaccessible. US private investors or institutions could make purchases of foreign securities through the machinery of stock exchanges, or foreign bonds expressed in foreign currencies, or foreign securities that could be bought in London, Paris, Johannesburg, Melbourne, Berlin, and so forth. However, these securities likewise carried currency risk, political risk, and nationalization risk. Investors could also participate in the expansion of American industrial and commercial concerns abroad, either alone or in partnership with British, French, German, or Latin American interests. These investments began on a small scale and the largest were oil companies investing in oil-producing countries. Hence, most American export capital was governmental and accomplished through the IBRD or Export-Import Bank.[33]

Eventually, significant changes occurred in the broader international lending picture prompted by a series of prominent bank mergers in the 1950s. These mergers included Manufacturers Trust with Hanover Bank, J. P. Morgan with Guaranty Trust, Chemical with New York Trust Company, and Chase's merger in 1955 with the Bank of the Manhattan Company. Each was viewed as a possible violation of antitrust laws, but all were ultimately approved, and the Chase merger made it the largest bank in New York and second only to the Bank of America nationally. A contest with Citicorp ensued in which size became an end in itself.[34]

Notably, David Rockefeller worked in the foreign department of the Chase Manhattan Bank to expand its international operations, particularly in Latin America and the Middle East, in the early 1950s. At a time when the senior leadership of Chase distrusted foreign lending, particularly in the less developed world, Rockefeller pushed to expand lending by building on its South American trade finance operations and good relations with central banks in such key countries as Peru, Chile, Argentina, Venezuela, Brazil, and Colombia. As a result of this expansion, Chase worked with the US Treasury and the IMF to provide a US$30 million loan to Peru to stabilize its currency. While the government did not provide collateral for the loan, it agreed to a program of fiscal reform laid out by the IMF in one of the first such transactions.[35] In subsequent years, other banks would expand their international operations and change the parameters of development finance directed through public IOs.

In the postwar years, banks gradually expanded their branches overseas to service corporate clients. Until the late 1950s, affiliates of multinational corporations had managed cash positions on a country-by-country basis. They raised funds locally and financed plan expansions from headquarters. Between 1960 and 1970, the book value of American direct foreign investment increased from $21 billion to $55 billion. The largest industrial firms held the bulk of this investment, and of the 187 firms accounting for three-fourths of all foreign direct investment in manufacturing, 165 were First National City (later Citibank) customers, making it the largest of the American banks overseas.[36] US firms sometimes had problems borrowing from local banks that tended to favor local firms. In countries such as Brazil and Argentina—where Citibank's branch system was large and well-established—the bank had high volumes of local currency deposits and a strong position in the local interbank markets. Hence, it could fund a large volume of local currency loans. The bank's working with American corporate clients overseas strengthened its banking relationships in the US as well.[37]

When Walter Wriston took command of First National City's overseas division in 1959, he and Bank president George Moore planned to create a financial services company that would perform every useful financial service, anywhere in the world, that could be performed at a profit.[38] First, they would put a Citibank branch in every commercially important country in the world; second, they would tap the local deposit market by putting satellite branches or minibranches in a country, and third, they would export retail services from New York. In a sense, Wriston and Moore rebuilt a network that had existed in the interwar period and deteriorated. First National City had established its first foreign branch in Buenos Aires in 1914 at the suggestion of American firms with affiliates there. In 1930, the bank had had 83 foreign branches. In 1955, there were only 61. Few Americans had worked overseas, and of the ones who had, fewer still had had contact with the head office or their counterparts in other regions. Between 1960 and 1967, First National City established 54 branches in Latin America and the Caribbean, 14 in the Far East, 15 in Europe, and 2 in the Middle East. By the end of 1967, Citibank had 148 direct foreign branches in 42 countries. In addition, it had 93 offices of bank subsidiaries or affiliates in 21 countries.[39] In the 1970s, Bankers Trust likewise expanded with the growth of US multinationals to have banking branches in more than 30 countries and a correspondent network of more than 1,200 banks.[40]

Chase Manhattan and the Bank of America were Citibank's nearest US competitors. Chase Manhattan's overseas facilities quadrupled between 1960 and 1970. Their leaders, Wriston and Rockefeller, would both become key supporters of the IMF when its role shifted in the 1970s and 1980s. Given his family background, David Rockefeller's commitment to the internationalization of the bank was personal as well as strategic. His extensive travels and network of government connections stirred criticism from within the bank that this work was unproductive. Rockefeller was viewed by his colleagues as "an internationalist, a person who believes that the world is best served by nations working with each other," and his activities outside the bank fostered the Council on Foreign Relations, Trilateral Commission, and semiannual Bilderberg meetings.[41] In the 1970s, Chase was called a "shadow State Department" since Rockefeller was so involved in promoting a public service role through its international operations.[42]

The machinery of the US government attached to the IMF and World Bank likewise evolved in these years. In the executive branch, PL 79–171 (the Bretton Woods Agreement Act) initially established that US interaction with the IMF and World Bank would be coordinated through the National Advisory Council on International Monetary and Financial Policies (NAC), the interagency committee established as part of the compromise that had secured passage. Chaired by the secretary of the treasury and including the assistant to the president for economic affairs, the secretaries of state and commerce, the chair of the board of governors of the Federal Reserve, and the president of the Export-Import Bank, NAC reviewed loan proposals through a committee of alternates. This committee was disbanded in 1965 and reestablished one year later under Executive Order 11269 on February 14, 1966.

With the 1966 order, the Department of the Treasury could instruct the US representatives to the multilateral development banks, and the National Advisory Council became more of an advisory body. In the mid-1970s, Treasury created the Office of Multilateral Development Banks (OMDB), which coordinated the loan- approval process and further diminished NAC's influence. Hence, by 1978 the Treasury had consolidated its near-complete authority over the executive directors to the Bank and the Fund, and retained this authority through its control of information over their proceedings. The Department of State did not challenge this autonomy.[43] Moreover, the bankers who had insisted on the creation of the NAC did not prevent its slide in the new environment.

Since the IMF did not even seek to increase its quotas until 1959, Congress did not pay significant attention to the Fund in its early years beyond some brief oversight hearings in the 1950s. In March of 1959, when the IMF did seek its first quota increase, William Swingle (then director of the National Foreign Trade Council) wrote committee chairs Senator Fulbright and Representative Spence in support of it. He quoted the NFTC convention of 1958 statement: "The Convention commends the International Monetary Fund for its sustained and insistent emphasis on monetary discipline as an essential condition for the provision of assistance."[44] In January of 1962, the NFTC notified its members of the new IMF arrangements for supplementary resources to increase international liquidity, and that the council supported the congressional approval that would be required for this initiative.[45] While they polled their members in January of 1962 for views, the previous 48th National Foreign Trade Convention final declaration had already expressed its favor for strengthening the resources of the IMF through suitable borrowing arrangements subject to appropriate safeguards.[46] Having been polled, the members supported the initiative. At the IMF, the executive board noted that Canada's willingness to take on more of a quota would "undoubtedly carry weight in the presentation of the whole matter to the United States Congress."[47]

## LEADERSHIP AT THE IMF AND THE BANKING COMMUNITY

One of the areas of tension between the IMF and the banking community had been the provision in the Bretton Woods Agreement Act over the liquidation of the Bank for International Settlements (BIS) in Basel. When it was resolved, the operations of the IMF in collaboration with the BIS further solidified the constituency for the IMF in the banking community that had opposed its creation.

Henry Morgenthau had sought the liquidation provision because the BIS was identified with appeasement and Nazi collaboration during the war. The Bretton Woods Conference avoided linking the BIS and the Fund in any way. For Morgenthau, the United Nations would tolerate no institution that did not "serve in the struggle for freedom and democracy."[48] However, the connection between the BIS and the Fund was not so easily broken in the banking community. In 1946, W. Randolph Burgess, one of the leaders in the opposition to the Fund's creation, attended a meeting of the Monetary Committee of the International Chamber of Commerce in Paris where he obtained a resolution of the BIS that had been prepared by Per Jacobsson on the question of foreign lending. Jacobsson was known in banking circles, since he had been an economics consultant at the League of Nations from 1920 to 1928 and later chief economist at the BIS. Burgess passed a copy of Jacobsson's resolution to Senator Robert Taft, Sr., who had likewise opposed the Fund's creation, with the suggestion that Jacobsson's resolution could "well be used as a charter by the International Bank."[49]

In order to liquidate the BIS, three-fourths of its members would have had to vote to dissolve it. In the years between the ratification of the Bretton Woods agreements and the beginning of operations of the new institutions, the BIS had greatly expanded its short-term lending. Moreover, officers of the BIS were working to rehabilitate its image. Jacobsson wrote an annual report praising the need for international financial institutions in general, and argued for support and cooperation among them. When John Snyder became secretary of the treasury, Andrew Overby left his position at the Federal Reserve Bank in New York to become an assistant secretary. Overby mentioned to Snyder that the BIS had never had a "fair hearing" and explained his own objections to White's stance against the BIS.[50] Hence, he is credited with "saving" the BIS with the Treasury.

The BIS also played a role. When Robert Triffin, then at the IMF, visited Basel in 1948 he reported that the Committee of Delegates of the BIS wanted to establish a closer collaboration with the Fund. The IMF had not sent a delegate to the 1947 Paris meeting; the BIS requested that they send a regular delegate in the future. Likewise, the Fund sent Jacques Polak to the BIS in 1952 to learn of the research work at the institution.[51]

The young IMF began to find its niche within the banking community when Ivar Rooth took over as IMF head in 1951. A lawyer and banker by training, Rooth met with Treasury and emphasized that were it to operate through the Fund, the US would not have to appropriate money to individual countries moving toward freer trade and convertibility. Despite the difficulties that the Fund had in convincing members to change their economic and financial policies, it was easier for an international organization to seek to do so than for those countries to take advice on technical and policy matters from another government.[52]

Rooth was successful in changing the opinion of prominent IMF critics such as Randolph Burgess, who hinted at his reasoning to the National Association of Manufacturers:

> The second thing which gave me encouragement in 1938 was the Tripartite Agreement, which was designed to place a check on competitive devaluations, avoid arbitrary and erratic exchange movements and promote a fuller mutual understanding among the participants. In 1953 we have improved considerably upon that mechanism. Fifty-five countries of the world are now joined together in the Monetary Fund with the stated purpose of avoiding competitive devaluations and erratic exchange movements. This organization exerts a constant beneficient pressure and stimulus towards honest interenational [*sic*] money.[53]

When Rooth left the office in 1956, Randolph Burgess proposed Per Jacobsson for the position. Jacobsson had visited the US with increasing frequency in the 1950s and made calls on the New York banks and Washington institutions. He spoke at the first joint seminar of the IMF, IBRD, and

Federal Reserve Board upon the invitation of Eugene Black of the IBRD. The event was so successful that it became an annual one.[54] When Jacobsson took over leadership in 1956, he requested freedom from both outside and inside pressures, and streamlined the functions of the executive board. While in office, he met regularly with House Banking Committee Chair Henry Reuss and Senators Prescott Bush and William Fulbright, often at critical negotiating stages.[55] Jacobsson was popular with the banking community because he disliked the idea of government controls over business, with the exception of the regulation of credit and tax incentives. He distrusted the arbitrary discipline of the old gold standard but advocated internal discipline practiced by countries themselves. Along with elements of the business community, Jacobsson opposed the US plan to create an IDA to lend soft currencies, arguing that countries did not need much of the aid they were getting.[56] He also circulated within the business community. In 1963, for example, he addressed the NFTC convention.

As the world economy expanded in the 1960s, the Fund needed additional resources to expand along with it. Jacobsson was successful in initiating the General Arrangements to Borrow (GAB), which allowed the Fund to borrow supplementary resources to deal with the wider swings in balances of payments, as well as movement of short-term capital to respond to investment interest-rate differentials and speculation.[57] Although the GAB expanded the resources, it was not without controversy. As negotiated, it was a set of conditional commitments by participants to lend to the Fund. They could refuse. This feature made it unpopular with officials outside the ten within the GAB because it led to the formation of the Group of Ten. That is, those participants needed to consult with one another each time the Fund asked to borrow under the agreement; hence the countries organized themselves to decide how to respond. Finance ministers and central bank governors of each of the ten (or twenty people) started to meet regularly and discuss some things that the executive board of the Fund likewise discussed. Those outside the arrangement blamed Jacobsson for the new situation.[58]

When Pierre-Paul Schweitzer took over as managing director of the IMF in 1963 upon Jacobsson's death from a heart attack, the number of Fund drawings had already grown, particularly in 1968 and 1969, two of the largest annual amounts since 1947. To help finance these drawings, Schweitzer instituted two general increases in quotas in 1964/5 and 1970 that nearly doubled the size of its operations.[59] The National Advisory Council issued statements supporting these increases, and in the 1965 increase, all of the supplementary letters submitted to Congress when they needed approval were supportive, including that of the American Bankers Association, which openly declared it had overcome its previous reservations about the Fund.[60] Thus, the international banking community had definitively emerged as a constituency for the IMF when it would need to turn to Congress for additional appropriations.

## Congress and a World Bank Group: New Agencies and Diversified Means of Lending for Development

The primary vehicle for congressional influence over the IFIs during the building stage remained amendments to legislation required for their establishment. New organizations continued to appear to meet needs that the early IFIs could not as they had been initially constructed. The Cold War and decolonization infused US foreign policy during these years with a sense of competition between capitalism and communism. Nonetheless, when decolonization initially occurred, the new states preferred to work within the UN system. Accommodating states with dramatically different levels of economic development had posed strains at the Bretton Woods and San Francisco conferences. While not all of the initiatives within the United Nations were successful, many did make important contributions to the later agencies that were established within the Bretton Woods system.

One such proposed institution was for the Special United Nations Fund for Economic Development (SUNFED).[61] The success of the Marshall Plan in the early years of the UN, combined with the perception of need for development transfers to developing countries, resulted in various attempts to create a major soft-aid mechanism within the UN itself.[62] In 1949, V. K. R. V. Rao proposed that an international agency be created within the UN to provide and coordinate technical assistance to developing countries, assist these countries in obtaining requisite materials for economic development, finance national development projects, and direct and finance regional development projects. Variations on this proposal dominated economic discussions in the UN in the 1950s, the most notable being SUNFED.

Led by China, India, and Yugoslavia, developing countries argued that SUNFED should be available to all countries and not serve as a means of foreign economic and political interference in their internal affairs.[63] Holding special observer status in the 1950s, the National Association of Manufacturers opposed it. Their rationale was that with SUNFED the US would have no control over the disposition of funds.[64] The US opposed SUNFED on the grounds that the money used should be through savings from worldwide disarmament, but some countries, like France, Denmark, Belgium, Luxembourg, Norway, the Netherlands, Italy, and Japan, came to support it between 1953 and 1954.

The failure of the US to support SUNFED would have important ramifications for the development of two agencies that did come to fruition within the World Bank group: the International Finance Corporation (IFC) and the International Development Association (IDA). They changed the shape of economic multilateralism because they complemented the increasingly outward orientation of US business interests. The IFC eventually assisted corporate expansion. The IDA assisted international agricultural interests. In addition, the creation of IDA necessitated an annual appropriation for its replenishment. Therefore, it bound Congress to the workings of the World Bank in a way that was not apparent at its birth.

## THE CREATION AND GROWTH OF THE INTERNATIONAL FINANCE CORPORATION

The IFC trajectory was similar to that of the World Bank and IMF insofar as its advocates were successful in getting the measure through Congress by working with the opposition to amend the agreement. Yet these amendments tended to hamper the early operations of the agencies established. It was only when these amendments were modified that the IO could function as planned.

Ideas about economic development were introduced into President Truman's official rhetoric when he argued in his inaugural address of January 20, 1949, that the US should embark on a program of making available the benefits of scientific advances and industrial progress for the "improvement and growth of underdeveloped areas." He then moved to develop a policy in this area when he tasked Gordon Gray to do a comprehensive study of US foreign economic policies and procedures and reconcile them toward a central objective. It was popularly understood to be an attempt to find a solution to the problem of the "dollar gap," although the authors of the study had little to say about the gap as such in the final report. When the report became public, Truman asked Nelson Rockefeller to chair a committee to consider Gray's proposals in underdeveloped areas.[65]

Despite criticism, and acting quickly in response to the outbreak of the Korean War, the International Development Advisory Board transmitted its "Partners in Progress" report to Truman in March of 1951. It echoed complaints from other quarters that despite the existence of the IBRD, private capital flows to less developed areas were insufficient. From 1946 to 1950, only approximately US$3.5 billion in private capital was transferred, according to the report, or about US$700 million a year, most of it concentrated in a small area. The report reflected Rockefeller's interest in the emerging economies by emphasizing the primary importance of increasing the flow of private investment from the US and Europe to Latin America, Asia, and Africa.[66]

An International Finance Corporation (IFC) was part of this proposal. Hence, the IFC proposed by the Rockefeller Board was an outgrowth of the emphasis on increasing private investment in what was then the Third World. Other initiatives for an IFC were under way at the same time—from the staff of the World Bank itself as a version of the UK colonial development corporation, and in competition with SUNFED.[67] After a delay of several years' time, pressures grew for some type of facility that would counter the USSR and its satellites, which was offering developing countries long-term exchange contracts for their products.[68]

Immediately prior to the transmission of the report in February, Mr. H. H. Schell of the United States Inter-American Council wrote Nelson Rockefeller that the council was disappointed in the emphasis the draft circulating placed on the "essential" role of national and international government agencies in the financing of economic development. The Council would have preferred an emphasis on the superiority of private, competitive enterprise and felt that the Rockefeller report overstressed the role of public financing and need for government agencies. They did not think that the Bank should be restricted to loans to governments. "We believe that the present efforts of the management of the International Bank to provide financing facilities to private enterprises in member countries whose capital markets are poorly developed, are sound and should be encouraged."[69]

In April, the NFTC held a meeting to discuss the report of the International Development Advisory Board that had been submitted in March. The committee was opposed to a centralized agency, concluding that a minimum of emphasis should be placed on grants and maximum attention given to the use of quasi-loans, even on an extremely long-term basis. While the committee appreciated the great need for equity investment abroad, it concluded that a proposed IFC was open to great risk. The US should not push this idea, since there were more important items on the development agenda to be accomplished first. Efforts in this direction should be undertaken by private concerns and not governments.[70] In an internal document, Mr. Hitchens argued that "if underdeveloped countries require financial assistance of this sort to keep them from going communist, I do not think there is enough money in the world to do the job."[71]

The NFTC thus opposed the IFC proposal despite its earlier support for an IMF and IBRD, and despite the support of some of its individual members. When the bill (S. 1894) proposing an IFC came before the 1st session of the 84th Congress, the NFTC testified against it. The representative argued that the articles did not prevent the IFC from providing venture or risk capital. They sent a letter to this effect to the House committee as well.[72] Thus, in practical (if not official) terms, the IFC would be engaged in equity financing. It was the NFTC's belief that the concept of an IFC ran afoul of the proper relationships between government and business. A public institution should not be endowed with the right and power to engage in financing of business.[73] Not surprisingly given David Rockefeller's association with the bank, the representative of Chase Bank wrote to the NFTC that he was a member of the finance committee and supported the proposal.[74] However, he was overruled on the NFTC committee.

While the Eisenhower administration had reservations about the proposal, Secretary of the Treasury George Humphrey and W. Randolph Burgess (now the undersecretary of the treasury) offered their support because the IFC would be prohibited officially from investment in equity and managing the firms. Other groups, such as the Chamber of Commerce, American Farm Bureau, Investment Bankers Association of America, Washington Board of Trade, and American Bankers Association testified in support.[75] The IFC proposal was approved, but for the first five years of its operation (1956–1961), it approved few loans. Forty-five projects had been endorsed in eighteen countries, mostly Latin American.[76] In 1961, the Treasury returned to Congress seeking an amendment to the IFC's articles in order that the Corporation could invest in capital stock, and again in 1965 so that the IBRD would be able to lend the IFC its resources to further stimulate private investment.[77]

The IFC's fortunes improved with the appointment of Eugene Black as World Bank president. In the mid-1960s, the IFC became a more experienced venture capital investor and a more successful partner with additional investors and projects. The expansion of its gross investments (as opposed to the net investments financed from its own funds) demonstrates that underwritings and syndications became an important part of its activities. Nonetheless, the emphasis on foreign investment meant that the IFC was going against a trend in its member countries where restrictions and regulations grew. In many of these countries, the investment climate worsened. Apart from promoting and financing development banks in the 1960s, the IFC invested in capital and intermediate goods industries like iron and steel, nonferrous metals, timber pulp and paper, and fertilizer.[78]

When Robert McNamara took over the Bank, poverty alleviation became a priority of the Bank's activities and many of the IFC's initiatives in industrial action shifted to the Bank itself. New leadership at the IFC (e.g., Executive Vice President William Gaud appointed by McNamara) leaned away from equity. More important, though, as inflation outstripped interest rates in the 1970s, borrowing was a more attractive way to finance commercial activities than equity. Oil money propelled commercial banks to expand lending to developing countries, and opportunities opened for the IFC to support and participate in that lending. Hence, the IFC's mode of operations shifted dramatically from equity investment to straight loans. Not surprising given its origins, the image of the IFC at the time was not of a development agency, but one that assisted multinational corporations' penetration of the developing world.[79]

## THE CREATION AND GROWTH OF THE INTERNATIONAL DEVELOPMENT ASSOCIATION

As discussed earlier, the initial concept for an International Development Association (IDA) began in the United Nations over the need for a concessional lending facility for developing countries. As the debate over the SUNFED proposal wore on, the debt level of developing countries grew. Eugene Black, then president of the World Bank, eventually became amenable to the concept of a soft-loan facility within the structure of the Bank.[80] When it was established within the World Bank Group, three of the four largest recipients were also among the twelve largest International Bank for Reconstruction and Development's major client countries who would have had considerable difficulty repaying Bank loans in the absence of IDA credits.[81] In so doing, the Bank was successful in using IDA to mobilize its own constituency of developing country governments. Unlike the IFC, the IDA was grounded in US domestic politics from its inception.

The congressional connection to the creation of IDA grew from the US food-aid program. In 1954, the program had begun to sell US agricultural surpluses overseas and thus to accumulate capital in nonconvertible foreign currencies. By the late 1950s, the US government needed a way to draw down these holdings to avoid embarrassment over their size. These resources could be used to make long-term loans at low rates of interest in local currencies to supplement IBRD loans that were at market rates.[82] Senator A. S. Mike Monroney (D-OK) proposed such a body in 1958.[83] At the time, Senator J. William Fulbright (D-AK) was the Banking Committee chair, as well as chair of the Subcommittee on International Finance. When Monroney proposed IDA, Fulbright surrendered his subcommittee chair to Monroney, who was not even then a member of it. In addition, he assigned a staff member to it so that Monroney could take the initiative.[84] Representatives from the Department of Agriculture testified before the Senate committee on behalf of the proposal, and agricultural interest groups submitted letters to the committee supporting it.

As with the earlier legislation on IOs, a group's broader ideological orientation toward multilateralism did not determine its position on the creation of a specific agency. Although generally supportive of foreign aid, the American Merchant Marine Institute opposed participation in IDA in 1960 because the US shipping industry at the time benefited from a congressional provision that 50% of the commodities or materials procured with government-assistance funds would be moved by US-flag commercial vehicles. Such an opportunity for US ships to participate in IDA was not included.[85] The Merchant Marine argued that IDA would not guarantee US producers their contracts and US shippers would likewise lose revenue. Thus, they could not support it.

Opponents who objected to specific provisions testified along with the "Citizens Foreign Aid Committee" and "Liberty Lobby" that opposed US participation because the groups opposed foreign aid on principle. Individual countries would be eligible for aid through IDA that were not the recipients of bilateral programs, such as Argentina, Brazil, and the United Arab Republic.[86] The lobby therefore argued that IDA was a "backdoor" form of aid over whose expenditures Congress had no effective control.[87]

Likewise, the NFTC had been supporters of multilateralism and the World Bank. Yet when members of the NFTC were sent information on IDA, they supported a recommendation in the Final Declaration of the Forty-fifth

National Foreign Trade Convention that the "Convention particularly questions the need for or desirability of creating an International Development Association, whether as a separate institution or as an affiliate of the International Bank for Reconstruction and Development."[88] The replies to NFTC's poll were virtually unanimous in expressing doubts as to the advisability of establishing an IDA, with some indicating outright opposition.[89] In February, when Eisenhower transmitted the articles to Congress, Donald Heatherington at the NFTC sent out another report to the members of the international finance committee. Again, he asked for their views by March 18 as to the position the NFTC might take on the matter. Should the resolution of the Forty-sixth Convention be revised or amplified, or specific provisions of the articles questioned?[90]

Members submitted their views and with one or two exceptions, respondents indicated doubts about IDA but thought that for political reasons the proposal would secure congressional approval. The NFTC board reviewed it and adopted a statement, transmitted to the secretary of the Treasury when the US adhered to the IDA formally.[91] In the statement, the NFTC pointed out that it had twice supported proposals to increase the authorized capital stock of the World Bank, but that two National Foreign Trade Conventions questioned the need to create another intergovernmental financial institution. Taking into account the limits written into the articles, the connection between IDA and the IBRD, assurances by officials of the US government, and the expected contribution of this institution to US foreign-policy objectives, NFTC did not express opposition at the hearings on H. R. 11001 and S. 3074 authorizing participation. Nonetheless, the council registered serious reservations about particular features.[92] The most significant was the acceptance of "local currency" in repayment of loans originally made in US dollars. No lending should injure private enterprise.

Consistent support for IDA during its creation in its early years came from David Rockefeller of the Chase Manhattan Bank, the League of Women Voters, the US Catholic Conference, the National Council of Churches, and the Society of Friends. These groups testified in order to voice support for American participation and did not offer policy suggestions. The Quakers referenced their own firsthand experience with poverty and development in Kenya and India, pointing out that one in five Quakers lived in Kenya in 1971.[93] When Bread for the World formed in the early 1970s, it likewise joined the supporters.[94] The business community supported IDA insofar as its infrastructure projects could promote economic development that would in turn fuel US imports.[95]

Therefore, IDA was established as a soft-loan facility for developing countries as part of the World Bank group and not the United Nations system. Key international groups, such as the NAM, had not supported the establishment of such a facility in the UN, although this was far from the only reason it did not come into being. IDA was, however, generally popular in Congress because it was perceived to be a mechanism to compete with communist development strategies and benefit elements of the multinational business community.

## Conclusion: The Building Stage

This chapter has shown that early efforts at congressional advocacy were initially achieved through the enactment of legislation establishing new international agencies that presented opportunities to shape their profiles. Then Congress backed off, mostly because it was not needed to provide funds. However, the internal operation of Congress mattered as well. During these years, it was relatively closed to interest-group politics, and committee chairs exerted a great deal of influence. In the building stage of the Congress-IFI relationship, there was little apparent need for their work in some business sectors, and it posed an apparent rivalry to others.

In the initial absence of a domestic American audience for their work, the IMF and World Bank each experienced early difficulties in their operations. Well into the 1960s, interbranch struggles over the role of the IFIs persisted. For example, the IMF created special drawing rights (SDRs) to augment the supply of the two reserves in 1969, gold and the US dollar.[96] SDRs were to be allocated according to the size of the IMF members' quota. Thus, advanced industrial economies would receive the highest proportion of "IMF money" when it was created. As the needs of the developing countries for investment capital grew, a proposal to link additional SDR creation and development assistance under IDA was recommended by the Joint Economic Committee in 1969. Rather than allocation according to the size of the member's quota, the proposal would have had the effect of tying the development work of the Bank and the Fund closer together. It would have doubled IDA's lending capacity, obviated both the balance-of-payments problem that inhibited aid-giving and the practice of tying aid purchases to donor countries, and lessened the need to budget and tax directly for foreign aid. However, the end result would also have been to eliminate the need to legislate annually for bilateral aid and cut into congressional jurisdiction.[97] It did not pass.

The situation changed only when the structure of international lending changed, and thus the coalition that had opposed multilateralism changed along with it. Some supporters, such as the NFTC, dropped out, and others began to see the advantage of having the IFIs. Thus, the new business environment created an audience for the work of the IFIs, who allied with those seeking to prevent communist expansion in the Cold War. Nonetheless, in the years from enactment through the 1960s, business support was tempered by key provisions included in legislation when the new organizations were established that affected their broadest operations by preventing any competition with American private enterprise. In the case of the IFC, the US joined because the new agency would not be allowed to invest in equity or manage firms. In the case of the IDA, the US joined over the objections of anti–foreign aid groups along more traditional lines: that the US would not be able to direct the resources of the new IO.

Nonetheless, during the building stage, the IMF rarely approached Congress for money directly. The Fund sought only five capital increases between its founding and the Mexican default in 1982.[98] Banks and business groups made appeals to committee chairs during these years, and for the most part the quota increases passed uneventfully under "suspension of the rules" in the House of Representatives.[99] Whether or not the IMF even needed a budget appropriation had been an open question until the 1967 President's Commission on Budget Concepts attempted to clarify it, because there was no outlay until the Fund needed the money to extend a loan.[100] The payments were considered exchanges of assets because they remained available to the US government as a member of the Fund, and they paid interest. The IMF only sought an appropriation in 1970 for an increase in the US quota, and in 1972 and 1973 to maintain the value of the US quota. In none of these cases did the appropriations result in any actual outlays. In 1975, the US made a maintenance-of-value payment to the IMF without an appropriation; in 1977, the quota increase did not receive an appropriation.[101]

The next chapter explores how a combination of changes in the internal operations of Congress and in the external operations of the financial community eventually made large appropriations politically possible, yet opened new channels of influence for new groups to press their interests.

# 4

# Domestic Constituencies Speak

## THE END OF FIXED PARITY AND THE RISE OF DEVELOPMENT LENDING

> Now, therefore, be it *Resolved by the Senate and House of Representatives of the United States of America in Congress assembled,* That the Treasury did not adequately consult the Congress with regard to the basic decision to support a possibly radical change in the character of the IMF and to accede to the use of IMF gold of aid to the less developed nations rather than to restitute the said gold to the member nations.[1]
>
> —S. J. Res. 161 94th Congress, 2nd Session

Whereas the World Bank had been engaged in issues associated with development lending from its outset, the IMF became increasingly concerned with these issues after the end of fixed parity and when the necessity of recycling oil revenues through the international financial system appeared. When Robert McNamara assumed the presidency of the World Bank in 1968, he expanded its scope beyond the assistance of poor countries to include poverty alleviation of people living in them. Thus, I refer to this stage as the "development stage" of the Congress-IFI relationship because the work mandates of both of the IFIs converged toward the promotion of economic development in poorer countries. This chapter details how the convergence was not, however, without political controversy.

Controversy occurred within the context of a series of exogenous shocks to the US political economy. Many of the long-term changes in the global economy discussed in the previous chapter were associated with rebuilding the global economy after World War II. Early in the process, the US had sustained a balance-of-trade surplus. Labor and big business were aligned on the issue of free trade since it brought jobs to the US economy. As the recovery succeeded, the surplus became a deficit, and the sectors of the US economy hit hardest by the new competition from abroad fell out of the free-trade coalition. The pressure on the US economy culminated with Richard Nixon's August 1971 decision to suspend gold sales and subsequent restructuring of the international financial system. Other exogenous changes discussed in this chapter were associated with the end of the US war in Vietnam.

Significant endogenous change also occurred in this stage, and offered new possibilities for the use of congressional procedure. Congressional committees' control over the legislative agenda eroded in the late 1960s and the power of political parties grew stronger. The institutional levers used in congressional advocacy efforts evolved as well. Following the passage of the Freedom of Information Act of 1966, new domestic US rules on access to information or records held by government bodies allowed groups access to information that had not been previously available. Once enacted, the "sunshine laws" in US domestic politics opened an array of governmental activities to public scrutiny both national and international, because they made so much more information on the IFIs available. Interest groups proliferated in the 1970s on a host of issues. In particular, the number of human rights groups grew as former anti-war activists sought new avenues of influence.

The result of the combined internal and external changes was that the groups and members of Congress active during the development stage began to seek specific international policy goals in their work that could now be conducted more openly in the new atmosphere on Capitol Hill. As Congress became a more distinct forum for groups seeking policy change, the necessity of an annual appropriation for IDA provided the hook for them to pressure the Bank. With increased access to information about what government agencies were actually doing, groups would seek an initiative with respect to the Bank and approach a sympathetic member of Congress. The member would then either write a letter to the appropriate authorities concerning the issue, hold a hearing to draw attention to it, or draft legislation to compel the US executive director to pursue a policy goal. Other groups, sympathetic members, and officials in IOs then joined the effort or opposed it in defense of the status quo. Members of a coalition did not always share a rationale for their involvement. For example, among business lobbies, the National Association of Manufacturers (NAM) supported aid for economic development. Nonetheless, their chief concern with aid was with the assets, contracts, and taxes of US citizens and corporations. Therefore, when specific aid proposals came up, NAM worked with or against other business and human rights groups, depending on how the legislation was constructed.

As institutional mechanisms of congressional advocacy toward the IFIs took on a more definitive shape, interest groups sought to withhold money through the budget process to alter their operations, rather than merely advocate for enactment of legislation establishing new agencies with certain provisions, as they had in the previous stage. Variation in the success or failure of these attempts can be explained by the wider number of groups brought into the struggle on either side. However, a very wide coalition is by its nature very fragile and not likely to survive into the next round. The distinct episodes of congressional advocacy detailed in this chapter—the Trust Fund arrangements, earmarks for human rights, the Witteveen Facility, and the Gold Commission—also demonstrate the limits of congressional advocacy once it took on the more definitive shape.

Since Congress is not a monolith, when members use congressional levers to advance a policy change in the IMF or World Bank, there is always the possibility that opponents to the change will attempt to use the same levers in reverse. The Jamaica Accord sparked a serious clash between the executive and newly assertive legislature over the ability of the US to commit money to establish the IMF Trust Fund. Some members opposed it, yet the Trust Fund was established while Congress preserved the *future* right to be consulted in areas where they had been bypassed, in a compromise over policy. Members sought to prevent the drift toward a development mission in the IMF; yet this drift continues. The US was never able to earmark funds or direct specific loans as Congress had attempted, although the president of the World Bank agreed not to extend further loans of the type that provoked debate because the Carter administration and World Bank had supporters on the Hill. The trend in the development stage was therefore toward more congressional activism on policy, but also more congressional support for multilateralism as a way to promote economic development in the world economy that came from the banking and business communities.

## The New Global Economy and Domestic American Politics

The end of the par-value system marked a clear turning point for the IMF and the World Bank. As the US imported more and exported less, exporters pressured the government to devalue the dollar to restore a degree of their competitiveness in the global economy. Yet the unique role of the dollar at the center of the fixed-parity system in the IMF complicated this action. In response to these growing tensions, the Burke-Hartke Trade Act represented the signature piece of legislation to address organized labor's concerns. Although Burke-Hartke failed, it cemented the rift between labor and big business over trade and changed the manner multinational firms sought to influence legislation to protect their interests through government affairs offices in Washington. The lack of a link between trade and finance during these years thus contributed to the collapse of fixed parity and reconfigured political alignments on the IFIs. In the wake of the struggle, labor became a critic of certain aspects of the work of the IFIs and introduced a new, significant, element of complexity in the constellation of interest groups active in this area.

### BREAKING THE POLITICAL ALLIANCE ON FREE TRADE

The division of responsibilities among the Bretton Woods institutions had always presented complications for the world economy, and the division between the General Agreement on Tariffs and Trade (GATT) and the IMF was perhaps the most notable. Since they were constructed as distinct institutions, a country could not exchange concessions in trade in the GATT for concessions in payments (i.e., its exchange rate) in the IMF. Exchange restrictions in other countries discouraged US exports and encouraged direct investments by US multinationals circumventing them.[2] Industrial competitors appeared on the American scene after the war, and they grew stronger in subsequent years. Growing competition provoked changes in US comparative advantage in some industries that the rigidities of the Bretton Woods system only exaggerated.[3]

The essence of the IMF's exchange-rate system was to establish an initial exchange rate for its currency stated in terms of gold. The maintenance of such an agreed-upon par value was a prerequisite for use of the Fund's resources within 1% of par. To change it, a member could submit a change to correct a fundamental disequilibrium in its balance of payments. Thus, the system came to be known as an "adjustable peg" since it was not one with purely fixed or fluctuating rates. Moreover, the operations of the system had always been challenged by broken cross-rates and suspended par values, problems that arose from nonconvertible currencies.[4]

During the late 1960s and early 1970s, inflation in the US rendered foreign goods cheaper, creating a growing balance-of-payments problem with American trading partners. Deficits in the Bretton Woods system needed to be addressed by the deficit country that had to change its patterns of overseas expenditures or adopt a deflationary fiscal regime to restore the balance-of-payments account. States could only devalue their currency if a fundamental disequilibrium existed. At the center of the IMF arrangements, the US was in a difficult position with respect to devaluation. It carried a good number of military and development assistance commitments that limited what items could be adjusted to lower expenditures. As a policy solution, deflation might have helped the export situation but would be a difficult political course. As the trade deficit worsened, certain key industries were hurt more than others. They began to call for protectionist trade legislation.[5]

Labor and big business had been aligned on free trade since the end of the Great Depression. For example, both groups supported the Reciprocal Trade Agreements Act and the Trade Expansion Act of 1962. Labor perceived overseas markets as contributing to US job growth. However, as the increasing number of imports entered US markets and US multinational affiliates increasingly operated overseas, this perception began to change. It broke into a full battle when the Foreign Trade and Investment Act of 1972 was proposed.[6] Also known as the Burke-Hartke Act, the bill would have given the president the ability to stop any overseas transfer of capital or technology that could result in a net reduction in US employment. It also proposed changes in the taxation of overseas income that would make multinational investment overseas more expensive. Goods that competed with American-made products would be subject to comprehensive import quotas.

Labor supported the bill. Nearly every US-based corporation opposed it.[7] During the Burke-Hartke hearings, the AFL-CIO presented its case in a series of hearings, press conferences, speeches, letters to members of Congress, and personal contacts on Capitol Hill. Labor argued that capital is mobile and labor is not. In response to labor's political activity, business groups formed to act on behalf of the multinational firms. The Emergency Committee for American Trade (ECAT) formed in 1967, and the NAM and Chamber of Commerce mobilized in favor of multinational activity and against the Burke-Hartke bill.[8]

Thus, despite the fact that Burke-Hartke was ultimately defeated, the debate over the taxation of transnational enterprise sharply increased the lobbying presence of all multinationals in Washington. Many studies were conducted on the contribution of multinationals for the US economy. The debate also provoked academic work on international trade that sought to include multinationals, intrafirm trade, economies of scale, and other factors.[9] In the new environment, groups sought to influence legislation in its formative stages, as opposed to waiting until it was complete for a response. For example, the NAM formed an international committee in 1971 on an ad hoc basis in reaction to the Burke-Hartke bill. It became a policy committee in 1973, then a series of ad hoc task forces. Eventually, NAM created a monetary and financial affairs subcommittee whose priorities would be international monetary reform, foreign aid, IDA, and balance-of-payment issues. Thus, the research and legislative influence of the multinational firm extended further into the work of the IFIs.

## ENDING THE PAR-VALUE SYSTEM

The link between an imbalance in trade and finance was well known to economists. The lack of ability of the international monetary system to generate adequate liquidity for the growing volume of foreign trade had also been a concern to economists since the 1960s. Historically, gold had provided liquidity; however, the supply of gold was not sufficient at its 1960s price to serve the enlarged demands for industrial and artistic uses. In one attempt to address the problem, the 1968 gold communiqué established a two-tier gold market, wherein monetary gold would be exchanged among official authorities at the official price and the free market would determine the price for all other uses. Monetary authorities agreed not to buy gold from the private market, including new production. Yet as pressure on the dollar mounted, President Nixon's foreign policy priorities remained East-West relations and China. He famously wrote,

> I do not want to be bothered with international monetary matters. This, incidentally, Kissinger should note also, and I will not need to see the reports on international monetary matters in the future. Problems should

> be farmed out, I would hope to Arthur Burns if he is willing to assume it on a confidential basis, and if not Burns to Houthakker who is very capable in this field. I have no confidence in the Treasury people since they will be acting in a routine way.[10]

Nonetheless, on August 15, 1971, Nixon took the dramatic step of suspending gold sales, floating the dollar, and imposing a 10% import tax. The Treasury had anticipated these measures three months earlier in a contingency paper. Secretary of the Treasury John Connally is widely considered to have been the chief architect of the plan.[11] Thus, the value of the dollar relative to other currencies dropped immediately. It could only have been devalued by one of three methods: raising the price of gold (which would have required congressional approval) and other countries *not* similarly raising the price in relation to their currencies; closing the facility wherein foreign central banks converted their dollar holdings into gold at $35 an ounce and other countries permitted the dollar to float against their own currencies until a new level was reached; or devaluing outright with advance negotiation among the major countries.

The day after Nixon announced his New Economic Policy, Paul Volcker, who was then at the Treasury Department, suggested a meeting among representatives of US allies to explain the reasoning behind the program and hear any initial reactions. He told the others that the US did not want a new Bretton Woods conference but were considering forums for negotiation. One potential group was the Group of Ten (G10), but it did not have developing-country participation. Volcker did not favor the IMF Board, because the executive directors did not necessarily have the authority of their governments and there was too much developing-country participation for this kind of negotiation.[12] The G10 ministers met at the Smithsonian Institution in Washington on December 17 and 18, 1971, and realigned exchange rates. By December 21, the US administration had still not made any communication to the IMF on the par-value issue or its willingness to propose a suitable means of devaluing the dollar price to gold. The IMF director did not expect such communication.[13]

The decision to devalue meant that the dollar value of three types of assets denominated in dollars rose: reserve assets, currency subscriptions in the IMF, and paid-in capital subscription to the international development lending institutions. These amounts totaled $2.5 billion in 1973. Reserve assets grew because the US held considerable gold assets. At the time, 75% of the US subscription to the IMF was paid in US dollars, but it was denominated on the books of the Fund as dollars of a fixed weight and fineness of gold. Thus, the value of the subscription increased in current dollars and allowed the US to increase drawing rights while maintaining its share of voting rights and allocations of special drawing rights. Paid-in investments in the World Bank, the IDA, the Inter-American Development Bank, and the Asian Development Bank were likewise denominated in dollars of a fixed weight and fineness of gold. Hence, US investments in those institutions increased in value as well.[14]

## LEGISLATIVE REQUIREMENTS FOR ENDING THE GOLD STANDARD

Gowa argues that in suspending the gold window, the Nixon administration made its decision within the structure and distribution of power among agencies involved in policy making in this area. The Treasury Department was preeminent.[15] While this assessment is correct for the time frame she examines, members of Congress began to assert the legislature's institutional authority after the years where her work ends. Formal congressional approval to close the gold window was not required; nonetheless, Congress asserted itself in later rounds of monetary negotiations that did require legislative approval to change the par value of the dollar and eventually terminate the link to an official price of gold.

The US could not technically implement its portion of the multilateral realignment of the exchange rates negotiated at the Smithsonian without Congress. Legislation was needed to authorize a change in the par value of the dollar in the IMF equivalent to $38 an ounce, and in effect revalue it. Section 5 of the Bretton Woods Agreement Act stipulated that the president may not propose or agree to a change in the par value of the dollar in the Fund unless Congress has given its consent. Hence, S. 3160, the Par Value Modification Act introduced in February 1972, was a key element of Nixon's efforts to strengthen the US international economic position.[16]

Given the domestic political circumstances, Nixon had support for this legislation insofar as its supporters perceived that it would help to restore a favorable trade balance for the US The cost and prices of foreign goods and services, when expressed in dollars, would rise relative to those produced in the US. This meant that imports would be more expensive. Domestic production should be stimulated. Exporters could quote lower prices in foreign currencies because they would receive the same amount in dollars under the new exchange rate. The new rate should have provided strong incentives to seek out foreign markets. Finally, the action would improve the asset-liability position of the US since, as discussed, the dollar value of the US gold and other reserve assets would increase by 8.57%, or $828 million, at the time. Gold certificates would be issued against this gold, so the equivalent cash gain for the Treasury would reduce borrowing needs with related savings on interest costs. Although some economists were calling for complete flexibility in the value of US currency, the business community was reluctant to go along with a fully free float because it sought a higher degree of price predictability in negotiations concerning international business transactions.[17]

In sum, little opposition to S. 3160 was expected, and little came. Nonetheless, the exchange rates were continually overwhelmed by market forces. In the first session of the next Congress, S. 929 again sought to amend the Par Value Modification Act, and it likewise passed. It authorized and directed the secretary of the treasury to establish the new par value of the dollar, and to maintain the value in terms of gold of the holdings in US dollars at the IMF, IBRD, and IDA. As anticipated, the legislation resulted in a $50 million increase in US assets held at the IMF. The dollar portion of $5 billion of Fund subscription was denominated in dollars of a fixed weight and fineness of gold. This subscription increased in current dollar value by .57%. Also, the US realized an 8.57% increase in its gold tranche of $1,675 million in the IMF.

## Congress Asserts Itself as an Agent: The 1976 Jamaica Agreements

After the collapse of fixed parity, the IMF had lost one of its core responsibilities and needed a new mandate. During these years, the oil shocks subjected developing countries to rapid and dramatic inflationary pressures. They borrowed huge sums to adjust. While the needs of the developing countries presented a new opportunity for the IMF, the opportunity intiated a turn toward development concerns that its framers at Bretton Woods had not intended in the original division of responsibilities they devised. Some members of Congress sought to prevent the drift—not because they opposed development lending in principle, but because they were concerned by attempts in the Nixon administration to bypass the congressional budget process and change the nature of the IMF without consulting the legislature. Thus, the gold sale agreement is one of the rare instances where members did not act in response to issues debated by groups elsewhere but sought to preserve the institution's Constitutional discretion to spend money. It is also an episode that elaborates on the role of individual members with personal interest in IFI issues.

### THE 1976 IMF GOLD SALE AGREEMENT

From 1974 to 1976, the IMF quotas were again under review. However, this review delved into multiple areas under the IMF's purview and the entire process culminated in a package of agreements on several issues. While the quota reviews were taking place, the board of governors of the IMF (generally the finance ministers) from the executive board states began to meet several times a year to address these and other problems. This meeting was initially the Committee of Twenty, then was institutionalized into the Interim Committee of the Fund in 1974.[18] The Committee sought to expand the Fund's financing activities for the benefit of the LDCs. However, the interbranch struggle between the executive and legislative branches of the US government would play a role in the manner the Trust Fund was structured and in the necessity of consulting Congress on future matters related to gold sales and trust fund creation.

The Treasury had entered the quota review process with three goals in mind. First of all, it sought to see gold phased out in order to erode support for a return to fixed parities. The Treasury feared that if the IMF continued to hold large gold stocks, it might borrow against it to provide aid to developing countries, since such activities are legal under its articles. The US would not be able to veto such proceedings. The objection, in addition to fears of excess credit and money creation, was that gold would remain in the Fund as backing for Fund securities and be dignified with a special role in the monetary system. Second, Treasury, together with the State Department, sought aid for the developing countries beyond their normal shares. Finally, Treasury sought to reach an accord with the French regarding a continuation of floating rates and their legalization. Some on the Joint Economic Committee sought to distribute proceeds from the sale of the full one-third of IMF total deposits to the developing world. This would have been about $1 billion of US money. Such a move, however, would dramatically alter the purpose of the Fund. Hence, the policy debate settled around the question of the IMF's new role as a development agency. Those who opposed this drift likewise opposed the distribution of gold to any group of countries disproportionately.

The solution appeared to be to sell a portion of the IMF's gold and establish a Trust Fund for developing countries through which to finance their balance-of-payments difficulties during the oil shocks. The Fund had regularly sold gold before the Trust Fund issue arose, because it needed to do so when industrial members made drawings and it needed currency. The IMF's holdings allowed it to lend without eliminating its balances of usable currencies. The situation in 1976 was different because the US and others sought to *dispose* of the assets at a time when the price of gold was high. When it did eventually come into being, the Trust Fund changed the nature of the Fund's financial assistance definitively, because by then it was clearly a lending institution to middle- and low-income states, not a stabilization fund among states with fixed exchange rates.[19]

The Department of the Treasury preferred the gold-sale option, because it did not want to have to wait for any amendments to be ratified and did not want to become embroiled in a congressional debate over the size or form of foreign aid. Secretary of the Treasury William Simon argued that the proposal would both phase out gold in the system and provide extra money for developing countries without the need for individual countries to allocate additional funds, including the US.[20] A Trust Fund appealed to the IMF as a legal instrument because under international law the Fund lacked the power to receive the type of gold-sale assets as part of its ordinary resources. That is, ordinary, or "general," IMF resources must have uniformity and could not be designated for any one group of states and not the others.[21] Hence, a general increase in the size of the IMF would increase every state's ability to borrow, not just the developing countries'. Moreover, the Trust Fund did not require an amendment to the

Articles of Agreement to establish, because it did not take the form of an agreement between the IMF and any of its members. Finally, a Trust Fund avoided the need to create new organizations with limited purposes.[22]

The French had been lukewarm to the proposal from the start. Nonetheless, the US and France presented a joint proposal to the IMF on Article 4, to permit floating exchange rates. The way it was arranged, Treasury would only need to present the amendment to the Articles to Congress, and the US executive director would vote in the IMF to go along with the Trust Fund. The review package was all the more important to the Nixon administration because Henry Kissinger had promised additional assistance to the developing countries at a UN Special Session in the same month. Were the US to back out of its commitment, it would jeopardize LDC support for the gold arrangement, and antagonize the Japanese, who did not want to renege on their promise to the LDCs because of their dependence on OPEC oil.

When the issue came to Congress, Robert Taft, Jr. (R-OH), and a Democratic colleague, Abraham Ribicoff (D-CT), opposed the package on the grounds that it changed the nature of the IMF without the legislature's having been consulted. Moreover, the gold sales mechanism circumvented the congressional budgeting process. Therefore, while they were not necessarily opposed to foreign aid in and of itself, they were concerned that Congress had not allocated it. Nonetheless, staff in Taft Jr.'s office perceived that it would not be wise to hold the amendment to the Articles hostage in order to demand that Treasury take an up or down vote on the issue of gold restitution. They thought that the amendment was necessary. Moreover, the US would find alternative uses for the gold to be worse than seeing part of it going into the Trust Fund. For example, there was the possibility that it could be retained to back IMF securities for the purpose of assisting developing countries with even *more* soft loans.

Thus, Taft Jr.'s office recommended that a joint resolution would first criticize the Treasury for not having kept Congress better informed and for not having tried to ascertain the views of Congress before negotiations began. The second part of the resolution would direct the US Governor of the Board of the IMF to emphasize that any loans coming out of the Trust Fund should be hard loans for traditional IMF purposes. The third part would expect that Congress be consulted on any move by the IMF to dispose of the remaining two-thirds of its gold. One of the amendments to be proposed to Congress would require that an 85% vote be needed for disposition of the remaining two-thirds of IMF gold, and this would give the US an effective veto. A staff document advised that the focus should be on getting a resolution through that would prevent the Treasury from doing something like this again with regard to the remaining IMF gold.[23] Taft Jr. and Ribicoff introduced a joint resolution along those lines to require Treasury to work for safeguards.

At the time, the BIS could purchase gold as an agent of its central bank members at market prices despite provisions in the Bretton Woods Act. To do so, however, the BIS would violate IMF Articles and flout the authority of Congress. Henry Reuss, who had assumed the House Banking Chair post, wrote to William Simon—then secretary of the treasury—to ask that no central bank or its agent be permitted to purchase gold at a price above the stated par value, plus the prescribed margin, until Congress ratified the proposed amendment to the IMF Articles permitting such purchases by abolishing the official price of gold. While Reuss disagreed with Taft and Ribicoff about the use of gold for developing countries, he did respect their opinions and urged that the Treasury delay action until the bill came before Congress.[24]

In mid-January of the next year, William E. Simon and other IMF representatives met at Kingston, Jamaica, and decided to establish the Trust Fund before Taft Jr. and Ribicoff's resolution could be enacted. Whereas market forces had compelled the previous devaluations, by 1976 the finance ministers were wantonly disregarding the IMF's articles. The Jamaica agreements included amendments to the IMF Articles of Agreement, an agreement on gold among the G10, and a general increase in Fund quotas. The Agreements reflected the reality that the Bretton Woods exchange system was dead. As the legislation proposed, the Interim Committee would dispose of about a third of IMF's gold holdings to members in proportion to their quotas at the official price of $35 SDR per ounce and the other two-thirds at public auction at market prices. Proceeds from the two-thirds would be used to benefit developing countries. Some would be transferred directly to developing countries according to their quotas, and the rest would be placed in a "Trust Fund" for balance-of-payments assistance on concessionary terms to the poorest developing country members.

Legislation would be needed to amend the Bretton Woods Agreement Act in order to authorize the US as a member to accept amendments to the IMF articles approved by the Fund's board of governors previously. In addition, legislation would authorize the US to accept the approximately $2 billion increase in its IMF quota also approved by the Board of Governors earlier in the year. It would make changes in US laws pertaining to US participation in the international monetary system and US intervention in the foreign-exchange markets. Finally, it would provide for enhanced congressional access to the information necessary for effective oversight of US international monetary and economic policy. However, Treasury argued that Congress was not legally entitled to act on the Trust Fund portion of the agreement. At the IMF, some members wanted grants to be available through the Trust Fund, but "they were prepared to move a long way toward formulating the provision in such a way as to give the least possible objection to the US Congress."[25]

Taft Jr. and Ribicoff continued to oppose the gold sale and Trust Fund on the grounds that it changed the nature of the IMF without Congress's having been consulted.[26] Therefore, Taft Jr. and Ribicoff developed a new joint resolution following the Jamaica meeting *requiring* the secretary of the treasury to work for safeguards in the Trust Fund to prevent waste or misuse of money, and to ensure that no additional agreements on gold disposal would occur without congressional review. They would also require annual reports on the Fund and notification of any discrepancies to Congress.

The measure was ultimately successful. When PL-94-564 was approved on October 19, 1976, neither the president nor the agency could "approve the establishment of any additional trust fund, for the special benefit of a single member or of a particular segment of the membership, of the Fund."[27] Likewise, the amendments were approved. Fixed exchange rates expressed in terms of gold were abolished, as was an "official" price of gold. The growth in quotas kept the IMF's resources in line with the growing balance-of-payments financing needs.

## MEMBER INITIATIVES AND THE IFIs

Robert Taft, Jr.'s, actions point to the complexity surrounding the IFIs and the significance of those members of Congress who follow these issues closely. This book argues that groups seeking change approach sympathetic members and coordinate their activities with those connected to other members. They do not try to change the positions of members where they have no connection, or commonality of purpose. As was the case with the Bretton Woods negotiations, a member's personal experience viewing the work of a development agency, or firsthand experience with the complexities of international negotiations, can compel them to take leadership on issues in the legislative arena. Once involved, their support cannot be easily categorized as pro or con.

Taft Jr.'s experience with development lending ran deep. Although his father had been one of the major opponents of the Bretton Woods Agreement Act, Taft Jr. had been one of the congressional advisors on the US delegation accompanying Secretary George Shultz to the Nairobi Meeting of the World Bank in September of 1973, when the IDA agreement was negotiated. He and the other members of Congress came away from the negotiations impressed that the negotiators had crafted a favorable outcome from the standpoint of the US. On the way to the conference, they also viewed the IDA projects in Senegal and Kenya.[28]

Shortly thereafter, the Foreign Relations Committee of the Senate voted to report S. 2665 to authorize the US participation of the fourth replenishment of the IDA. S. 2665 would provide for the authorization of a total commitment of $1.5 billion in four installments of $375 million. The US share was lower than its previous one, down to 33.3% from 40% of the total replenishment. The House, however, had defeated the IDA replenishment on January 23, 1974, out of a sense of frustration with the Arab oil embargo. However, that frustration was misplaced, because the oil-producing countries' per capita incomes exceeded $375 by that time; thus, they did not qualify for IDA loans. Were IDA to be cut off, developing countries without oil or other rich mineral resources would be the most severely affected, since IDA does not subsidize oil imports. Senators Jacob K. Javits and John Sparkman wrote to their colleagues to secure authorization of the fourth replenishment so that it would remain "live" in a conference, arguing:

> Support for IDA by the Senate is an important means for emphasizing our own commitment to the needs of the developing countries, and providing the necessary example that will induce the newly rich oil producing countries to undertake their fair share of the burden.[29]

Taft Jr. joined the effort. When the bill came to the Senate floor, he pointed out that his support stemmed from his personal involvement in the formulation of the proposal and personal observation of what IDA does in the field. He shared the opinion that if the Senate did not come though so that IDA funding would be revived in the conference committee, the organization would be finished, and the US would be blamed. It was revived, and the money was eventually appropriated.

When considered as a whole, Taft Jr.'s position cannot be characterized as antagonistic toward multilateralism, or development lending in particular. In the case of the IMF, he opposed the institution's drift to development lending and the attempted circumvention of the congressional budget process because the legislature had not been consulted. At the same time, he supported development lending in IDA. As more members became aware of and involved with the work of the IFIs, their motivations and policy orientations were similarly difficult to pigeonhole. Many had direct experience with the work of the IFIs. Such involvement comes with a desire to shape the work of the agency in question.

## Congress as a Forum for Organized Groups Seeking Change

Individual members of Congress figured prominently in the Jamaica dispute because they perceived the institution's budgetary authority to be under attack by the executive. Thus, they did not act in response to issues debated elsewhere but sought to preserve the institution's Constitutional discretion to spend money. More commonly, congressional advocacy with respect to an issue stems from organized groups who approach members on issues of concern. The configuration of these groups had changed in the wake of the end of fixed parity and the split over free trade between organized labor and multinational corporations. The split introduced new problems in gaining passage for legislation on IFI issues since the former allies now sought different goals.

In addition, in the later years of the development stage of the relationship, the institutional changes in the legislature opened possibilities for interest groups to initiate new procedural maneuvers that would go beyond issuing directives to executive directors. Congress passed the Legislative Reorganization Act in 1970, which recommended the opening of congressional committee hearings to the public. Later "sunshine law" reforms included publication of roll-call votes in open reports, increases in committee staff resources, and an expansion of the Congressional Research Service. Eventually, the US Congress floor proceedings were televised. As a result of these initiatives, the information available to the public about Congress grew exponentially, and committee chairs became more responsive to their members and less dominant.[30] These domestic reforms eventually affected IFI activity when congressional staff and others began to ask the IMF and World Bank for information about specific lending and project arrangements that enhanced the debate both inside and outside the formal organizations. They resulted in more definitive procedural levers through which members of Congress could seek to influence policy in the IMF and World Bank.

## EARLY DIRECTIVES TO US EXECUTIVE DIRECTORS

Although lending in the IFIs had a political element from the start, economics and politics appeared to be separate in the Bank and the Fund during IDA's initial years, because the atmosphere of the World Bank permitted the US to express its preferences silently and effectively. As the regional development banks grew, and US supremacy at the Bank declined, policy makers began to make their positions more public. Congress was able to observe votes taken by the US executive directors, and members sought to specify which political considerations should govern US behavior in the banks.[31]

Organized groups had always attempted to transmit preferences on the voting behavior of the US representative, or executive director, toward specific loans with legislative directives. For example, the US executive director did not support loans to Asian palm oil producers that competed with US soybean and cottonseed oils.[32] Individuals sought to prevent loans to countries where expropriation of assets had occurred without compensation to US multinational corporations as well.[33] The Nixon administration had wanted to cut off Bank aid to Chile after Salvador Allende in 1970, but the Bank's president sent a message to the Chilean former president of the Inter-American Development Bank that he hoped the Bank would maintain its relations with the new regime.[34] The 1974 IDA replenishment became enmeshed in the question of individual ownership of gold after the Senate added a nongermane amendment to the authorization bill H.R. 15231. In 1975, the Foreign Assistance Appropriations Act sought to prevent the US executive director to IDA from voting in favor of loans to countries with nuclear devices and those that had not acceded to the Non-Proliferation Treaty. Before this provision was repealed in 1977, the US executive director voted "no" against loans to India twenty-six times.[35]

These attempts to alter the lending profile of the Bank usually failed, since the US executive director would vote no and the other executive directors would nonetheless form a majority necessary for the loan's approval.[36] With the increased availability of information, however, groups were not satisfied with this outcome. Furthermore, new groups entered the debate and sought new ways of using the more open environment on Capitol Hill to press for policy change beyond simply seeking to mandate the executive directors' vote.

## ATTEMPTING TO EARMARK FUNDS: HUMAN RIGHTS AND THE CARTER ADMINISTRATION

When the US war in Vietnam ended, many individuals involved in the peace movement of the 1960s increasingly turned their attention to human rights causes, thus raising the number of groups active on these issues. When Jimmy Carter was elected president, interest-group strategy changed from seeking to issue directives to executive directors to attempts to develop more comprehensive policies, such as earmarking US contributions away from certain projects that might benefit human rights offenders. Therefore, the old question of the ability of the US to direct loans toward friendly states and away from Cold War adversaries became intertwined with questions of human rights. At first, the outlook for influencing the World Bank through earmarks was bright. In the Nixon and Ford administrations, human rights concerns had just added to the tension between a Republican executive and a Democratic Congress. Once elected, a Democratic president presented a new opportunity. Yet in the course of the Carter administration, the human rights community split among factions: One camp wanted to give Carter free rein on these issues and the other wanted to develop a human rights code.[37] Eventually, the groups grew disenchanted, and the legislative activity decreased and ultimately retrenched.

The Carter administration initially attempted to pursue its human rights policy by refusing to vote for loans to select countries whose regimes they disapproved of. World Bank president Robert McNamara refused to bend the Bank's rules for these human rights concerns, arguing that lending must be based on economic considerations alone. The board supported him. As with the previous pattern, the US executive director would vote no on loans that would then pass with the other members voting unanimously to approve them.[38] Others in the Carter administration sought to use loans to promote a human rights policy, yet they did not want US funds earmarked for a specific agenda because they did not believe that IDA would be able to accept such contributions legally.

By 1977 inflation, the expanding need for credit in developing countries, and higher oil prices caused the IFC and the IBRD to approach Congress for replenishments, in this case the first replenishment for the IFC and the first since 1959 for the IBRD.[39] At that time, groups such as the Women Strike for

Peace and the Women's International League for Peace and Freedom pressured Congress to include human rights earmarks in appropriations bills. The most ardent pro–human rights groups worked with anti–foreign aid groups toward this goal.[40]

Knowing that the fifth IDA replenishment would likewise be a problem, the administration stretched out the payment installments for IDA IV over four years. In March, Secretary of the Treasury Michael Blumenthal invited members of the Senate Subcommittee on Foreign Assistance to attend the actual IDA replenishment negotiations in Vienna. Although the senators could not attend, they sent two staffers in their place.[41] Nonetheless, in the House, Representative Robert A. Young (D-MO) attempted to attach country-specific human rights amendments to appropriations bills prohibiting loans to Cambodia, Vietnam, Laos, and Uganda. In this round, Congress compromised with the Carter administration after the administration agreed to vote "no" on loans to the countries in question. Although the 1977 amendment was defeated, Young introduced a similar amendment the following year but limited it to Vietnam and IDA.[42] Members voting "no" to the amendment would have gone on record opposing a measure to halt aid to Vietnam. Thus, it passed. A similar amendment with respect to human rights and Cuba likewise passed by voice vote; yet the amendments were deleted in the conference committee.[43]

The next round was not so easily deflected. In September of 1979, Vietnam invaded Cambodia while further loans were in the process of being negotiated between Vietnam and the Bank. At the same time, Congress was debating the sixth replenishment of IDA. Young offered his amendment prohibiting the use of US funds to FY 1980 appropriations bill H. R. 4473 on the House floor. He made the argument that while the initial agricultural loan to Vietnam had been for irrigation on the Mekong River, and the six pending loans were for railroad development, port rehabilitation, roads, and railways, these projects freed up money for the Vietnamese government to pursue war with its neighbors.[44] Moreover, the IDA VI replenishment of US$12 billion was an increase over the IDA V replenishment of US$7.64 billion. While the US percentage of the contribution had been lowered from 31.2% of the total to 27%, members argued that they had expressed reservations over the size during the negotiations and were thus not compelled to support the larger amounts requested.

As members made their positions public, Senate conservatives supported the amendments, whereas moderate Democrats supported Carter's stand against earmarking. After the invasion, Young refused more compromises with the administration and the negotiations reached an impasse.[45] McNamara's role was complicated by his past involvement as secretary of defense when the war in Vietnam escalated. He intervened directly in the matter by signing a letter to the chair of the House Banking Committee that no further loans to Vietnam would be made.[46] The action was controversial because the Treasury Department had the chief responsibility for interfacing with Congress, and

McNamara had sent the letter directly to Congress. Most likely, however, the Department of the Treasury had not been excluded. The assistant US secretary of the treasury for international affairs and acting US executive director of the Bank supervised drafting of the offending letter. Officials in Congress and the US Treasury Department had approved it before McNamara signed it.[47]

Nonetheless, the Bank's board protested that in signing a letter to Congress, McNamara had bypassed the established practice of dealing only with executive-branch authorities. Thus, the events in 1979 were significant not only because McNamara pledged not to extend further loans to Vietnam but because they marked a shift in Congress's involvement. As an institution, Congress no longer deferred to the executive branch on World Bank policy. The monies for the sixth IDA replenishment were not appropriated for the rest of McNamara's tenure. In the absence of US contributions, other countries made advance contributions until the situation could be resolved. Nonetheless, these countries threatened that they would make proportionate cuts to any cuts made by the US from the amount negotiated in the round. Members of the Carter administration eventually admitted that they handled the foreign-aid issue badly insofar as they assumed that congressional approval simply required the acceptance of a few key political players.[48]

## ATTEMPTING TO BLOCK LEGISLATION: THE IMF AND THE WITTEVEEN FACILITY

When the IMF began to figure more prominently on the interest-group radar groups sought to block legislation that might enable its growth into certain areas. Efforts to block legislation are not always successful, because they can be countered by supporters who seek to move it along. Nonetheless, the IMF and the Witteveen Facility represents one early effort by critics of the IMF to prevent US money from being contributed as a "bailout" mechanism. The maneuver failed because the House and Senate committee chairs were allied with Treasury on the matter, and the budgetary implication was arguable.

The idea for a facility grew out of the end of the fixed-parity system and the lack of a clear development mandate for the IMF. On one hand, the Fund's critics were correct that it was not designed to be a development agency. On the other hand, its supporters had used its lending in the developing world as a rationale for funding quota increases as far back as the 1960s. For example, in the first increase, C. Douglass Dillon from the Department of State argued to Congress that less developed countries were beginning to accept the IMF's advice more and more, particularly Turkey and Argentina. Were the IMF to have an increase in funds available, it would likewise increase the influence of the Fund itself.[49] The amount and types of assistance to developing countries grew during the early years, particularly when the Fund extended its compensatory financing facility to assist primary commodity-producing members with shortfalls in export earnings as well as a facility to finance buffer stocks. After the end of the parity system, lending to developing countries appeared to be a logical extension of the Fund's purpose and global economic events contributed to the need for such a role.

Although the oil shock of 1973–1974 and subsequent worldwide recession did not provoke a full-blown debt crisis, it did strain the ability of less-developed, oil-importing countries to pay the higher energy costs. This episode foreshadowed the events to come in the 1980s. The IMF created an oil facility in 1974 and later expanded it. In planning for the facility, Sam Cross, then US executive director to the IMF, reported to the board that if it borrowed large amounts of dollars even for a day, as the draft was then written, "his authorities were concerned that appropriations would have to be sought from Congress in order to cover the value of the dollars held."[50] The US authorities hoped to avoid holding currencies unnecessarily, and thus the need to approach Congress to seek an appropriation. The OECD had proposed a Financial Support Fund for developing countries in 1976 to address the problem of current account deficits; however, Congress had objected to these proposals due to the belief that the fund would be used to bail out commercial banks. When the IMF considered its own mechanisms, it sought to avoid encountering the same problem by *not* emphasizing the question of Fund cooperation with commercial banks.[51]

In 1977, the IMF under Managing Director H. Johannes Witteveen proposed a Supplementary Financing Facility—that is, "the Witteveen Facility." It would serve as an emergency-loan mechanism that would prevent the collapse of the world's private banking system resulting from the severe balance-of-payments problems of some countries associated with the quadrupling of oil prices. The initial proposal was for seven Western countries, including the US, and seven OPEC countries, including Saudi Arabia, to raise approximately $10 billion. The OPEC countries would supply 48% of the planned financing of the facility. In exchange, the Arab contributors would gain a greater role in managing the Fund on the basis of weighted voting. Western governments opposed the original plan and the facility was recast as a series of bilateral agreements outside the IMF machinery, excluding Arab states from a greater role in decision making. It would offer OPEC countries a depository vehicle at favorable interest rates and with exchange-rate guarantees.[52]

Many of the elements of the later IMF bailouts of the 1980s were evident in the facility. It involved a high degree of conditionality for countries to qualify for their loans. It expanded the role of the IMF as a lender of last resort to developing countries, contrary to the role envisioned at the Bretton Woods conference. Despite the efforts of individuals at the IMF to downplay the connection between the Fund and commercial banks, they were firmly fused in the minds of many observers. For example, the editorial page of the *Wall Street Journal* described it as relief for bankers who would be bailed out by the IMF.[53]

This was not an accident. Bankers such as Irving S. Friedman at Citibank openly supported the creation of the facility. As private banks became more reluctant to lend to these same countries given their buildup of debt, countries such as Peru, Mexico, Brazil, and Zaire were reaching the limit of their abilities to service the loans without new credits. In the absence of IMF lending, they may have defaulted on these obligations and triggered a collapse of some large banks.[54]

When the issue of the Witteveen Facility came up for approval in Congress, the possibility of a coalition of anti–foreign aid conservatives and anti-"bailout" liberals existed. However, Henry Reuss, then chair of the House Banking Committee, and Senator Frank Church (D-ID), then a member of the Senate Foreign Relations Committee, were allied with the Treasury. Moreover, the budgetary implication of the facility was an open question. The Treasury argued that participation would not require an appropriation; thus, it would not have to pass through the additional set of appropriation committees.[55]

As the bill moved through Congress, it encountered a high degree of opposition despite the fact that a Democratic president and most members of the Democratic Congress supported it. Some members were angry at the OPEC cartel and wanted OPEC to finance the balance-of-payments deficits of non-oil developing countries themselves.[56] In addition, similar human rights opposition to that forming against the World Bank in the same years emerged against the Witteveen Facility. In March, Representative Thomas Harkin (D-IA) successfully inserted an amendment that would require the US executive director to oppose loans from the Witteveen Facility that would contribute to the deprivation of basic human needs or the violation of basic human rights. The idea to use the IMF's lending to overtly promote political goals threatened to become a serious conflict with both the Bank and the Fund's constitutions. The provision was struck from the bill in the Senate, and the appropriation question did not become a major stumbling block to passage. Hence, the measure was authorized within thirteen months of the initial request. However, by the late 1970s the IMF executive board minutes contain increasing references to the desirability of operating without needing congressional approval for any given course of action.

## INVESTIGATING THE WORK OF THE IFIs: THE GOLD COMMISSION

In a third major episode where groups sought to use increasingly sophisticated methods of congressional advocacy over the activities of the IMF and World Bank during the late 1970s, groups opposing additional resources were successful in creating a congressional commission. In this instance, the recommendations of the commission would be dead on arrival. The IMF gained the resources it needed. However, the episode set a precedent for a later commission that would have more lasting results, the Meltzer Commission.

In 1980, Treasury requested a permanent IMF quota increase in Congress. In response, a group of fiscally conservative members joined liberal member Thomas Harkin to oppose the increase. Harkin sent out a "Dear Colleague" letter to approximately fifty other liberals that led with the question "How would you like to cast a fiscally conservative vote and feel good about it?"[57] The letter targeted the IMF, and other opponents of the increase joined the effort, including tax-reduction advocates Andrew Jacobs, Jr. (D-IN), and Republican House leaders Jack Kemp (R-NY) and David Stockman (R-MI). Overall, critics argued that the IMF was a poor manager of international credit.[58] When the Senate considered the 1980 quota increase, it was approved with a much narrower margin than earlier IMF votes.

As part of the bargaining necessary to gain his acceptance, Senator Jesse Helms (R-NC) added an amendment to the bill on June 16, 1980, that directed the Treasury to establish and chair a commission to "conduct a study to assess and make recommendations with regard to the policy of the US Government concerning the role of gold in domestic and international monetary systems" and to report its findings and recommendations to Congress.[59] Commissions, such as the Gold Commission, are regarded as part of a broader tradition between Congress and the executive branch to either provide bipartisan cover for unpleasant topics that need to be addressed, or bury them. Base closings and the social security reforms of 1983 are regarded as an example of the former, and the Gold Commission as an example of the latter.[60] Thus, PL 96-389 both enlarged the quota assigned to the US by the IMF and created the Gold Commission to please gold merchants and their legislative allies.

When Carter lost the presidential election, the task of appointing members of the Commission fell to the Reagan administration and the chair of the Joint Economic Committee, Henry Reuss. Reuss designated Chalmers Wylie to represent the House side, despite the fact that Wylie was a Republican. The vice chair of the Joint Economic Committee, Senator Roger Jepsen (R-IA), designated himself to represent the Senate side. Thus, two Republicans were the Joint Economic Committee members. Reuss then named himself as the Democratic representative from the House side, and the commission had three members, rather than the two members prescribed by the law.

Regardless of the reason for its formation and problems with selection of members, Schwartz argues that the Commission had no clear sense of direction when it came into existence.[61] The pro-gold members were in the minority, although this was not evident from the start. The three Federal Reserve governors on the commission had a strong self-interest in opposing a large role for gold in the system; nonetheless, their primary concern was to prevent an extended discussion of the role of the Federal Reserve in the current economic situation. The three pro-gold members did not agree on the institutional arrangements they sought.

Helms and other sponsors of the amendment to the bill had been motivated by the postwar peak in the consumer price index of 1980. However, as with other IFI activists, the actions of the House and Senate members were motivated by different views on inflation that informed their actions. In the Senate, Helms was informed by the neoclassical view of the economist Arthur Laffer, whereas in the House, Congressman Ron Paul (R-TX) was informed by the "Austrian School" economists. The distinction mattered, because Helms and Laffer sought a variant of a traditional gold standard with a fixed, but adjustable, price of gold and some modification of the existing institutional arrangements under the Federal Reserve System. Paul and the Austrian School approach sought a 100% coin gold standard, with no face value for the coins other than prices expressed in weights of gold and a complete break with the existing institutional banking system.[62]

The main proposal to emerge from the commission was that the Treasury issue gold-bullion coins of specified weights, without dollar denomination or legal-tender status, to be sold at a small mark-up over the market value of the gold content. The coins would be exempt from capital gains taxes and from sales taxes. Senator Helms sought to exempt the coins from US and state capital gains taxes, and Representative Paul sought to issue the coins without legal-tender status. This proposal could serve as a first step toward achieving the objective of relinking the entire monetary system to gold, since it would provide a form of currency that would serve as an alternative to paper dollars.[63]

While these proposals did not come to fruition, the creation of the commission served the objective of promoting a discussion of gold in the media insofar as laypersons understood gold to be "honest" money. The commission issued its report on March 31, 1982, and pleased many individuals, including participants who learned that those who supported an enlarged role for gold did not comprise a significant percentage of the economics profession.[64] Prior to the submission of the report to Congress, the House Banking Committee issued a statement opposing its recommendation that the Treasury issue gold-bullion coins. Such an issue without legal tender would confuse monetary conditions. Congressman Reuss led the opposition to the commission's recommendations.[65] Hence, the commission accomplished little beyond its heavily detailed report and role in securing passage of the 1980 IMF quota increase. A later IMF quota increase would likewise come with the mandate for a commission attached—and more profound results.

## Conclusion: The Development Stage

In the development stage of the Congress-IFI relationship, the institution of Congress opened up to further interest-group activism at the same time the international financial system was transformed, bringing the needs of developing countries to the fore. The alliance between big business and labor on the issue of free trade broke down, and the increasingly contentious groups attached to the IFIs attempted to use the legislative machinery in new ways.

The direction of the trend was not conclusive at first. On one hand, the specific initiatives were mostly unsuccessful. The IMF Trust Fund and Witteveen Facility were established over attempts to prevent them. Funds were not earmarked for the World Bank. And the Gold Commission had no visible policy outcome. On the other hand, the legislative maneuvering attached to these initiatives did shape the broad policy outlines of the IFIs in the years ahead. Congress did successfully assert its own authority against the executive over the Trust Fund Agreement by inserting the provision for a *future* role in any IMF gold sales. The World Bank terminated its lending programs in Vietnam in those years. The Witteveen Facility cemented the political alliance between the money center banks and the IMF. The Gold Commission foreshadowed the later congressional commission on the IFIs, the Meltzer Commission, that would offer more substantive policy recommendations. Moreover, the mechanisms of congressional advocacy initiated in these years, either on behalf of members or acting for organized groups, did raise the political stakes.

The trend became more clearly supportive of the IFIs in the next stage as appropriations increased and the legislature provided even larger sums of money. However, as these issues became more publicly controversial, members did not want to have to take a formal stand that could be interpreted as support for an enemy of the US, or a "bailout." The next chapter shows that congressional procedures to gain support for the IFIs would have to change so that activities were moved "inside" politics and avoided the public arena.

5

# Iron Triangles Go Global

## THE 1982 DEBT CRISIS AND END OF THE COLD WAR

> No country can duck below the waves or disappear from the surface of the Earth, unlike a corporation which goes out of business. So the most believable future course of events would be a reshaping of the debt . . . But I do not foresee the kind of development in the case of a country that might take place in a commercial bankruptcy—that a country might just shake off its debts.
>
> —Henry C. Wallich, Member, Board of Governors of the Federal Reserve System[1]

The initial coalition of support for the IFIs among banks, big business, and anti-communist members of Congress had been challenged when organized labor defected from the free-trade coalition and human rights activism grew during the development stage in the 1970s. However, supporters of economic multilateralism had been successful in obtaining necessary legislation for IDA replenishments, IMF quota increases, and overriding amendments despite delays. In the "debt stage," described in this chapter, backers of the IMF and World Bank received consistent support from Congress in terms of providing funds with the fewest policy prescriptions attached by domestic groups. This financial support came even from presidents like Ronald Reagan, who had been openly adversarial toward multilateralism prior to his election. Therefore, during the debt stage, conflict over the IFIs persisted, yet business support solidified even further through organized channels in favor of Treasury's positions. Opponents to the IMF were not organized.

I term this the debt stage of Congress-IFI relations because it was characterized by the exogenous changes associated with the accumulation of sovereign debt and default in developing countries, followed by the collapse of communism and the end of the Cold War that prompted new problems with debt in the former Soviet satellites. As the debt stage progressed, it was no longer possible to divide the interest community active on IFI issues into a domestic and an international component. The end of the Cold War did not initially end the coalition of support for economic multilateralism. It arguably enhanced it. But the collapse of communism did usher in a new dimension to transnational advocacy networks that were no longer hemmed in by the old ideological and political boundaries. As banks expanded their lending and diversified into international bond issues, domestic interest groups connected to financial concerns developed international ones. As NGOs campaigning on behalf of the environment and poverty alleviation looked beyond the American borders, they connected with groups overseas to press for policy changes in the IMF and World Bank.[2] This chapter argues that the debt stage of the Congress-IFI relationship reshaped the "iron triangle," or policy-making relationship characterized by limited outside participation and deference to experts, by adding an international angle.

Endogenous change also occurred within Congress. The expanded use of omnibus legislation facilitated the provision of funds for the IMF and World Bank despite the popular opposition to government "bailouts" of banks during a major recession. In short, IFI measures were rolled into larger bills and individual members were not accountable for votes that could be used against them politically. The first such successful new budgetary mechanism was the Omnibus Reconciliation Bill of 1981. Whereas riders have often been attached by members to kill an initiative, an omnibus bill is a comprehensive bill that unites diverse bills. It is constructed to get something passed. Attention is focused away from the controversy and negotiations involve the president.[3] Therefore, omnibus bills served as a perfect vehicle for IFI issues because party leaders could prevent individual members from having to take a public stand on unpopular issues, like "bailing out" banks through the IMF. Yet their increasing use had the effect of taking control over the IFI issues out of the committees' domain and placing it more squarely with party leaders and the executive who negotiated the specifics of a bill.[4] A concentrated lobby, such as that representing the banking industry, could thus secure funding by working within congressional channels and thwart an unorganized, incoherent opposition that now openly questioned the practices of the Fund and the Bank.

The pattern of congressional advocacy continued wherein groups would approach a member of Congress with an initiative and the member would then draft a letter, hold a hearing, or consider legislation to pursue a policy goal. Other groups would either join or stay out of the newly constituted "floating coalition," which rarely shared a rationale. As in previous years, the World Bank retained a degree of its own agency within these same networks. James Wolfensohn took over as president in 1995 and attempted to include nongovernmental organizations in the working of the Bank in a more comprehensive manner, as well as cultivate personal relations on the Hill. Policy goals would need to be reconciled in compromise legislation.

These maneuvers resulted in policy changes at the IMF and World Bank ranging from raising the rate of remuneration coefficient (the amount the

IMF charges borrowers), to increasing lending to Africa, to the World Bank inspection panel. These policy goals obviously pointed in different directions. The contradictions would only grow more profound with the ultimate resolution to the debt crisis of the 1980s, which transformed the bulk of developing-country debt from bank loans into bonds, and splintered the commonality of purpose in the financial and activist communities. Yet the debt stage was one where members of Congress used procedure, chiefly omnibus legislation, to advocate successfully for IFI funding in the face of serious opposition. By the end of the stage, the cracks created by the end of the Cold War were apparent, and the possibilities of using procedure allowed new groups to impose a substantive policy change on the World Bank, like the inspection panel that had been resisted by many members of the IFIs themselves.

## The Background of International Banking and the Debt Crisis of the 1980s

Interest groups active on Capitol Hill reflect the broader American economy and society, and in this case the American role in the international banking system. That system changed dramatically after the collapse of the fixed-parity system, but the results were not immediately apparent in 1971. As discussed in Chapter 3, US banks expanded their branch banking in the 1960s and became identified with the operations of the IFIs. Their role deepened in the 1970s when sovereign debt to private banks built up through the volume of receipts to oil producers. These receipts, or "petrodollars," were recycled through eight primary US banking organizations that specialized in managing large syndicated loans and came to be included in the "money-center banks."[5] These banks kept dollar deposits outside the territorial US and re-lent them to developing countries through what were then called the "eurodollar markets." In addition, new lending procedures, like credit syndication and floating-rate loans, broadened lender participation.[6] Thus, mid-sized regional and other non-money-center banks also participated in these credits and competed for smaller, trade-related ones. The result was that international lending exploded. Figure 5.1 demonstrates the dramatic growth after 1977.

In addition, lending to developing countries by US banks increased rapidly in the 1970s. As Figure 5.2 shows, by year-end 1978, the eight money-center banks on average held approximately 9% of their total assets in outstanding credits to Latin America.[7]

The typical loan was a syndicated medium- to long-term credit priced with a floating-rate contract tied to the London Interbank Offering Rate (LIBOR). Since the interest rate was priced approximately every six months, and approximately two-thirds of this debt was tied to LIBOR, these loans were vulnerable

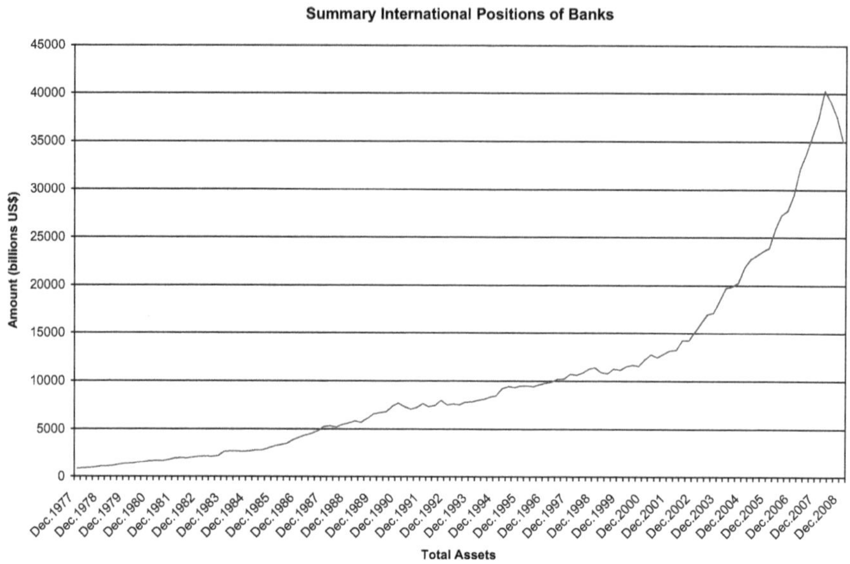


FIGURE 5.1 Summary International Position of Banks.

*Source*: Data from BIS Quarterly Review: June 2009.

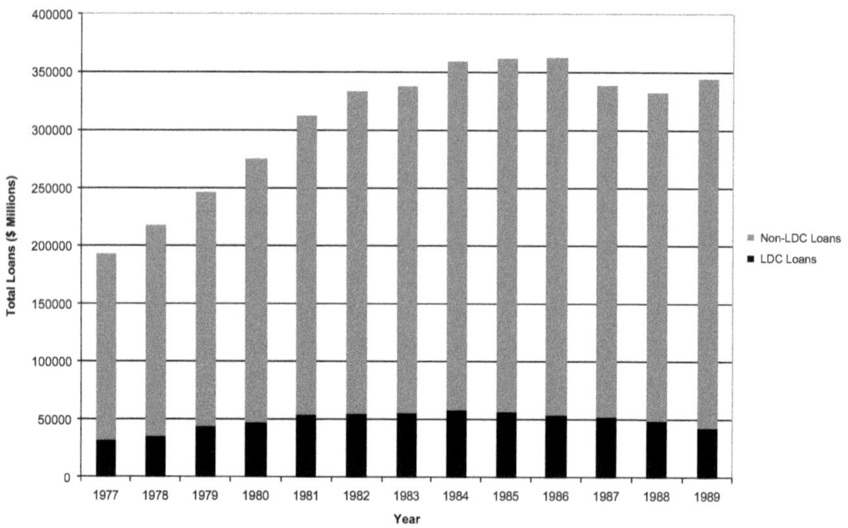


FIGURE 5.2 Aggregate Loans for Eight Money Center Banks.

Source: Data from FDIC History of the Eighties.

to interest-rate risk in the US and other creditor countries.[8] This private debt was heavily concentrated in a few countries. Brazil alone accounted for 30% of all non-oil developing countries' debt. A limited number of states in Latin America and East Asia accounted for most of the rest. Conversely, in 1981 all of the non-oil, less-developed African states owed less than 9% of the total.[9]

The resolution to the crisis would thus reflect the economic circumstances of a very specific group of states that threatened a specific segment of the private banking system.

The buildup did not go unnoticed. Congress held hearings on the debt issue as early as 1975 and expressed concern about the threat of the concentration of developing country loans to the capital position of US banks. In 1977, the Senate Subcommittee on Foreign Relations published a staff report noting that the US banking system, and by extension the international financial system, could be jeopardized by the massive balance-of-payments lending done by commercial banks after the oil price hike.[10]

By the late 1970s, the managing director of the IMF and his staff held talks with officers of commercial banks about the debts owed to them, and capital markets in general. As they began to encounter problems, a member state would negotiate with the Fund and the private banks at the same time; therefore, the banks and the Fund had a shared interest in the financial position of some IMF members. Eventually, the managing director spoke publicly on this issue and set a policy of *not* sharing Fund reports with the banks, and of keeping records of the informal contacts between IMF staff and officials of commercial banks.[11] The perception of collusion among banks and the IMF, together with the political fallout from it, would be more difficult to eradicate.

As mentioned earlier, large commercial banks began lending to states on a large scale in the 1970s because they were awash in cash deposited by oil exporters themselves benefiting from the boom in oil prices during those years. Sentiment at the time, articulated by Walter Wriston, who had been responsible for a good deal of the initial international expansion of branch banking, was that "countries don't go bankrupt."[12] Citibank and J. P. Morgan led many of the syndicates, and smaller banks relied on the larger banks to scrutinize the loans. Some 1,500 banks worldwide were eventually involved, especially in Brazil.[13] In the 1970s and 1980s, J. P. Morgan lent US$1.2 billion to Mexico, $1.8 billion to Brazil, and US$750 million to Argentina.[14] Chase had extended the major portion of its loans in dollars, $11.6 billion in all, between 1979 to 1981—that is, after the second oil-price explosion.

When the general commodity price boom ended in the late 1970s, it was accompanied by the second oil shock. The severity of the world recession of 1981–1982 that reduced world trade, commodity prices, and export earnings came as a surprise to most analysts. In the months prior to the Mexican crisis, the Falkland Islands war contributed to a mood of uncertainty in Latin American lending. When Argentina invaded the Falklands/Malvinas, Britain froze the London-based assets of Argentina. This combination of factors continued the need for high levels of borrowing in oil-importing countries yet diminished the resources to service the debt. Eventually, the interest rates on these loans rose, since they were not fixed, and an overall squeeze in international liquidity made the debt service unmanageable.

The possibility of Mexican default in August of 1982 was not the first crisis of its kind, but it was the first that posed the possibility of systemic collapse to the International Monetary Fund.[15] When Jesus Silva Herzog, the Mexican secretary of finance, informed Jacques de Larosiere, then managing director of the IMF, of the government's position, de Larosiere responded that the Fund would help but that Mexico would have to avoid default.[16] The US government provided immediate emergency funding. Paul Volcker, who was now the Federal Reserve chair, attempted to arrange a meeting of the G10 Central Bank governors through the Bank for International Settlements (BIS).[17] The BIS provided a bridge loan that was shared among participating central banks. Anthony Solomon next hosted a creditors meeting at the Federal Reserve Bank of New York. The main Mexican creditors were British, American, and then Japanese, in that order. However, when Herzog met with the chair of the four major New York banks, Walter Wriston of Citibank, Willard Butcher of Chase, John McGillicuddy of Manufacturers Hanover, and Donald Platten of Chemical, they agreed that a "coordinating committee" of banks would take the lead. Paul Volcker of the Federal Reserve and William Rhodes of Citibank cochaired the Banks' Advisory Committee.

Prior to the crisis, banks and the IMF made lending decisions independent of one another. The crisis created a situation where the banks needed the Fund's country analysis and leverage in dealing with governments, and the Fund needed the banks' resources. States involved needed both the analysis and the funds.[18] A bailout could have been arranged without the IMF, but at a higher cost to all of these parties. The problem that faced the IMF and other actors in the crisis was that the banks needed to *increase* their exposure at a time when they were particularly reluctant to lend new funds. At the meeting with the banks, Herzog presented the government's position as one willing to work *with* them.[19]

When the Mexican crisis hit, investors began to close their short-term Brazilian loans. The Brazilian finance and planning ministers met the senior vice president for Latin America at J. P. Morgan Bank to try to arrange an emergency loan of US$2.5 to $3 billion. When a larger package was needed, the Brazilian relationship with J. P. Morgan was such that they requested that this bank lead the rescheduling, a role generally reserved for the bank with the greatest exposure. More than half of Brazil's debt was held by non-American banks, yet Citibank and J. P. Morgan were the key decision makers in the Brazil crisis.[20] As cochairs of the rescheduling, they aroused suspicions from Europeans that they gave Brazil lenient treatment. Steering committees of later crises were also similarly American, and tensions built. Regional banks with smaller exposure sought to cut their losses, but they participated because they were reluctant to antagonize the Federal Reserve and the larger Wall Street banks.[21]

The IMF of the 1980s appeared to be an organization helping countries get enough new financing that they could service their debts on normal market terms. The Mexican negotiations proved to be a model for later crises. A separate bank committee of twelve to fourteen banks was formed for each country, and these banks would negotiate a new schedule of payments. Each bank on the committee would keep the other creditor banks in its country or region informed, and under pressure to agree.[22] Later rescue packages managed by William Rhodes sought a greater participation of creditor governments, at the IMF, World Bank, US Treasury, Federal Reserve, and State Department.[23] Tensions among banks diminished and a spirit of shared sacrifice resulted.

These individual country meetings forged a common purpose in the banking industry by the time legislation emerged on the Hill. That is, bankers were not working at odds with one another other in the political system, nor did they seek to change the policies the IMF and World Bank implemented in the bailouts. These types of concerns had been handled in the previous meetings. Once the appropriation reached Congress, the banks simply wanted the funds.

Despite lingering issues over how public-sector debt would be handled in bailouts, the relationship between the IMF and commercial banks had come a long way from where it had been in the 1940s when the industry had attempted to prevent the establishment of the organization. The IMF was successful in cultivating new forms of participation owing to Jacques de Larosiere's activism as well as its ability to construct financing packages by withholding its endorsement until it was assured of a "critical mass" from both commercial banks and government creditors.[24] The new conditions also altered the attitude of the US toward the IO. Whereas the early Reagan administration had sought to limit the role of the Fund, when the financial threats reached large American financial institutions, it felt compelled to act.

## Ronald Reagan, Congress, and the 1983 IMF "Bailout"

When Ronald Reagan assumed office in January of 1981, Congress had still not appropriated monies for the sixth IDA replenishment, stalled over the Vietnamese invasion of Cambodia. Members of his administration were reluctant to increase IMF funding early in the 1982 crisis because they believed it would contribute to the problem of moral hazard. Moreover, the Reagan administration posed an obstacle for IFI funding because Ronald Reagan had opposed the operations of many UN agencies as well as US foreign aid as far back as the 1960s. Despite Reagan's skepticism toward international organizations, his administration sought to make good on the IDA commitment for the sixth replenishment once in office. When the issue first came before the House appropriations committee, he was recuperating in the hospital after an assassination attempt. The secretary of the treasury, Donald T. Regan, testified that he had seen the president in the hospital and Reagan had told him, concerning IDA, "But we are going to support those commitments that have been made by the previous Administration and on which our allies are counting on us for our support."[25]

The 97th Congress is notable because the reconciliation bill that approved US contributions to four international development banks passed. House leaders, banking committee leaders and members, and the president were all in favor of the funding for the IOs. Yet it was controversial with the American public, and previous efforts had failed. The leaders attached the measure to the omnibus reconciliation bill, it passed overwhelmingly, and the president signed it.[26] This would mark a shift in procedure on later IMF/World Bank funding issues wherein unpopular measures could be included in larger packages and assembled as budget compromises.

With this omnibus bill and those that follow to the present day, party leaders behave strategically insofar as they attempt to assemble bills that will succeed. There is evidence that they are nearly perfect in doing so, since all of the omnibus bills examined in Krutz's comprehensive work on the topic were enacted.[27] Conversely, the overwhelming majority of standard bills fail at some point. Thus, there is no variation between successful and unsuccessful omnibus bills, and the most significant question is what gets attached to an omnibus bill. Krutz argues that "omnibus legislating in effect inserts an important decision about policy outcomes (what will be incorporated into a must-pass bill) into the pre-floor legislative process."[28] Presidents have something to gain in these omnibus bargains because they can negotiate to have their own items included. Congress will accommodate these requests to avoid a veto. Paradoxically, bills opposed by the president and agenda items supported by him are also more likely to become attached.[29] Krutz finds that when an issue is fragmented across committees, it is more likely to be attached to omnibus bills, and those considered in times of divided government are 17% more likely to be attached to omnibus bills than those in unified government. Thus, they help chambers avert a stalemate.[30]

## LEGISLATIVE LOGROLLING TO GAIN IMF SUPPORT

The next debate over IMF funding surpassed the vitriol of the IDA-Vietnam issue and divided the Republican members, just as earmarking IDA funds had divided the Democrats earlier. The ambivalence of the Reagan administration to the IMF stemmed from Reagan's own conflicting sentiments on international organizations, as well as that of many officials in his administration who shared his views. Moreover, his team of economic advisors was drawn from all schools of conservative thinking and did not agree about how to control inflation, further complicating their views on the role of the Fund. Monetarists, such as Milton Friedman, sought to regulate money aggregates. Supply-siders preferred a return to the gold standard.[31] David Stockman, who had been an IMF critic when he was a member of Congress, moved to the role of director of the Office of Management and Budget (OMB).

Although Treasury Secretary Donald Regan had testified on behalf of the US commitments to IDA already made, he opposed increased IMF funding for most of 1982, arguing that any move to expand the IMF would only encourage lax lending.[32] As late as November of that year, the executive board of the IMF noted that "the US Administration was still in the process of consulting the Congress regarding the size of any contribution that the United States might make."[33] In December, the US indicated that a 50% increase in Fund quotas would raise difficulties in Congress. The administration proposed designating a portion of the increase to quotas and a portion to an increase in the General Arrangements to Borrow (GAB).[34] Although the US executive director, then Richard D. Erb, did not want to say that the congressional climate was the sole reason for dividing the increase, he did take the view that a two-pronged approach of seeking an increase in quota together with an increase in the GAB was considered more practical than simply seeking a quota increase.[35]

The IMF eventually proposed to increase the total capital pool by $43 billion, and the US was asked to contribute $7.8 billion. Reagan submitted the proposal to Congress, although the ambivalence of his administration persisted. Direct conflict over the bill emerged. The Bankers Association for Foreign Trade (BAFT) led the bank lobbying efforts in favor of the increase.[36] The labor movement and management in traditional industries regarded it as a giveaway to banks and corporations that had exported US jobs. For example, William Hoppe, a steel industry representative, argued that foreign lending had created a problem of overcapacity in the steel industry because the debt had financed steel production in middle-income countries that competed with American producers.[37]

In April of 1983, the Senate authorized increased funding for the quota increase by a vote of 55 to 34. When the bill reached the House, the debate grew stronger. In July, groups such as the Citizens' Coalition Against the IMF Increase (an ad hoc group of environmentalist, church, conservative, taxpayer, and free-market organizations) worked to defeat it. Thus, perceived as a "bailout," the bill only narrowly passed the House, with a six-vote majority (217 to 211) and after the administration campaigned in its favor. In order to achieve passage, the House bill had been amended to prohibit IMF loans to communist nations. Hence, despite passage in both chambers, the House and Senate versions needed to be reconciled.

As the crisis over the Mexican default unfolded, the IMF's resources went from approximately $13 billion at the end of 1982 to $6 billion by October 1983. Reconciliation of the two versions of the bill was complicated by the fact that in the interim, the National Republican Congressional Committee had sent news releases and mailed letters to selected voters in some of the districts where members had voted against the anti-communist amendment, interpreting their votes as supporting communism. David Obey (D-WI) was among those targeted, and he, together with Speaker Tip O'Neill (D-MA), demanded a letter of apology from the president that would make it clear his vote had the backing of the administration.[38] Therefore, the legislation took on unpleasant partisan overtones even after the Reagan administration issued a letter to address the problem of the amendment, and the money was still not appropriated.

In a classic example of legislative logrolling, the chair of the House Banking Committee and an IMF supporter, Fernand J. St. Germain (D-RI), linked further action on funding it to the passage of a housing bill.[39] This housing legislation had been deadlocked for a number of years and had not had the support of the administration, whereas the IMF now did have its support. The more the administration sought the IMF increase, the more vulnerable it was to these types of tactics. Frieden argues that St. Germain took a publicly hostile position on the IMF in order to maintain his reputation and defuse opposition. He would act as a critic during the public committee meetings and privately assure the bankers that he would remove restrictive amendments in the House-Senate conference committee.[40] Eventually, the combined bill attracted enough votes in the House and Senate to gain approval with few substantive reforms required. Thus, it became a classic example of an omnibus vehicle that advances a controversial cause by forcing members to accept a measure that couldn't survive alone because they want the entire bill (or another part of it) to pass.[41]

Despite the Reagan administration's reluctance to support the Fund and its success with the bill, opponents to international organizations and foreign aid in general remained. Centrist internationalists from both the Democratic and Republican Parties now confronted liberal opposition that joined free marketers. The cement in this emerging anti-IMF coalition was the notion that the money-center banks had caused the debt crisis and were being bailed out in a recession. During the course of the debate, an IMF loan to apartheid South Africa threatened to take the Congressional Black Caucus over to the side of the opposition.[42] Hence, even though the bill eventually passed, the legislative fight over the IMF quota increase revealed major opposition to the Fund in Congress.[43] Moreover, its image as a good manager was seriously weakened.[44] Academics were already publishing papers on the problem of moral hazard associated with IMF lending, because the IMF's willingness to assist nations with trouble increases the likelihood that such difficulties will occur.[45]

In this round, the funding passed because supporters of the IMF were more prepared to present their case. They were defending a position that had media support, represented conventional wisdom, and had the backing of many powerful groups, including corporate ones, the (reluctant) administration, the Chamber of Commerce, the National Association of Manufacturers and Agribusiness, public interest groups such as the League of Women Voters and the Consumers for World Trade, along with think tanks such as the Institute for International Economics. The League support came from its belief that the IMF promotes international trade and development.[46] Large American banks contacted their major manufacturing customers and asked for their help with lobbying Congress. One answered the call. Aircraft manufacturer Boeing's treasurer calculated that the firm attempted to sell aircraft in more than thirty countries where the IMF had, or was negotiating, programs.[47] From the perspective of IMF officials involved, Congress was ultimately persuaded by members' desire to maintain the US veto power.[48]

In terms of organization and effectiveness on the Hill, the coalition of critics of the IMF lacked explanatory materials to make their case to those who needed substantive knowledge of the IMF in Congress; hence, they were forced to develop them at the same time they were finding ways of talking about the issue. Many members of Congress did not care to meet with anti-IMF coalition members because the IMF question was not a significant part of their normal agenda. Moreover, the IMF's detractors generally sought reforms, which further complicated their actions because few could agree on the specifics that would make the IMF increase acceptable, whereas the banks were unified. Some favored regulatory supervision over those banks involved in lending; others favored language requiring the US representative to the IMF to promote human rights or environmental values. The groups could not develop a uniform position given the time pressures.[49] Nonetheless, they learned from this experience for subsequent legislative fights.

By the end of Reagan's second term, most members of his administration had developed a more positive view of the IFIs than they had had when Reagan was elected. A degree of the change can be attributed to the actions of the 1982 debt crisis in Latin America, when Reagan commissioned a Treasury report on US participation in the multilateral development banks. Although it argued that US funding should be decreased due to US budgetary concerns, the report's generally supportive posture toward the IFIs turned the tide in favor of the IMF and World Bank. By 1985, the US was current in its commitments to the World Bank. President Reagan later attended an annual meeting of the World Bank and lobbied on behalf of IDA. His Treasury Department supported the IMF.[50]

## THE POLICY DEBATE ON DEBT

The debt crisis provoked an international economic debate. Religious missionaries of every denomination were joined by international development organizations, such as Oxfam in the UK, and by left or progressive organizations, such as the Institute for Policy Studies and the Development Group for Alternative Policies (D-Gap) in the US.[51] Discussions in the US explored the possibility of some kind of reduction in debt stock. However, internal divisions over US foreign policies and other matters, combined with fatigue, caused the first coalition of debt activists to disintegrate. Development experts independent of the activist community, such as Professors Peter Kenen of Princeton,

Jeffrey Sachs of Harvard, and investment bankers Felix Rohatyn and James D. Robinson, argued for the establishment of some type of fund for debt relief.[52] They presented their views to Congress throughout the 1980s and were eventually joined by individuals working at the Jesuit-related Center of Concern in Washington, DC.[53]

Outright debt forgiveness, however, contradicted notions of the sanctity of the contract and the property rights of international banks. In 1985, the Reagan administration offered the Baker Plan as an initial programmatic response to the problem of large debt that would allow for an increase in commercial and multilateral bank lending over three years, in addition to debt swaps for equity, environmental and social projects, and conversion of debt into "exit bonds." The plan failed to resolve the situation. Nonetheless, in 1986 Mexico agreed to the terms that rescheduled approximately 83% of the country's pre-1985 public-sector debt to be paid over twenty years. In 1988, the subcommittee chair of the House Banking Committee, Walter Fauntroy (D-DC), sought a general capital increase for the IBRD that would be linked to debt relief. The policy goal was to encourage *banks* to voluntarily shoulder some of the burden of debt relief.[54] He viewed the situation as a "pass through arrangement" where money from the World Bank freed other money to be used for IMF or commercial payments.

In 1989, the administration offered the "Brady Plan," which would allow banks to restructure a volume of syndicated bank debt to developing countries off of their balance sheets and onto individual investors by issuing bonds. The plan offered debtors a menu of options that contained roughly the same discounted present value of the current price of their bank debt in the secondary market. This meant that in exchange for 65% of the value of the loans, countries issued longer-term "Brady Bonds," which were dollar-denominated instruments collateralized by US Treasury zero-coupon bonds. Thus, the concentration of risk would be spread throughout the global financial system.

Mexico was the first to negotiate terms under the Brady Plan through Brady Bonds. Mexican loans were exchanged for bonds that would allow the debt to be traded in financial markets where it could be priced according to its market value. This value was enhanced by the use of US Treasury securities to guarantee part of the interest and principal payments.[55] Mexico converted US$43 billion into Brady Bonds; Venezuela converted $9 billion into the bonds. Citibank lent an additional amount of money rather than convert its $2.4 billion.[56] Settlements with Argentina and Brazil followed in 1992. As a result, Latin American debt was not only to private sources, it created a growing market for sovereign debt outside of direct loans from commercial banks. The trend continued. In the current era, emerging market bond issues have grown four times as quickly as syndicated bank loans. The variety of debt instruments and derivatives used has also grown among the debt stock. The political interests of the holders of these different debt instruments diverged.

The resolution of the debt crisis matters because the new holders of Latin American sovereign debt would eventually become active in Congress and elsewhere to press for different political interests connected to their individual investment concerns. By the end of the debt stage, the financial community was no longer a political monolith.

## Lending to China and India and the Growing Role of NGOs

As discussed earlier, when Ronald Reagan assumed the presidency, Congress had not appropriated funds for the sixth IDA replenishment. Reagan himself was not an advocate of multilateralism, but he sought to make good on the American commitment. Therefore, his administration sought the funding for the sixth, while negotiating a dramatically reduced seventh, replenishment. Also in 1980, China joined the World Bank as part of its broader package of domestic economic reforms. The two issues became linked when the annual appropriations for the round unfolded. The Reagan administration and members of Congress sought a decrease in the amount of development assistance IDA directed at only two countries: China and India. During the same years, a new, more vocal, set of actors emerged in support of IDA from the business community and religious groups. They would be successful in securing resources for the World Bank, but also in shaping the direction of the Bank's lending.

### IDA AND AFRICA

The seventh IDA replenishment was smaller than the sixth when adjusted for inflation. When the IDA deputies met in February 1983 to negotiate it, the US representative did call for a lower allocation to India and China combined than the Bank had proposed. Regan argued that the round was smaller because the administration had had so many difficulties gaining passage for the sixth.[57] Members of the Senate authorizing committee expressed concerns that the lower level reflected a lack of support for IDA overall. Senators Charles Percy (R-IL), Charles Mathias (R-MD), John Glenn (D-OH), and Christopher Dodd (D-CT) wrote a letter to the secretary of the treasury requesting a higher figure.

Another senator, John C. Danforth (R-MO), had visited Africa, and he saw IDA as a good use of the US government's money and an effective way to seek internal policy change. He argued: "If the United States were to embark on a very heavy-handed effort to try to change domestic policies within recipient countries, we would be viewed as the ugly American. But when the international community as a whole does so, then I think real changes can be put into place, and that is what is needed in a lot of these countries."[58] As the hearings for the seventh round progressed, other individuals and groups, such as Terence Cardinal Cooke, the Chamber of Commerce, the National Council for

US-China Trade, the US Catholic Conference of Bishops, and M. W. Kellogg Co. (an engineering construction company that had received IDA contracts), pressured the Reagan administration on the grounds that it was "moral" to support IDA and it was good for American business. In April of 1984, the Senate Committee on Foreign Relations passed an amendment out of the committee directing the US executive director of IDA to negotiate that the amount of development credits made available to Africa in the seventh replenishment equal or exceed those of the sixth.[59]

Although the US did not increase its contribution, Danforth offered a compromise that an additional $500 million would be added, provided the president report to Congress that the seriousness of the condition in countries warranted a supplemental contribution. The president must ask Congress for the additional amount, and Congress must appropriate it. Once the round was completed in 1985, H. R. 1949 was brought to the House Banking Committee. H. R. 1949 would allow the US to participate in a Special Facility for Africa through IDA. Thus, the US could contribute more to IDA while directing money at a special purpose. Although the Reagan administration did not support the initiative, groups and academics rallied to support its passage.[60] Public laws 99–500 and 99–591 authorized and appropriated $64.8 million for the Special Facility.[61] Thus, when the contention surrounding the sixth replenishment dissipated and the seventh round was completed, congressional advocacy efforts had been successful in increasing the amount of money appropriated to IDA and Africa in particular.

## NEW GROUPS AND LOBBYING FOR THE IFIs

The controversy attached to the IMF and IDA appropriations generated more institutionalized forms of support from the groups and individuals concerned with their activities. New organized groups were needed to press for the IFIs' concerns on Capitol Hill, since the IMF and World Bank cannot hire lobbyists to represent themselves.

One of the first was associated with the Treasury. In 1982, two scholars at the Brookings Institution organized a conference and asked former Secretaries of the Treasury Henry Fowler and Charls Walker to host it. The sense among these individuals was that the IFIs' main constituent had been the secretary of the treasury, yet no organized group existed to promote the department in Congress. Forty people attended the initial meeting and wanted to create an ongoing entity that would support the Treasury Department's budget request for the IFIs and their broader legislative agenda.[62] Hence, the Bretton Woods Committee was formally established in 1984 to build public understanding of the Bretton Woods institutions and international development banks in a bipartisan manner within the corporate community. Eventually, it attracted more than 600 members from a range of leadership positions in business, government, national associations, and education. Elliot Richardson was a member of the executive committee of the Bretton Woods Committee. Honorary cochairmen were Jimmy Carter and Gerald Ford. Cochairs were Henry Owen, Paul Volcker, and Charls Walker.[63]

Other groups acted similarly to present favorable views on multilateralism to Congress and the American public at large. The Overseas Development Council (ODC) had been established in 1969 to provide research, analysis, and education on US interests in, and relations with, developing countries under the initiative of David Rockefeller and with Rockefeller Foundation funding. In addition to foundation finance, it received its major support from export-oriented multinational business, and banking in particular. By the late 1980s, the ODC put a high priority on Third World debt, on the environment/development relationship, and on the interplay of economic and political development.[64] The organization commissioned two studies in these years on the future of the IMF and World Bank. Both studies concluded that the institutions should be strengthened and allocated more resources for lending, not less.[65]

Connected more closely to the events of 1982, the Institute for International Finance (IIF) was established in 1983 as a global trade group for internationally active financial institutions from around the world concerned with ways to protect their interests in borrowing countries during the Latin American debt crisis. Its initial concern was that the only information on these markets available was through the IMF, which was reluctant to share it and perhaps unreliable. Therefore, the IIF would serve as its own source of information. Later, the IIF broadened its mission to attempt to influence the policy directions of the IFIs. By 2002, the IIF represented more than 300 banks and other financial institutions from fifty countries.[66]

During these years, the World Bank ramped up its external relations department and the IMF established its own. With the Bretton Woods Committee, ODC, IIF, and other new groups joining the network of interest groups attached to IFI issues, the IMF and World Bank had a more organized channel of access in successive rounds of budget appropriations. In 1989, the House passed a foreign assistance appropriations measure that did not include funding for the hard-loan windows of the World Bank and the Inter-American Development Bank (IDB) for FY 1990. To ensure that the amounts were added in the Senate, the Bretton Woods Fund wrote Elliot Richardson and asked him to sign a letter that would be sent to members of the Senate Appropriations Committee at a strategic point in their deliberations.[67] They also asked for a personal letter and, if he was willing, visits to the Hill, where their staff would be happy to schedule appointments. Overall, the Fund planned to contact 400 American firms awarded procurement contracts through the World Bank and ask that they write their legislators expressing support for the multilaterals. The Bretton Woods Fund also coordinated a coalition of DC-based representatives of national trade associations, multinational corporations, and other business groups to make the business sectors' case for multilateral foreign assistance programs.[68]

Nonetheless, a diversity of policy views persisted even among allies on debt. At a Bretton Woods Committee–Brookings Institution Conference, Senator Paul Sarbanes (D-MD) welcomed the US Treasury's recognition that debt reduction was necessary. But he said that the approach outlined by Brady was only the beginning of the beginning. Debt reduction means acceptance of losses by banks. Senator Bill Bradley (D-NJ) called the Treasury's acceptance of the need for debt reduction "a significant change of direction." But he questioned whether or not it was sufficient. Representative Jim Leach (R-IA) thought that the Brady Plan was insufficient but a step in the right direction. He had no sympathy for commercial-bank quid pro quo's of a regulatory forbearance nature. In his view, it had gotten the thrift industry into trouble and should not be tolerated in commercial banking. Banks doubled LDC lending from 1979 to 1982, and taxpayers should not have been expected to accommodate the mistakes of financial institutions.[69]

As the new groups increased their activities, they became more savvy about the members to approach and the techniques that would resonate with the public. Support that was too overt was frowned upon. For example, large newspaper ads were discouraged. Conversely, former members of the House and Senate could approach current members with greater degrees of success.[70] Yet other organized interest groups became more sophisticated as well.

By the late 1980s, environmental groups became increasingly engaged in the work of the World Bank. In the process of seeking advocates for their positions, they approached individual members of Congress who could affix measures from inside the institution. Environmental activists gained an important new ally in 1987 when Nancy Pelosi (D-CA) won a special election for the House of Representatives and was assigned to the banking committee. In the next, 101st, Congress, Pelosi worked with Walter Fauntroy (D-DC) on the International Development and Finance Act of 1989, which when passed amended the International Financial Institutions Act with specific environmental provisions in what came to be known as the "Pelosi Amendment." As with previous efforts to influence the bank through directives to executive directors, the Pelosi Amendment mandated certain abstentions or "no" votes on projects that would have a significant effect on the human environment that had not been assessed, or whose assessments had not been made public at least 120 days before a vote. In specifically referencing environmental assessments of certain projects, the amendment gave indigenous peoples and NGOs an important new tool in their struggles over individual projects.

After the amendment came into effect two years later, all of the major multilateral development banks adopted environmental-assessment and information-access procedures. A much greater amount of information became available than had been before. Nonetheless, the multilateral banks exhibited major gaps in the analyses contained in their assessment reports. The rapid appraisal techniques and outdated material they used left much work to be done. However, the entrance of the environmental groups into the community of IFI activism would prove to be momentous after the Soviet alliance system broke down, the Soviet Union collapsed, and the Cold War ended shortly thereafter. New states joined the IFIs seeking development finance. In the years that followed, the sense of competition between the IMF and World Bank's capitalist development strategies and communist ones dissipated in the outlook of many members of Congress who had supported the IFIs out of a sense of rivalry with the Soviets. Like Robert Taft, Jr., Nancy Pelosi would emerge as a strong defender of the IFIs, ensuring that they received funding throughout her tenure in Congress. At the same time, her support was tempered by a strong concern for their environmental policies and, later, the role of women in development.

## The End of the Cold War

The end of the Cold War did not initially appear to threaten the IMF and World Bank. In 1992, the George H. W. Bush administration preferred that any economic assistance for the former Soviet republics be channeled through the IMF and supported $12 billion in new contributions. Once again, a Republican president facing a Democratic Congress was able to gain material support for IFI budgetary measures by attaching them to other bills. In this instance, the problem was with other items rolled into the foreign-aid bill, not with the substance of the IMF's work program or allegations of "bailing out" banks. However, the sense of Cold War competition with communism had united a disparate coalition supporting economic development. When that connection was gone, the groups did not necessarily share an orientation on appropriate development-policy measures. The nature of the World Bank's work in project lending left it more immediately vulnerable to shifting political alignments associated with the end of the Cold War now that the cement was gone. Omnibus legislation allowed key players in Congress to assert a stronger policymaking role in the Bank on their behalf because they were willing to work inside the machinery to gain policy goals on behalf of those interested parties.

### THE IMF NINTH GENERAL QUOTA REVIEW IN CONGRESS

After the difficulties with the eighth general quota review at the end of 1983, the IMF's board discussed objections raised in the US Congress about the somewhat concessional nature of Fund lending. Members of Congress viewed the Fund as a commercial institution and not a cooperative one. However, it charged a rate of interest that was below the rate the US government paid when it borrowed money. While the Fund's management did not agree that it was commercial in nature, they did realize that they had to get the rate of remuneration coefficient (i.e., the amount paid by borrowers) to almost 100% of the borrowing price (i.e., the market rate) before they could establish a Committee of the Whole on Quotas. That is, the rate could not be concessional. The non-US executive directors were reluctant to change the remuneration coefficient but agreed that the next quota increase would need to be successful. Therefore, if the rate was increased to an appropriate level at an earlier date and not limited to the completion of the next quota review, the US authorities would be more willing to discuss the timing of the ninth general review. The cost to the US of Fund programs would be an important factor influencing their decision in that regard. Thus, in anticipation of this problem, management eliminated it before considering a quota increase.[71] Aside from the issue of the remuneration coefficient, Congress was favorably disposed toward the IMF at this time because members sensed a need to support it to help the former Soviet Union and other regimes.

Despite the positive sentiment, when the ninth review came before Congress in 1992, it became embroiled in an unrelated issue in the foreign-aid bill. The government of Israel sought $10 billion in housing loan guarantees from the US to obtain more favorable loan rates to build housing for Soviet and East European Jews who emigrated there at the end of the Cold War. The US proposed that it would provide the amount only if Israel stopped building new settlements in the occupied West Bank and Gaza Strip. The US also proposed deducting any funds that Israel spent in the territories from the guarantees that it would make. Senator Patrick Leahy (D-VT), chair of the Senate Appropriations Subcommittee, stated that there would be no aid bill unless the conditions were met. Leahy did not want to fight for a foreign-aid bill in an election year, when public opposition to it was overwhelming.

Because the ninth quota review increase was contained in the foreign-aid bill (and packaged with an amendment to the Articles of Agreement), the IMF money and amendment would also be blocked.[72] A continuing resolution kept the funding for other foreign-aid programs constant. However, the IMF had not received funding the previous year and was thus cut off despite the degree of support. Members of the board of the Fund considered writing to President George H. W. Bush regarding the matter, but the US executive director, Thomas Dawson, advised against it. He argued that in an election year the Fund could try to influence congressional members and staff, but must avoid any actions that could be used by those who did not want the quota increase to pass. A letter to the president was potentially such a problematic action.[73]

As the impasse dragged on, the Senate considered dropping the loan guarantees from the bill to ensure that the IMF would be funded and that the former Soviet Union would get its relief. However, were the Senate to drop the guarantees, Israel's supporters in Congress most likely would not have supported the bill, and it would not have passed. Resolution came from within the Israeli political system. Yitzhak Rabin was elected prime minister in 1992 and modified Israel's settlement policy. Nearly eight months later, in October of that year, the Senate approved the request as well as the IMF increase and aid to Russia.[74]

Therefore, the stall in IMF funding was not related to the operations of the Fund. Rather, it resulted from the manner the legislation was packaged to gain support. At the end of the Cold War, the IMF appeared to be more in sync with the business community than the World Bank did.[75] The stall was caused by other interest groups, attached to unrelated issues, who were nonetheless needed to construct enough support for the foreign-aid bill in an apathetic environment.

## IDA AND PROPOSALS FOR A WORLD BANK INSPECTION PANEL

The wider range of programs and their deeper integration into the societies of developing countries made World Bank projects more immediate targets for criticism when the Cold War ended. The cycle of its annual IDA appropriation also put it on the congressional agenda more repeatedly. Whereas the sixth replenishment had strengthened the role of Congress in concluding a round of negotiations and directing monies at certain countries and regions, albeit indirectly, the subsequent years strengthened the role of groups in pressing for specific policy changes by withholding support for IDA. Moreover, these groups sought a more direct and ongoing vehicle through which to participate in World Bank activities, and Congress supported these efforts in its appropriations.[76]

Initially, those seeking a greater role for Congress encountered legal obstacles. Some aspects of legislative oversight may have conflicted with the World Bank's Articles of Agreement, which established contact with member states through their finance ministries. Therefore, as the NGO role in the World Bank's operations grew, parliamentarians began to explore alternate accountability mechanisms through democratic legislation that might be within the parameters set by the articles. Representative Barney Frank (D-MA) commented that when he took over the subcommittee chair, a colleague from Australia approached him about the possibility of convening an informal group of parliamentarians to talk about the IFIs directly, without any one country being accused of undue familiarity with the Bank or the Fund. In response, Frank arranged an international meeting of parliamentarians so that they could perhaps coordinate on what they would ask of their official government representatives. The all-day event was held in the Rayburn Office Building and presided over by Frank. Rather than a formal hearing, participants engaged in a "seminar-style hearing" with a panel of experts, including the first deputy managing director of the IMF, Stanley Fischer, and the vice president and chief economist of the World Bank, Michael Bruno.[77]

Whereas the international meeting of parliamentarians did not develop into an ongoing oversight mechanism, NGOs did continue to approach the new chair on the accountability of the Bank to civil society. In the next case, a new set of environmental activists entered the ring. A great deal of media attention had been focused on the construction of the Narmada River development in India. The controversial project would provide drinking water, irrigation, and electricity for 40 million people; yet it also meant that 40,000 households would be displaced. As a result of the controversy, the Bank commissioned an independent review of the Narmada project by a former member of Congress and UNDP official, Bradford Morse, which concluded that the Bank had breached its own environmental guidelines.

NGOs stepped up their efforts to stop the project when the tenth replenishment came before Congress. During the hearing, several members questioned what specifically they could do to change IDA and the World Bank.[78] As the Domestic and International Monetary Policy Subcommittee chair, Frank sought to institutionalize the results of the Morse Commission so that it would not be an ad hoc mechanism for each World Bank project. When the IDA authorizations came before the subcommittee, he insisted on the creation of the World Bank inspection panel as well as country reports on projects.

Hearings were held on the topic during which time NGOs and the Bank negotiated the specific details of the panels.[79] As Frank recalled the event, former congressman Matthew McHugh, who served as an assistant to the president of the World Bank, told him, "'Look, you can't order us to do anything'. I [Frank] said: 'I agree, and you can't order me to pass the bill with the money.'"[80] At a time when arrearages from previously unfunded replenishments were accumulating, Representative John Kasich (R-OH) offered an amendment totally eliminating funds for the World Bank on the House floor. It was defeated by a margin of six votes.[81] Moreover, opposition to the inspection panel at the World Bank came from developing countries that viewed the panels as an infringement on their sovereignty. The environmental groups were thus able to broaden the scope of the conflict over World Bank policy by first joining with fiscal conservatives in Congress, such as Robert Kasten (R-WI), and then with other members of Congress, such as Frank, who sought reform.[82]

As the negotiations dragged on, the financial services committee marked up the authorization bill and the Bank's board authorized a resolution for the panels. However, outstanding questions concerning their independence and operation remained. Using congressional procedure to his advantage, Frank proposed a two-year authorization and then a one-year authorization in the third year to see how the panels had been operating. In this way, the authorizing lever would remain in place to ensure that the panels would be an effective accountability mechanism. The Bank objected that authorization could only be for the entire replenishment, and not an increment of it. Frank's staff sought a legal opinion on his capacity to change the authorization. Whereas the

Bank's legal interpretation was that the round had to be authorized as a package, the interpretation rendered by the Congressional Research Service was that Article I of the US Constitution gives Congress the power to approve appropriations and the power to set its own rules. Congress has created a system whereby two steps are necessary to release funds from the US Treasury. No international organization and no department of the executive branch has the right or capacity to change that system, no matter what legislation they might think is necessary.[83]

In this example, an important legal principle was at stake between the executive and legislative branches of government beyond the specifics of the policy proposals brought to Congress by the NGOs. When the World Bank's board issues a replenishment resolution and countries pay their first installments, the US then engages in a *two*-step process. Admittedly, it is the only country that observes this practice. The Treasury must authorize participation in the replenishment round, and Congress must authorize funding for it. This arrangement cannot be altered by an international agreement. Therefore, in creating the inspection panel, Frank and the committee were using Congress as a forum for groups seeking change, and also asserting the prerogative of the congressional budget process, and specifically the rules of the House, which cannot be changed from outside.

The view of some environmental groups, that IDA should be cut off, was directly challenged by business interests that benefited from World Bank contracts and many others. Both arguments carried the day. The inspection panel was created, and IDA was funded over the objections of the few groups that opposed it. In a later episode, where members of Congress clashed with Bank member states, Nancy Pelosi together with sixty members of Congress wrote to World Bank president Wolfensohn protesting the Qinghai project in China in May and June of 1999. In the course of the exchange, the US threatened to cut IDA funding over it, and China threatened to cut off its borrowing.[84] The Chinese government later withdrew its request for the project.[85]

When the Democrats lost control of the House in 1994, Bill Clinton faced the same partisan scenario as Reagan and Bush before him, albeit in reverse. The 1995 Congress zeroed out IDA, and by the end of the tenth IDA replenishment, US arrears had grown to be so considerable that Secretary of the Treasury Robert Rubin proposed skipping a contribution and spreading the eleventh replenishment over two payments instead of three. In return, the US would be barred from bidding on approximately $500 to $600 million in procurement financed from a special fund that the US had not contributed to. US firms could, however, bid on procurement financed from reflows and IBRD transfers. Although members of Congress expressed concern over these arrangements, they did eventually provide for some appropriations to cover a percentage of the arrearages.[86] At an IDA deputies meeting, the Japanese and Canadian donors were quietly convinced to moderate their positions on the US procurement issue until Congress caught up.[87]

Therefore, even though the percentage of US contributions to IDA declined dramatically in these years, Congress became a more influential external lever because the institution had evolved beyond the closed structure of the 1950s and 1960s, and omnibus budget legislation in the debt stage offered new channels for groups to pressure the IFIs. Some of the groups involved were willing to cut off the IOs completely, and not just an individual country pursuing questionable policies, as had been the case in the 1970s with human rights initiatives. Members concerned with IDA issues, such as Frank, asserted congressional agency and used the institution as a forum simultaneously.

By the end of the debt stage, the IMF actively sought to avoid congressional involvement where possible. For example, in 1992 the board considered a reallocation of SDRs that would need congressional approval on the part of the US. Then IMF managing director Michel Camdessus remarked that this was "a prospect that no administration will be looking forward to with much enthusiasm."[88] When the issue of the tenth review of quotas came up, Tom Dawson, then the US executive director, told the IMF board that Congress was suffering from "quota fatigue" and it would be tough to convince the Treasury to go for it.[89] No increase was proposed. Likewise, in 1995 the board considered using Special Contingency Account refunds to finance the subsidy component of the Enhanced Structural Adjustment Facility, concluding that "some chairs stated this would require parliamentary or congressional approval, something we would want to avoid."[90]

## Conclusion: The Debt Stage

In the debt stage, the work of the IMF and the money-center banks was tightly interwoven. Support for funding with minimal policy provisions was high, and members used omnibus legislation to provide it without having to take a public stand on the issue. By the end of the stage, the situation had changed dramatically. The structure of lending changed from one that had been channeled through money-center banks to one channeled through a variety of financial instruments. Support for IFI funding from traditional sources began to diminish, whereas the newer groups active on IFI issues demanded policy changes in the way the World Bank operated its development projects.

In the evolution of congressional advocacy, these omnibus bills make it less clear to constituents where members stand on important issues of the day. However, those members willing to negotiate to get a measure included almost always meet with success. Therefore, omnibus legislation was initially a useful vehicle for providing financial support for the IFis in the face of considerable opposition. It became one that could be used in reverse as well, compelling change from a very specific number of legislators in key procedural positions. Not surprisingly, the World Bank was the initial subject of these types of policy changes because the broad range of project loans attracted a greater variety of interest groups and NGOs, and the World Bank needs an annual appropriation for IDA. The next chapter examines how the IMF's need for funds in a crisis would reveal even deeper cracks in the coalition of support that broke open in the Asian financial crisis of 1997.

# 6

# Widening the Circle, Narrowing the Outcome

## THE 1997 ASIAN FINANCIAL CRISIS

> I got to read the *Wall Street Journal* article, and I do notice that it takes two positions: one, we should abolish the IMF; but only after we pass this bailout.
>
> —Representative Barney Frank (D-MA)[1]

This chapter describes the next, "moral hazard stage." As with the other stages, congressional advocacy efforts resulted from a mix of changes in the international environment and in the institution of Congress, yet here the trend ran against the IFIs. During the previous debt stage, the IMF and World Bank had grown controversial, yet pivotal, to the functioning of the world financial system in resolving the debt crisis. Bankers and their lobbyists approached members individually, testified in committees, worked through trade organizations, and contributed to public advocacy organizations, like the Bretton Woods Committee and Overseas Development Council, that supported a strong US multilateral posture. The ultimate resolution to the debt crisis of the 1980s was achieved only when a significant portion of the debt of developing countries was converted into bonds and taken off the books of the major money-center banks. This transfer allowed participating countries to negotiate substantial reductions in their levels of debt and debt service. It diversified sovereign risk away from commercial bank portfolios and spread it more widely in the investment community. When the middle-income countries regained access to capital markets for finance, new financial instruments and loosened regulations expanded the availability and movement of capital around the globe.

In the stage examined here, the exogenous environment of international finance changed when many of the old money-center banks merged. The upshot was that the banking community did not need the IMF as it had in the previous stage, and the corporate community needed the World Bank less than it had since its creation. The results of these changes as they were filtered through the American political system ultimately splintered the political support for the IFIs in Congress and left apathy and criticism in its place. While the changes had been slow-growing, they became acutely apparent when the 1997 Asian financial crisis occurred.

The chief criticism from the right was that the IMF had created a problem of "moral hazard." Since they knew that the official sector would rescue them in the event of a default, the bailouts permitted the banks and private investors to extend riskier loans than they might otherwise have. Bondholder groups, hedge funds, and private equity brought in new organized interests and lobbies that represented them in Washington, DC. Whereas the financial community had common interests in resolving the series of national defaults in the previous decade, international bondholders did not even have the same interests in repayment among themselves, since each had a different investment objective and time horizon in the new one. New critics also came from the left. The environmental critics that entered the arena at the end of the Cold War continued to insist on reforms in the IFIs. Nongovernmental organizations (NGOs) active on the environment, poverty, labor, and women's rights reinforced the congressional predisposition to provide funds but insist on policy reforms, such as transparency initiatives, debt relief, and a deemphasis on loans in IDA.

Endogenous change occurred within the institution of Congress when the Republican Party gained control of the House of Representatives for the first time in more than forty years. The Republican net gain of fifty-four seats in the House of Representatives in the midterm election of 1994 reversed the partisan arrangement of the 1980s: A Democratic president now faced a Republican Congress whose leadership had achieved its success by focusing the campaign on the party and enforcing its discipline. Yet the election represented more than just a reverse of majority party. The Republican Party of the time came in with a very specific agenda, the "Contract with America," which its leadership used to combine party ideology with a specific legislative agenda in the national discourse. Having won, they argued that the Contract had received an electoral mandate. For some of the newest members, the Contract had implications for the IFIs. Congressional committee chairs became less autonomous and even more tightly connected to the (now Republican) majority party.[2] In the newer structure, the appropriations committees became particularly important vehicles to cut the federal budget and replace spending priorities. Expanding on the existing trend toward omnibus legislation, the Republican leadership used appropriations bills to change the direction of public policy despite a House rule against including substantive legislation in them.[3] Members of Congress ambivalent on IFI issues thus had greater incentives to work within the stronger "team" mentality of the new Congress.

The combination of exogenous economic change with endogenous congressional change meant that some groups on the right began to openly argue that the IMF should be abolished. Ultimately, the dramatic growth of international lending opportunities and new forums operated outside the confines of any formal government venues. A patchwork of cooperative arrangements led international relations theorists to depict a system of "global governance" wherein authority was vested in some combination of state and private agencies.[4] The IMF and World Bank that emerged in the moral hazard stage were less relevant to the banking and transnational business communities, and were the object of criticism by NGOs, divided in the degree of their support for the IFIs. With the trend toward private markets in the first decade of the twenty-first century, individuals and groups openly debated the fundamental need for these organizations, and the IMF looked to alternative sources of funds, such as gold sales, to finance its daily operations budget.

This chapter argues that the circle of interest with respect to IFI issues was widened as a direct result of the financial turmoil in middle-income countries in the 1990s, but the outcomes were limited to extremely specific policy changes because any one coalition was so fragile. Variation in achieving a successful outcome can be seen in the widening of this circle. When a wide range of groups agree on a goal, they can achieve a significant outcome, as with debt relief. Yet as the circle widens, so much more opposition must be mitigated that advocacy networks become highly vulnerable to fragmentation and deadlock, as with the proliferation of groups after the Asian financial crisis. Politics must then be pushed further "inside" to achieve any specific reform and appropriation.

## Disintermediated Capital Markets and Divided Government in Reverse

Although the Clinton administration sought to work within the multilateral framework as the Reagan and George H. W. Bush administrations had done in the debt-crisis years of the 1980s, the resources of the IMF were stretched, and the political base of support had shifted dramatically. With the Cold War over, both institutions were very unpopular with civil society groups because of the high levels of debt service required in developing countries. Big business no longer relied on the World Bank for major projects, since multinational corporations had internalized transnational production within the firm. The more liberal environment for foreign direct investment likewise worked against the Bank, since countries competed for investment and private capital markets and banks provided funding, lessening the need for Bank involvement. Banking interests splintered into bank and nonbank intermediaries and a widening number of capital market participants. The international developments met with equally substantive developments in the internal operations of the institution of Congress. The political party's hold on chairs strengthened, whereas the influence of individual members' preferences on the IFIs diminished. The first episode of congressional advocacy in the new environment over the Mexican crisis in 1995 would set the stage for the explosion over the IMF in 1997.

## THE CONTINUING EVOLUTION OF THE INTERNATIONAL BANKING INDUSTRY

On the international side of the equation, Chapter 5 left off in 1989, when the Brady Plan resulted in the restructuring of a volume of syndicated bank debt to developing countries in "Brady Bonds." Named after Secretary of the Treasury Nicholas F. Brady, the basic principles of the plan were derived from corporate workouts. Creditors would grant relief in exchange for a greater assurance of collectability. Debt relief would be linked to some assurance of economic reform. And finally, the resulting debt was tradable so that creditors could diversify their risk widely. Although each issue was unique, the plan exchanged loans for bonds that would allow the debt to be traded in financial markets where it could be priced according to its market value. This value was enhanced by the use of US Treasury securities to guarantee part of the interest and principal payments.[5] As a result, Latin American debt was not only to private sources, it was disintermediated.

In the current era, emerging market bond issues have grown four times as quickly as syndicated bank loans. The variety of debt instruments and derivatives used has also grown among the debt stock. Figure 6.1 depicts the expansion of international lending that followed the crisis years of the early 1980s. While syndicated credit facilities (indicated in the figure as signed international credit facilities) grew more than sevenfold between 1992 and 2006, this growth was dwarfed by the expansion of the issuance of

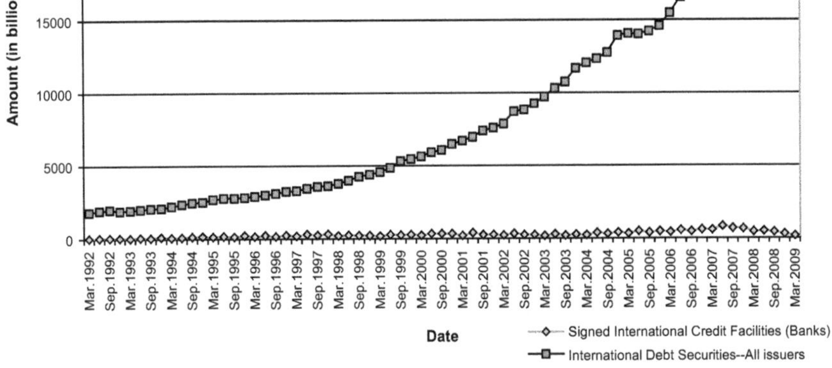


FIGURE 6.1 Expansion of International Lending 1992–2008.

*Source*: Data from BIS Quarterly Review: June 2009.

international debt securities from US$985 billion in 1987 to US$25 trillion in 2008.[6]

The rising use of disintermediated credit that had been propelled by the Brady Bonds altered the commonality of creditors' interests, even eroding the premise that all creditors seek repayment as their primary goal. The shift in political interests had political ramifications for the IMF and World Bank. That is, the large-scale crises that threatened many middle-income Latin American countries in the 1980s had involved private creditors and were handled with the active involvement of the IMF and World Bank. Reschedulings occurred in a reasonably orderly manner, despite the controversy associated with them. In the 1980s, a steering committee of approximately fifteen creditor members, responsible for holding approximately 85% of a given country's debt, could conduct a given rescheduling. Most of the major creditors to Latin American states were commercial banks, and thus the negotiators had strong incentives to cooperate. They desired to maintain good relations with the debtor state to ensure future business. As similar financial institutions, they were subject to similar regulations. If a holdout creditor chose to pursue its claims through litigation, the creditor would have to share its proceeds with the others. This obligation rendered such action rare.

As creditor institutions and debt instruments diversified, their interests did as well. Some bondholders continued to seek a rapid and orderly restructuring to preserve the value of their claims. Others preferred a disorderly process that resulted in debt that could be purchased cheaply on the secondary market. In general, bondholders have more legal leverage than banks and are less subject to the influence of official regulators.[7] Private equity or hedge funds may specialize in purchasing certain kinds of distressed debt, and bring attachment and recovery actions against a sovereign issuer. Many of these claims are settled out of court. Although fears of disruptive litigation may prove to be overly pessimistic, an aggressive creditor holds the potential to upset the entire process of debt workout. In one notable case an aggressive holdout creditor, Elliott Associates, bought US$20 million of Peru's debt on the secondary market for $11 million, which was approximately half its actual value. Elliott then persuaded courts in the US and Europe to prevent Peru from servicing its Brady debt until Elliott was paid. Rather than go into default, Peru settled, paying Elliott Associates $58 million (full payment of the debt plus capitalized interest). Individuals involved in this and other such "vulture fund" cases have pursued similar activities with the debt of Panama, Ecuador, Poland, Côte d'Ivoire, Turkmenistan, and the Democratic Republic of Congo.

These splits in creditor interests would eventually be cycled into the mix of organized interest representation in Washington on financial matters. The money-center banks continued to support the IMF either through their own offices or larger organizations, such as the American Bankers Association or Bretton Woods Committee, that had been formed in response to the 1980s crises. Yet entirely new groups also joined the debate, such as the Emerging Markets Traders Association (EMTA), which formed in 1990 in response to the opportunities created by the Mexico and Venezuela debt reschedulings under the Brady Plan, and whose membership is primarily large institutions such as Goldman Sachs and J. P. Morgan. The Managed Funds Association was established in 1991 as a voice of the global alternative investment community. Its membership includes professionals in hedge funds, funds of funds, managed futures funds, and industry service providers.

The rise of private capital markets and the fragmentation of views in the financial services industry strengthened the voices of critics of the IMF who argued that formal international organizations were no longer necessary to facilitate global finance. As in previous eras, these groups did not line up neatly along party lines. By the mid-1990s, money-center banks were thus not the chief constituency of the IMF, but one of many interests among the Treasury, some elements of the financial services community, trade-oriented business, and the growing community of NGOs.

## PROCEDURAL CHANGES IN THE REPUBLICAN-MAJORITY CONGRESS

On the domestic side of the equation, Bill Clinton assumed the presidency in January 1993. Yet the Democratic majority in Congress suffered a staggering loss of seats in the House of Representatives in the 1994 midterm election. Hence, divided government remained, yet the parties had reversed from the 1980s. The new partisan arrangement was significant because the Republican revolution had completed a transformation of the role of committee chairs that would have important ramifications for the way IMF–World Bank legislation would be tied to broader ideological concerns of the party.

First of all, rather than being leaders of somewhat autonomous units, chairs became representatives of the majority party.[8] Moreover, many were new to the legislature and had no connection to the old interest groups active on IMF and World Bank issues, let alone the new ones. Chairs were new because Representative Newt Gingrich's chairmanship of GOPAC—a political action committee to recruit and assist candidates for state and local offices—changed its emphasis from simply supplying money to supplying ideas, rationales, and motivation to candidates in the 1980s. Large Republican classes of 1992 and 1994 included many members who had received help from GOPAC.[9] Because there had been no Republican committee chairs for more than forty years and so many members were new, only five of the new chairs had served for more than two years as ranking minority members when the Republicans took control.[10] Moreover, House Republicans adopted a rule that seniority would no longer be the sole criterion for advancement to chair, and that chairs would be limited to three consecutive Congresses. In 2001, when the term limits set in, the House Republican Steering Committee cast secret ballots for the 107th

Congress committee chairs, further centralizing power in the hands of the leadership.[11] The Republican Party leadership thus became much more active on major legislation, from shaping it, structuring the procedure of floor votes, mobilizing votes, and assisting with other legislative strategies.[12]

Second of all, the role of appropriations bills changed with the Republican ascendancy, and deemphasized the authorization step. The FY 1996 spending bills marked a decided upturn in the use of appropriations to force changes in public policy. When Republican leadership pressured committee leaders to include a large number of provisions in their bills, the Rules Committee wrote special rules for those bills, waiving points of order against what would have otherwise been impermissible legislative provisions. The Senate did not enforce its rule against legislation in appropriations bills. During that period, Clinton resisted many of the provisions. Many were removed in conference. Clinton vetoed four appropriations bills in 1995, partly over provisions to prohibit federal agencies from spending monies to enforce environmental laws and additional restrictions on abortions.[13] However, these controversial social issues became linked to IMF/World Bank appropriations as part of the larger contextual change.

Difficulties in passing *all* US budget legislation meant that continuing resolutions and omnibus appropriations became the rule. Congress passed omnibus appropriations bills in every calendar year but 2001 and 2005. The most complete breakdown was in 2006, when Congress passed only two stand-alone appropriations bills, for Defense and Homeland Security. The remaining 2006 bills (for FY 2007) were combined into an omnibus and passed by the new Democratic-controlled Congress in February 2007.[14] As with other omnibus legislation, the fragile IMF and World Bank funding deals included in these bills were vulnerable to collapsing if a high degree of media attention was directed at the specifics. The next sections will show that the IMF funding responding to the exogenous shock of the 1997 crisis took almost a year to achieve. The opposition was brought around with Treasury-agreed reforms and the establishment of a congressional commission to consider the issue of reform.

## THE MEXICAN CRISIS IN 1995

The Mexican peso crisis was the first to demonstrate the new constellation of interests and arrangements on Capitol Hill. The crisis grew out of the same set of international circumstances connected to the rise of the bond market for sovereign debt. As the opportunities for international lending improved, the Mexican banks issued *tesobonos,* or bonds whose redemption value was linked to the movement of the dollar-peso exchange rate. When the peso depreciated, the redemption value increased. The government had accepted this increasing share of the exchange-rate risk of foreign borrowing during 1994 in order to calm foreign investors after the Chiapas uprising and the assassination of the leading Presidential candidate. When President Ernesto

Zedillo was inaugurated, the Mexican Congress devalued the peso, commencing a downward spiral in the movement of the peso against the dollar in December of 1994. In a first attempt to resolve the crisis, President Bill Clinton attempted to provide US government guarantees for up to ten years on repayment of the principal and interest on private-sector loans to the Mexican government, including bond issues. The plan had the bipartisan support of leadership in both houses of the new Congress: Speaker Newt Gingrich (R-GA), Richard Gephardt (D-MO), Robert Dole (R-KA), and Thomas Daschle (D-SD). Similar to the IMF process, the guarantees would be recorded in the budget but incur no outlay or need for an appropriation.[15]

While the leadership in Congress supported the rescue strategy, membership did not. The Republican gain in the midterm election meant that when Clinton introduced his first plan in January of 1995, the party controlled both the House and Senate for the first time in forty years. The rescue contradicted the spirit of the Contract with America. As large numbers of senators and representatives expressed public opposition to the Clinton plan, it could not be hidden in a larger piece of legislation, as other measures had been. Action was needed quickly, as a Mexican default was imminent. Rather than continue to seek the guarantees, Clinton announced that he would direct the secretary of the treasury to extend up to $20 billion in credits to Mexico through the Exchange Stabilization Fund (ESF). The congressional leadership joined Clinton in affirming the statutory authority of the president to act unilaterally. The executive board of the IMF also approved its contribution to the unprecedented package.

Members of Congress were surprised to learn that their approval would not be required to finance the rescue. Committees held numerous hearings on it throughout 1995. Henning details the various proposals created to change or restrict the Treasury's discretion to lend to Mexico from the ESF.[16] Representative Steve Stockman (R-TX) introduced a bill to prohibit the use of federal funds for any swap, loan, loan guarantee, or grant to Mexico without the approval of Congress. On the Democratic side, Representative Gene Taylor (D-MS) introduced a bill to instruct the comptroller general to investigate this use of the ESF for Mexico. Citing Congress's rights and prerogatives, the chair of the Senate Banking Committee, Alfonse D'Amato (R-NY), asked Secretary of the Treasury Robert Rubin to suspend support until his committee could hold hearings, at which time he proposed an amendment to an unrelated bill stipulating that ESF loans larger than $5 billion be approved by Congress. Similar legislation was introduced in the House.[17] Congress passed the Mexican Debt Disclosure Act, which Clinton signed on April 10, 1995, and which specified an array of reporting and disclosure requirements. The Mexican government repaid the US as well as the IMF's component of the package with interest.

Therefore, congressional leadership facilitated a bailout of the Mexican government over the opposition of many members. However, in this case legislation for a direct IMF appropriation was never formally entered or defeated. The IMF acted as part of a broader rescue package that included the ESF. Nonetheless, congressional discontent remained over yet another "bail-out" of a foreign government with the IMF's involvement.

## Congress, the Asian Financial Crisis, and Related Contagion

The ability of the IMF and World Bank to respond to a full-blown liquidity crisis was severely tested in the 1997 Asian financial crisis. Like the 1982 debt crisis, the 1997 crisis served as a source of international systemic pressure on congressional politics. Unlike the 1982 crisis, the Asian financial crisis occurred after the Cold War had ended definitively. In seeking resources for the IMF, traditional supporters could no longer be relied on to confront the stronger free-market and social ideologies driving the team operations in the Republican Congress.

The crisis was rooted in many causes that varied by country, among them a credit boom, weak financial sectors, and growing mismatches between liquidity and currencies. Foreign capital flows have two kinds of associated risk: the risk that the investment itself will fail, and the risk that the currency in which it is denominated will devalue relative to the currency of the foreign investor. Most of the affected countries had practiced some type of preferential credit allocation whereby governments directed investment capital toward selected businesses and industries on generous terms; as a result, firms operated with high debt-to-equity ratios, which had the effect of concentrating risk in exchange markets as well.[18] When the real estate bubbles burst, stock and property prices fell dramatically, and the government of Thailand devalued its currency in order to make its goods cheaper relative to others. Devaluation raised the cost of debt outstanding and triggered capital flight from the region. Similarly, currency rates dropped in Indonesia, Malaysia, the Philippines, and South Korea. Servicing loans became a problem in these circumstances, and banks demanded repayment of both principal and interest on loans outstanding. At the height of the crisis, key firms in the Japanese economy began to file for bankruptcy.

Thus, the IMF was embroiled in the crisis through multiple bailout packages that attempted to stabilize the economies at risk but that also stretched its resources to the point where countries began to consider new vehicles through which to address the crisis. On January 27, 1997, the executive board of the IMF approved the New Arrangements to Borrow (NAB), essentially a set of credit arrangements between the Fund and twenty-five members and institutions to provide supplementary resources to cope with a problem in the international monetary situation, or to deal with an exceptional situation that poses a threat to stability. The NAB became effective November 17 of the following year, when the US and Germany signed on to the agreement.[19]

However, the appropriation struggle that accompanied the expansion of IMF and World Bank activity as a result of the crisis uncovered fierce political wrangling where it had not appeared to exist before. This section will show that the opportunity to bargain for inclusion in omnibus legislation now worked against the IFIs' supporters. Jesse Helms (R-NC) in the Senate sought to reform the US foreign-policy-making apparatus in the entire development field—the United Nations, Department of State, US Agency for International Development, and so on. Appropriations struggles led by Representative Chris Smith (R-NJ) in the House sought to reintroduce the Reagan-era Mexico City Policy, which prohibited US funds from being spent on organizations that performed abortions in other countries. Some in the House formed their individual preferences with the House leadership succession question in mind. In addition, many Republicans who opposed the funding in both chambers simply opposed the Clinton administration. Hence, as the debate unfolded and groups chose sides, left-leaning alliances such as the Fifty Years Is Enough Network admitted that they were in an odd partnership with Dick Armey (R-ND) and Jesse Helms against their old allies Barney Frank and David Bonior (D-MI).[20]

## THE IMF QUOTA DEBATE IN CONGRESS

The debates surrounding IMF funding in the 1997 crisis would transform the dynamic of coalition formation in Congress because the wider number of participants and stronger ideological viewpoints made the funding measures difficult to conceal in larger spending packages. The executive branch was in Democratic hands with a commitment to international intervention, and the legislature in ideologically disciplined Republican hands with stronger control over committee activity. Therefore, the negotiations broke down repeatedly. Nonetheless, the IMF was eventually funded as it had been in the past.

As the Asian crisis unfolded at first, President Bill Clinton included $3.4 billion in his November 1997 Foreign Operations spending bill for the New Arrangements to Borrow, which was approved by the Senate. The administration also sought a $14.5 billion quota increase for the Fund. However, as discussed earlier, Clinton faced a different legislature than the previous administration had when it sought an increase. The 105th Congress (1997–1999) comprised 206 Democrats and 228 Republicans in the House, and 45 Democrats and 55 Republicans in the Senate.[21] With the Republican majority in the Senate, Jesse Helms became the chair of the Committee on Foreign Relations. As chair, Helms sought to restructure the foreign policy agencies of the Federal government and stalled a series of ambassadorial appointments and other measures until the executive branch addressed this issue. On the House side, Representative Christopher Smith sought to restructure authorization and appropriations bills to restore the Reagan administration's policy of withholding US contributions to agencies and NGOs that performed or promoted abortion as a method of family planning.[22] Thus, an additional split in the Republican support occurred between the House and Senate.

When Clinton's initial appropriations bill with the IMF provisions came before his committee, Helms worked with Senate Democrats and the White House to arrange a deal on funding the State Department, pay US arrears on UN dues, and reorganize the foreign affairs agencies. Smith's initiative in the House threatened Helms's work in the Senate because he refused to drop the abortion provision in the House bill, even under pressure from Senate Republicans.[23] Thus, when the initial bill went to the conference committee, Smith pledged to work to defeat it if the committee dropped his antiabortion language. House Speaker Newt Gingrich did agree to take it out of the appropriations bill, *along with* the $3.4 billion for the IMF, the $1 billion for the UN, and the reauthorization for the State Department. Hence, the House appropriations committee stripped the IMF funding from the Foreign Operations bill and, when it finally passed, Clinton's original request for the IMF died.[24]

In October, William Simon, the former secretary of the treasury in the Nixon and Ford administrations, published an editorial in the *Wall Street Journal,* which was reprinted in the *Congressional Record,* suggesting that the IMF should be abolished entirely since it had not solved a major currency crisis or promoted stability.[25] A later editorial making the same argument to the *Journal* was authored by Simon, George P. Shultz, and Walter Wriston.[26] Later joined by many from both the right and left who had never been comfortable with the bailouts in the 1980s, the debate on the IMF thus shifted to the far more serious question of whether or not it should even exist. The cacophony of voices stalled the legislative provision further.

Without the funds in the appropriation bill, the IMF nonetheless had enough resources to proceed with the Indonesian package. In December, long-standing internationalist supporters of the IFIs from the Nebraska agricultural business community mobilized and met with Senator Chuck Hagel (R-NE), a member of the Banking Committee, to discuss the situation with respect to Asian export markets and the diminished capacity of the Fund to address the crisis as it spread. Working across party lines, Hagel turned to Secretary of the Treasury Robert Rubin to express his support for the IMF funding measure. Therefore, it was again included in the 1998 emergency supplemental appropriations bill. Members of the Clinton administration approached Republicans on the Appropriations Subcommittee on Foreign Operations, such as Mitch McConnell (R-KY), and provided evidence that US workers would lose jobs connected to the Asian crisis. After Clinton's State of the Union address, Hagel openly supported the IMF funding and groups began to take sides on the issue once again. This time, support for the measure came from traditional sources, such as Boeing, the American Farm Bureau Federation, the US Chamber of Commerce, and other groupings of Fortune 500 CEOs.[27]

The secretary of defense, William Cohen, testified on behalf of the measure to the House Banking Committee and resurrected the old links between the Fund and security by emphasizing the importance of the overall investment climate in Asia.[28] A representative from Boeing China testified that 86% of the content of commercial airplanes built by the Boeing Commercial Airplane Company were from content in the United States. Were the crisis to persist, the US firm would lose orders.[29] Nonetheless, some members of the committee openly challenged these traditional security and business concerns. Others were still stung by Clinton's perceived evasion of Congress in the 1995 Mexican crisis. For example, banking committee member Spencer Bachus (R-AL) questioned the administration's use of the Exchange Stabilization Fund on the grounds that it had been used inappropriately in the Mexican bailout.[30]

Also at issue were the numerous "voice and vote" restrictions placed on US executive directors on workers' rights and other provisions that seemed to have no effect.[31] In a subsequent hearing with the US executive director of the IMF, Karin Lissakers, Bachus and Bernie Sanders (I-VT) pressed the issue of the "voice and vote" provisions by asking her to detail how she had followed the congressional mandate. In frustration, Sanders told Lissakers:

> [F]or 20 years Members of the Congress have obviously been wasting their time by passing all kinds of fine-sounding legislation . . . saying to use your voice and your vote. The only problem is you don't vote. Maybe you might have come up here and told us that and it would have saved us a lot of time so we would have developed another mechanism to kind of tell you what we thought would reflect the best interest of the United States.[32]

With the inclusion of the independent progressive Sanders, criticism of the IFIs also came from the left. Labor representatives urged the House committee to investigate IMF procedures and labor conditions in recipient countries. George Soros and Jeffrey Sachs, then a Harvard professor, opposed the IMF austerity programs. The *Wall Street Journal* opposed funding the request, and some Republicans, such as Steve Forbes, who was then a presidential candidate, opposed the IMF altogether.[33]

Scott and Carter argue that the negotiations evolved into a "four-cornered bargaining and negotiating game among members of the Senate and the administration."[34] In the first corner, Senator Pete Domenici (R-NM), Paul Sarbanes (D-MD), Joseph Biden (D-DE), and others supported the IMF funding with minimal conditions. In the second, Republican senators such as Helms, Jon Kyl (R-AZ), and Lauch Faircloth (R-NC) supported funding with strong restrictions from the right, such as adoption of market principles and conditions on borrowers. In the third corner, Patrick Leahy (D-VT) and Paul Wellstone (D-MN) similarly supported funding, but with restrictions from the left, such as on workers' rights and environmental protections. In the fourth corner, the Clinton administration supported the IMF funding without restrictions or conditions. Moreover, Smith continued to press for antiabortion provisions in the bill in the House. Not surprisingly, these groups likewise reached an impasse.

In March of 1998, with the measure still not approved, Hagel again mobilized support from government, business, and agriculture groups and openly opposed the language the appropriations committee in the Senate had reported out on the bill. He worked with the Clinton administration to release a report showing the percentage of US exports to Asia, broken down by state, and others broken down by congressional district. Others placed ads in major newspapers and organized letter-writing campaigns to Congress, with signatures supplied by top corporate executives. Nonetheless, by May it still appeared unlikely the proposal would pass. Further opposition from the Democratic representatives in the House surfaced when a group signed a letter to Secretary Rubin stating they would withdraw their support unless Rubin withdrew his from the IMF's plan for unrestricted capital movements. These members sought reforms similar to those the Senate Democrats did, insofar as they wanted the IMF to link capital movement to protection of the environment and workers' rights, although they later retreated on some of the stronger wording in the letter.

The bill had passed the House committee earlier with a 40–9 vote. At that time, Barney Frank had crafted a compromise among members to join forces with Chairman Jim Leach to provide the funding but request positive reforms, including reforms on labor, the environment, institutional openness, and Treasury cooperation with NGO and labor representatives. All of the "no" votes were Republican, together with Sanders.[35] Yet the IMF funding bill remained stalled in the House over the demand for the IMF reform and the antiabortion proposals. Two days after the Lissakers hearing on April 21, David Obey (D-WI) proposed that the House instruct its representatives to the conference committee to support the Senate's attachment of the $18 billion to a disaster-relief spending bill then being reconciled by the two houses. Newt Gingrich objected, and the measure was rejected 222–186.[36] Various compromise measures emerged in both the House and the Senate well into the fall of that year, as world markets were shaken by fears that Asia and Russia would melt down.

Eventually, in October 1998, the IMF funds and Helms's foreign-affairs reorganization plan were included in an omnibus appropriations bill that passed the House and Senate, and that Clinton signed. Thus, the full $17.9 billion IMF measure passed nearly one year later. Nonetheless, it included more reforms than the Clinton administration had wanted. Borrowing countries would no longer have access to loans at concessional rates for periods beyond two and a half years. The IMF would have to make its agreements with recipients public, and the G7 countries would have to endorse disclosure of IMF activities. The Treasury would have to certify that the IMF lending did not subsidize industries that competed with those in the US, such as semiconductors, steel, textiles, and automobiles. Finally, under pressure from Phil Gramm

(R-TX) (then chair of the Senate Banking Committee) and Dick Armey (then House majority leader), Congress and the Treasury would create their own advisory committees to review IMF operations as the crisis continued to spread to parts of Latin America.[37] Although the Treasury Department had opposed the creation of the International Financial Institution Advisory Commission (later referred to by the name of its chair, Allan Meltzer), Deputy Secretary Lawrence Summers was forced to comply under pressure from President Clinton, who sought the congressional appropriation.

## THE INTERNATIONAL FINANCIAL INSTITUTION ADVISORY COMMISSION

The congressional commission that came out of the funding debate extended and transformed the role of congressional advocacy. Not by accident, it was a microcosm of the struggle, because members of Congress who had been active on the issue appointed members of the commission who shared their views. For example, Dick Armey recommended Allan Meltzer, who became its chair when former treasury secretary William Simon could not for health reasons. On the Democratic side, Jerome Levinson was a candidate because he had written op-eds in the *Washington Post* on related topics and had helped to draft legislative amendments directing US executive directors to vote in support of workers' rights at the IMF and World Bank in 1994. Although Treasury Secretary Rubin and his deputy, Lawrence Summers, opposed Levinson as too leftist, Barney Frank (chair of the Domestic and International Monetary Policy Subcommittee) and Richard Gephardt (then House minority leader) supported his appointment. Jeffrey Sachs, who had experience with the Fund from his work on the communist transition, lobbied heavily to be included as a member of the commission from the Democratic side.[38]

Thus, substantive contradictions existed among the Democratic appointees from the start: Levinson was a critic of the IFIs on the workers' rights issue, yet held the view that they should not be stripped of their development finance function. Sachs was a critic of the IFIs, but he was not a supporter of including the issue of workers' rights in the work of the commission. With Sachs's affinity for some of the Republican criticisms, the Republicans on the commission were a more ideologically coherent unit and were better able to control its agenda and outcome. Nonetheless, viewpoints on either side were hardly monolithic. Democratic appointees found themselves in the odd position of defending the functions of the institutions, despite their serious ideological reservations. Meltzer chose not to appoint a co–vice chair from the Democratic appointees, arguing that he did not want partisan differences to cloud the outcome.

The primary objectives of the commission were to consider the roles of the institutions, how they could be improved, and what duties they should assume in the future. Its operations were quite different from those of the Gold

Commission approximately twenty years earlier. Whereas the Democrats and Republicans on the Gold Commission both sought to thwart any move to restore the gold standard in the world economy, the Meltzer Commission members shared only the belief that the IFIs needed reform. On the questions of degree and direction of that reform, they disagreed and were supported in these disagreements by congressional and Treasury sponsors. According to the congressional rules, Treasury had a representative at each meeting. The press had access as well that, incidentally, it chose not to exercise. Moreover, Treasury controlled the commission's budget. Hence, Treasury officials were able to follow the operations each day. The chair of the commission met with relevant congressional committee chairs and ranking members during the process, although Richard Gephardt declined the meetings.[39]

At the same time as the Meltzer Commission, Treasury had its own group on reform of the IFIs that sought to blunt any major issues that might emerge from the commission's report when it was finalized. Thus, modest reforms occurred as part of the process and in anticipation of the report's publication (as the work of the commission continued), so that the Treasury could indicate that it had already complied with many of the requests.[40] Then Treasury Secretary Lawrence Summers gave a speech in late December 1999 outlining his own vision for the IMF with a heavy emphasis on collecting and disseminating information for investors and markets, and on serving on the front line in the international response to financial crises. Summers also sought an institutional governing structure at the IMF that was more representative of the world economy. Along these lines, he organized the Group of Twenty (G20) finance ministers and central bank governors, wherein participants from both developed and systematically significant developing countries would gather annually in the autumn at the ministerial level to discuss key issues related to the global economy.[41]

The Meltzer Commission met for twelve days and held public hearings for three days as well. Approximately fifty leading economists and officials of international institutions testified, including Stanley Fischer, deputy managing director of the IMF, and James D. Wolfensohn, president of the World Bank. Most of the commission's findings related to the IMF. The final report criticized the expansion of IMF programs into providing long-term financial assistance and advice in all areas of economic and social development. Growth in this direction is inconsistent with the Fund's charter and has failed to produce results. The commission report also criticized the conditionality requirements on loans, and the failure of the Fund to encourage local political institutions to reform laws, regulations, and institutions so that they can act more responsibly. In addition, the report pointed out that the Fund frequently failed to enforce its own conditionality.

The result was that the commission favored lending to countries in financial crisis, but with serious reforms so that the time period between negotiation and disbursement of the release of funds could be shortened. Moreover, borrowers had to be solvent. With respect to the World Bank, the commission pointed out that 70% of its nonsubsidized loans went to eleven countries that could borrow on private capital markets. Loans to countries with access to private markets should do so, and aid to the heavily indebted countries should be in the form of grants. For both organizations, efforts should be focused on achieving real reforms for sustained development and not for making the loans themselves. In short, the Fund should adopt preconditions in its lending so that it could help countries with viable credit and leave others on their own.

All of the splits in the policy community were apparent in the final report. Four out of five commission members nominated by the Democrats filed a dissent from the majority's recommendations (Levinson, Fred Bergsten, Richard Huber, and Esteban Torres), although Huber both voted for the majority report and joined the dissent. Other studies followed, which either examined the global financial architecture or responded to the Meltzer Commission.[42] Jerome Levinson's dissenting statement questioned the connection between moral hazard and the 1997 financial crisis, as well as the commission's charge that in the 1995 Mexican bailout the administration had actually circumvented Congress in using the Exchange Stabilization Fund. From Levinson's perspective, American policy in the Clinton administration with respect to core worker rights was at odds with itself. He felt that there was no forum in which these apparent contradictions could be seriously discussed with the administration, and he pressured the commission to include the issue.

Despite the differences, the Meltzer Commission report made two unanimous recommendations. The first was to write off debt against heavily indebted poor countries (HIPC), and the second was for the IMF to limit its lending to short-term loans, leaving the long-term loans for poverty reduction to others. Instead, the IMF created the Poverty Reduction and Growth Facility (PRGF) in 1999 as its low-interest lending facility for the poorest countries. Shortly thereafter, in June of 2000, the Treasury issued its response to all parts of the Meltzer Commission report (including dissenting statements), noting its agreements and disagreements along the lines of Summer's December speech. Moreover, the Treasury report emphasized the issues of transparency and debt relief. It took issue with the Meltzer Commission's report recommendation that the IMF limit lending to a number of prequalified emerging market countries on the grounds that it would fundamentally change the nature of the organization. It questioned the recommendations for the multilateral development banks on the grounds that these measures would limit the ability of the organizations to increase development assistance. One section of the report detailed the reforms completed to date.[43]

Therefore, any evaluation of the effects of the Meltzer Commission is complicated by the nature of the bureaucratic involvement during the congressional and subsequent processes. Nonetheless, it does represent a new avenue for congressional advocacy efforts to change policies, insofar as Treasury and the IFIs may respond to preempt further legislative action. The groups that pressed for specific reforms made these positions public during the 1998 IMF funding debates in Congress. The selection of the commission's members was openly partisan and reflected conference members' preferences on specific issues, such as workers' rights. The Treasury began its response as the commission held hearings and finalized its report. Thus, when the Treasury issued its own response to the report, some reforms were already under way and the battle lines on others were clearly drawn.

Cross-cutting connections existed and operated throughout the process. For example, Allan Meltzer and Stanley Fischer (who was then first managing director of the IMF) had been friends prior to 1997. Meltzer briefed Fischer frequently on what would be proposed in the commission report. When the issue of dropping Article IV consultations for developing countries arose in the committee, a seven-to-one majority voted to end them, with Levinson as the sole dissenter.[44] However, Fischer also voiced his opposition to the proposal privately to Meltzer, and Meltzer accommodated him by dropping it from the report.[45] On the larger suggestion concerning preconditions for IMF lending, however, the IMF did not follow the proposals, which would have been a major change for the operation of the Fund. Opposition came from representatives of other countries, such as the Canadian and African directors, when members of the commission met with IMF staff. Congress did not have a lever to impose on the Fund until the next crisis, at which time it was not taken up by the Democratic president or Democratic Congress.

## New Groups and New Groupings after the Crisis

The 1997 financial crisis and resulting congressional involvement thus led to a resurgence of interest in all of the international organizations concerned with the international financial system. Their response generated new groups in civil society and new groupings of states. Among the resurgent international organizations, the United Nations had not played a role in resolving the 1982 debt crisis but renewed its interest in finance after 1997.[46] The UN debated policy proposals to reform the global financial architecture and how to best integrate global trade and investment regimes within it. The rediscovered interest culminated in the UN Monterrey Conference on Financing for Development (FfD). In preparatory meetings for the conference as early as 1998, the UN reached out to NGOs active in other issue areas and encouraged them to expand their involvement in financial topics, thereby purposefully expanding the dynamic of interest-group involvement once again. That is, many NGOs that may not have thought they had a vested interest in the FfD issue area became involved in it nonetheless.[47] The UN perceived that it needed to change its image on financial matters and build NGO confidence in the institution. These networks among NGOs that formed for the Monterrey meetings also turned their attention to Congress.

Academic forums reignited interest in this area as well. The Reinventing Bretton Woods Project aimed to rethink global solutions to systemic problems, and not national ones, by serving as a platform for academics to share ideas prior to major international meetings with national finance ministries. A tradition emerged wherein the ministerial- or deputy-ministerial-level chair of the meeting (i.e., the UK, Brazil, South African representative) would offer a seminar before they went to the meeting. The Bretton Woods Project commissions papers from academics and then invites policy makers and academics to exchange ideas. Prior to the 1999 G20 meeting in Canada, the focus was on financial regulation.

The Overseas Development Council convened another task force of development experts to discuss the role the IMF, in particular, should play in development. The report, and subsequent working group, concluded that its role should be focused on providing short-term liquidity lending to all countries hit by macroeconomic crises; advising through policy dialogue; and collecting information on countries with regard to macroeconomic policy and financial markets. While it should be the lead IFI analyzing macroeconomic issues and lending, it should cease to provide long-term development finance and its involvement in deeper structural issues in economies, even in times of crisis.[48]

The Group of Seven (G7) governments also established venues to address weaknesses in the financial architecture.[49] Among them, the finance ministers and Central Bank governors of the G7 countries sought recommendations for new structures for enhancing cooperation among national and international supervisory bodies and international financial institutions to promote financial stability in October 1998. In 1999, the ministers and governors sought a Financial Stability Forum (FSF), which was first convened April 14, 1999, in Washington. The forum seeks to bring together national authorities (such as treasuries, central banks, and supervisory agencies), sector-specific international groupings of regulators, international financial institutions charged with surveillance, and committees of central-bank experts concerned with market infrastructure and functioning.[50] Likewise, the Group of Twenty (G20) finance ministers and central-bank governors was established in 1999 to include systemically important developing countries in discussions of the global economy. It is an informal forum, with no clear voting mechanism that would resolve the contradiction among wealthier and poorer members. However, a regular dialogue with a constant set of partners was institutionalized by the regular meetings. These venues did not include NGOs in the discussion, nor did they use the UN as a vehicle for policy change.

## THE DEBT-RELIEF MOVEMENT AFTER THE IMF FUNDING DEBATE

What was the result of this new activism across forums? As mentioned earlier, one of the few areas of agreement among all parties to emerge from the Meltzer Commission was the issue of some kind of debt relief. Hence, it was the one area with the greatest possibility for a successful outcome, since there was bipartisan support in Congress, as well as initiatives within the Treasury. The issue had been one of concern for activists, because the high debt levels in some developing countries had been a problem since the 1970s. As mentioned in Chapter 4, the earliest debt-relief movement had divided over strategies to promote human rights.

Within the antiglobalization networks, a loose coalition of NGOs began to focus specifically on the issue of Third World debt in the 1980s. Their activities were informed by the notion that developing-country debt places an immoral burden on the backs of the poor.[51] In 1990, the Jubilee movement formed in Britain and spread to other countries, similarly promoting notions of biblical forgiveness that should be associated with onerous debt. Thus, individuals had been concerned with the issue but had not promoted specific legislative proposals to address it. Moreover, an uneasy tension had always existed among groups whose commitment to the cause was informed by dramatically different intellectual orientations: debt relief as a human right, debt relief as a biblical obligation, or debt relief as a necessary corrective for the bad debt on the books of the IMF and World Bank, which were not taking responsibility for the poor decisions they had made in the past.

Matters were different on the ground in developing countries. A genuine grassroots movement on debt relief had begun to develop prior to the 1997 crisis. James Wolfensohn took over the presidency of the World Bank and traveled to Uganda in 1995. He met with local NGOs in Kampala who repeatedly raised the issue of debt relief. The Oxfam representative argued that a country like Uganda could not pursue all of the orthodox economic reforms that the World Bank had urged and make headway against poverty when it was carrying the burden of old debts.[52] Thus the issue, combined with Wolfensohn's desire to work with NGOs, moved front and center on the development agenda. The result was the creation of the Heavily Indebted Poor Countries (HIPC) initiative in the Bank and the Fund in 1996, which would provide low-interest loans to bring debt levels to manageable levels in qualifying countries, subject to conditionality.

In 1997, the Jubilee 2000 coalition called for a cancellation of debt, which it portrayed as a new form of slavery. Most members of the coalition had a religious orientation and opposed the condition-based lending programs of the IMF and World Bank. As the grassroots activity associated with the Jubilee movement progressed, the G7 leaders created an Enhanced HIPC initiative that would speed the process of debt relief. In 2005 at the Gleneagles Summit meeting, the G7 eventually endorsed the concept of full cancellation, subject to a degree of conditionality. The Bush administration's actions on debt relief can be explained by aspects of the US military intervention in Iraq, and the economic and conservative religious ideology of its members.[53] Yet specific legislative proposals for debt relief must also be placed in the context of the Meltzer Commission process and the ability of activists to work across party lines on reform proposals most could agree upon. Moreover, as of late 2010, the total amounts to fund the Gleneagles initiative have not been appropriated.

In 1999, the Clinton administration requested $120 million for several initiatives, including the Bilateral Paris Club Initiative, contributions to the HIPC, and funds to support the debt for rain forest legislation. In the early round, Sonny Callahan (R-AL) chaired the Appropriations Subcommittee on Foreign Operations and opposed debt relief. Nancy Pelosi (D-CA) served as ranking member on the subcommittee and was more supportive of debt relief, but backed the liberal set of reforms.[54] Nonetheless, following the Cologne G7 summit in June of 1999, advocates made direct appeals to congressional committee chairs on both the liberal Democratic and conservative Republican sides on the grounds of causal beliefs, religious morality, and political pressure.[55] Networks among key policy makers allowed the advocates to work across party lines. For example, Bono met Arnold Schwarzenegger through the Democratic Shriver family; Schwarzenegger advised him to work with the Republican Kasich.[56]

The problem of debt relief is a problem of how to pay for it. If the IFIs cover the bad debts themselves, their resources for further operations will be severely diminished. Yet if governments do so, they must find the funds within their own budgets to save the unpopular institutions, which, needless to say, is not an easy task in the US Congress. The initial British proposal was for a gold sale by the IMF so that the institution itself would absorb the cost. The US sought a draw on the IMF's earnings from the 1998 reevaluation of its gold reserves and from its Poverty Reduction Growth Facility. During the debate on financing the Enhanced HIPC initiative in 1999–2000, the Meltzer Commission had opposed gold sales along with many economic conservatives in Congress. They argued that gold sales would depress world prices and was legally questionable because the gold was technically owned by IMF member countries and their taxpayers. Gold sales are also generally opposed by gold-mining companies and representatives from Western gold-producing states. They were also opposed by other G7 countries, such as Germany, France, and Canada.[57]

The Joint Economic Committee of the US Congress issued a report on the issue in August 1999, arguing against the sale on the grounds that it would help perpetrate and reinforce the IMF's drift toward becoming another development bank such as the World Bank. Moreover, a sale would weaken the IMF's balance sheet at a vulnerable time and reinforce the existing moral hazard problem by leading to expectations that future gold sales would occur for the same purpose.[58] Ultimately, the proposal died under congressional opposition.

Congress did authorize the revaluation of the portion of the reserves to cover the program, and in 1999, the executive board authorized some off-market transactions in gold.[59]

Thus, debt relief began to move on the agenda because more specific proposals emerged at the conclusion of the Meltzer Commission. Moreover, the coalition associated with it expanded and included broader segments of the right and the left. Events intervened that brought the presidential administration closer to congressional sentiment, chiefly the US war in Iraq. The economic reconstruction of Iraq required a dramatic reduction in its external debt. Members of the Republican-controlled Congress would not approve aid to Iraq that would be used to pay off other Middle Eastern countries, or countries that had refused to support the war.[60] The French and Germans drew parallels between Iraq's debt and the HIPC debt, and thus the two issues became intertwined. When the US announced its support for HIPC debt relief, it immediately undercut the French and German arguments against Iraqi debt relief.[61]

The new groups that joined the anti-debt coalition, and to a degree replaced some of the dwindling Republican internationalist business support for the IFIs, came from the Christian right. The conservative movement had been influenced by the Jubilee campaign's lobbying efforts drawing on notions of biblical forgiveness. Spencer Bachus, himself a Baptist, worked with Maxine Waters (D-CA) and Barney Frank, liberal internationalists, on the Jubilee Act of 1999, which called for debt cancellation. The conservative movement was also influenced by the argument presented in the Meltzer Commission report from more traditional Republican sources arguing that the IFIs simply lent funds to cover interest payments to themselves. This benefited the IFIs but raised the level of developing-country debt. In March 2000, twenty-six Republicans voted against the Republican House leadership to back debt relief and the motion passed. By fall of that year, prominent celebrities joined the campaign, Bush endorsed the concept, and on October 25, 2000, Congress passed Clinton's previous request for the HIPC relief plan.[62]

As the debt and war issues converged, Jubilee supported Bachus's and Jim Leach's proposed bill to eliminate Iraqi debt. Supporters made open appeals to President George W. Bush's religious convictions. At the grassroots level, the Jubilee network, joined by the US Catholic Bishops, mobilized letter-writing and phone-call campaigns to the White House, Treasury, and members of Congress.[63] In 2005, the G7 agreed to cancel the debt to the IMF, IDA, African Development Bank, and Inter-American Development Bank through the creation of the Multilateral Debt Relief Initiative (MDRI) in the IMF. The MDRI would be financed through the Fund's Poverty Reduction Growth Facility Trust Subsidy Account, the HIPC Umbrella Account, and the Special Disbursement Account, which is used for receiving profits of the aforementioned 1999 off-market gold sales. In 2007, the IDA deputies began to negotiate the fifteenth replenishment round, which will be the first to cover the resources that have been drawn down from the MDRI. After the 2005 G7 agreement was announced, Jubilee USA continued to press for more debt cancellation to a wider set of countries and without conditionality.

Thus, the debt-relief movement represents one instance of a wide, bipartisan coalition that achieved success on an issue. However, the outcome must be evaluated within the context of the overall aid program. Payment for the MDRI drew upon IDA. As of the end of FY 2006, IDA held $102.9 billion in total assets, down $32.1 billion from FY 2005, when monies were used to write off debt under the MDRI. Replacement monies for these funds must come in the current, fifteenth, round. Thus, they must come from a new presidential administration and a new Congress. In the absence of replenishment funds, debt relief will have been achieved at the cost of the future IDA resources for grant- and loan-making.[64]

## IDA FUNDING AND THE MELTZER COMMISSION REPORT

Another result of the renewed activism across forums after the 1997 crisis was the shift in IDA loans to grants. The proposal to transform IDA in this way came from the Meltzer Commission report. The idea that IDA should provide grant aid to developing countries, and not loans, overturned decades-long development thinking that countries should repay these amounts.[65] Through its IDA deputy, the Clinton administration had inserted a grants provision into the thirteenth replenishment IDA negotiations before Clinton left office.

As soon as President George W. Bush nominated John Taylor for the position of undersecretary for international affairs at Treasury, many of the same prominent academics in the field of development economics who had made the suggestion that it be included in the report contacted him.[66] When President Bush's administration sought an issue in preparation for the 2001 G8 meeting that would not be overly expensive, his advisors formally proposed that IDA make 50% grants, in place of loans, to the poorest countries. Since IDA monies would not be replaced by repayment funds, such a change would be more generous in the present period yet more expensive later when the IDA credits would have otherwise been repaid. Taylor considered IDA reform to be a moral commitment. He created a package of reforms for the organization that also included a results-measurement system and an increase in funding from the US. In his memoir of the period, Taylor recalled that the Bush administration discussed the grants proposal prior to the G8 summit with many of the same religious, environmental, and nongovernmental organizations that had been active on the issue before, such as Friends of the Earth and the US Conference of Catholic Bishops.[67]

Thus, discussions of the proposal were conducted at many international meetings of groups concerned with the issue. Allan Meltzer continued his personal involvement in the issue, traveling to European countries to discuss it with officials. He encountered differences in the positions of national treasuries (that supported the move to grants) and development agencies (that opposed it). The Europeans opposed the move to grants on the grounds that it would contribute to a culture of dependency and hinder countries' ability to develop creditworthiness. They also viewed the US as stingy and overly slow to pay its IDA commitments. Unless the US government was committed to dramatically increasing its contributions, it would ultimately bankrupt the World Bank as well as reduce its policy leverage.[68] At the House hearing requesting reauthorization, Reverend David Beckmann, a former World Bank economist and president of Bread for the World, argued that the European reluctance to move to grants had been "nutty."[69] In another example from the same hearing, Raymond Offenheiser of Oxfam America referenced discussions of the multilateral institutions at the World Social Forum.[70]

Ultimately, the thirteenth replenishment contained provisions for as much as 21% grants to be made through IDA, as opposed to loans. As a part of an additional reform proposal, the US conditioned $100 million during the second year of the thirteenth IDA replenishment, and $200 million during the third year, on satisfactory progress toward select, high-development impact objectives. Once again, a wide number of groups had become involved in a proposal, yet far from turning the IDA into a grants-making organization, it funded approximately one-fifth of its activities with grants. In this case, the dampening effect on the grants provision came not from groups fighting it, but from other countries whose total IDA replenishment contributions had grown to encompass a greater percentage of the whole, giving them additional leverage.

## A Diminished Role for the IMF, an Increased Role for Congress

By the end of the twentieth century, the IMF was clearly engaged in development issues. Whereas the Meltzer Commission report recommended separating the roles of the IMF and World Bank with respect to development, any distinction grew even more muddied after its release. Further issues, such as debt relief and gold sales, affected both organizations. The 1997 crisis had exposed the vulnerability of Western financial markets to crises in middle-income countries. The issue of moral hazard also came to the fore, as repeated bank bailouts were challenged by a more aggressive, market-based ideology. The Meltzer Commission had heightened awareness of several "inconvenient" features of the international lending system, such as the Fund's lending to cover interest payments on its own debt and the inadequacy of the international system to work out unsustainable debt levels in an orderly manner.

As a result of the contagion connected to the crisis, officials in a variety of formal public organizations commenced discussions concerning the inadequate nature of the international financial architecture. New groupings of states and

IOs, both formal and informal, emerged to consider the future. In response, the IMF adopted a strategy of "duck and cover" from Congress. This strategy meant the IMF avoided taking any action that required legislation for fear a fight would break out on the Hill. Nonetheless, groups continued to take their concerns with the IMF to individual members of Congress.

When a subsequent crisis ensued in Argentina and the IMF was involved in resolving it, the Treasury did not seek funds from Congress. Argentina had built up a large debt burden that the government could not service by the end of 2001. The result was one of the largest defaults by a debtor nation in history. The month after the collapse, there were five successive presidents. When President Nestor Kirchner came to office in May 2003, Argentina had defaulted on foreign debt obligations of approximately $140 billion. The debt was to private creditors, mostly holding sovereign bonds in excess of $80 billion.

In the immediate stage after the crisis, the government gave no indication of when, or how much, of the defaulted debt it intended to repay. The politicians stressed that the repayment of foreign debt was not a priority. The Bush administration did not challenge this approach. In September of 2003, the US supported a second IMF assistance program, which was primarily to be used to repay the IFIs. Thus, while the terms were popular with Kirchner, they were controversial with private creditors. After the IMF deal was announced, Kirchner offered the private bondholders not more than 25% of the nominal value of the principal of its debts. Creditors described these terms as morally unacceptable, and they sought terms more in line with what they had accepted after the Russian and Ecuadorian defaults of 1998 and 1999. They were also outraged that the offer did not include accumulated interest that had not been paid since the default. Nonetheless, the US did not raise objections.[71] The next year, the Argentine government suspended its IMF program until it could reach an agreement with the bondholders. Although the bondholders objected to the suspension of the program, the US did not intervene.[72]

Helleiner argues that the Bush administration's approach to the Argentine crisis can be explained by the need for the administration to cultivate Argentina's political support in the region, its neoliberal ideology that sought yet again to address the problem of moral hazard in international lending, and Republican members of Congress who had opposed the Clinton request for the IMF.[73] Prominent members of the administration agreed that international investors should be made to pay for their own mistakes. Republicans in Congress drew upon the Meltzer Commission report and continued to seek his advice in testimony. Meltzer had advised that Argentina should be encouraged to default. Default and the subsequent losses would deter other speculative capital flows in international markets. In addition, the Bush administration and IMF realized that any subsequent new increases in funding for the IMF were unlikely. This fact gave politicians in Argentina additional leverage during the negotiations with their bondholders, because the size of the IMF's outstanding liabilities to the country forced it to remain in any negotiations.[74]

## Conclusion: The Moral Hazard Stage

The change in majority party in Congress, combined with its years in the minority and the ideological leanings of some new members, moved the issue of "moral hazard" to the center of the IFI debate. With an understanding that the IMF, in particular, contributed to global instability and did not help to resolve it, members that might not have participated in these issues worked to block funding. Social concerns both helped and hurt the IFIs, as they were connected to the Christian right in the party: Abortion concerns contributed to the 1997 delay, whereas onerous debt concerns helped solidify a coalition in support of debt relief after that. Therefore, although the parties changed branches, many of the legislative strategies with respect to the IFIs remained essentially intact. Supporters aimed to include funding measures in large omnibus bills where attention was deflected away from the amounts and onto the nucleus of the package. Detractors tried to focus attention on these issues to get them out of the packages.

The trend revealed in this chapter is that a major challenge to the IFIs over time has been the disintegration of the banking industry into a variety of bank and nonbank institutions, whose interests in multilateral coordination via the IMF range from substantive to nonexistent. As a result of this industrial change, many promoters fell off, particularly large firms and the shadow financial services industry that did not need the IMF or World Bank to support their activities.[75] By 2007, it appeared that the core base of constituents for the IFIs had gone and only the critics remained. The IMF did not approach the George W. Bush administration with a quota increase. The administration never submitted to Congress the "Fourth Amendment" to the IMF's Articles of Agreement approved by the board in 1997.[76] However, his administration did write reforms for IDA into the language of appropriations bills that carried over into the next divided government—in 2007, when the Democrats regained control of the House.

# 7

# Reviving a Role for the Bretton Woods Institutions

## THE FINANCIAL CRISIS OF 2008

> A stronger and more responsive IMF is essential to the restoration of confidence in the global economy and financial system and thus to our own economic recovery. We urge Congress to move expeditiously on the President's request.[1]
>
> —Letter to Speaker Nancy Pelosi and Majority Leader Harry Reid from James A. Baker III, Nicholas F. Brady, Harold Brown, Frank C. Carlucci, Lee H. Hamilton, Henry Kissinger, W. Anthony Lake, Robert McFarlane, Paul H. O'Neil, Henry Paulson, Colin L. Powell, Condoleezza Rice, Robert Rubin, Brent Scowcroft, Paul A. Volcker

In the "revived stage" of the Congress-IFI relationship explored in this chapter, the international financial community suddenly needed a way to restore some elements of the international payments system that had broken down unexpectedly after the collapse of Lehman Brothers in the US. Next, it needed to prevent the collapse of some weaker European states without appealing directly to taxpayers in wealthier, industrial, European countries. Therefore, just as the US banking community used the IMF as a buffer in imposing conditionality during earlier crises in emerging markets, the Europeans needed the IMF to achieve a multilateral solution among themselves.

This chapter details the revival of the IFIs as a result of the exogenous shock of the 2008 financial crisis. Their revival in the wake of the 2008 crisis cannot be discounted. Prior to the crisis, their strategy had been to "duck and cover" from Congress. Countries built up their reserves to avoid having to seek assistance from the IMF. The traditional base of support for the IMF in the banking sector existed on government life support for a time, and could not be called on to marshal public sentiment in the Washington policy community. In the new era, the IMF has resumed a role in Europe, but as part of larger international rescue packages. With the resurgence of the state in international financial matters, the use of the IMF has allowed other IOs like the European

Union to craft their own rescue packages and deflect a degree of political fire from nation-states whose taxpayers will ultimately bear the cost of state-sponsored bailouts. Avoidance of the IMF is thus no longer an option for many countries in crisis. However, the stigma attached to an IMF package following the emerging-market crises of the 1980s and 1990s remains.

The picture of domestic American politics changed with the election of Barack Obama in the midst of the crisis in November 2008. For the first two years of the Obama administration, the partisan arrangement between the presidential administration and Congress was unified. A Democratic president and Democratic Congress strongly endorsed increased funding for the IMF and World Bank out of a wholehearted policy concern with achieving a multilateral solution to the spreading international crisis.

The result was that Congress funded both an additional replenishment round for the International Development Association (IDA) in the World Bank and authorized an increase in the New Arrangements to Borrow (NAB) in the IMF. Within Congress, divisions remained in both political parties over the work and necessity of the Bretton Woods institutions in the current era of transnational capital flows. Passage was facilitated, but far from guaranteed, by the Democratic leadership in the House, which did not want to see the new president unable to fulfill his initial foreign policy commitments during the financial crisis. Despite the relatively strong alignment of party and financial policy goals, the funds came with strong congressional advocacy to change some IFI policies on behalf of initiatives prompted by organized labor and sympathetic Democratic members. As with previous episodes, almost all of the negotiations surrounding the IMF funding were conducted out of public view. In fact, the issue of the funding was perceived to be so controversial in Congress that they were purposefully not included in any public hearings to avoid an unpredictable response in the media. The needs for a future general capital increase for the IMF, and/or future funding for the World Bank, are complicated by the unfolding crisis in the European Union that has reoriented the institution of the IMF toward more advanced, industrial democracies than it had been previously.

This chapter shows that the trend line toward irrelevance has been arrested in the revived stage, but the question, For how long? remains open. In the 2010 midterm election, the Democratic Party lost its majority in the House of Representatives and thus ended the period of unified government. As with previous alignments of interests in this area, the question of divided government must be placed in the broader context of the international political economy. The IMF and World Bank have received bipartisan support during these periods, but they have had a unified political constituency in the banking industry, support from multinational corporations, and an external rivalry with the Soviet Union. The resolution of the current crisis and the role that the Bretton Woods institutions will play in the world economy as it recovers will depend on the shape of the international lending arrangements to come and how they connect with the work of the IFIs. The need to generate bipartisan support in the 112th Congress has never been greater, since the IMF and World Bank plan to make additional requests to augment their resources. If the trend toward irrelevance is to be halted definitively, the IFIs will need constituencies in American politics willing to work on their behalf.

## The 2008 Crisis and the International Financial Institutions

The 2008 crisis marks another pivotal event for the IMF and World Bank. In the years prior, a series of congressional oversight hearings had focused on the problem of corruption related to the development banks. In response to whistle-blower reports, Senator Richard Lugar (R-IN), who was then chair of the Senate Foreign Relations Committee, directed the committee staff to begin a comprehensive study of the IFIs.[2] Between 2005 and 2009, the staff observed the projects of the multilateral development banks and met with officials in a range of countries. They concluded that the banks present an opportunity for the US to maintain its influence, address national security issues, and provide global leadership, despite the decline in size of the American economy relative to the rest of the world.[3] Yet the need for substantive reform remains.

The IMF became increasingly irrelevant as the Financial Stability Forum, Monterrey Conference and follow-ups, the Group of 20, and other forums created after the Asian crisis broadened the number of venues where states could air concerns. New outlets meant that officials and groups "forum-shop" for favorable participants and terms if they were not satisfied with the direction in one venue.[4] Recipient countries began to hold higher levels of reserves to avoid having to go to the IMF in the future. Traditional think tanks that had contributed to the debate on economic development, such as the Overseas Development Council, disbanded when its foundation support dried up. The situation came to a head at the 2006 Singapore meeting of the IMF and World Bank boards of governors. The IOs began to explore governance-reform options in the face of protests openly. By 2007, the IMF's resources had dropped so low that it needed funds to cover its administrative operations that it had previously covered out of its lending activities. Immediately prior to the financial crisis of 2008, the IMF reduced its staff for the first time in its history to make up an annual deficit of $400 million.[5]

Realizing that the IMF faced an uncertain future, departing director Rodrigo de Rato concluded a reform effort. On March 28, 2008, the executive board approved an agreement on a package of reforms, some of which required US congressional authorization. By that time, de Rato had been replaced as director of the Fund by Dominique Strauss-Kahn. Although the agreement was modest in scope and did not include any proposals for change in the composition or size of the executive board, NGOs objected immediately. As part of the proposals, the IMF needed a one-time authorization from Congress to sell a percentage of its gold reserves to establish an endowment that would provide monies for its future operations.

The use of congressional advocacy via the budget mechanism remained as influential as ever. In June of 2008, civil society groups based in the US wrote to the US Congress regarding the potential gold sale, pointing out that were it to succeed, it would impair future congressional leverage over Fund activities. The groups urged Congress to condition its authorization on the IMF's acceptance of reforms to its policy mandates and prescriptions for developing countries.[6] The IMF was openly searching for a mission, and it considered taking on issues such as codes of conduct for sovereign wealth funds. At the close of 2008, the Fund sent draft legislation via the Treasury to Congress at a time when the legislature was mired in the 2008 financial crisis and US auto company bailouts. Thus, there was little chance it would pass before the close of the 110th Congress.

Nonetheless, the severity of the crisis, combined with the speed with which it threatened some national economies, brought the IMF firmly back into the center of the global economic response with new programs and dramatically increased resources to lend. The outcome for the World Bank has been less clear.

## SEPTEMBER TO OCTOBER 2008

The 2008 financial crisis unfolded through a sequence of events beginning with the collapse of the American subprime-mortgage market in August 2007.[7] German asset-management firms were among the first to close to protect investors. While the American and German problems could be handled within the context of their domestic financial systems, it was apparent that any systemic problems would pose a more serious challenge to banks located in small economies yet overexposed in foreign markets, because any disruption would threaten their solvency and overwhelm the ability of their country's central bank to serve as a lender of last resort.

Such was the case with Iceland, a country whose three largest banks relied on short-term financing for 75% of their funds. Money markets and the short-term interbank market had provided these funds in the period when the Icelandic banking sector deregulated and expanded. Yet by March 2008, investors were increasingly reluctant to lend to the Icelandic banks, given their dependence on short-term funds.[8] After the collapse of the American investment bank Lehman Brothers in September, short-term markets reassessed the risk once again. A good deal of lending in short-term markets and interbank lending across Europe terminated suddenly. The freeze-up meant that Iceland's three largest banks could not find adequate funds in the interbank market at the same time that the cost of their deposit insurance rose dramatically, and the krona depreciated. As a result, the Financial Supervisory Authority of Iceland took control of these banks between October 7 and 9, 2008, to try to stop further depreciation of the krona. Nonetheless, the problems spread immediately to Great Britain, where hundreds of thousands of citizens had online accounts with Icelandic banks. The government of British prime minister Gordon Brown froze the British assets of one of the banks until the situation could be resolved.[9]

As the magnitude of the crisis mounted, it became apparent that the IMF was in no position to lend to the US or other affected Western economies, with the possible exception of Iceland. At the time, the IMF's total resources were $352 billion, of which $257 billion was usable. The most the IMF had ever lent in one year was $30 billion.[10] In comparison, the US Troubled Asset Relief Program of approximately $700 billion was itself only one component of the overall measures needed to stop the run on institutions in the US. At the IMF's October 2008 annual meeting, Strauss-Kahn announced that the IMF had activated its Emergency Financing Mechanism (EFM) to speed up the approval process for loans.

There were alternatives to a multilateral strategy, chiefly bilateral or regional ones. When Iceland initially failed to secure loans from its NATO allies, the government approached the Russian government.[11] On November 19, 2008, Iceland and the IMF finalized an agreement on an economic stabilization program supported by a $2.1 billion two-year standby arrangement from the Fund. The reasons for the delay in finalizing an agreement are debated. Nonetheless, as Icelandic banks began to default, other countries feared that the Icelandic banks would shift funds back to Iceland. British, Dutch, and German officials were particularly concerned with the disposition of accounts. After the IMF's decision was announced, Denmark, Finland, Norway, and Sweden agreed to lend an additional $2.5 billion to Iceland.[12] The immediate European crisis was averted, but future problems loomed.

## THE IMF RESPONDS

Therefore, in the cascade of events surrounding the global crisis, the debate over the relevance of the IMF ended immediately. It was nonetheless left to the Fund to explain how it had changed and why it merited a central role. To address concerns with the Fund's controversial conditionality requirements, its new managing director, Dominique Strauss-Kahn, met with the IMF's staff and instructed them that they should only include conditionality requirements that were directly related to the crisis in loan packages associated with it.[13] Strauss-Kahn also met with the House Financial Services Committee chair, Barney Frank, who laid out the agenda he sought in exchange for his and the committee's support: lowering of conditionality requirements, ending use of the World Bank's controversial *Doing Business* report, and concessional assistance for low-income countries. Strauss-Kahn felt that he could work within this framework, and Frank likewise thought they shared common ground.[14]

Thus, the IMF once again reshaped its image as a crisis fighter. In the first phase of the crisis following the Icelandic collapse, the banks in trouble were those in Europe who had lent to others in Eastern Europe. Yet a series of sovereign debt crises next threatened the Eurozone. The IMF was poised to intervene because it appeared to be a somewhat neutral outsider with a European chief. In return for increased contributions and pledges from its members, the Fund agreed to set aside its more onerous lending conditionality and develop arrangements that were more suitable to all parties affected.

One of the first plans was the creation of a new three-month short-term lending facility aimed at middle-income countries such as Mexico, South Korea, and Brazil. The Short-Term Liquidity Facility (STLF) would have no policy conditionality. The IMF was eager to change its image, but the borrowing countries were not as quick to believe that it had. No countries made drawings on the STLF, most likely due to a perceived stigma attached to accepting assistance from the IMF.[15] Moreover, the need for additional resources continued to be apparent. At the end of 2008, British prime minister Gordon Brown and French president Nicolas Sarkozy called for a "new Bretton Woods" conference, a "Bretton Woods II."[16]

The historical analogies used in these discussions were largely rhetorical. The world economy had changed dramatically from the World War II environment that existed when Keynes and White circulated their initial plans. Perhaps most important, a multilateral framework exists in the present era and is perceived to have failed to prevent the crisis from spreading, unlike the interwar era, where there was no stabilization fund. As discussed earlier, the Bush administration submitted a package of IMF reform proposals, including gold sales to the Congress in late 2008. Yet the proposed legislation was stalled in the transition to the administration of President Barack Obama and in the numerous bailouts of the US auto and financial services industry that overwhelmed the congressional agenda.

In response to the crisis at the World Bank, President Robert Zoellick proposed a "facebook for economic multilateralism" that would comprise a flexible network maximizing the strengths of interconnecting and overlapping actors and institutions, public and private.[17] Zoellick's vision of multilateralism is dramatically different from what Gordon Brown and Nicolas Sarkozy proposed. The former is far more formal, negotiated among governments, with clearly defined rules of behavior. The latter leaves a high degree of ambiguity concerning the obligations of states and private actors. These distinctions are not academic. With China managing its exchange-rate system and the permissive regulatory environment in the US prior to the crisis, analysts argue that some countries need more government intervention in their financial markets and some need less, seriously complicating the calls for reform.

In 2009, IMF first managing director John Lipsky proposed doubling the lending resources of the Fund to around $500 billion. This action would include the gold sales, additional capital from members, and bond sales. The IMF had been reluctant to issue bonds in the past, most likely because the US and Europe argued it would lessen their hold on its policy direction were it to become less dependent on members for financial resources.[18] The proposals would need to gain the political support of the new presidential administration, whose Treasury Department would have to shepherd them through Congress.

## The IMF and World Bank Legislative Sequences: Economic Multilateralism and the Financial Crisis of 2008 in Congress

Once President Barack Obama took office, discussions began as to whether the reform package submitted by the Bush administration should be adjusted or be scrapped altogether. The G20 placed IMF reform on its negotiating agenda as part of the "New Bretton Woods." At the London G20 summit meeting in April of 2009, Obama followed through by proposing an additional $1 trillion to be funneled through the IMF and World Bank. Groups began to take sides. The funding was secured by a new presidential administration that proved willing to expend a great deal of political capital to deliver on its promise at the G20, and the cooperation of key members of Congress who worked with the administration out of policy concerns related to the ongoing crisis. Nonetheless, the manner in which it was obtained left some with the impression that the administration had introduced an unnecessary element of partisanship into the process, complicating the issue ahead.

### FUNDING FOR THE WORLD BANK

The first item on the Obama administration's agenda for the World Bank was the fifteenth IDA replenishment, which needed both a three-year authorization and its annual appropriation. As with other policy issues, members of Congress sought to use the procedural lever of legislation to influence policy in the World Bank. The IDA replenishment had carried over from the Bush administration and received almost no attention in the media.

The requisite authorization to participate in the replenishment had become mired in the issue of labor rights and the use of the IFC's *Doing Business* report to allocate aid as a component of the World Bank's Country Policy and Institutional Assessment (CPIA) indicator.[19] *Doing Business,* an influential annual report in the business community, attempts to produce a quantitative measure of regulations for starting a business, dealing with construction permits, employing workers, registering property, getting credit, protecting investors, paying taxes, trading across borders, enforcing contracts, and closing a business as they apply to domestic small and medium-size enterprises. The "employing workers" measure specifically examines the difficulty of hiring, nonstandard work schedules and paid annual leave, and the costs and rules governing redundancy termination.

The AFL-CIO, the International Trade Union Confederation (ITUC), and the Carnegie Endowment for International Peace have opposed the use of this indicator since its adoption in 2003 because it promotes certain practices in the treatment of workers that contradict the World Bank's greater goal of improving the distribution of wealth in developing countries in order to fight poverty.[20] Critics of the "employing workers" standard point to specific examples, such as the Marshall Islands and Palau. These two are top ranked, yet they lack labor codes and are not members of the International Labor Organization. Hence, they do not adhere to the core labor standards framework of that organization.[21]

While the IDA replenishment was being negotiated, members of the Financial Services Committee criticized the use of this report and threatened to withhold payments if it was not changed. In addition, committee chairman Barney Frank spoke directly with IMF managing director Dominique Strauss-Kahn and World Bank president Robert Zoellick about his concerns, given the report's increasingly global mandate and scope.[22] He assigned senior committee aide Daniel McGlinchey to follow the issue persistently.[23] Individuals within the Bank shared some of the concerns the critics expressed. For example, the Independent Evaluation Group report on the *Doing Business* report argued that regulations generate social benefits as well as private costs. What is good for an individual firm might not benefit the economy or society as a whole. The right level and type of regulation is a matter of choice in each country.[24]

The IDA authorization passed the House and Senate in the 110th Congress, but the different provisions in each version were not reconciled. Thus, it did not become law. In the 111th Congress, the authorization could have been included in the omnibus spending bill but was not, because the workers' rights issue had not been resolved with the relevant committee chair in the House. The annual appropriation passed first; however, the Treasury could not release the funds without the requisite authorization.

To move the issue forward, Frank proposed a one-year authorization after which time the issue could be revisited, as had been done with the inspection panel in the 1990s. When the deadline to include the authorization in the supplemental appropriations bill approached, Frank's staff negotiated with the Bank's staff over the issue. During the course of the negotiations, however, those opposing the promotion of specific policy goals through the congressional process also attempted to use procedure to fight the policy change. They argued that an individual member could not forward a one-year authorization of IDA. In agreement with these individuals, the Treasury Department argued that Congress must pass a full three-year authorization of the appropriation in order for Treasury to send a qualified letter of commitment to the Bank.

Those involved sought a legal opinion on the matter.[25] The Congressional Research Service determined that neither the Treasury nor the World Bank could determine the US contribution process. The IDA Act (PL-86–565) specifies what steps must be taken before the US may be committed to an IDA replenishment agreement. The IDA-15 agreement also states that "necessary appropriation legislation" may be enacted after a country submits its qualified instrument of commitment, and no country but the US has a two-step authorization/approval process for appropriations. The ultimate arbiter of the ability of Congress to authorize the replenishment for one, two, or three years is not an international agreement but Article I of the Constitution, which gives Congress the power to approve appropriations and set its own rules. It designates its own system to release funds from the US Treasury under these rules. No international organization and no department of the executive branch has the right or capacity to change that system.[26]

Therefore, Congress's use of procedure was affirmed legally, but this affirmation did not end the political struggle. While protesting that the Bank should not be accountable to only one member of Congress, its management eventually did agree that it would cease to use the *Doing Business* "employing workers" indicator in the CPIA, and that they would publicize this decision. At the end of April 2009, a statement to this effect appeared on the *Doing Business* website.[27] To ensure that both the Bank and Treasury would comply with the arrangements, H. R. 2346 includes language in the bill detailing the future policy.[28] The Bank employee responsible for the indicator resigned his position, citing family considerations.

In this example of congressional advocacy, Congress continued to provide funds for the Bank and use procedure to press for policy changes simultaneously. The issue initially came to the committee's attention from the work of groups investigating the labor rights issue. These individuals and groups had long-standing connections with the office on a variety of issues, and the committee staff was known to have the ability to deal with the knotty issues surrounding IDA appropriations and authorizations from their experience with the inspection panel.

### FUNDING FOR THE INTERNATIONAL MONETARY FUND

The IMF sequence was conducted over a shorter period of time than the IDA authorization and no public hearings were held. Nonetheless, it was equally thorny, and procedural issues mattered as much, or more. As stated earlier, newly inaugurated President Barack Obama agreed to participate in pledges for $500 billion in new funding for the IMF at the G20 summit in London. This money was to be targeted for helping developing countries hard hit by the economic crisis. The administration included the $108 billion appropriation for the US contribution into the supplemental budget request for funding the war submitted in April of 2009, perhaps to avoid the debate over the IMF's policies.

Some elements of the proposal required congressional action and others did not.[29] Nearly ten years after its approval by the IMF's board, the administration also sought approval for the "Fourth Amendment" to the IMF's Articles of Agreement. The Fourth Amendment would balance allocations of SDRs by giving some states more SDRs than their quota share would dictate. These countries did not have allocations proportionate to their quotas, because no SDRs had been issued after 1981, when they joined. This action required congressional approval, but it was not submitted after it was approved in 1997 because it had become embroiled in the abortion debates and dropped from active consideration.

Supporters mobilized to obtain the funding. Prior to the crisis, the IMF staff had devoted some resources to its public relations efforts on the Hill. They had organized seminars at the Fund for congressional staff on issues of concern and to provide information on IMF programs that might be of interest to individual members. Through development and follow-up within this network, IMF staff cultivated connections on the Hill in hopes of mending the bad feelings that surrounded the 1997 quota-increase struggle. The goal was that if they had to make a request on the Hill again, they would be able to work through the authorizing committees and Congressional Research Service staff to get relevant information to the appropriate individuals.

Also attempting to mitigate any policy concerns, IMF staff and Treasury officials organized a campaign to build on the old support and eliminate any opposition once Obama's request was official. Senator Richard Lugar (R-IN) and John Kerry (D-MA) immediately issued a statement to show bipartisan support for the IMF from the Foreign Relations Committee. Strauss-Kahn met with skeptical members of Congress such as Maxine Waters and activists such as Bob Geldoff on the gold sales proposal to convince them of his sincerity in changing the organization. On May 14, a group of former government officials coordinated by the Bretton Woods Committee sent a letter to House Speaker Nancy Pelosi and Senate Majority Leader Harry Reid (D-NV) urging that they enact the president's request. The Treasury Department released the letter to bolster support in Congress, using the old "national interest" argument. Likewise, the Chamber of Commerce sent a letter to members of Congress urging support. To convince progressives, the coalition reached out to Doug Rediker, the director of the Global Strategic Finance Initiative of the New America Foundation, to write an op-ed supporting the IMF. Perhaps most significantly, Fund staff reached out to organized labor, specifically the ITUC and AFL-CIO, to convince them *not* to campaign against funding.[30]

Despite the support, the request stalled over the nuances of the IMF funding requirements. Given its unique nature, the Fund is a lending institution that can release funds to the US on demand. In budget terms, this is perhaps no different from placing money in a demand-deposit account at a bank. Thus, the debate centered around whether the request for the New Arrangements to

Borrow needed an appropriation for the entire $108 billion (with no outlay), none of it (under the old "exchange of assets" concept), or a percentage of it perceived to be at risk.[31] Including the entire $108 billion with no outlay posed a major political problem, as the bill requested only $106 billion to fund the wars in Afghanistan and Iraq. The larger amount for the IMF would most likely attract a good deal of media attention. Moreover, it was not clear that it was even necessary to request the entire amount. As previous chapters have detailed, before 1967 the US had used public debt transactions and payments from the Exchange Stabilization Fund to make its contribution to the IMF. In 1966, the US payment came in the form of a letter of credit to the IMF, which the US borrowed back. In 1967, the Commission on Budget Concepts recommended that payments be treated as monetary exchanges. However, later Congresses were unhappy with this arrangement and argued for an appropriation.[32]

In the 2009, Peter Orszag, a former director of the Congressional Budget Office who had moved to a position as the director of the Office of Management and Budget, entered the fray. Together with a representative from the Treasury, he pressured his old colleagues to make it easier to include the IMF funds in the bill.[33] All parties agreed to include $5 billion in the appropriation (the percentage perceived to be at risk), which would leverage $108 billion for the IMF for a five-year term. The smaller amount would then be included in the war supplemental that would attract the greater part of the media's attention.

Eventually, the campaign for IMF funding succeeded, but not without the usual bargaining on related and unrelated issues. The war supplemental passed out of the House of Representatives 368–60 on May 14. At the time, fifty-one antiwar Democrats opposed it. The Senate attached the IMF funding to the bill. It passed, along with a ban on the release of any photos depicting abuse of war detainees. Sherrod Brown (D-OH) also attached an amendment to the IMF measure requiring that the US executive director to the IMF oppose loans and programs that did not exempt certain spending by the governments of HIPC countries from health, education, food security, and other social safety-net programs.

The two chambers needed to reconcile their differences with the presumption that "funding our troops" would be "must pass" legislation when it returned to the House. At this stage, the Republican congressional leadership protested the bill with the IMF funding on the grounds that it was a "bailout" for European banks hit by the crisis. The Republican defection meant that the Democrats who opposed the ban on release of the photos would need to be brought in to achieve a majority. Eventually, the photo ban was stripped from the war supplemental and the bill passed the House. Thus, the IMF funding measure passed, together with the IDA authorization. PL 111–32 did, however, contain Brown's amendment concerning the social safety-net programs. Members of the House, led by Maxine Waters, were not satisfied that the reforms went far enough and immediately began to attach additional measures to the annual foreign-assistance spending bill, such as mandating the release of IMF board documents within two years and requiring that parliaments in borrowing countries approve any IMF loans or agreements.

The tension with the executive branch over control of US foreign policy persisted. When signing the bill, President Barack Obama issued a "signing statement" stating that the sections of the bill dealing with workers' rights and the Brown amendment would interfere with his constitutional authority to conduct foreign relations.[34] The statement angered the relevant Democratic committee chairs in the House and Senate, who wrote a letter to the president objecting to the statement.[35] The White House countered that the statement was issued to preserve core presidential prerogatives in the area of foreign policy; nonetheless, the House reinstated Obama's restrictions with a bipartisan vote of 429–2 on a Foreign Operations appropriations bill.[36]

The first 2008-crisis legislative struggle over the IMF revealed the Treasury to be its chief supporter. The perception in Washington policy circles was that the new president had made an international commitment and did not want to lose a floor vote over that commitment.[37] No hearings were held on the IMF issue, and thus no one testified publicly in support or opposition. Passage was facilitated by the partisan work of Democratic leaders in the House and Senate who agreed to a budget score along the lines of Orszag's argument that only a percentage need be included in the congressional estimate of the cost.

Nonetheless, the funding did not come without a considerable struggle. When the Republicans demonstrated their commitment to vote against it, House Speaker Nancy Pelosi and the Democratic leadership had to apply a high degree of pressure to persuade antiwar Democrats to support it. That such pressure was needed is remarkable, given that the funding measure was proposed in the first unified, Democratic, government in both chambers and the executive since the 103rd Congress, when Bill Clinton was president in 1993–1995. It is doubtful, however, that ideological opposition falls neatly along party lines. Republican opposition to the IMF measure appeared to end on the floor of the House. In public appearances and various media outlets, Republican members made no outward efforts to call attention to the matter or strip the IMF funding from the bill. A group of NGOs retain a degree of opposition to the funding, given their uncertainty that the IMF is truly committed to reform.[38] Rather, the Democrats and Republicans worked as legislative teams with a stake in the outcome of winning or losing the overall package. Individual members had supported or opposed the measure—for example, Richard Lugar (R-IN), who was an early supporter, and Sherrod Brown (D-OH), who was a critic.

Therefore, despite the completion of a legislative sequence wherein the IMF expanded its resources to lend through the NAB, the question of whether or not a "new" or "old" IMF will be doing the lending remains outstanding, as is the question of legislative support for the Bretton Woods institutions.

Some components of the answer will emerge from the use of the funds, and whether or not they are indeed used to bail out Eastern European banks. Others will be revealed in the conditionality agreements attached to the future packages the Fund arranges with borrowing states. The ultimate component, however, will be the connection between the banking systems and state system that is being reconfigured as the crisis wears on. As these components fall into place, future legislative sequences will indicate the degree of support, or lack thereof, that the resurgent IMF has achieved with its domestic, American, political constituencies.

## The IMF and the European Union

If the first wave of the 2008 financial crisis was the collapse of financial institutions in the US, and the second was the subsequent collapse of others across the globe, the third wave has come in the form of sovereign debt crises, one of the most notable being Greece in late 2009 and Ireland in late 2010. In this new challenge to the IMF, sovereign debt within the Eurozone exposed major flaws in the design of the Eurozone arrangements, as well as the ongoing stigma attached to using IMF funds. The questions to emerge from the Greek and Irish crises concern the operations of regional currency unions in sovereign issues, and their connection to the broader multilateral institutions that have states as members. Members of Congress have expressed a high degree of concern with any IMF funding that could be perceived as a "bailout" of the Eurozone, despite their ongoing support for traditional multilateral institutions.

The *Wall Street Journal* reported that two months after the collapse of Lehman Brothers in the fall of 2008, a group of European leaders created a small, secret task force to devise a plan to head off a default by a country in the sixteen-nation Eurozone.[39] The group was unable to agree on a strategy before the Greek crisis emerged. The problem, exposed by the crisis, was that the Eurozone has no tools to prevent default by one of its own members. Whereas Hungary had used an existing facility at the IMF earlier, European Union treaties do not allow the other countries to use it.

### THE GREEK CRISIS

In October 2009, the newly elected government of Greece announced that the country's budget deficit was headed for 12.5% of GDP (at 13.6% of GDP in late 2010), a figure more than three times the previous government's official forecast. The announcement triggered a crisis as investors questioned the ability of the government to finance its debt.

The country turned to other Eurozone member states and the IMF for financial assistance, yet there was no consensus on how to provide it. For

French president Nicolas Sarkozy, Eurogroup president Jean-Claude Juncker, and European Central Bank (ECB) chief Jean-Claude Trichet, using the Washington institution would be an admission of European weakness.[40] Only Germany's Angela Merkel dissented; the IMF's involvement would allow her to convince German voters that aid to Greece was part of an IMF program of economic adjustment. IMF conditionality would deter other indebted Eurozone countries from seeking aid. For its part, the US was content with the EU countries staying away from the IMF, because the Fund could then concentrate its limited resources elsewhere.[41] The leaders of France and Germany had different stakes in the outcome. Sarkozy saw that the crisis could threaten the entire zone, and he used the issue to prove his leadership and shore up his popularity at home. He sought greater freedom for national governments to provide support to one another as they wished. Merkel worried more about a backlash from domestic voters, and her own supreme court, were she to contribute taxpayer money to Greece, with its history of massive deficits. The Germans wanted any aid to come from individual countries, not the EU, so that they could control the process and insist on certain reforms. Germany and France broke their stalemate in May of 2010, but not without pushing the Eurozone to the brink of collapse.

The $143 billion Greek package assembled in May 2010 was a standard IMF program combined with resources from the European Commission and the European Central Bank. Nonetheless, it was unusual because the IMF had not previously lent money to a Eurozone member, since the zone had not been created when it last lent to a European state in the 1970s. It is also a relatively large program. The hope was that assistance, combined with austerity measures, would prevent the government from default or abandoning the euro and returning to a national currency.[42] In June, the Europeans committed about US$575 billion in guarantees to create the European Financial Stability Facility (EFSF). They hoped that the action would convince financial markets that further assistance would be available despite the lack of an institutional European mutual fiscal insurance mechanism that could impose conditionality and remove members from the zone who defaulted. Member states of the EU pay into the fund in proportion to their contribution to the paid-up capital of the European Central Bank (ECB), plus 20% to ensure that the fund can repay its obligations even if one country defaults. The EFSF itself issues bonds, then takes the proceeds to lend to other countries. Thus, the amount for the facility was not lending capacity of $575, it was *guarantee* capacity, which dropped immediately when Greece's guarantee was removed from the package. Nonetheless, it sought and received a AAA rating, which allowed it to obtain funding at a lower rate than the individual members of the EU could obtain, since only six had AAA ratings in June 2010.

As with developing countries' stabilization plans, the citizens of Greece will need to enact a massive fiscal contraction to produce the primary budget surplus needed for the plan to work. Projections in 2010 were that a surplus could not be expected until 2012. It is unlikely that this degree of contraction will be politically feasible. The IMF appears to want some type of "bail-in" of private investors along the lines it has negotiated in previous crises. A "Plan B" would extend official support for a longer period. Conversely, no such plan will be needed if Greece is able to sell short-term bonds in the near future. Greece's history of unsustainable policies and creative accounting makes this outcome unlikely soon.

After the IMF made the Greek loan, the US Senate adopted an amendment to S. 3217 that directs the US executive director at the IMF to evaluate any IMF loan to a country whose public debt exceeds its gross domestic product, to determine and certify to Congress that the loan will be repaid. Since that information is likely unavailable to the executive director, the impact of this provision, if it is adopted, is unclear. Other pieces of legislation that seek to block use of the IMF's resources to fund loans to EU member countries have also been introduced. One seeks to oppose any use of US-provided funds to help support assistance under the proposed EU stability plan. As with S. 3217, the impact of these measures, if they are eventually adopted, is uncertain.[43] They will most likely die in the 111st Congress, yet they could be reconsidered in the 112th, Republican, Congress, which began in January 2011.

## THE IRISH CRISIS

Instability within the Eurozone did not end with the Greek bailout. Domestic financial crises can affect other economies through trade connections, economic similarities among them, or financial risks that link them. All three factors are at work within the European Union. For example, a collapse in one country can trigger a crisis of confidence in the banks of another, depending on the assets the banks in each state hold. Spanish bank stocks have been threatened by their exposure to Portugal. Similar problems in countries that have sovereign debt problems may cause investors to question the stability of others. For example, Portugal does not have budget deficits the size of Greece's, but it does have a similar combination of deficits, government debt, and low growth. Bond markets became wary of lending to both Portugal and Spain following the Greek bailout.[44] Disagreement among the governments of the stronger European economies, and the degree of involvement private lenders will need to have in future rescues, has contributed to ongoing sovereign bond market uncertainty across the Eurozone and propelled the IMF further into the resolution of sovereign European insolvency.

The first country to apply for help from the EFSF was Ireland. Unlike the Greek crisis, the Irish debt and banking crises were triggered by a housing boom and bust, and the government's pledge in 2008 to guarantee the deposits and debt of Irish banks. As the difficulties in honoring this pledge mounted, budget deficits grew along with it, and depositors withdrew funds. The banks borrowed from the ECB to cover their deposits and the Irish government worked to contain the damage nationally and avoid seeking assistance from the UK, EU, or IMF, which it perceived to be an infringement on its hard-won sovereignty. Nonetheless, Ireland did seek aid in November 2010 and reached an agreement with the EU and IMF for roughly $90 billion on November 28, 2010. The IMF would lend approximately half as much money to Ireland as the EU. Yet Germany and the other European members made the use of the EFSF conditional on reaching an agreement with the IMF, likewise to be included in any future European bailouts.

Therefore, the Irish deal signaled that the Eurozone would aid its own members, but as part of the agreement, creditors of countries considered insolvent could be forced into a restructuring before the fund dispensed aid in the future. The new mechanism is planned through "collective-action clauses" on Eurozone bonds that will be inserted from June 2013 onward. On a case-by-case basis, the IMF, the European Commission, and the ECB will decide whether a country's payment problems are due to insolvency or a short-term cash shortage. If the analysis of these institutions is that the country is insolvent, Eurozone finance ministers would need to vote unanimously that this analysis is correct. The government would then have to negotiate with its private-sector creditors. Although it appears unlikely a government would choose to vote itself into insolvency, it might do so to pass a degree of loss on to its bondholders and avoid the imposition of further austerity on its citizens.[45]

## Conclusion: The Revived Stage

The IMF and, to a lesser degree, the World Bank have been revived in the aftermath of the 2008 financial crisis. Each IO has progressed through a successful funding sequence in Congress. Therefore, there are preliminary indications as to how groups will line up looking forward, and how the legislature will operate. This book has argued that any one individual vote, or even one sequence of votes, does not structure the relationship between the IFIs and constituency groups in the US economy. The work of the IFIs ultimately needs to be grounded in domestic US politics in order to have a solid base of support in Congress among those groups affected; or conversely, they need to threaten a constituency in order for their existence to be threatened. The crisis has revealed the deep integration of major US banks and nonbank financial institutions in the structure of the world's financial system, and the necessity of drawing middle-income countries into any plan for a global recovery.

The ultimate success of economic multilateralism in the US legislature will therefore depend on the contours of the US banking structure that survives the crisis and its connection to the state. Second, successful economic multilateralism will require this new banking structure to throw the weight of its support behind a multilateral, and not a bilateral, approach. No doubt the shape of the recovery packages that the IMF designs with member states will play a significant role in determining that outcome as well. Yet simply extending a credit line to the IMF or authorizing an IDA replenishment will not be enough to secure these organizations' futures.

In the run-up to the crisis, entirely new lobbies formed to protect their interests in Washington, and others have added to their resources—for example, the Private Equity Council formed late in 2006 by leaders in the company buyouts business, such as Blackstone Group, Carlyle Group, and Kohlberg Kravis Roberts. In the same year, the Security Industry Association and the Bond Market Association merged to form a group they hoped would have more influence, the Securities Industry and Financial Markets Association (SIFMA). The Managed Funds Association added to its staff in Washington at the same time, when all groups feared additional regulation of the private-equity industry.[46] If these groups realize material gains from the new European bailout mechanisms, they will promote and support the IMF's role. If the sovereign bailouts impede their collection on debt, they will oppose a role for the political institutions, including the IMF, in the future. Irish banks had US$58.6 billion outstanding to US banks at the end of 2009, compared to the US$16.6 billion outstanding by Greek banks to US banks. The amount of exposure of US financial institutions through credit default swaps based on the sovereign debt of these countries is not known, because the amount of the swaps could raise or lower US bank exposure. If the swap was taken to lower exposure by insuring the loans, the risk to the banks that took it would be low; whereas if the US banks sold credit protection, it could be orders of magnitude larger because the bank would have to cover the loans that defaulted.[47]

The new problem in the Congress-IFI relationship is that the traditional bedrock of support for the IMF in the banking community is gone. The Dodd-Frank Wall Street Reform and Consumer Protection Act enacted by Congress in July of 2010 did not seek to stop the progress of disintermediation of the world's capital markets, associated with the highly engineered financial products at the heart of the American crisis. Rather, it sought to regulate the existing process more effectively. Therefore, the new lobbies' connections to the IMF and World Bank policy issues as bondholders, and not banks, will serve as a potential new constituency, or rival. With a global recession, the World Bank's remaining political constituency in the corporate community in the US is also weakened. NGO activity has been threatened by cutbacks in foundation support. The result is that the Treasury Department remains the top promoter of the IMF and World Bank. In the short term, the Democratic presidential administration–Democratic Congress alignment augured well for financial support, particularly since the Secretary of the Treasury and top economic advisor had direct work experience with the Bank and the Fund.[48] As the banks recover and the economy emerges from the recession, however, the future of formal, organized multilateral cooperation is far less certain.

8

# Conclusions

Global institutions require support from formal domestic political institutions in order to flourish. In recent years, studies of global governance have explored the operations of transnational networks and IOs operating across state boundaries.[1] Yet the endpoint of most major decisions concerning funding and programs remains within the institutions of member states, particularly legislatures, which have not received a great deal of either theoretical or empirical attention. This investigation into Congress has shown that the relationship between the legislature and multilateral organizations poses a challenge to American democracy because it distorts the complex balancing arrangements designed by the Constitution's framers to diffuse and limit the exercise of power. Features of accountability and the checks and balances unique to American democracy need to be incorporated into the multilateral framework. To get requisite legislation passed, therefore, some degree of congressional advocacy toward the IMF and World Bank is a necessary component of successful multilateral cooperation. When using congressional levers, individual members bring together ideas and material interests to pursue specific policy goals. As in the domestic process, even one powerful lawmaker who chooses to pursue a specific policy objective can appear to hamstring an outcome in an IO by manipulating legislative procedure. Yet in the absence of congressional involvement, these same IOs would lack a crucial independent accountability mechanism, with its unique power to drive change from the outside.[2]

Given the existing degree of apathy and opposition to IFIs in Congress, how is it that the US joined them and has provided funding at all? This history has shown that there is not one fixed resolution to the puzzle. All three institutions are in a constant state of change emanating from both internal and external causes. That is, there has not been one IMF, one World Bank, *or* one Congress from 1945 to the present. Studies of the intersection of domestic and international politics acknowledge that the "second image" can reverse, or that international factors can cause domestic outcomes and domestic factors can influence the state system.[3] The interaction of national and international politics has meant that constituencies for the IFIs have materialized and receded in response to the structure of the world political economy, chiefly the emergence of the Cold War, the resumption of international lending, increasingly disintermediated international lending arrangements, and the end of the Cold War. Across time, allies of the IFIs have used congressional procedure as it operated in that time to graft IMF and World Bank measures onto legislation that must pass. At pivotal moments, they have influenced the broad policy parameters of the IMF and World Bank. These activities have occurred at the highest levels of the party leadership, the presidential administration, the Treasury, and the top management of the Bretton Woods institutions.

Looking to the future, it is clear that multilateral institutions must have constituencies in US domestic politics in order for them to flourish. While at first glance this conclusion may appear obvious, the history of coalition building explored in this book demonstrates that the Bretton Woods institutions need to find the widest possible base of grassroots support to continue to receive funding from the American political process, because the coalition building that is necessary to achieve that result carries the seeds of its own destruction. As greater numbers of groups are brought into the process and participate in its functioning, they hold the potential to break away and oppose a measure in the future. Coalitions can form across party and ideological lines, and they can re-form shortly thereafter. Therefore, while the policy community may seem stable at any one moment in time, it is highly vulnerable to shocks from external events, primarily from the global economy.

## Evaluating Trends in Congressional Advocacy for Policy Change

As I stated at the outset, I use the term *congressional* advocacy to refer to the process wherein American legislators use the institutional mechanisms of Congress to influence public policy and resource-allocation decisions outside of formal American institutions of rule and within international organizations. Members of Congress pull the levers they have available to pull. Although the US supplies a smaller percentage of the funds to the IMF and World Bank than it did when they were founded, the internal mechanisms available through omnibus legislation allow individual members willing to work within the budget process a considerable degree of power to promote their individual preferences. As with all omnibus legislation packages, inside deals are vulnerable to external media scrutiny that can compel leadership to remove an individual provision. To overcome these obstacles, supporters of the IFIs and multilateralism need promoters on the inside and outside of the institution who are willing to expend political capital on their behalf. While ideas and ideology operate among members, American notions of "liberalism" and "conservatism" are not expanded to cover every policy issue. On many issues, such as the IFIs, party cleavages can be driven by partisan responses to presidential leadership, or party coordination on procedural and parliamentary control.[4]

## EXPLAINING LEGISLATIVE SUCCESS ACROSS TIME

The legislative struggles explored in each of these stages echo the conclusion Oleszek makes to his classic study of congressional procedures and the policy process that American lawmaking is a dynamic process wherein the interests, pressures, perceptions, and prejudices of members of Congress change rather quickly as a result of the election cycle and other conditions.[5] While members use procedures to effect policy change, the procedures themselves perpetuate the messiness, openness, pragmatism, compromise, and deliberateness that is characteristic of American policy making. At every stage of a bill's passage, promoters must form a new winning coalition to advance to the next rung. While coalitions form in favor of it, others form to oppose it. If promoters fail in one session, they can always try again when the environment improves. Multilateralism is exactly this type of issue in politics: There are not correct answers, but a flow of compromises.

Each empirical chapter of this study depicted a phase in the relationship between Congress and the IMF and World Bank that provided evidence for this contention. Congressional advocacy in each phase is a product of both the domestic institutional procedures available and the international environment. Any explanation for congressional behavior that relies on one dimension without the other is incomplete, because both the context of the international political economy and the institution of Congress have changed across time, and thus mechanisms of influencing policy outcomes in the IFIs have changed as well.[6] Different kinds of bills were needed in each phase and were easier or harder to pass, depending on the composition and degree of support in the business community and civil society.

The result in each chapter is that the way congressional politics respond to exogenous shocks depends on the internal procedures and institutional arrangements of the day. Conversely, internal procedural and institutional arrangements, such as amendments to bills added with an "open rule" in the House, omnibus legislation, and concepts such as divided government, operate within a particular context configured by the global political economy. For example, the outcome of legislation that included provisions for the IMF or World Bank during periods of divided government during the Cold War and the use of omnibus legislation differed from the negotiations with the executive branch during periods of divided government in the twenty-first century after the Cold War had ended.

Table 8.1 summarizes the major legislative struggles investigated in each phase of the book, as well as the congressional advocacy efforts for policy change that were associated with them. The summary reinforces the conclusion that in phases where a clear constituency has understood why the IFIs are needed, and how their work provides a material benefit, Congress has passed legislation with minimal policy demands.

TABLE 8.1

**Summary of Phases in the Congressional-IFI Relationship**

| Phase/(Years) | Major Legislative Struggles | Associated Congressional Advocacy for Policy Change |
|---|---|---|
| Enactment (1944–45) | Bretton Woods Agreement Act | The IMF and World Bank are established with the US as a member. The National Advisory Council would formulate US policy and report to Congress every six months on participation in the Bank and the Fund. |
| Building (1945–1971) | IFC established | IFC established with restrictions on holding equity and managing firms. |
| | IDA established | IDA established as a concessional lending facility under the World Bank umbrella, and not the United Nations, to compete with communist development strategies. |
| Development (1971–1982) | PL-94-S64 | Trust Fund created with reservations attached to US participation in future Trust Fund Agreements, future gold sales require congressional approval. Second Amendment to the IMF Articles of Agreement approval ended fixed parity. |
| | IDA-6 replenishment | Replenishment eventually funded without earmarked funds, despite dispute over World Bank loans to Vietnam. |
| | "Witteveen Facility" | IMF Supplementary Financing Facility established over objections of human rights and other groups. |
| | 7th general IMF quota review | Request funded. Gold Commission created, but no policy result. |
| Debt (1982–1997) | 8th general IMF quota review | Request funded over objections of labor movement, steel producers and others that opposed it. Banks and business organizations organize support. |
| | IDA-7 replenishment | H. R. 1949 Special Facility for Africa funded. |
| | International Development and Finance Act of 1989 | Adds "Pelosi amendment" on environmental impact assessment studies to executive director votes on multilateral development banks. |
| | 9th general IMF quota review | Request funded despite delay over unrelated matters in the foreign-aid bill. |
| | IDA-10 replenishment authorization | World Bank Inspection Panel created with efforts of environmental groups that joined the debate as both promoters and critics. |
| Moral Hazard (1997–2008) | 11th general IMF quota review request and increase in NAB | Both IMF quota increase and NAB funded despite anti-IMF activism associated with abortion, reform of US foreign aid bureaucracy, and organized labor. The Meltzer Commission established with reform agenda to follow. |
| | IDA-13 replenishment | Replenishment funded with shift in IDA from loans to grants, debt relief. Performance targets added to appropriations. |
| Revived (2008–) | IDA-15 replenishment | *Doing Business* labor indicator taken out of CPIA. |
| | 2009 IMF increase in NAB | NAB approved with modifications in IMF conditionality and transparency. |
| | The Eurozone crisis and IMF | Direct use of US funds avoided in European bailouts. |

In the first of these stages, the legislative goal was to secure US membership in the postwar multilateral institutions despite the previous experience with the League of Nations. Therefore, in the enactment phase, the Treasury organized the initial constituency to support passage by working through the National Foreign Trade Council and making the case that American membership would help to restore the global economy and prevent another economic catastrophe, like the Great Depression, through an extensive public relations effort. Promoters of the Bretton Woods Agreement Act had been careful to work with bipartisan congressional leadership when it was being negotiated. Committee chairs and ranking members were invited to attend the conference in New Hampshire and therefore understood the difficulty of obtaining an agreement among so many states. Committee chairs were key to congressional procedure in those years. As the legislation moved through the House and Senate, Treasury, committee members, and key members of organized interest groups negotiated compromise measures that allowed the act to pass.

Once the IOs began operations in the building stage, their support in the business community remained divided, as it had been when the legislation passed. Congress was a closed institution then, and committee chairs held a good deal of control over each committee's agenda. The international economy was in the process of recovering from the war. As the IFIs became established in this environment, the compromise measure reached during the Bretton Woods Agreement Act's passage limited the scope of their activities. Two additional pieces of legislation during this phase allowed for US membership in the newly created IFC and IDA, with additional compromise measures over the scope of their activities. Some groups that had supported the Bretton Woods Agreement Act, such as the NFTC, opposed the creation of the IFC.

Nonetheless, the phase is a "building" phase because constituencies were built during these years as a result of both domestic and international developments. Domestic securities laws were changed so that the World Bank could raise money in private American capital markets. The perceived communist threat in developing countries prompted the broader business community to support the IFIs as a means to open foreign markets. Moreover, the IFIs built constituencies as the world economy recovered from the war. Banks came to understand that their interests were aligned with, and did not compete with, the IMF. They did not object when Treasury approached Congress with an early quota review request, and Congress funded it. By the end of the phase, the business community was far more coherently in support of them than when they were created.

In the development phase, banks, multinational firms, and their related interest groups in US politics changed in reaction to changes in the world economy that ended fixed parity and created a need for greater development resources. The internal workings of the institution of Congress opened up with the rise of single-issue advocacy groups and the "sunshine laws" that exposed the government (and by extension the IMF and World Bank) to public view. Major legislation was needed during these years in response to these external shocks—namely, to clarify the role of the IMF following the end of fixed parity, replenish IDA, provide additional resources to the IMF for a Supplementary Financing Facility, and fund the IMF's seventh general quota review. The newly solidified constituencies for the IMF and World Bank in the banking and business communities worked with allies on Capitol Hill to fend off challenges to their programs from single-issue groups, chiefly in the issue area of human rights. The result was that in each of these legislative struggles, the bill eventually passed and the funding was provided.

However, the episodes explored in the development stage revealed deep ideological divisions among members of each political party on multilateralism. In addition, members of Congress fought to preserve the institution's budgetary prerogatives with respect to the foreign-aid bill. Despite passing the IMF legislation, members inserted provisions that would provide future tools through which to influence the course of the IFIs' development. The individual measures did not have as much of a policy impact as they would in the next stage. Yet the necessity of blocking the various amendments and commission recommendations exposed the weaknesses of the IFIs that would have to be addressed with new procedures in the future as domestic interests became increasingly concerned with global ones, like human rights and poverty alleviation.

In the debt stage, the world economy changed again after the Mexican default in 1982 and severe recession in the US, as did the internal institution of Congress with the new era of divided government in the Reagan administration. Nonetheless, the banking community clearly needed the IMF as part of the solution to the series of sovereign debt crisis that followed in the decade. To pass major legislation, party leaders in Congress increasingly used the technique of bundling measures around a nucleus that must pass, with additional measures that members and the presidential administration negotiated for inclusion in order to win their support. During this stage, the eighth general IMF quota review was funded over the objections of an ad hoc group of labor and steel producers, and environmental, church, conservative, taxpayer, and free-market organizations. It was buried in complex budget negotiations and then packaged into omnibus legislation. A later Republican administration expended political capital on the ninth IMF quota review, yet it was stalled in a protracted delay over the foreign-aid bill and the unrelated issue of Israeli housing guarantees. The IDA-7 replenishment was perceived by some to have been inadequate. Congress provided funds for a Special Facility for Africa in order to direct funds toward that continent.

At the beginning of the debt stage, Congress made few policy demands because the goal was merely to secure funding. By the end of the debt stage, the struggle over the authorization for the IDA-10 replenishment allowed environmental groups acting as both supporters and critics of the World Bank to pressure the Bank to create an inspection panel over the objections of some of its state members. This change in congressional advocacy occurred because banks had initially reached agreements with their creditors and the IMF before the quota review reached Congress. They needed only to secure an appropriation and not seek specific policy measures. However, toward the end of the stage, those seeking policy change began to use the same lever of omnibus negotiations. As the Cold War receded into memory, members concerned with the environment grew in number and influence, whereas the number of staunchly anti-communist ones decreased.

In the moral hazard phase, change came from the exogenous international political economy when new forms of finance made capital widely available outside traditional banking arrangements, fracturing the solidarity and degree of support of the banking and business community. In short, the interests of banks, bondholders, and those firms that provide derivative financial products were no longer aligned. Likewise, poverty and environmental activists did not necessarily agree on appropriate courses of policy for the IFIs. The IFIs came to be viewed as part of the problem of international instability, not the solution. Endogenous legislative change came in the form of the Republican takeover of Congress, which brought on another episode of divided government, this time with the parties holding the White House and Congress reversed. The upshot of the change in majority party after forty years was that budgetary power intensified in the authorizing committees. The changes in Congress and the international context within which it works were solidified with Treasury's eleventh general IMF quota review request and increase in the NAB during the Asian financial crisis of 1997. The measures were funded, yet not without protracted legislative struggles and significant pressure for policy change.

Therefore, while Congress funded the IMF and World Bank requests during the moral hazard phase, it triggered an ongoing process of reform. The new committee chairs held wildly diverging views on the IFIs. Some long-serving senators, such as Jesse Helms, sought to reform the US foreign-aid bureaucracy. Other new House members who had been recruited and funded for their ideological stands on some social issues associated with the Contract with America pressured leadership to attach abortion and other social policy issues to IFI funding. Organized labor likewise sought to work through democratic leadership. It was thus necessary for the majority in the House to work with the minority on these issues in order to secure a majority in the new ideological environment. In a notable example, the Meltzer Commission revealed a consensus among critics on the need for multilateral debt relief. Groups also worked with allies in the executive and legislative branches to raise the proportion of IDA grants, lower the proportion of aid it assigned through loans, and fight corruption. Although all of the efforts at congressional advocacy were not successful in this stage, divided government splintered support for the IFIs, and the uniquely independent features of the US budgeting process allowed individual members of Congress concerned with these issues to retain their ability to influence policy outcomes. In such an environment, bipartisan support is critical to crafting a legislative package that includes IFI measures. Hence, common policy goals such as transparency, anticorruption, and debt relief allowed members and the executive branch to find common ground.

At present, the IMF and, to a lesser degree, the World Bank have reassumed a central role in the world economy in addressing the international ramifications of the 2008 financial crisis. In the revived phase, a new round of congressional advocacy associated with the crisis achieved success in obtaining new funding for the IMF and the World Bank. These requests were facilitated by the unity among American political institutions during the first two years of the Obama administration, when a Democratic president and Democratic Congress worked together to package legislation that would honor the policy commitments President Obama made to the Group of 20. But the details of the legislation that provided these funds reveal that the future remains unclear, given the collapse of support for them in traditional interest groups, remaining criticism in the newer groups involved, and the depth and nature of the unresolved issues.

Among the issues outstanding are the role of the IMF in the European sovereign debt crises and the future structure of US financial markets in the housing area. The IMF has returned as a crisis lender to some European, as well as developing, countries. It has been a partner with European arrangements to bail out sovereign debt in the Eurozone; however, it has been careful to avoid openly using US funds to avoid giving any impression that the US is bailing out the Eurozone.[7] Moreover, the internal institutional arrangements supporting the Eurozone are inconclusive in mid-2011. The relationship between the American state and financial markets has been reformulated with the passage of the Dodd-Frank Wall Street Reform and Consumer Protection Act in 2010. But the ultimate conclusion to the direction of change will not occur until the outstanding issue of the final disposition of the government-sponsored enterprises (GSEs) Fannie Mae and Freddie Mac is resolved. Only then will the contours of American financial markets of the future begin to emerge—that is, what interest groups are attached to them and how they will be connected to the work of the IMF.

At present, there are few interest groups left in the US policy community that outright support the IMF or the World Bank. Those interests remaining on IMF legislation appear to be primarily political elites that support the Treasury (such as those organized by the Bretton Woods Committee to support the supplemental legislation in 2009), what is left of the large money-center banks, and some NGOs that seek to maintain the ability of developing countries to finance exports. Those financial actors most affected by the volatility in the Eurozone are potential supporters, such as sovereign debt holders and financial intermediaries that may have provided credit default swap insurance on euro-denominated instruments. Interests active on World Bank legislation are concentrated in the NGO sector.

In each phase, success in achieving the dependent variable—that is, funding and concomitant policy change in the IMF and World Bank—is best explained by the existence of a clear budget item in play to act as a vehicle, a bipartisan coalition supporting an initiative attached to it that has a material stake in the work in the IFIs, and a few members committed to passage at senior leadership levels in the House and/or Senate who can negotiate with the executive branch on specifics.[8] Since neither party is ideologically unanimous in how it views the IFIs, the parties also lack unanimity in terms of how they translate ideology into policy on these issues. A bipartisan coalition helps to cut across lines to forge a majority. In fact, the minority party may matter even more in the House on these issues, because assembling a majority of votes on an IFI issue nearly always requires including minority party votes to do so. Rather than trying to bring a large number of supportive members of Congress into their coalition, these coalitions work best when a wide range of allies on the issue can work to eliminate opposition to the measure that exists in either party or in civil society.

## THE STRUCTURE OF THE BANKING SYSTEM TO COME

What conditions will promote the expansion of the coalition of support? The broader question of the relationship between the banking and state systems in the world political economy is being negotiated as the 2008 crisis has passed, and states must decide how to unravel the complex bailout shareholder arrangements configured to address the immediate situation. It is unlikely that the banks will go back to their precrisis independence in each of the industrial states that engaged in massive intervention. Nonetheless, in these individual cases, it is not clear if a form of intervention might remain through ownership of shares, regulation, or a combination of the above. In addition, it remains to be seen how these entities will operate across borders once the outline of their public/private shareholder arrangements and regulatory framework emerges. At present, indications are that the US Treasury will work closely with the IMF and the IFIs will reach out to states.

In light of the Greek, Irish, and other sovereign debt crises, it appears that there will be some type of collaborative relationship between major industrial states and large international banks located in them for the foreseeable future. Therefore, there needs to be some type of official international collaboration to support lending when the market is too anemic to provide it. The IMF and World Bank have been shown to be well-suited to this role. As evidence, future Eurozone bailouts will require an IMF agreement in order to receive funds from the European stability facility. The IFC embarked on a partnership as part of a US$50 billion global trade financial initiative through the World Bank.[9] However, for these efforts to flourish, broader segments of the populations of advanced, industrial democracies need to be brought into the effort and see its benefits, not simply the austerity measures associated with them. In the US, geographic constituencies need to understand their connection to the work of the Bank and the Fund—for example, through contracts received by local firms that employ local workers, firms that provide local food supplies, or environmental causes that relate to their daily lives. The planners at Bretton Woods incorporated such an educational effort into their efforts at passing the original agreement in Congress. A successful public dialogue considers objections and attempts to work with broad constituencies to achieve the multilateral cooperation that will be necessary to fundamentally resolve the present crisis.

There *are* alternatives to a multilateral strategy. Some regional arrangements exist, and bilateral operations as well. Iceland failed to get funding from its NATO allies for a period during the financial crisis. Before the IMF stepped in, the government approached the Russian government.[10] Other changes will emanate from the future of US-China bilateral financial relations. In the short run, the Chinese government has continued to purchase US Treasury securities. Some analysts have predicted a US-China condominium in the short to medium term, although the Chinese central bank has denied that it seeks such a role. Given the complexity of resolving the needs of the global financial system on a multilateral basis, certain interests in the US may prefer to pursue bilateral arrangements, coordinated through loose "governance" arrangements, that mix public and private agreements.

## CONGRESSIONAL ADVOCACY AND THE STUDY OF POLITICS

When does Congress matter the most? It matters the most when the IMF and World Bank need money, generally during a financial crisis or an authorization for a capital replenishment, and when there are clear policy initiatives circulating for institutional reform. Literature in American politics and international relations points to similar long-term trends and short-term threshold events. For Polsby, the social base of change is domestic and reflects technological advances that made demographic and then party realignment possible within the US.[11] For Mayhew, war can serve as a cause for change in American politics because it can give movements a chance to achieve what they wanted to achieve anyway, and that they might never have achieved otherwise.[12] This book has added the structure of international lending as a cause for long-term change—lending that expanded when the Cold War receded and splintered the interests of the financial community among investors, banks, bondholders, private equity, hedge funds, and other users of disintermediated capital.

When does Congress matter the least? The sheer size of the legislature and lack of expertise in a narrow segment of economics by most members' staffs ensures that the legislature does not play a systematic role in specific World Bank project designs or IMF austerity packages. Nor does Congress enter into the specifics of IDA negotiations, outside of broad reform proposals congressional staffs contribute during briefings on the negotiations by Treasury. Anecdotal evidence exists that members make calls on behalf of constituents bidding on World Bank contracts.[13] However, there is little evidence that such lobbying by a member has any systematic influence. Moreover, US executive directors follow congressional directives and vote against specific loans or projects. They know, however, that they will be outvoted by the rest of the board in most of these cases. Hence, the most significant role Congress plays in specific loans and projects is in its oversight function, whereby a member can write a letter to the secretary of the treasury or president of the IMF or World Bank, or conduct a hearing in order to call attention to an issue connected to a project. Generally, an organized group, media coverage, or contact in the office triggers these activities because congressional staffs lack the resources or inside information to generate them.

The international relations literature on IOs misses an understanding of how the arrangement of political institutions in the American system and institutional procedure channel the normative orientations of international actors. Congress is a forum where ideas interact with material interests to produce policy outcomes in IOs. Indeed, ideas are omnipresent in the political world. Members of Congress are human, with ideas that inform their actions. However, this study shows that *many* ideas operate on a given issue. On any one specific piece of legislation, support for ideas like "multilateralism" or "cooperation" is very concrete and connected to specific proposals. Support on one bill does not necessarily translate into support on the next one, depending on how each bill is written. The assembly of a piece of legislation determines whether or not many groups or members join an effort or stay out of it. In each stage, the connection of the international financial and corporate communities to the work of the IMF and World Bank explains more about congressional advocacy, and the direction of policy measures included or excluded, than the power of ideas does.

The American literature on Congress misses the political role that members of Congress can play on certain issues that do not attract a great deal of attention on the congressional agenda—as health care, the military, and social security do—as well as the international context within which concepts like "divided government" and "omnibus legislation" operate. On a practical level, the American arrangements have given US representatives to the IMF and the World Bank a useful tool insofar as they can deflect a degree of responsibility for a measure onto Congress. Fairly or unfairly, they can seek a certain goal or block another by manipulating the perception of whether or not they could get it through the legislative process. The career paths and necessity of Senate confirmation for high-level positions ensure that representatives to the multilateral institutions will, at minimum, avoid antagonizing senators. But Congress is far more than a veto player. The resolve of a member of Congress who invests him- or herself in an issue and wants to do something about it can result in policy change, even if that member does not generate the policy proposal. To make a difference, the member must successfully navigate the inside arrangements made when large bills are packaged and be able to count on support from party leadership should opposition decide to fight an item's inclusion.

When taking US and international politics to be a unified field of activity, we see that economic dislocations do more than just rearrange coalitions in this area. They contribute to ongoing policy change in both domestic and international institutions. On the domestic institutional side, the increased tendency to construct ever-larger legislative packages was set in motion many years prior to the 1981 omnibus budget reconciliation bill. On the international side, the IMF emerged from the 1982 debt crisis as a different type of institution than it had been in the era of fixed parity, when industrial countries made drawings. Much of the direction of that change was propelled by the needs of domestic banking interests in the US that, together with the Treasury Department, found it useful to work to resolve the debt crisis through a multilateral institution. The alternative, in their view, was the imposition of conditionality by the US government alone, or the perception of it. The IMF was preferable. Incidentally, some members of the European Union appear to have reached the same conclusion: that it is useful to resolve sovereign debt crises with the involvement of the IMF and not the alternative—imposition of conditionality by the European Union, or bilateral arrangements.

Therefore, the features of IMF and World Bank legislation as both necessary and unpopular with many segments of the American public required that they be joined with other issues so that multilateral funding is not the focus of a big bill. The resolutions of crises eventually spin off new players in the global economy with new interests, whereas others decline. These new interests may or may not support the multilateral framework. The ebbs and flows in support of the banking community for economic multilateralism have been strong indicators of periods of ascendancy, growth, and decline in the IMF. Hence, when IOs lose constituents, as was the case with the IMF prior to the financial crisis of 2008, they must seek alternative sources of revenue to continue to staff even their normal operations, such as economic surveillance.

The picture of the legislative sequence that is repeated over time thus illustrates the changing location and exercise of power operating through policy networks that can cooperate with one another on one bill, compete with one another on the next, and/or remain out of the third struggle, depending on their business interests (for for-profit entities), mission, or funding sources (for NGOs and other issue-advocacy groups).

## Congressional Advocacy for Other International Organizations

What about other issue areas? Is the issue area of financial politics in Congress unique? Do the interactions among Congress and other IOs operate similarly? In his examination of foreign economic policy, Zysman argues that the government's ability to act in one policy area differs from others. Policy tasks vary, as do patterns of interest organization.[14] Yet the changes in the institution of Congress have interacted with the same international crises in these other areas that should lead to comparative outcomes in terms of support for other IOs that lack mass domestic constituencies. The World Trade Organization (WTO) is the most obvious comparative example with the financial issues, because the American balance of trade and international financial positions are so closely connected. The United Nations presents another comparative example in the security area. A brief comparison shows that both the WTO and UN have worked to generate domestic constituencies throughout their histories in their own ways, and have likewise been caught up in the same mix of internal and external causes that have shaped congressional advocacy in the financial area.

### THE WORLD TRADE ORGANIZATION

Although monetary and trade issues are closely related in politics, they are considerably different in terms of the national and international arrangements that support them. When goods are traded, businesses exchange concrete items across national borders; whereas when money crosses borders, financial institutions swap an intangible store of wealth, unit of account, and unit of exchange. Therefore, the concepts associated with money require some understanding of economic concepts not familiar to most Americans. The degree of economic expertise necessary for groups and individuals to participate in financial politics, combined with the secrecy necessary in many banking transactions, makes the field inaccessible to many scholars who specialize in the study of Congress, and generalists who study broader issues of American politics. Therefore, trade differs from finance at the most basic level because individual citizens mostly have an innate understanding of what is going on with trade, and not with finance. Their participation in trade-related political issues reflects this greater degree of comprehension; political institutions that address financial matters are also structured differently. In attempting to clarify an earlier debate about relative state strength in the trade and monetary policy area, Gowa points out that American trade and international monetary policy are political goods whose susceptibility to collective action is a function both of characteristics inherent in those goods and of the institutional framework within which they are produced.[15] Others, such as Helleiner, have pointed out that the possibilities for collective action in the institutions of trade and finance are notably different.[16]

The most notable institutional difference between the trade issue area and the financial one has been the lack of a corresponding international trade organization (ITO) as a third pillar of the Bretton Woods system for many years.[17] Legislation proposing an ITO that had been detailed in the Havana Charter died in Congress under pressure from the business community, which argued against its antitrust provisions and full-employment provisions as socialist planning. Unlike the Bank and the Fund, the legislation was not proposed when the postwar enthusiasm for multilateralism was at its high point. The ITO did not devote attention to the economic needs of the underdeveloped countries, nor did it make a timely attack on the transitional problem of the rapidly changing world of 1947.[18] In the absence of an ITO, groups supporting free trade worked with official state negotiators within the ad hoc GATT framework to reduce trade barriers in a series of negotiating rounds. When the Truman administration announced in 1950 that it would not continue to seek congressional approval of the ITO, the General Agreement on Tariffs and Trade (GATT) was forced to fill the void. The GATT grew to *resemble* an international organization but had many differences that altered the opportunity structure for congressional advocacy efforts.

Since there was no provision in the GATT for a secretariat, an interim commission had been created to prepare for the work of the ITO after the Havana meeting proposed that one be formed. Performing secretariat services for the GATT, this commission became the de facto GATT secretariat under an arrangement that technically existed until the Marrakesh Accords were signed in 1994.[19] In legal terms, the US president had entered into a trade agreement pursuant to advance delegation of authority from Congress in the Trade Agreements Act of 1945. That agreement simply dealt with commitments, not an international organization. In order to create a vehicle for multilateral decisions without the appearance of an organization, the Trade Agreements Division of the State Department insisted that references in the General Agreement to an "organization" be replaced with the phrase "CONTRACTING PARTIES acting jointly."[20] With this device, the GATT could avoid having the appearance of a formal organization, which it was not, and avoid using the word "members," which connotes an organization and would have had to come before Congress.[21] Likewise, the position of director general within the GATT was one of conciliator and not one of compulsory legal power. He or she could hold consultations and information negotiations with contracting parties to reach a consensus, yet had to rely on the power of persuasion to achieve results.[22]

Therefore, without any status as a formal IO, Congress did not have the type of budgetary leverage over the GATT secretariat that it held over the IMF and World Bank.[23] Congress appropriated monies for the GATT under the International Conference Fund of the State Department, and not a specific appropriation for the GATT.[24] The GATT secretariat lacked the capacity to make policy that the IMF and World Bank's headquarters did. Even if Congress had done a direct appropriation, it most likely would not have had the same impact, because the IO does not distribute the type of loans or project assistance the IFIs do.[25] Interest groups were certainly involved in the GATT negotiations, but they worked directly through the negotiating and treaty-ratification process.

Despite the unique features connected to the IFI issues, there is nonetheless evidence that many features of the framework offered in this book can be applied to trade. In both trade and financial politics, the same changes in the structure of the international economy altered the operation of the US economy, and corresponding new interest groups appeared that influenced the passage of unpopular tariff legislation. The chief international causes highlighted in this study of finance have been the end of World War II, the expansion of money-center banks' lending during the 1950s and 1960s, the end of fixed parity in the IMF system, the 1982 debt crisis, the end of the Cold War, and the 1997 financial crisis, which furthered the process of financial disintermediation and deregulation in the international banking system. There is some evidence that the same pivotal events provoked changes in interest groups, their congressional activities, and IOs in the trade area in the long run.

As was true with IFI-related issues, the working relationship between interest groups and Congress changed after the Burke-Hartke episode. Groups no longer sought to exert influence on the process after the legislation had been proposed, but sought instead to participate in formulating it prior to the proposal stage. Many of the same groups operated in the trade area as with the IFIs. The US 1974 Trade Act established a private-sector advisory committee for multilateral trade negotiations wherein forty-five committees and nearly a thousand advisors gave broad policy advice to a top-level committee. The negotiators, who drew their authority from Congress and needed congressional approval for the results to be implemented, formulated objectives with the private-sector advisory committees. Later, the negotiators reported any deviations from these objectives to the business advisors when deviations were necessary. The business advisors in turn reported their views to Congress when the final agreements were presented for ratification to minimize protectionist sentiments.[26] Since the private-sector advisory process in the US had helped to ensure passage of the Tokyo Round in the US Congress, the 1988 Omnibus Trade Act essentially reconfirmed it. The US trade representative managed private-sector committees in cooperation with the Departments of Commerce, Agriculture, Labor, and Defense under the authority of a top oversight committee, the Advisory Committee for Trade Policy and Negotiations.

The congressional advisory system enhanced the private sector's understanding of the constraints on the individual state negotiators, and it created a degree of the private sector's personal identification with the negotiations success. In the later stages of the Uruguay Round, American business groups formed the "MTN Coalition" to promote their interests in the intellectual property, investment measures, and goods and services negotiations to the US government. The group, cochaired by Jimmy Carter's trade representative, Robert Strauss, and Ronald Reagan's trade representative, William Brock, was a coalition of eleven business, farm, and consumer groups, and 13,000 companies to raise public awareness of the Uruguay Round and to provide support for Carla Hills (then Bush's trade representative).[27] Strauss in particular spoke at the coalition's organizational press conference about the importance of lobbying Congress to overlook narrow parochial interests in favor of trade liberalization. As Miles Weiss reported for UPI in "Business Group to Push for GATT Approval" on May 15, 1990, Strauss said that during the Tokyo Round "I literally talked to every single Congressman and Senator, which is a big job . . . I personally listened to their complaints, and that is an even bigger job."[28]

When the time for ratification came in the US Congress, the multilateral trade negotiations coalition become the Alliance for GATT NOW. At this time (February 1994), the US Chamber of Commerce was on board, as was the National Association of Manufacturers. GATT NOW coordinated a three-pronged campaign of Washington lobbying, grassroots campaigning, advertising, and public relations. Boeing assumed the lead lobbying role in the aerospace industry and its home state of Washington. Monsanto took the lead among chemical companies, and Warner Lambert Co. took the lead among pharmaceutical companies. The GATT round's opponents, led by Ralph Nader and environmental, consumer, labor, and conservative activists, focused their opposition on the WTO.

Therefore, the GATT round was successful in mobilizing a constituency for its successful passage. Yet, as with the IMF and World Bank, these constituencies were not always stable. For example, the Dispute Settlement Understanding of the World Trade Organization (WTO) was one of the major controversies attached to the Uruguay Round of legislation in the Clinton administration. Groups sought to prevent the WTO from becoming a Supreme Court of Trade controlled in Geneva, making decisions directly that would affect American policy. Opposition to the measure came not from protectionist manufacturing industries but from a coalition of labor, environmental, and consumer protection groups. They were joined by some business associations and conservatives, like Newt Gingrich, Ross Perot, and Pat Buchanan.[29] On subsequent issues, these same groups and individuals have had little in common.

## THE UNITED NATIONS

There is clear evidence that the same international causes that changed the context of interest-group activity on the IMF, World Bank, and WTO also changed the context within which groups worked through congressional channels to change policy in the United Nations. As with the IMF and World Bank, the

UN emerged from a set of postwar negotiations, was transformed by the new and diverse members entering after the decolonization movement, lost its leadership role as the IMF and World Bank assumed it in the development field, and suffered a further crisis of mission as the financial crises of the 1980s and 1990s splintered the Group of 77 coalition that had existed among developing countries in response. Similar to the IMF and World Bank, the UN lacks a natural constituency in US domestic politics. Thus, the trajectory of the United Nations Organizations in Congress is closer to the Bretton Woods institutions than the WTO is, because the United Nations was established immediately after the war and offered the budgetary lever from 1945 to the present.

Key differences exist as well. The UN is not "orphaned" in the congressional committee structure as the IFIs are, because there is not the same competition for jurisdiction between foreign affairs and banking/financial services. Other differences existed between the Bretton Woods talks and the Dumbarton Oaks talks that followed them from August to October of the same year.[30] The differences tied the organizations to the Washington foreign-policy establishment differently. For example, the Dumbarton Oaks talks were held in Washington, DC, and the Bretton Woods talks had been held in New Hampshire. The location allowed Roosevelt to follow, and intervene in, the Dumbarton Oaks talks more readily, whereas he had been much less interested in the progress at Bretton Woods. In addition, the planners at Bretton Woods had commenced their talks with a more substantive agenda, derived from the Keynes and White discussions. The negotiators at Dumbarton Oaks did not have the same unified vision to take as a starting point.

The UN's planners also faced different sets of opposition in the international political economy. At Dumbarton Oaks, the Soviets sought to design a peace and security organization that would ensure postwar cooperation among allies. The Soviets had not posed a challenge to the design of the IMF because they did not join the organization. Therefore, the task of individuals planning the United Nations was challenged from the start by the fundamental incompatibility of economic systems in the US and USSR, and the resulting differences during the Cold War that followed. Whereas the Bretton Woods institutions came to represent an alternative economic model to the Soviet one, the UN embraced Soviet membership and the possibility of cooperation.

Finally, the IMF and World Bank received organized political support only after the budget struggles of the 1970s and early 1980s; yet the United Nations has always received organized political support from the United Nations Association, which had initially existed as the American Association for the United Nations, and the earlier League of Nations Association. The United Nations Association has been focused on programs and education efforts to build constituencies for the UN through individual chapters throughout the US. When Eleanor Roosevelt left her position at the United Nations, she became a vocal supporter for the organization until her death. Other prominent Americans have served in leadership roles in the United Nations Association, including former chairs of major corporations, diplomats, and top-level government officials.

The chief similarity between the Bretton Woods institutions and the UN in Congress is the availability of the budget lever. The unique agencies of the United Nations have each required both authorizations and appropriations since the UN was founded. Peacekeeping is likewise segmented in the US budget, giving ample opportunities for members of Congress to use the budgetary lever to influence the pace and scope of myriad reform proposals by withholding allocations. Moreover, representatives to the UN are enmeshed in the same policy networks as representatives to the IMF and World Bank insofar as they must be confirmed by the Senate. The principle of NGO representation had been introduced at the San Francisco Conference of the UN, and provisions were made for consultative arrangements to the organization's proposed Economic and Social Council (ECOSOC). Many of the same interest groups thus had a direct vehicle through which to work in the UN for an even longer span of time than they have in the IFIs.

With the budget lever it holds over the UN, which is similar to that over the IMF and World Bank, members of Congress grew more assertive in their advocacy efforts during the same years. In 1984, during the Reagan administration, the US—together with Great Britain and Singapore—officially withdrew from the United Nations Educational, Scientific, and Cultural Organization (UNESCO), given its lack of satisfaction with UNESCO's political orientation and management.[31] The US rejoined in 2003 as part of its struggle against global terrorism. Similarly, the US repeatedly threatened to withdraw from the United Nations Conference on Trade and Development (UNCTAD) during the1980s, but this action was complicated by the fact that UNCTAD is an organ of the UN General Assembly. In 1986, the US withheld 20% of its annual dues in an attempt to force weighted voting on UN budgetary matters. In response, the UN began the practice of consensus-based budgeting, giving the US an effective veto over major budgetary decisions.[32] In all three cases of congressional advocacy, the UN agencies maintained operations with nongovernmental organizations and universities in the US through a variety of programs. In all cases, the threat to exit, and the exit with enticement to rejoin, enabled the US to exert a high degree of influence over internal reforms.

When divided government reversed from the 1980s to the 1990s, and the Democrats held the White House in the Clinton administration and Republicans controlled the Senate, additional congressional advocacy struggles over policy reforms broke out. In the notable 1994 funding dispute over the United Nations, Senator Jesse Helms fought to reform the entire US foreign-aid bureaucracy and held up UN funding as a part of his overall strategy. At that time, the UN General Assembly authorized creation of the Office of Internal Oversight Services in response to American pressure for an "inspector general" to detect and eliminate waste, fraud, and abuse, recommend efficiency measures, and evaluate the effectiveness of UN programs. As the conflict dragged on, the Clinton administration failed to defend the UN enthusiastically.[33]

The debate over US arrears went on for several years, and many compromise efforts failed. On these issues, as with the financial areas, the differences were not so much over ideology but partisan responses to presidential leadership, or party coordination in packaging legislation that would be needed to fund the federal government. As with the IMF and World Bank, partisan ideology is not consistently translated into policy measures. For example, some accounts of these years note that in seeking compromises with Democrats, Helms disagreed with abortion activist Christopher Smith (R-NJ) in the House and sought to exclude Senator Richard Lugar (R-IN) from conference participants selected to work out differences in legislative proposals.[34]

In sum, successful congressional advocacy toward the UN is best explained by the existence of a clear budget item in play to act as a vehicle, a bipartisan coalition supporting it, and a few members committed to passage at senior leadership levels who are willing to expend political capital on the issue and negotiate with the executive branch on specifics, as it is with the IMF and World Bank.[35] The political parties do not translate ideology into policy on the UN identically. Some elements of the Republican Party are more concerned with social issues, others with free-market ideology, and still others with America's role in the world. Some elements of the Democratic Party have concern for labor rights, others for spreading the New Deal ideology to other parts of the world through multilateral institutions. A bipartisan coalition cuts across lines to forge a majority. Compromise is a frequent feature of the process as legislation moves through each chamber.

## Conclusion: Congressional Advocacy toward International Institutions

This study has explored the exchanges between the US Congress and the Bretton Woods institutions in order to explain how legislation succeeds despite formidable obstacles. A notion of congressional advocacy is needed to understand congressional behavior with respect to the IFIs, because the institutional levers of the legislature provide a mechanism wherein competing national and international demands can be transmitted to an international organization in return for support. The construction of policy at the intersection of domestic and international political institutions contributes to theoretical literature on both sides of the American/international relations divide with respect to how institutions change and how powerful states exert influence over IOs. It requires a conceptual shift away from the notion that the international system of states is subject to rules created by international institutions that are above the states. The process of congressional advocacy toward the IFIs demonstrates that globalization has occurred both "from the top down" and "from the bottom up" as domestic concerns have become increasingly entangled in international matters, beginning with the expansion of international branch banking after the war and continuing to the present.

To understand both dimensions of the process, theorists on both sides of the American/international relations divide must consider how members of Congress work as policy makers in areas that are not of mass interest on the larger congressional agenda. The transmission route for this process is generally not through the formal diplomatic channels established for US representation, such as the executive directors of the Bank and the Fund, but in hearings, meetings, and the day-to-day maneuvers of commissions wherein the IMF and World Bank adjust policy to accommodate the preferences of a variety of actors.

A presidential administration lasts for a maximum of eight years, and the tenures of the secretary of the treasury and the US executive director to the IMF or World Bank are frequently far less than that. Conversely, the congressional careers of many key committee members active on these issues are far longer than those of either the president or treasury officials. For example, Senator Robert Taft, Sr.'s congressional career spanned eighteen years; Senator J. William Fulbright's career spanned thirty-two years; Senator Jesse Helms's career spanned thirty; Senator Chuck Hagel's career spanned twelve; Representative James Leach's career spanned thirty; and Representative David Obey's career spanned forty years. As of 2011, Senator Richard Lugar's career has spanned thirty-five years; Representative Barney Frank's career has spanned thirty-one; and Representative Nancy Pelosi's career has spanned twenty-four.

The long tenure of these individuals does not mean that they are always on the same side of an issue, or that support for the IMF and World Bank automatically translates into support for funding a given budgetary appropriation. In fact, frequently it does not. Thus, the same individuals have been among the harshest critics of the IMF and World Bank, and also among their strongest supporters. Nonetheless, in rising to the top of key committee leadership positions and maintaining an active interest in these issues, their initiatives on the IMF and World Bank are far from indiscriminate. Interest groups with wider access to information and more time to devote to an initiative approach sympathetic legislators to promote policy change outside the formal governance structure of the IOs. While this process can tend to detract from the autonomy of the IO, it does promote accountability to some democratically elected body in a governance system that has been described as having a democratic deficit.[36] Those working to design new systems of economic multilateralism for the twenty-first century would be well served to incorporate such parliamentary accountability into governance process and not to evade it.

# NOTES

## Introduction

1. For the understanding drawn from American politics, see David B. Truman, *The Governmental Process: Political Interests and Public Opinion* (New York: Knopf, 1951), 322.

2. For some examples from a range of literature in international relations, see Keith Krause and W. Andy Knight, "Introduction: Evolution and change in the United Nations System," in *State, Society, and the UN System*, ed. Keith Krause and W. Andy Knight (New York: United Nations University Press, 1995); Leon Gordenker and Thomas G. Weiss, "Pluralizing Global Governance: Analytical Approaches and Dimensions," in *NGOs, the UN, and Global Governance*, ed. Leon Gordenker and Thomas G. Weiss (Boulder, CO: Lynne Rienner Publishers, 1996); Margaret E. Keck and Kathryn Sikkink, *Activists Beyond Borders: Advocacy Networks in International Politics* (Ithaca, NY: Cornell University Press, 1998); Margaret E. Keck and Kathryn Sikkink, "Transnational Advocacy Networks in the Movement Society," in *The Social Movement Society: Contentious Politics for a New Century*, ed. David S. Meyer and Sidney Tarrow (New York: Rowman & Littlefield Publishers, Inc., 1998); Sydney Tarrow, *The New Transnational Activism* (New York: Cambridge University Press, 2005).

3. For some examples from a range of literature on Congress, see Christopher J. Deering and Steven S. Smith, *Committees in Congress*, third ed. (Washington, DC: CQ Press, 1997); Roger H. Davidson and Walter J. Oleszek, *Congress and Its Members*, seventh ed. (Washington, DC: CQ Press, 2000); Barbara Sinclair, *Unorthodox Lawmaking: New Legislative Processes in the U.S. Congress* 2d ed. (Washington, DC: CQ Press, 2000); Eric Schickler, *Disjointed Pluralism: Institutional Innovation and the Development of the U.S. Congress* (Princeton, NJ: Princeton University Press, 2001); Nelson W. Polsby, *How Congress Evolves: Social Bases of Institutional Change* (New York: Oxford University Press, 2004); Thomas E. Mann and Norman J. Ornstein, *The Broken Branch: How Congress Is Failing America and How to Get It Back on Track* (New York: Oxford University Press, 2006).

4. Devesh Kapur, "The Changing Anatomy of Governance of the World Bank," in *Reinventing the World Bank*, ed. Jonathan R. Pincus and Jeffrey A. Winters (Ithaca, NY: Cornell University Press, 2002); William Ascher, "The World Bank and US Control," in *The United States and Multilateral Institutions*, ed. Margaret P. Karns and Karen A. Mingst (Boston: Unwin Hyman, 1990); Michael Goldman, *Imperial Nature: The World Bank and Struggles for Social Justice in the Age of Globalization* (New Haven: Yale University Press, 2006).

5. Mann and Ornstein, *The Broken Branch: How Congress Is Failing America and How to Get It Back on Track*; Frances E. Lee and Bruce I. Oppenheimer, *Sizing Up the Senate: The Unequal Consequences of Equal Representation* (Chicago: University of Chicago Press, 1999).

6. See Marie T. Henehan, *Foreign Policy and Congress: An International Relations Perspective* (Ann Arbor, MI: University of Michigan Press, 2000); Cecil V. Crabb, Glenn J.

Antizzo, and Leila E. Sarieddine, *Congress and the Foreign Policy Process: Modes of Legislative Behavior* (Baton Rouge, LA: Louisiana State University Press, 2000); Don Wolfensberger, "The Founders and Foreign Policy: An Introductory Essay," in *Congress Project Seminar on Congress' Role in Foreign Policymaking* (Woodrow Wilson International Center for Scholars, 2009); Christopher J. Deering, "Congress's Role in Foreign Policymaking," in *Congress Project Seminar on the Role of Congress in Foreign Policymaking* (Woodrow Wilson International Center for Scholars, 2009).

7. President Woodrow Wilson, for example, argued in *Congressional Government* that the separation of powers was a mistake because it led to deadlock. See Woodrow Wilson, *Congressional Government: A Study in American Politics*, 7th ed. (Boston: Houghton, Mifflin and Company, 1890).

8. See the poll accessed May 31, 2009, at http://www.gallup.com/poll/1600/Congress-Public.aspx.

9. Susan Strange, "The Persistent Myth of Lost Hegemony," *International Organization* 41, no. 4 (1987): 571.

10. J. Lawrence Broz and Michael Brewster Hawes, "Congressional Politics of Financing the International Monetary Fund," *International Organization* 60, no. 2 (2006); J. Lawrence Broz and Michael Brewster Hawes, "US Domestic Politics and International Monetary Fund Policy," in *Delegation and Agency in International Organizations*, ed. Darren G. Hawkins, et al. (New York: Cambridge University Press, 2006); J. Lawrence Broz, "Congressional Voting on Funding the International Financial Institutions," *Review of International Organizations* 3, no. 4 (2008).

11. Henehan, *Foreign Policy and Congress: An International Relations Perspective*; Crabb, Antizzo, and Sarieddine, *Congress and the Foreign Policy Process: Modes of Legislative Behavior*.

12. Polsby, *How Congress Evolves: Social Bases of Institutional Change*; Mann and Ornstein, *The Broken Branch: How Congress Is Failing America and How to Get It Back on Track*; Deering and Smith, *Committees in Congress*; Davidson and Oleszek, *Congress and Its Members*.

13. Omnibus legislation is legislation that addresses numerous and not necessarily related subjects, issues, and programs, and therefore is usually highly complex and long. They are typically assembled to get something passed. The bill has a locus of attention (nucleus) and draws the support of important players. They are powerful because they divert attention from other controversial items. See Barbara Sinclair, *Unorthodox Lawmaking: New Legislative Processes in the US Congress* (Washington, DC: Congressional Quarterly Press, 1997), 64; and Glen S. Krutz, *Hitching a Ride: Omnibus Legislating in the U.S. Congress* (Columbus, OH: Ohio State University Press, 2001), 45.

14. Jeffrey M. Chwieroth, "Normative Change from Within: The International Monetary Fund's Approach to Capital Account Liberalization," *International Studies Quarterly* 52, no. 1 (2008); Jeffrey M. Chwieroth, *Capital Ideas: The IMF and the Rise of Financial Liberalization* (Princeton, NJ: Princeton University Press, 2010).

15. See Nitsan Chorev, "A Fluid Divide: Domestic and International Factors in US Trade Policy Formation," *Review of International Political Economy* 14, no. 4 (2007); and Philip G. Cerny, *Rethinking World Politics: A Theory of Transnational Neopluralism* (New York: Oxford University Press, 2010), 7.

16. Donald R. Wolfensberger, *Congress and the People: Deliberative Democracy on Trial* (Washington, DC, and Baltimore Maryland: Woodrow Wilson Center Press and Johns Hopkins University Press, 1999), 92.

17. Henning makes an earlier version of this argument. See C. Randall Henning, "Political Economy of the Bretton Woods Institutions: Adapting to Financial Change," *The World Economy* 19, no. 2 (1996): 173.

18. IMF Articles of Agreement, I (i). Accessed January 16, 2009, at http://www.imf.org/external/pubs/ft/aa/aa01.htm.

## Chapter 1

1. William Clark's career at the World Bank ranged from 1968 until 1980. As quoted in The World Bank/IFC Archives, Oral History Program, October 5, 1983, transcript by Robert Asher. Accessed online 04/30/09 at http://siteresources.worldbank.org/EXTARCHIVES/Resources/William_Clark_Oral_History_Transcript_1983_10_05_44_02.pdf.

2. John Gerard Ruggie, "Multilateralism at Century's End," in *Constructing the World's Polity* (New York: Routledge, 1998), 112.

3. Kathryn C. Lavelle, "Exit, Voice, and Loyalty in International Organizations: US Involvement in the League of Nations," *Review of International Organizations* 2 (2007).

4. Allan J. Cigler, "Interest Groups: A Subfield in Search of an Identity," in *Political Science: Looking to the Future*, ed. William Crotty (Evanston, IL: Northwestern University Press, 1991), 116. See also Richard A. Smith, "Interest Group Influence in the US Congress," *Legislative Studies Quarterly* 20 (1995): 15.

5. Gary W. Cox and Mathew D. McCubbins, *Legislative Leviathan: Party Government in the House* (Los Angeles: University of California Press, 1994). John H. Aldrich and David W. Rohde, "The Consequences of Party Organization in the House: The Role of the Majority and Minority Parties in Conditional Party Government," in *Polarized Politics: Congress and the President in a Partisan Era*, ed. Jon R. Bond and Richard Fleisher (Washington, DC: CQ Press, 2000).

6. See Barbara Sinclair, "Parties and Leadership in the House," in *The Legislative Branch*, ed. Paul J. Quirk and Sarah A. Binder (New York: Oxford University Press, 2005), 233.

7. See Steven S. Smith, "Parties and Leadership in the Senate," in *The Legislative Branch*, ed. Paul J. Quirk and Sarah A. Binder (New York: Oxford University Press, 2005), 276.

8. Frances E. Lee, *Beyond Ideology: Politics, Principles, and Partisanship in the U.S. Senate* (Chicago: University of Chicago Press, 2009), 191.

9. See, for example, Barbara Sinclair, *Legislators, Leaders, and Lawmaking: The U.S. House of Representatives in the Postreform Era* (Baltimore: The Johns Hopkins University Press, 1995); Barbara Sinclair, *Unorthodox Lawmaking: New Legislative Processes in the U.S. Congress* 2d ed. (Washington, DC: CQ Press, 2000); Barbara Sinclair, *Party Wars: Polarization and the Politics of National Policy Making* (Norman, OK: University of Oklahoma Press, 2006).

10. Sinclair, *Legislators, Leaders, and Lawmaking: The U.S. House of Representatives in the Postreform Era*.

11. Robert A. Dahl, *Congress and Foreign Policy* (New York: Harcourt, Brace and Company, 1950), 10.

12. Ibid., 12. For a later view of the ability of members to vote their conscience on many foreign-policy issues, see James M. Lindsay, *Congress and the Politics of U.S. Foreign Policy* (Baltimore: The Johns Hopkins University Press, 1994).

13. Pluralism is an orientation toward the study of politics wherein any group can organize, find a voice for their concerns, and compete for these interests within the institution of rule. "Pluralist American-style democracy" refers to conceptions of interest- group organization derived from Madison and Tocqueville. See Alexander Hamilton, James Madison, and John Jay, *The Federalist Papers* (New York: Bantam Books, 1988), No. 10, pp. 42–49. See also Alexis de Tocqueville, *Democracy in America*, ed. J. P. Mayer and M. Lerner, trans. G. Lawrence (New York: Harper, 1966), and Marvin Zetterbaum, "Alexis de Tocqueville," in *History of Political Philosophy*, ed. Leo Strauss and Joseph Cropsey (Chicago: University of Chicago Press, 1972). For some examples of theorists that discuss the term explicitly in international relations, see Leon Gordenker and Thomas G. Weiss, "Pluralizing Global Governance: Analytical Approaches and Dimensions," in *NGOs, the UN, and Global Governance*, ed. Leon Gordenker and Thomas G. Weiss (Boulder, CO: Lynne Rienner Publishers, 1996); Nayef H. Samhat, "International Regimes and the Prospects for Global Democracy," *The Whitehead Journal of Diplomacy and International Relations* 6, no. 1 (2005); Rodger A. Payne and Nayef H. Samhat, *Democratizing Global Politics: Discourse Norms, International Regimes, and Political Community* (Albany, NY: SUNY Press, 2004).

14. Lindsay, *Congress and the Politics of U.S. Foreign Policy*, 13.

15. Dahl, *Congress and Foreign Policy*, 17. For a view of networked politics from work in international relations, see Miles Kahler, ed., *Networked Politics: Agency, Power, and Governance* (Ithaca, NY: Cornell University Press, 2009).

16. For a discussion of this issue, see Glenn P. Hastedt, *American Foreign Policy: Past, Present, Future*, 6th ed. (New York: Pearson Prentice Hall, 2006), 92.

17. Mancur Olson, *The Logic of Collective Action: Public Goods and the Theory of Groups* (Cambridge, MA: Harvard University Press, 1971); Raymond A. Bauer, Ithiel De Sola Pool, and Lewis Anthony Dexter, *American Business and Public Policy: The Politics of Foreign Trade*, 2nd ed. (Chicago: Aldine, Atherton, 1972); E. E. Schattschneider, *The Semisovereign People: A Realist's View of Democracy in America* (New York: Harcourt Brace Jovanovich College Publishers, 1975); Frank R. Baumgartner and Bryan D. Jones, *Agendas and Instability in American Politics* (Chicago: University of Chicago Press, 1993), 7; Frank R. Baumgartner and Beth L. Leech, *Basic Interests: The Importance of Groups in Politics and Political Science* (Princeton, NJ: Princeton University Press, 1998); John W. Kingdon, *Agendas, Alternatives, and Public Policies* (Boston: Little, Brown and Company, 1984); Jeffrey M. Berry, *The New Liberalism: The Changing Power of Citizen Groups* (Washington, DC: Brookings, 1999); Jeffrey M. Berry, "Interest Groups and Gridlock," in *Interest Group Politics*, ed. Allan J. Cigler and Burdett A. Loomis (Washington, DC: CQ Press, 2002).

Margaret E. Keck and Kathryn Sikkink, *Activists Beyond Borders: Advocacy Networks in International Politics* (Ithaca, NY: Cornell University Press, 1998).

18. The author is grateful to Jon Sanford for suggesting this analogy.

19. For example, Karin Lissakers, IMF Executive Director (12-01-93 to 8-6-2001) was the staff director of the Foreign Economic Policy Subcommittee in the Senate. Colbert King, World Bank Executive Director (12-21-79 to 3-31-81) was the minority staff director of the Senate Committee on the District of Columbia.

20. Confidential interview, former Treasury official, Washington, DC, 2008.

21. Kent Higgon Hughes, *Trade, Taxes, and Transnationals: International Economic Decision Making in Congress* (New York: Praeger Publishers, 1979), 144.

22. Susan Strange, "Towards a Theory of Transnational Empire, 1989," in *Authority and Markets: Susan Strange's Writings on International Political Economy*, ed. Roger Tooze and Christopher May (New York: Palgrave MacMillan, 2002), 149.

23. Specifically, the IMF was established with the US contributing one-third of its original quota subscriptions. It is similar to other bank and nonbank financial institutions in that it relies on income from lending to finance its administrative expenses, meet funding costs, and build precautionary balances. At least every five years, the IMF reviews its quotas and determines whether or not to request infusions of capital to enlarge the size of its lending. In addition, the IMF maintains two standing borrowing arrangements, the New Arrangements to Borrow and the General Arrangements to Borrow, should the Fund believe that its forward commitment capacity might fall short of its members' needs. In the 1997 financial crisis, the Fund did need to request capital, and Congress was able to use that need to press for major reforms within it.

The budgetary mechanism used for IMF appropriations has varied. Before 1967, the US funded its participation through a variety of procedures, including public debt transactions and payments from the Exchange Stabilization Fund. In 1966, the US gave the IMF a letter of credit and borrowed its own money back during the next years. In 1967, the US adopted a budget procedure wherein IMF payments were handled as an exchange of assets. Thus, they were excluded from budget receipts and expenditures. Congress authorized payments, but they were not included in the budget. In 1976, Congress again treated payment to the IMF as an exchange of assets. After a debate over the matter in 1980, it was agreed that US participation would be appropriated as budget authority. However, no outlays would be counted. See Jonathan E. Sanford and Martin A. Weiss, "The Global Financial Crisis: Increasing IMF Resources and the Role of Congress" (Washington, DC: Congressional Research Service, 2009).

In 2003 and 2008, the Fund chose not to ask for an increase. During those years, developing countries began to avoid it altogether and turned to alternative sources. It began to run an operating deficit and look toward its own alternate sources of finance, such as a proposed trust fund from gold sales that would require congressional approval. The financial crisis of 2008 changed this picture dramatically when world leaders called for the coordination of international economic policies and propelled questions of reform of the International Monetary Fund and World Bank to the center of the international agenda at the G20 Summit. When the Obama administration took office, the Treasury requested a $100 billion increase in the IMF's New Arrangements to Borrow.

24. U.S. Congress, House of Representatives, Committee on Appropriations, *Par Value Modification Appropriations*, 93rd Cong., 1st sess., September 14, 1973, 8.

25. Unlike the IMF, the IBRD has grown since 1945 to encompass four IOs under the umbrella "World Bank Group." Members realized that the initial subscriptions to the IBRD would not be adequate to finance the major development needs of the postwar era. Therefore, they allowed the organization to borrow money in private capital markets and lend it to finance large-scale development projects. The IBRD thus generates income from the spread between the market rate available to the organization given its high credit rating, and the higher rate charged to borrowers on projects. The amount it borrows depends on the level of projects it seeks to finance, which peaked in 1998 after the Asian financial crisis. The income pays the IBRD's operating expenses, goes into reserves, and allows it to transfer a certain amount to the International Development Association each year. Therefore, while governments have paid only $11

billion in capital to the IBRD since 1947, it had financed more than $400 billion in loans by 2008.

An affiliate of the World Bank, the International Finance Corporation (IFC) was established in 1956 to provide financing to private-sector initiatives in developing countries. The IFC is a distinct legal entity from the IBRD, with its own Articles of Agreement, share capital, financial management, and staff. However, membership in the IFC is available only to members of the World Bank. The president of the World Bank is also the president of each of the other World Bank institutions, including the IFC. Similar to the IBRD, members pay subscriptions and periodic capital increases. However, since the IFC's portfolio generates income, it rarely requests funds for a capital increase, and it is able to finance its activities through earnings and its own borrowings on private markets. It is rarely subjected to direct oversight, although as a part of the World Bank Group it responds to indirect congressional pressure.

In 1960, member states of the World Bank established the International Development Association (IDA) as an agency within the World Bank Group that would provide long-term, low-interest loans to poor countries in order to reduce poverty and extreme inequalities in global living conditions. Unlike the IBRD and IFC, IDA does not raise money to finance its activities on secondary capital markets or generate income from lending. Rather, it solicits contributions from its wealthier member states through periodic replenishment rounds. These rounds are significant not only because IDA lending has increased as a percentage of the World Bank total, but because they involve a series of discussions of the allocation criteria that will be used by the Bank in its lending procedures for the three years ahead. Thus, when IDA was established, the official representatives of states and interest groups gained their most important vehicle through which to press for policy changes in IDA itself, in the World Bank Group, and ultimately in the broader system of postwar institutions of multilateral development finance because periodic replenishment monies must be appropriated on a well-established schedule.

The Multilateral Investment Guarantee Agency (MIGA), established in 1988, and the International Center for the Settlement of Investment Disputes (ICSID), established in 1966, are also affiliated with the World Bank "umbrella" but do not approach Congress for appropriations. The World Bank covers the administrative expenses of the ICSID together with income from fees and the sale of publications. MIGA is financially self-sustaining.

26. Allen Schick, *Congress and Money: Budgeting, Spending and Taxing* (Washington, DC: The Urban Institute, 1980), 6.

27. Appropriations bills can be general, continuing, or supplemental. A continuing appropriation is passed when the fiscal year begins without a regular appropriations bill having been passed. It holds spending at rates based on previous years. A supplemental appropriation is passed after the regular appropriation for "unanticipated" expenses; however, the use of supplemental appropriations in funding the war in Iraq has called the practice into question.

28. In 1994, such a meeting took place in a congressional hearing room during discussions for the inspection panel. See U.S. Congress, House of Representatives, Subcommittee on International Development, Finance, Trade, and Monetary Policy, *Oversight of the International Monetary Fund and the World Bank: A Meeting of a Multinational Group of Parliamentarians Involved in Oversight of the IMF and the World Bank*, 103rd Cong., 2nd sess., November 21, 1994.

29. Lewis G. Irwin, "Dancing the Foreign Aid Appropriations Dance: Recurring Themes in the Modern Congresses," *Public Budgeting & Finance,* Summer (2000). See also Joseph White, "Making Connections to the Appropriations Process," in *The Interest Group Connection: Electioneering, Lobbying, and Policymaking in Washington*, ed. Paul S. Herrnson, Ronald G. Shaiko, and Clyde Wilcox (Washington, DC: CQ Press, 2005).

30. White, "Making Connections to the Appropriations Process," 165.

31. Diana Evans, "Appropriations in the Republican Era," *Extensions: A Journal of the Carl Albert Congressional Research and Studies Center,* Spring (2007).

32. Executive Office of the President, "The Budget for Fiscal Year 2009," ed. OMB (US Government Printing Office, 2008), 850.

33. See 22. Foreign Relations and Intercourse, U.S. Code, Chapter 7, "International Bureaus, Congresses, etc.," secs. 262r-4(b).

34. Confusion over committee jurisdiction in the Senate was created with the passage of the Bretton Woods Act that technically gave it to the Senate Foreign Relations Committee. However, the Banking Committee handled IFI matters in the Senate as in the House. When Democrats regained control of the Senate in 1955, J. William Fulbright became chair of the Banking Committee and took a particular interest in them. When he resigned his chair in 1959 to assume the chair of the Foreign Relations Committee, jurisdiction was quietly transferred back. No members objected, because foreign lending had been considered Fulbright's domain. See John Bibby and Roger Davidson, *On Capitol Hill: Studies in the Legislative Process* (New York: Holt, Rinehart and Winston, Inc., 1967), 178.

35. Schick, *Congress and Money: Budgeting, Spending and Taxing*, 7.

36. David R. Mayhew, *Divided We Govern: Party Control, Lawmaking and Investigations, 1946–2002* (New Haven, CT: Yale University Press, 2005), 131–132.

37. Lisa L. Martin, *Democratic Commitments: Legislatures and International Cooperation* (Princeton, NJ: Princeton University Press, 2000).

38. Glen S. Krutz and Jeffrey S. Peake, *Treaty Politics and the Rise of Executive Agreements* (Ann Arbor, MI: University of Michigan Press, 2009).

39. The procedure is called a discharge petition. If the chair of a committee, generally in the House of Representatives, refuses to put an item onto the committee's agenda, a discharge petition removes it from further consideration in that committee and brings the bill or resolution directly to the floor. A successful petition requires the signatures of an absolute majority of the House.

40. Harrison W. Fox, Jr., and Susan Webb Hammond, *Congressional Staffs: The Invisible Force in American Lawmaking* (New York: The Free Press, 1977), 4.

41. Michael J. Malbin, *Unelected Representatives: Congressional Staff and the Future of Representative Government* (New York: Basic Books, 1979).

42. Frank Klingberg, *Postive Expectations of America's World Role* (Lanham, MD: University Press of America, 1996); Hastedt, *American Foreign Policy: Past, Present, Future*. Other authors argue for a more nuanced view. See Walter Russell Mead, *Special Providence: American Foreign Policy and How It Changed the World* (New York: Alfred A. Knopf, 2001).

43. Marie T. Henehan, *Foreign Policy and Congress: An International Relations Perspective* (Ann Arbor, MI: University of Michigan Press, 2000). For a more nuanced historical view, yet one that avoids a discussion of the IMF and World Bank, see Robert David Johnson, *Congress and the Cold War* (New York: Cambridge University Press, 2006).

44. Susan Strange, "The Persistent Myth of Lost Hegemony," *International Organization* 41, no. 4 (1987): 553.

45. Lee, *Beyond Ideology: Politics, Principles, and Partisanship in the U.S. Senate*, 65.

46. I. M. Destler, *American Trade Politics*, 3rd ed. (Washington, DC: Institute for International Economics, 1995); Helen V. Milner and B. Peter Rosendorff, "Trade Negotiations, Information and Domestic Politics: The Role of Domestic Groups," *Economics and Politics* 8, no. 2 (1996); Helen V. Milner, *Resisting Protectionism: Global Industries and the Politics of International Trade* (Princeton, NJ: Princeton University Press, 1988).

47. David R. Mayhew, *Parties and Policies: How the American Government Works* (New Haven: Yale University Press, 2008), 4.

48. R. Douglas Arnold, *The Logic of Congressional Action* (New Haven, CT: Yale University Press, 1990).

49. David Epstein and Sharyn O'Halloran, "A Theory of Strategic Oversight: Congress, Lobbyists, and the Bureaucracy," *Jounal of Law, Economics, & Organization* 11, no. 2 (1995): 232. Epstein and O'Halloran relate other models addressing the question of third-party signaling.

50. Ibid., 248.

51. J. Lawrence Broz and Michael Brewster Hawes, "Congressional Politics of Financing the International Monetary Fund," *International Organization* 60, no. 2 (2006).

52. J. Lawrence Broz, "Congressional Voting on Funding the International Financial Institutions," *Review of International Organizations* 3, no. 4 (2008).

53. Ibid., 358.

54. Eric Redman, *The Dance of Legislation: An Insider's Account of the Working of the United States Senate* (Seattle, WA: University of Washington Press, 2001).

55. R. Douglas Arnold, *Congress, the Press, and Political Accountability* (New York: Russell Sage Foundation, 2004), 92.

56. Richard L. Hall, *Participation in Congress* (New Haven: Yale University Press, 1996).

57. Arnold, *Congress, the Press, and Political Accountability*, 92.

58. Theodore J. Lowi, *The End of Liberalism: The Second Republic of the United States* (New York: W. W. Norton, 1969).

59. "Hyperpluralism" refers to the current state of excessive representation in which groups protect their interests tenaciously and effectively, making policy making highly responsive to individual interests and less so to broad societal challenges. Allan J. Cigler and Burdett A. Loomis, "Always Involved, Rarely Central: Organized Interests in American Politics," in *Interest Group Politics*, ed. Allan J. Cigler and Burdett A. Loomis (Washington, DC: CQ Press, 2002), 381.

60. Jeffrey M. Berry, "Subgovernments, Issue Networks, and Political Conflict," in *Remaking American Politics*, ed. Richard Harris and Sidney Milkis (Boulder, CO: Westview Press, 1989).

61. The author is indebted to David Klaus for this insight.

62. John J. Mearsheimer, "The False Promise of International Institutions," *International Security* 19, no. 3 (1994).

63. Michael N. Barnett and Martha Finnemore, *Rules for the World: International Organizations in Global Politics* (Ithaca, NY: Cornell University Press, 2004), 43.

64. Ibid.

65. Daniel L. Nielson and Michael J. Tierney, "Delegation to International Organizations: Agency Theory and World Bank Environmental Reform," *International Organization* 57 (2003): 242.

66. Jeffrey M. Chwieroth, "Normative Change from Within: The International Monetary Fund's Approach to Capital Account Liberalization," *International Studies Quarterly* 52, no. 1 (2008).

67. For a similar discussion of the limits of the constructivist understanding with respect to the structural or material aspects of globalization, see Philip G. Cerny, *Rethinking World Politics: A Theory of Transnational Neopluralism* (New York: Oxford University Press, 2010), 88.

68. Sarah Babb, *Behind the Development Banks: Washington Politics, World Poverty, and the Wealth of Nations* (Chicago: University of Chicago Press, 2009), xii.

69. Catherine Weaver, *Hypocrisy Trap: The World Bank and the Poverty of Reform* (Princeton, NJ: Princeton University Press, 2008).

70. Erica R. Gould, "Money Talks: Supplementary Financiers and International Monetary Fund Conditionality," *International Organization* 57, no. 3 (2003); Erica R. Gould, *Money Talks: The International Monetary Fund, Conditionality and Supplementary Financiers* (Stanford: Stanford University Press, 2006); Erica R. Gould, "Delegating IMF Conditionality: Understanding Variations in Control and Conformity," in *Delegation and Agency in International Organizations*, ed. Darren G. Hawkins, et al. (New York: Cambridge University Press, 2006).

71. Ngaire Woods, *The Globalizers: The IMF, World Bank, and Their Borrowers* (Ithaca, NY: Cornell University Press, 2006).

72. See Sebastian Mallaby, *The World's Banker: A Story of Failed States, Financial Crises, and the Wealth and Poverty of Nations* (New York: Penguin Press, 2004); Paul Blustein, *The Chastening: Inside the Crisis That Rocked the Global Financial System and Humbled the IMF* (New York: Public Affairs, 2002).

73. Bauer, Pool, and Dexter, *American Business and Public Policy: The Politics of Foreign Trade*, xi.

74. Lester W. Milbrath, *The Washington Lobbyists* (Chicago: Rand McNally, 1963).

75. Richard L. Hall and Alan V. Deardorff, "Lobbying as Legislative Subsidy," *American Political Science Review* 100, no. 1 (2006). See also Marie Hojnacki and David C. Kimball, "The Who and How of Organizations' Lobbying Strategies in Committee," *Journal of Politics* 61, no. 4 (1999).

76. Robert D. Putnam, "Diplomacy and Domestic Politics: The Logic of Two-Level Games," *International Organization* 42, no. 3 (1988); Joseph M. Grieco, *Cooperation Among Nations: Europe, America, and Non-Tariff Barriers to Trade* (Ithaca, NY: Cornell University Press, 1990); Joseph M. Grieco, "Anarchy and the Limits of Cooperation: A Realist Critique of the Newest Liberal Institutionalism," *International Organization* 42, Summer (1988); H. Richard Friman, "Side-Payments Versus Security Cards: Domestic Bargaining Tactics in International Economic Negotiations," *International Organization* 47, no. 3 (1993).

77. See Ruth W. Grant and Robert O. Keohane, "Accountability and Abuses of Power in World Politics," *American Political Science Review* 99, no. 1 (2005).

## Chapter 2

1. U.S. Congress, House of Representatives, Banking and Currency, *H. R. 2211 A Bill to Provide for the Participation of the United States in the International Monetary Fund*

*and the International Bank for Reconstruction and Development*, 79th Cong., 1st sess., March 7, 8, 9, 12, 13, 14, 15, 16, 19, 20, 21, 22, and 23, 1945, 165.

2. John Gerard Ruggie, "Multilateralism: The Anatomy of an Institution," in *Multilateralism Matters: The Theory and Praxis of an Institutional Form*, ed. John Gerard Ruggie (New York: Columbia University Press, 1993), 14.

3. Richard N. Gardner, *Sterling-Dollar Diplomacy in Current Perspective: The Origins and the Prospects of Our International Economic Order* (New York: Columbia University Press, 1980), 134.

4. Thomas W. Lamont, *Across World Frontiers* (New York: Harcourt Brace, 1951), 192.

5. Arthur Sweetser to Eric Drummond, March 21, 1920. Folder "US Willing to Join League 1920," Box 13, Papers of Arthur Sweetser, Manuscript Division, Library of Congress, Washington, DC.

6. Denna Frank Fleming, *The United States and the League of Nations: 1918–1920* (New York: G. P. Putnam's Sons, 1932), 54.

7. Ibid., 57.

8. Ibid., 111.

9. Ibid., 476.

10. Daniel D. Stid, *The President as Statesman: Woodrow Wilson and the Constitution* (Lawrence, Kansas: University Press of Kansas, 1998), 158.

11. Ibid., 157.

12. Ibid., 155.

13. Frances E. Lee, *Beyond Ideology: Politics, Principles, and Partisanship in the U.S. Senate* (Chicago: University of Chicago Press, 2009), 191.

14. Fleming, *The US and the League of Nations*, 43.

15. Arthur Sweetser to Eric Drummond, March 21, 1920. Folder "US Willing to Join League 1920," Box 13, Papers of Arthur Sweetser, Manuscript Division, Library of Congress, Washington, DC.

16. John J. Raskob to Senator Heisler Ball, October 4, 1919. Papers of John J. Raskob, Accession #473 Files 1324–1355. "Liberty Loan Committee" NAM Folder: NAM Accession 1411, Series I 100-LL. Box 105, Hagley Museum and Library, Hagley, DE.

17. Fleming, *The US and the League of Nations*, 398.

18. Bernard Baruch, *Baruch: The Public Years* (New York: Holt, Rinehart and Winston, 1960), 124.

19. See Raymond B. Fosdick, *Letters on the League of Nations from the Files of Raymond B. Fosdick* (Princeton, NJ: Princeton University Press, 1966), vii and 118. See also Robert Skidelsky, *John Maynard Keynes: The Economist as Saviour 1920–1937*, 3 vols., vol. 2 (New York: The Penguin Press, 1986); Robert Skidelsky, *John Maynard Keynes: Fighting for Freedom 1937–1946*, 3 vols., vol. 3 (New York: Viking, 2000).

20. Gary B. Ostrower, "The United States and the League of Nations, 1919–1939," in *The League of Nations in Retrospect*, ed. United Nations Library (New York: Walter de Gruyter, 1983), 130.

21. Ibid., 134.

22. Louis W. Pauly, *The League of Nations and the Foreshadowing of the International Monetary Fund*, vol. 201 (Princeton, NJ: Princeton University Essays in International Finance, 1996). n. 11.

23. Kathryn C. Lavelle, "Exit, Voice, and Loyalty in International Organizations: US Involvement in the League of Nations," *Review of International Organizations* 2 (2007).

24. Ibid.

25. Charline Pelly to Senator Taft, "Memorandum," April 23, 1945. Folder "Bretton Woods Agreement 1945," Box 497. The Papers of Robert A. Taft, Sr., Manuscript Division, Library of Congress, Washington, DC.

26. Townsend Hoopes and Douglas Brinkley, *FDR and the Creation of the UN* (New Haven: Yale University Press, 1997).

27. This history is covered in several historical and theoretical accounts. See Eric Helleiner, *States and the Reemergence of Global Finance: From Bretton Woods to the 1990s* (Ithaca, NY: Cornell University Press, 1994); Jacqueline Best, *The Limits of Transparency: Ambiguity and the History of International Finance* (Ithaca, NY: Cornell University Press, 2005); Skidelsky, *Fighting for Freedom*, 3.

28. Gardner, *Sterling-Dollar Diplomacy*, 95.

29. Memoranda, "Treasury Meeting," October 2, 1943. File #343, Box 36, Bretton Woods Conference Files, Bretton Woods Collection, IMF Archives, Washington, DC.

30. Minutes of the 34th Annual Meeting, April 30, 1946, p. 11. Chamber of Commerce of the U.S. Box 2, Accession 1960 Series 4, U.S. Chamber of Commerce. Hagley Museum and Library, Hagley, DE.

31. "Final Memorandum to the Economists' Committee on the Bretton Woods Program," July 20, 1945, page 1. Folder: Bretton Woods Agreements: Documents 2 of 3, Box 131, NFTC Accession 2345, Hagley Museum and Library, Hagley, DE.

32. Gardner, *Sterling-Dollar Diplomacy*, 129.

33. Eric Helleiner, "Reinterpreting Bretton Woods: International Development and the Neglected Origins of Embedded Liberalism," *Development and Change* 37, no. 5 (2006).

34. Jacques Fomerand, "Mirror, Tool, or Linchpin for Change: The UN and Development" (Waterloo, Ontario: The Academic Council on the United Nations System, 2003).

35. Kevin M. Casey, *Saving International Capitalism During the Early Truman Presidency: The National Advisory Council on International Monetary and Financial Problems* (New York: Routledge, 2001), 43.

36. Arthur Sweetser, "Memorandum," July 19, 1944. Folder "UN Monetary and Financial Conference," Box 38, Papers of Arthur Sweetser, Manuscript Division, Library of Congress, Washington, DC. See also Edward H. Collins, "A Lynching Party That Failed," January 4, 1954. *The New York Times,* p. 35. Leon Fraser had been vice president of the BIS at one time. He began by working with General Dawes on the reparation question in its functions to receive payments from Germany on its reparation account, and distribute them. At the time of the Bretton Woods hearings, he was president of the First National Bank of New York.

37. "Memorandum. Re: Conversations with Treasury Department Representatives in connection with Bretton Woods Plan for an International Monetary Fund and International Bank," September 1, 1944, page 2. Folder: International Finance Committee—Bretton Woods Agreements-Conferences, #13, Box 130, NFTC Accession 2345, Hagley Museum and Library, Hagley, DE.

38. "Memorandum. Re: Conversations with Treasury Department Representatives in connection with Bretton Woods Plan for an International Monetary Fund and International Bank," September 1, 1944, page 2. Folder: International Finance Committee—Bretton Woods Agreements-Conferences, #13, Box 130, NFTC Accession 2345, Hagley Museum and Library, Hagley, DE.

39. "Memorandum. Re: Conversations with Treasury Department Representatives in connection with Bretton Woods Plan for an International Monetary Fund and International Bank," September 1, 1944, page 1. Folder: International Finance Committee—

Bretton Woods Agreements-Conferences, #13, Box 130, NFTC Accession 2345, Hagley Museum and Library, Hagley, DE.

40. "Memorandum. Re: Conversations with Treasury Department Representatives in connection with Bretton Woods Plan for an International Monetary Fund and International Bank," September 1, 1944, page 1. Folder: International Finance Committee—Bretton Woods Agreements-Conferences, #13, Box 130, NFTC Accession 2345, Hagley Museum and Library, Hagley, DE.

41. "Memorandum. Re: Conversations with Treasury Department Representatives in connection with Bretton Woods Plan for an International Monetary Fund and International Bank," September 1, 1944, page 2. Folder: International Finance Committee—Bretton Woods Agreements-Conferences, #13, Box 130, NFTC Accession 2345, Hagley Museum and Library, Hagley, DE.

42. "Memorandum. Re: Conversations with Treasury Department Representatives in connection with Bretton Woods Plan for an International Monetary Fund and International Bank," September 1, 1944, page 2. Folder: International Finance Committee—Bretton Woods Agreements-Conferences, #13, Box 130, NFTC Accession 2345, Hagley Museum and Library, Hagley, DE.

43. "Memorandum. Re: Conversations with Treasury Department Representatives in connection with Bretton Woods Plan for an International Monetary Fund and International Bank," September 1, 1944, page 2. Folder: International Finance Committee—Bretton Woods Agreements-Conferences, #13, Box 130, NFTC Accession 2345, Hagley Museum and Library, Hagley, DE.

44. A. E. Mallon to C. E. Hunter, December 19, 1944, page 3. Folder: International Finance Committee—Bretton Woods Agreements-Correspondence 1944–1945, #14, Box 130, NFTC Accession 2345, Hagley Museum and Library, Hagley, DE.

45. Mr. C. E. Hunter to Mr. A. E. Mallon, December 21, 1944. Folder: International Finance Committee—Bretton Woods Agreements-Correspondence 1944–1945, #14, Box 130, NFTC Accession 2345, Hagley Museum and Library, Hagley, DE.

46. H. Salinger to C. E. Hunter, January 19, 1945. "Re: Bretton Woods Proposals," Folder: International Finance Committee—Bretton Woods Agreements-Correspondence 1944–1945, #14, Box 130, NFTC Accession 2345, Hagley Museum and Library, Hagley, DE.

47. "Report of the International Finance Committee on the Bretton Woods Agreement to the Board of Directors of the National Foreign Trade Council, Inc.," February 23, 1945. Folder: International Finance Committee—Bretton Woods Agreements-Conferences, #13, Box 130, NFTC Accession 2345, Hagley Museum and Library, Hagley, DE.

48. "Report of the International Finance Committee on the Bretton Woods Agreement to the Board of Directors of the National Foreign Trade Council, Inc.," February 23, 1945. Folder: International Finance Committee—Bretton Woods Agreements-Conferences, #13, Box 130, NFTC Accession 2345, Hagley Museum and Library, Hagley, DE.

49. "Recommendation of the International Finance Committee to the Directors of the National Foreign Trade Council," January 26, 1945 (draft), page 1. Folder: International Finance Committee—Bretton Woods Agreements-Conferences, #13, Box 130, NFTC Accession 2345, Hagley Museum and Library, Hagley, DE.

50. "Recommendation of the International Finance Committee to the Directors of the National Foreign Trade Council," January 26, 1945 (draft), page 2. Folder: International

Finance Committee—Bretton Woods Agreements-Conferences, #13, Box 130, NFTC Accession 2345, Hagley Museum and Library, Hagley, DE.

51. *H. R. 2211 A Bill to Provide for the Participation of the United States in the International Monetary Fund and the International Bank for Reconstruction and Development*, 445.

52. "Draft of Report of the Committee on Special Activities of the ABA and the Special Committee of the Association of Reserve City Bankers on the Bretton Woods proposals," page 16. Folder: International Finance Committee—Bretton Woods Agreements-Conferences, #13, Box 130, NFTC Accession 2345, Hagley Museum and Library, Hagley, DE.

53. "Draft of Report of the Committee on Special Activities of the ABA and the Special Committee of the Association of Reserve City Bankers on the Bretton Woods proposals," page 1. Folder: International Finance Committee—Bretton Woods Agreements-Conferences, #13, Box 130, NFTC Accession 2345, Hagley Museum and Library, Hagley, DE.

54. Thomas L. Stokes, "Banks and Peace," March 9, 1945, *New York World-Telegram*.

55. Randall Bennett Woods, *A Changing of the Guard: Anglo-American Relations 1941–1946* (Chapel Hill: University of North Carolina Press, 1990), 231.

56. *H. R. 2211 A Bill to Provide for the Participation of the United States in the International Monetary Fund and the International Bank for Reconstruction and Development*, 9.

57. Ibid., 166.

58. Casey, *Saving International Capitalism*, 43.

59. Ernest M. Hopkins to NFTC, February 17, 1945. Folder: International Finance Committee—Bretton Woods Agreements-Correspondence 1945—, #15, Box 130, NFTC Accession 2345, Hagley Museum and Library, Hagley, DE.

60. Charline Pelly to Senator Taft, "Memorandum," April 23, 1945, p.7. Folder "Bretton Woods Agreement 1945," Box 497. The Papers of Robert A. Taft, Sr., Manuscript Division, Library of Congress, Washington, DC.

61. "Speeches for Congressmen," Richard B. Brenner Series, Bretton Woods Collection. Box 6, File #66, IMF Archives, Washington, DC.

62. Charline Pelly to Senator Taft, "Memorandum," April 23, 1945, p. 3. Folder "Bretton Woods Agreement 1945," Box 497. The Papers of Robert A. Taft, Sr., Manuscript Division, Library of Congress, Washington, DC.

63. *H. R. 2211 A Bill to Provide for the Participation of the United States in the International Monetary Fund and the International Bank for Reconstruction and Development*, 723.

64. Charline Pelly to Senator Taft, "Memorandum," April 23, 1945, p. 8. Folder "Bretton Woods Agreement 1945," Box 497. The Papers of Robert A. Taft, Sr., Manuscript Division, Library of Congress, Washington, DC.

65. *H. R. 2211 A Bill to Provide for the Participation of the United States in the International Monetary Fund and the International Bank for Reconstruction and Development*, 679.

66. Ibid., 1015; Ibid., 1183. Carey also testified in the Senate; see U.S. Congress, Senate, Banking and Currency, *H. R. 3314 An Act to Provide for the Participation of the United States in the International Monetary Fund and the International Bank for Reconstruction and Development*, 79th Cong., 1st sess., June 12, 13, 14, 15, 16, 18, 19, 20, 21, 22, 25, and 28, 1945, 604.

67. *H. R. 2211 A Bill to Provide for the Participation of the United States in the International Monetary Fund and the International Bank for Reconstruction and Development*, 784; Ibid., 1036.

68. Ibid., 647.

69. Ibid., 650.

70. John Quirk to Carlos Donayre, March 28, 1945. Folder: International Finance Committee—Bretton Woods Agreements-Correspondence 1945—, #15, Box 130, NFTC Accession 2345, Hagley Museum and Library, Hagley, DE.

71. John J. O'Connor to Finance Department Committee, March 6, 1945. Folder: Bretton Woods Agreements: Documents 2 of 3, Box 131, NFTC Accession 2345, Hagley Museum and Library, Hagley, DE.

72. "Draft of Report of Finance Department Committee on the Bretton Woods Program," March 6, 1945, p. 4, Folder: Bretton Woods Agreements: Documents 2 of 3, Box 131, NFTC Accession 2345, Hagley Museum and Library, Hagley, DE.

73. Memorandum to Secretary Morgenthau and Mr. Luxford, April 5, 1945, Richard B. Brenner Series, Bretton Woods Collection, Box 5, File #47, IMF Archives, Washington, DC.

74. Casey, *Saving International Capitalism*, 49.

75. "Statement of Robert A. Taft on the Plan for an IMF," July 12, 1944. Folder "Bretton Woods Agreement 1944," Box 496. The Papers of Robert A. Taft, Sr., Manuscript Division, Library of Congress, Washington DC.

76. *H. R. 3314 An Act to Provide for the Participation of the United States in the International Monetary Fund and the International Bank for Reconstruction and Development*, 35–36.

77. For an early example, see Raymond A. Bauer, Ithiel De Sola Pool, and Lewis Anthony Dexter, *American Business and Public Policy: The Politics of Foreign Trade*, 2nd ed. (Chicago: Aldine, Atherton, 1972).

78. W. Randolph Burgess to Jesse P. Wolcott, June 4, 1945. Folder: "Bretton Woods Agreement 1945," Box 497. The Papers of Robert A. Taft, Sr., Manuscript Division, Library of Congress, Washington, DC.

79. Memoranda, "Senator Taft's Criticisms," July 18, 1944, Bretton Woods Collection, Bretton Woods Conference Files, Box 31, File 291, IMF Archives, Washington, DC.

80. "Recommendations of the American Bankers Association for Safeguarding the Monetary Fund," June 25, 1945. Folder "Bretton Woods Agreement 1945," Box 497. The Papers of Robert A. Taft, Sr., Manuscript Division, Library of Congress, Washington, DC.

81. *H. R. 3314 An Act to Provide for the Participation of the United States in the International Monetary Fund and the International Bank for Reconstruction and Development*, 483.

82. Ibid., 472.

83. "Statement by W. Randolph Burgess," July 6, 1945. Folder "Bretton Woods Agreement 1945," Box 497. The Papers of Robert A. Taft, Sr., Manuscript Division, Library of Congress, Washington, DC.

84. "Statement by W. Randolph Burgess," July 6, 1945. Folder "Bretton Woods Agreement 1945," Box 497. The Papers of Robert A. Taft, Sr., Manuscript Division, Library of Congress, Washington, DC.

85. Gardner, *Sterling-Dollar Diplomacy*, 134.

86. H. Richard Friman, "Side-Payments Versus Security Cards: Domestic Bargaining Tactics in International Economic Negotiations," *International Organization* 47, no. 3 (1993).

87. Gardner, *Sterling-Dollar Diplomacy*, 143.

## Chapter 3

1. Remarks made extemporaneously by Mr. Randolph Burgess at the National Foreign Trade Council Convention in November 1953. File 176, Box #12, Ivar Rooth Sous-Fonds, Office of the Managing Director Fonds, IMF Archives, Washington, DC.

2. Barbara Sinclair, *Unorthodox Lawmaking: New Legislative Processes in the US Congress* (Washington, DC: Congressional Quarterly Press, 1997), 20.

3. Kevin M. Casey, *Saving International Capitalism During the Early Truman Presidency: The National Advisory Council on International Monetary and Financial Problems* (New York: Routledge, 2001), 225.

4. Bruce Muirhead, *Against the Odds: The Public Life and Times of Louis Rasminsky* (Toronto: University of Toronto Press, 1999), 110.

5. Ibid., 111.

6. Sidney Dell uses the term "grandmotherly" to describe the desired characteristic of the IMF. See Sidney Dell, *On Being Grandmotherly: The Evolution of IMF Conditionality*, vol. 144 (Princeton, NJ: Essays in International Finance, Department of Economics, Princeton University, 1981).

7. Richard N. Gardner, *Sterling-Dollar Diplomacy in Current Perspective: The Origins and the Prospects of Our International Economic Order* (New York: Columbia University Press, 1980), 258–259.

8. Raymond Frech Mikesell, *The Bretton Woods Debates: A Memoir*, vol. 192 (Princeton, NJ: Princeton Essays in International Finance, 1994), 52.

9. Casey, *Saving International Capitalism*, 211–223.

10. Per Jacobsson, "Trade and Financial Relationships Between Countries: The Progress Towards Multilateralism," in *Some Monetary Problems International and National*, ed. Per Jacobsson (New York: Oxford University Press, 1958), 286.

11. Dell, *On Being Grandmotherly: The Evolution of IMF Conditionality*, 144, 10.

12. Louis W. Pauly, *Who Elected the Bankers? Surveillance and Control in the World Economy* (Ithaca, NY: Cornell University Press, 1997), 112; Ibid.

13. R. H. D. "Memorandum for the Files," August 20, 1946. Folder "International Bank Staff Memoranda, Etc. 1946," Box 128, The Papers of Eugene Meyer, Manuscript Division, Library of Congress, Washington, DC.

14. Eugene Meyer to Russell Leffingwell, December 30, 1946. Folder "International Bank, Resignation," Box 128, The Papers of Eugene Meyer, Manuscript Division, Library of Congress, Washington, DC.

15. Edward S. Mason and Robert E. Asher, *The World Bank Since Bretton Woods* (Washington, DC: The Brookings Institution, 1973), 129.

16. "Hurdle for World Bank's Bonds," *Finance Week,* December 13, 1946. Folder "International Bank, Resignation," Box 128, The Papers of Eugene Meyer, Manuscript Division, Library of Congress, Washington, DC.

17. Jacques J. Polak, *The World Bank and the International Monetary Fund: A Changing Relationship* (Washington, DC: The Brookings Institution Occasional Papers, 1994), 2.

18. Miles Kahler, "The United States and the International Monetary Fund: Declining Influence or Declining Interest?," in *The United States and Multilateral Institutions: Patterns of Changing Instrumentality and Influence*, ed. Margaret P. Karnes and Karen A. Mingst (Boston: Unwin Hyman, 1990), 94.

19. Kai Bird, *The Chairman: John J. McCloy* (New York: Simon & Schuster, 1992), 286.

20. Ibid., 289.

21. Robert E. Asher, Walter M. Kotschnig, and William Adams Jr. Brown, *The United Nations and Economic and Social Co-Operation* (Washington, DC: Brookings Institution, 1957), 165.

22. Mason and Asher, *The World Bank Since Bretton Woods*, 130.

23. McCloy lived in a house owned by Nelson Rockefeller with Garner and Black in 1947.

24. A graduate of Yale, Leffingwell received a law degree from Columbia University. He was assistant secretary of the treasury from 1917 to 1920, when he resumed his law practice in New York. He became a partner of J. P. Morgan in 1923. He also served as chairman of the Carnegie Corporation of New York. See Abraham Flexner, *Funds and Foundations: The Policies Past and Present* (New York: Harper & Brothers Publishers, 1952), 119.

25. Ron Chernow, *The House of Morgan: An American Banking Dynasty and the Rise of Modern Finance* (New York: Atlantic Monthly Press, 1990), 487.

26. Ibid., 518.

27. Mason and Asher, *The World Bank Since Bretton Woods*, 132.

28. "World Bank to Raise $50,000,000 Here in Negotiated Underwriting," *New York Times,* April 29, 1952.

29. Morgan Stanley & Co., *A Summary of Financing: 1935–1953* (New York: Morgan Stanley & Co., 1954), 17.

30. "World Bank and Wall Street Join in $50,000,000 Loan to Belgium," *New York Times,* December 15, 1954.

31. Mason and Asher, *The World Bank Since Bretton Woods*, 342.

32. Ibid., 134.

33. Sir Arthur Salter, *Foreign Investment*, vol. 12 (Princeton, NJ: Princeton Essays in International Finance), 54.

34. David Rogers, *The Future of American Banking* (New York: McGraw-Hill, Inc., 1993), 85.

35. David Rockefeller, *Memoirs* (New York: Random House, 2002), 134.

36. Harold van B. Cleveland and Thomas F. Huertas, *Citibank: 1812–1970* (Cambridge, MA: Harvard University Press, 1985), 266.

37. Ibid., 268.

38. Ibid.

39. Ibid., 264.

40. Rogers, *The Future of American Banking*, 148.

41. John Donald Wilson, *The Chase: The Chase Manhattan Bank, N.A., 1945–1985* (Boston, MA: Harvard Business School Press, 1986), 325.

42. Rogers, *The Future of American Banking*, 81. Well into the late 1970s, Chase was known as "the bank of the Rockefellers" or "David's bank" after David assumed the head in 1960. An uncle of the Rockefeller's, Winthrop Aldrich, had been the chief executive officer of Chase. Identified with Rockefeller family interests, it serviced blue-chip corporations, financial institutions, governments, and highly affluent individuals. At the same time, the bank reflected the family's longtime commitment to public service.

43. Lars Schoultz, "Politics, Economics, and US Participation in Multilateral Development Banks," *International Organization* 36, no. 3 (1982): 540.

44. William S. Swingle to Hon. J. W. Fulbright, March 6, 1959, page 2. Folder: International Monetary Fund 1959–1962. Box 167, Accession 2345 National Foreign Trade Council, Hagley Museum and Library, Hagley, DE.

45. "New IMF Arrangements for Obtaining Supplementary Resources," January 11, 1962. Folder: IFC Committee Releases, 1962–3. Box 132, Accession 2345 National Foreign Trade Council, Hagley Museum and Library, Hagley, DE.

46. Donald F. Heatherington to National Foreign Trade Council, January 15, 1962. Folder: IFC Committee Releases, 1962–3. Box 132, Accession 2345 National Foreign Trade Council, Hagley Museum and Library, Hagley, DE.

47. EBM 5855, Minutes of Executive Board Meeting, 12/12/58, page 6. IMF Archives, Washington, DC.

48. Henry Jr. Morgenthau, "Bretton Woods and International Cooperation," *Foreign Affairs* 23, no. 2 (1945): 192.

49. W. Randolph Burgess to Robert Taft, Sr., December 27, 1946. Folder "Bretton Woods Agreement 1945," Box 497. The Papers of Robert A. Taft, Sr., Manuscript Division, Library of Congress, Washington, DC.

50. Erin E. Jacobsson, *A Life for Sound Money: Per Jacobsson: His Biography* (Oxford: Clarendon Press, 1979), 190.

51. See "Robert Triffin to Mr. Gutt," Report #2 from Basel, March 9, 1948. File 5, Box 150, Central Files Collection, I300, Bank for International Settlements, IMF Archives, Washington, DC.

52. Notes by Rooth for talks with Treasury, File 190, Box 12, Ivar Rooth Sous-Fonds, Office of the Managing Director Fonds, IMF Archives, Washington, DC.

53. Excerpt from a speech made by W. Randolph Burgess, Deputy to the Secretary of the Treasury, at the National Foreign Trade Council meeting on November 16, 1953, in New York, File 176, Box 12, Ivar Rooth Sous-Fonds, Office of the Managing Director Fonds, IMF Archives, Washington, DC.

54. Jacobsson, *A Life for Sound Money: Per Jacobsson: His Biography*, 279.

55. Ibid., 322.

56. "Per Jacobsson: World Currency Cop," *Time* magazine, September 28, 1959, accessed 10/30/2008 at http:///www.time.com/time/printout/0,8816,811323,00.html.

57. U.S. Congress, House of Representatives, Committee on Banking and Currency, *Bretton Woods Agreement Act Amendment*, 87th Cong., 2nd sess., February 27 and 28, 1962.

58. Margaret Garritsen de Vries, *The IMF 1972–1978 Cooperation on Trial*, vol. I: Narrative and Analysis (Washington, DC: IMF, 1985), 588.

59. Margaret Garritsen de Vries, *The IMF in a Changing World: 1945–85* (Washington, DC: The IMF, 1986), 90.

60. U.S. Congress, House of Representatives, Banking and Currency, *US Quota Increase in the IMF*, 89th Cong., 1st sess., March 23 and 24, 1965, 124.

61. John Toye and Richard Toye, *The UN and Global Political Economy* (Indianapolis: Indiana University Press, 2004), 36–37.

62. D. John Shaw, "Turning Point in the Evolution of Soft Financing: The United Nations and the World Bank," *Canadian Journal of Development Studies* 26, no. 1 (2005): 44.

63. Ibid., 48.

64. "UN 100-LL 1959," NAM Folder, Box 105, NAM Accession 1411, Series I 100-LL. Hagley Museum and Library, Hagley, Delaware.

65. For an additional discussion of the growth of the IFC, see Kathryn C. Lavelle, "The International Finance Corporation and the Emerging Markets Funds Industry," *Third World Quarterly* 21, no. 2 (2000), and Kathryn C. Lavelle, *The Politics of Equity Finance in Emerging Markets* (New York: Oxford University Press, 2004), 49–51.

66. B. E. Matecki, *Establishment of the International Finance Corporation and United States Policy* (New York: Frederick A. Praeger, 1957), 46.

67. Asher, Kotschnig, and Brown, *The United Nations and Economic and Social Co-Operation*, 216.

68. Jonas Haralz, "The International Finance Corporation," in *The World Bank: Its First Half Century*, ed. Devesh Kapur, John P. Lewis, and Richard Webb (Washington, DC: The Brookings Institution Press, 1997), 811.

69. Mr. H. H. Schell to Mr. Nelson Rockefeller, February 19, 1951, p. 3. Folder "IFC: Committee Meetings, 1951–1954," Box 131, Accession 2345, National Foreign Trade Council, Hagley Museum and Library, Hagley, DE.

70. "Report of the Meeting of International Finance Committee," April 18, 1951. Folder "IFC: Committee Meetings, 1951–1954," Box 131, Accession 2345, National Foreign Trade Council, Hagley Museum and Library, Hagley, DE.

71. Mr. Hitchens to Mr. Swingle. April 27, 1951. Folder: TPC: Studies: BS Advisory group, Rockefeller Committee. Box 162, Accession 2345, National Foreign Trade Council, Hagley Museum and Library, Hagley, DE.

72. U.S. Congress, House of Representatives, Committee on Banking and Currency, *H. R. 6228*, 84th Cong., 1st sess., July 11 and 14, 1955, 103–106.

73. "Statement Concerning S.1894," June 7, 1955. Folder "IFC: Documents 1953–1955," Box 131, Accession 2345, National Foreign Trade Council, Hagley Museum and Library, Hagley, DE.

74. D. F. Heatherington to R. F. Loree, "Comments of Mr. A. E. Schumacher re Statement on International Finance Corporation," Memo May 27, 1955. Folder: IFC Committee Correspondence 1945–1955, Box 131, National Foreign Trade Council Accession 2345, Hagley Museum and Library, Hagley, DE.

75. U.S. Congress, Senate, Subcommittee on International Finance, Committee on Banking and Currency, *S. 1894 A Bill to Provide for the Participation of the United States in the International Finance Corporation*, 84th Cong., 1st sess., June 6 and 7, 1955.

76. Haralz, "The International Finance Corporation," 819.

77. U.S. Congress, Senate, Committee on Foreign Relations, *HR 6765: An Act to Authorize Acceptance of an Amendement to the Articles of Agreement of the IFC*, 87th Cong., 1st sess., July 31, 1961; U.S. Congress, House of Representatives, Committee on Banking and Currency, *H. R. 8816 and S. 1742*, 89th Cong., 1st sess., July 8, 1965.

78. Haralz, "The International Finance Corporation," 820.

79. Ibid., 845.

80. Shaw, "Turning Point," 56.

81. Ronald T. Libby, "International Development Association: A Legal Fiction Designed to Secure an LDC Constituency," *International Organization* 29, no. 4 (1975): 1068. The International Bank for Reconstruction and Development was the initial organization established at Bretton Woods that became known as the "World Bank." Nonetheless, it is a distinct legal entity from the other parts of the World Bank Group, like IDA. The IBRD borrows money on international capital markets and lends to poor countries at market rates. It also makes contributions to IDA.

82. Shaw, "Turning Point," 57.

83. Jonathan E. Sanford, "World Bank: IDA Loans or IDA Grants?," *World Development* 30, no. 5 (2002): 744.

84. John Bibby and Roger Davidson, *On Capitol Hill: Studies in the Legislative Process* (New York: Holt, Rinehart and Winston, Inc., 1967), 174.

85. U.S. Congress, House, Committee on Banking and Currency, *International Development Association Act*, 86th Cong., 2nd sess., March 15, 16, and 17, 1960, 117; U.S. Congress, Senate, Committee on Foreign Relations, *To Provide for the Participation of the United States in the International Development Association*, 86th Cong., 2nd sess., March 18 and 21, 1960, 104.

86. U.S. Congress, Senate, Committee on Foreign Relations, *Amendments to the Inter-American Development Bank and International Development Association Acts*, 86th Cong., 1st sess., November 15 and December 4, 1963, 43; U.S. Congress, House, Committee on Banking and Currency, *International Development Association Act Amendment*, 86th Cong., 2nd sess., March 23 and 24, 101.

87. U.S. Congress, Senate, Committee on Foreign Relations, *Increased Resources for International Development Association*, 90th Cong., 2nd sess., May 21, 1968, 41; U.S. Congress, House, Committee on Banking and Currency, *To Provide for Increased Participation by the United States in the International Development Association*, 90th Cong., 2nd sess., May 8 and 9, 1968, 147.

88. "International Development Association Ref. No. M-262," September 22, 1959. Folder: IFC Committee Releases, 1958–1959, Box 132, Accession 2345 National Foreign Trade Council, Hagley Museum and Library, Hagley, DE.

89. Donald F. Heatherington to International Finance Committee, "International Development Association," December 9, 1959. Ref. M-405. Folder: IFC Committee Releases, 1958–1959, Box 132, Accession 2345 National Foreign Trade Council, Hagley Museum and Library, Hagley, DE.

90. Donald F. Heatherington to International Finance Committee, "International Development Association," February 25, 1960. Folder: IFC Committee Releases, 1960, Box 132, Accession 2345 National Foreign Trade Council, Hagley Museum and Library, Hagley, DE.

91. "Statement of the National Foreign Trade Council Concerning US Participation in the International Development Association," August 10, 1960. Folder: IFC Committee Releases, 1960, Box 132, Accession 2345 National Foreign Trade Council, Hagley Museum and Library, Hagley, DE.

92. Donald F. Heatherington to International Finance Committee, "International Development Association," August 12, 1960, Ref. M-944. Folder: IFC Committee Releases, 1960, Box 132, Accession 2345 National Foreign Trade Council, Hagley Museum and Library, Hagley, DE.

93. U.S. Congress, House, Committee on Banking, Finance, and Urban Affairs, *To Provide for Increased Participation by the U.S. in the International Development Association*, 92nd Cong., 1st sess., July 6, 1971, 131.

94. U.S. Congress, House, Committee on Banking, Finance, and Urban Affairs, *To Provide for Increased Participation by the U.S. in the International Development Association*, 93rd Cong., 2nd sess., June 11, 1974, 81.

95. Ibid., 73.

96. The need to create additional SDRs lessened when the fixed-parity system collapsed in the 1970s and governments borrowed in private capital markets. It does, however, remain the unit of account in the IMF and some international organizations. A recent proposal for additional SDR allocations to members has been included in

solutions to the 2008 financial crisis, thus returning discussions of SDRs to center stage.

97. U.S. Congress, Joint Economic Committee, *A Proposal to Link Reserve Creation*, 91st Cong., 2nd sess., August 1969.

98. The capital increases were in 1959, 1965, 1970, 1976, and 1978.

99. "Suspend the rules and pass the bill" in the House of Representatives is a motion for noncontroversial matters that must receive a two-thirds majority vote to succeed. No amendments can be offered. If the motion fails, the bill may be reconsidered apart from the suspension calendar.

100. The World Bank expenditures required an appropriation because they always involved a real transfer of resources. The amount of resource transfer associated with IMF lending was always questionable.

101. Congressional Budget Office, "US Participation in the Witteveen Facility: The Need for a New Source of International Finance" (Washington, DC: Congress of the United States, 1978), 39.

## Chapter 4

1. U.S. Congress, S. J. Res. 161, 94th Cong., 2nd sess., February 2, 1976, page 3, line 1.

2. Kent Higgon Hughes, *Trade, Taxes, and Transnationals: International Economic Decision Making in Congress* (New York: Praeger Publishers, 1979), 90.

3. Ibid., 205.

4. Margaret Garritsen de Vries, *The IMF in a Changing World: 1945–85* (Washington, DC: The IMF, 1986), 42.

5. Hughes, *Trade, Taxes, and Transnationals: International Economic Decision Making in Congress*, 82.

6. Ibid., 17.

7. Kent H. Hughes, *Building the Next American Century: The Past and Future of American Economic Competitiveness* (Washington, DC: Woodrow Wilson Center Press, 2005), 34.

8. Hughes, *Trade, Taxes, and Transnationals: International Economic Decision Making in Congress*, 90.

9. Hughes, *Building the Next American Century*, 34.

10. National Archives, Nixon Presidential Materials, NSC Files, Subject Files, Box 341, HAK/RN Memos 69/70 as reprinted in Bruce F. Duncombe, ed., *Foreign Economic Policy, 1969–1972; International Monetary Policy, 1969–1972*, vol. III, Foreign Relations of the United States, 1969–1976 (Washington, DC: US Government Printing Office, 2001), 95.

11. Katz to Rogers August 13, 1971, as reprinted in ibid., 463.

12. "Memorandum of Conversation," August 16, 1971, as reprinted in ibid., 473.

13. EBM 71129, Minutes of Executive Board Meeting, 12/21/71, p. 5, IMF Archives, Washington, DC.

14. U.S. Congress, House of Representatives, Committee on Appropriations, *Par Value Modification Appropriations*, 93rd Cong., 1st sess., September 14, 1973, 11.

15. Joanne S. Gowa, *Closing the Gold Window: Domestic Politics and the End of Bretton Woods* (Ithaca, NY: Cornell University Press, 1983), 88.

16. See U.S. Congress, S. 3160, 92th Cong., 2nd sess., February 1972.

17. "Par Value Modification Legislation," Folder 8, "Dollar Devaluation, 1972–73," Box 134, Papers of Robert Taft, Jr., Manuscript Division, Library of Congress, Washington, DC.

18. This grouping is currently known as the International Monetary and Financial Committee (IMFC). It advises, and reports to the board of governors on matters relating to the board's functions in supervising the management and adaptation of the international monetary and financial system, reviewing developments in global liquidity and the transfer of resources to developing countries; considering proposals by the executive board to amend the Articles of Agreement; and dealing with disturbances that might threaten the system.

19. Margaret Garritsen de Vries, *The IMF 1972–1978 Cooperation on Trial*, vol. I: Narrative and Analysis (Washington, DC: IMF, 1985), 647 and 661.

20. Ibid., 661.

21. Joseph Gold, "Trust Funds in International Law," in *Legal and Institutional Aspects of the International Monetary System, Selected Essays*, ed. Joseph Gold (Washington, DC: International Monetary Fund, 1984), 868.

22. Ibid., 866.

23. "IMF Gold Agreement," Folder 3, "IMF 1974–76," Box 138, Papers of Robert Taft, Jr., Manuscript Division, Library of Congress, Washington, DC.

24. Henry S. Reuss to William Simon December 24, 1975. Folder 3, "IMF 1974–76," Box 138, Papers of Robert Taft, Jr., Manuscript Division, Library of Congress, Washington, DC.

25. EBM 76131, Minutes of Executive Board Meeting, 3/3/76, page 6, IMF Archives, Washington, DC.

26. See Robert Taft, U.S. Congress, Senate, Volume 122, *Congressional Record*, 94th Cong., 2nd sess., February 2, 1976, 1.

27. See ibid., June 22 and July 27, considered and passed House; October 1 considered and passed Senate. According to press release—October 5, Congress passed 13955 containing provision by Taft to "clear with the Congress any US vote to transfer IMF assets into a trust fund for Third World nations."

28. U.S. Congress, Senate, *Congressional Record*, 93rd Cong., 2nd sess., May 20, 1974, S8517.

29. Jacob K. Javits and John Sparkman, United States Senate, to Colleagues April 30, 1974. Folder 24, "S. 2665 provide increased participation in IDA, 1974," Box 111, Papers of Robert Taft, Jr., Manuscript Division, Library of Congress, Washington, DC.

30. Donald R. Wolfensberger, *Congress and the People: Deliberative Democracy on Trial* (Washington, DC, and Baltimore Maryland: Woodrow Wilson Center Press and Johns Hopkins University Press, 1999), 92.

31. Lars Schoultz, "Politics, Economics, and US Participation in Multilateral Development Banks," *International Organization* 36, no. 3 (1982): 539.

32. Ibid., 552.

33. Ibid., 554.

34. William Clark, "Robert McNamara at the World Bank," *Foreign Affairs* 60, no. 1 (1981): 176.

35. Schoultz, "Politics, Economics, and US Participation," 558.

36. Clark, "Robert McNamara at the World Bank," 180.

37. Jo Marie Griesgraber, "Implementation by the Carter Administration of Human Rights Legislation Affecting Latin America" (Ph.D. diss., Georgetown University, 1983), 32. See also Kathryn C. Lavelle, "Multilateral Cooperation and Congress: The Legislative Process of Securing Funding for the World Bank," *International Studies Quarterly* 21, no. 2 (2011): 193-214.

38. Clark, "Robert McNamara at the World Bank," 180.

39. U.S. Congress, House of Representatives, Subcommittee on International Development Institutions and Finance, *H.R. 5262*, 95th Cong., 1st sess., March 22, 1977, 3. See also U.S. Congress, Senate, Committee on Foreign Relations, *International Financial Institutions*, 95th Cong., 1st sess., March 9, 10, 1977, 102.

40. *H. R. 5262*, 81.

41. *International Financial Institutions*, 856.

42. Schoultz, "Politics, Economics, and US Participation," 567.

43. Ibid.

44. U.S. Congress, House, Committee on Appropriations, *Foreign Assistance and Related Programs Appropriations for 1980. Part 6: International Financial Institutions*, 96th Cong., 1st sess., March 14, 27, 28, April 3, 25, 1979, 569.

45. Schoultz, "Politics, Economics, and US Participation," 568.

46. U.S. Congress, House of Representatives, *Congressional Record*, 96th Cong., 1st sess., September 5, 1979, H7294.

47. Therefore, it was odd when McNamara later apologized to the Carter administration for not working through the Treasury Department, although he may not have known the circumstances. For a discussion of the episode, see Bartram S. Brown, *The United States and the Politicization of the World Bank* (New York: Kegan Paul International, 1992), 189.

48. "Aid: Little and Late," *The Economist,* October 7, 1978. The World, American Survey, p. 54.

49. U.S. Congress, House of Representatives, Committee on Foreign Affairs, *Briefing on Current World Situation*, 86th Cong., 1st sess., January 28 and 29, 1959, 40.

50. EBM 74151, Minutes of Executive Board Meeting, 5/24/74, p. 22, IMF Archives, Washington, DC.

51. EBM 7754, Minutes of Executive Board Meeting, April 13, 1977, pages 6 and 19; EBM 7758, Minutes of Executive Board Meeting, April 18, 1977, page 5, IMF Archives, Washington, DC.

52. "No Sign of That Saudi Money," *BusinessWeek,* May 2, 1977 World Trade, the IMF, p. 36.

53. U.S. Congress, Senate, Committee on Banking, Housing, and Urban Affairs, *IMF Supplementary Financing Facility*, 95th Cong., 1st sess., October 13, 1977, 2.

54. "The Lender of Last Resort," *Time* magazine, August 15, 1977, accessed online June 10, 2009, at http://www.time.com/time/magazine/article/0,9171,915265-2,00.html.

55. Congressional Budget Office, "US Participation in the Witteveen Facility: The Need for a New Source of International Finance" (Washington, DC: Congress of the United States, 1978), 46.

56. de Vries, *The IMF 1972–1978 Cooperation on Trial*, I: Narrative and Analysis.

57. Letter quoted in Fred L. Smith, Jr., "The Politics of IMF Lending," *Cato Journal* 4, no. 1 (1984): 214.

58. Ibid.

59. Anna J. Schwartz, "Reflections on the Gold Commission Report," *Journal of Money, Credit and Banking* 14, no. 4 (1982): 539.

60. Confidential interview, staff member, US House of Representatives, January 27, 2009.

61. Schwartz, "Reflections on the Gold Commission Report."
62. Ibid., 543.
63. Ibid., 545.
64. Ibid., 550.
65. Ibid., 551.

## Chapter 5

1. U.S. Congress, Senate, Committee on Banking, Housing, and Urban Affairs, *Oversight on International Economic Policy as It Affects United States Monetary Affairs, Credit, and Financial Institutions: In Particular on International Debt*, 95th Cong., 1st sess., August 29 and 30, 1977.

2. Leon Gordenker and Thomas G. Weiss, "Pluralizing Global Governance: Analytical Approaches and Dimensions," in *NGOs, the UN, and Global Governance*, ed. Leon Gordenker and Thomas G. Weiss (Boulder, CO: Lynne Rienner Publishers, 1996).

3. Glen S. Krutz, *Hitching a Ride: Omnibus Legislating in the U.S. Congress* (Columbus, OH: Ohio State University Press, 2001), 5.

4. Ibid.

5. The money center banks of the 1970s and 1980s were BankAmerica, Bankers Trust New York, Chase Manhattan, Chemical New York, Citicorp, First Chicago, Manufacturers Hanover, and J. P. Morgan & Company.

6. Charles Lipson, "The International Organization of Third World Debt," in *Toward a Political Economy of Development*, ed. Robert Bates (Berkeley, CA: University of California Press, 1988).

7. Federal Deposit Insurance Corporation, *An Examination of the Banking Crises of the 1980s and Early 1990s* (Washington, DC: FDIC, 1997), 195.

8. Ibid.

9. Lipson, "The International Organization of Third World Debt," 22–23. Lipson cites *World Financial Markets* (January 1981): 4, Table 5.

10. Staff report by the US Senate Committee on Foreign Relations, Subcommittee on Foreign Relations, *International Debt, the Banks, and US Foreign Policy,* 95th Congress, 1st session, 1977, p. 5, as quoted in Federal Deposit Insurance Corporation, *Banking Crises of the 1980s and Early 1990s*, 198.

11. Margaret Garritsen de Vries, *The IMF 1972–1978 Cooperation on Trial*, vol. I: Narrative and Analysis (Washington, DC: IMF, 1985), 963. See also *IMF Survey,* Volume 15 (May 3, 1976), 138–40, for Witteveen's speech on the topic.

12. Wriston's precise quote was that countries "don't go out of business." See Harold James, *International Monetary Cooperation Since Bretton Woods* (New York: Oxford University Press for the IMF, 1996), 352.

13. Ron Chernow, *The House of Morgan: An American Banking Dynasty and the Rise of Modern Finance* (New York: Atlantic Monthly Press, 1990), 639.

14. Ibid., 638.

15. This account of the Mexican crisis relies heavily on Boughton. See James Boughton, *Silent Revolution: The International Monetary Fund 1979–1989* (Washington, DC: International Monetary Fund, 2001), 281.

16. Ibid., 291.

17. Ibid., 293.

18. Ibid., 297.

19. Ibid.

20. Chernow, *House of Morgan*, 643.

21. Ibid., 645.

22. James, *International Monetary Cooperation*, 369.

23. Chernow, *House of Morgan*, 646.

24. Miles Kahler, "The United States and the International Monetary Fund: Declining Influence or Declining Interest?," in *The United States and Multilateral Institutions: Patterns of Changing Instrumentality and Influence*, ed. Margaret P. Karnes and Karen A. Mingst (Boston: Unwin Hyman, 1990).

25. U.S. Congress, House, Committee on Appropriations, *Foreign Assistance and Related Programs Appropriations for 1982, Part 4*, 97th Cong., 1st sess., April 7, 9, 10, June 2, 1981, 176.

26. Krutz, *Hitching a Ride*, 6.

27. Ibid., 5.

28. Ibid.

29. Ibid., 65.

30. Ibid., 73.

31. William Greider, *Secrets of the Temple: How the Federal Reserve Runs the Country* (New York: Simon and Schuster, 1987), 366.

32. Fred L. Smith, Jr., "The Politics of IMF Lending," *Cato Journal* 4, no. 1 (1984): 215.

33. EBM 82162, Minutes of Executive Board Meeting, 11/19/82, page 11, IMF Archives, Washington, DC.

34. The General Arrangements to Borrow is a credit arrangement between the IMF and the U.S. government that allows the IMF to borrow under certain circumstances for a five-year period. Because it requires an additional level of U.S. approval to activate and is negotiated for five-year increments, it is generally easier to move through Congress.

35. EBM 82162, Minutes of Executive Board Meeting, 12/17/82, pages 19 and 24, IMF Archives, Washington, DC. The General Arrangements to Borrow enable the IMF to borrow from a country under certain circumstances at a market rate of interest. When the 1982 agreements were being negotiated, the IMF paid a rate below market interest. It currently pays a market rate, as the later history will show.

36. Jeffrey A. Frieden, *Banking on the World: The Politics of American International Finance* (New York: Harper & Row, 1987), 183.

37. Ibid., 184.

38. Smith, "Politics of IMF Lending," 216. See also *Time* magazine, October 10, 1983, "Trouble at the Credit Union," accessed 12/11/2008 at http:///www.time.com/printout/0,8816,955232,00.html.

39. "Logrolling" is a term used to describe common legislative behavior wherein two members agree to support a project that is not important to them in exchange for a vote on a project that is.

40. Frieden, *Banking on the World*, 188.

41. Krutz, *Hitching a Ride*, 5.

42. Kahler, "The United States and the International Monetary Fund," 107.

43. The appropriation was included in an amendment to another bill. Since it was so controversial, it was not debated in a conference committee and was on the House floor under the tightest rule possible. That is, the bill had to pass with the amendment or not at all.

44. Smith, "Politics of IMF Lending," 216.

45. Roland Vaubel, "The Moral Hazard of IMF Lending," in *International Lending and the IMF*, ed. Allan H. Meltzer (Washington, DC: The Heritage Foundation, 1983). Vaubel referred to in Smith, "Politics of IMF Lending."

46. Smith, "Politics of IMF Lending," 236.

47. James C. Orr, "Business Associations and Global Financial Governance," in *Civil Society and Global Finance*, ed. Jan Aart Scholte and Albrecht Schnabel (New York: Routledge, 2002), 205.

48. EBM 9046 Executive Board Minutes, 3/26/90, page 8. IMF Archives, Washington, DC.

49. Smith, "Politics of IMF Lending," 237.

50. Confidential interview, World Bank official, February 24, 2009.

51. Jo Marie Griesgraber, "Influencing the IMF," in *Critical Mass: The Emergence of Global Civil Society*, ed. James W. St.G. Walker and Andrew S. Thompson, *Studies in International Governance* (Waterloo, CA: Wilfred Laurier University Press, 2008), 154.

52. James, *International Monetary Cooperation*, 480.

53. Griesgraber, "Influencing the IMF," 154.

54. U.S. Congress, House of Representatives, Committee on Banking, Finance, and Urban Affairs, *General Capital Increase for the World Bank*, 100th Cong., 2nd sess., June 15, 1988, 3.

55. Randall Dodd, "Sovereign Debt Restructuring," *The Financier,* 2002.

56. Richard B. Miller, *Citicorp: The Story of a Bank in Crisis* (New York: McGraw-Hill, Inc., 1993), 112.

57. U.S. Congress, House, Committee on Appropriations, *Foreign Assistance and Related Programs Appropriations for 1985, Part 5*, 98th Cong., 2nd sess., March 14, 15, 29, April 10, 12, 1984, 507.

58. Ibid., 115.

59. Executive Office of the President, "Appendix: The Budget of the United States Government," ed. OMB (US Government Printing Office, 1986), D9.

60. U.S. Congress, House, Committee on Appropriations, *Foreign Assistance and Related Programs Appropriations for 1987, Part 3*, 99th Cong., 2nd sess., March 4–6, 12, 13, 1986, 669.

61. Executive Office of the President, "Appendix: The Budget of the United States Government," ed. OMB (US Government Printing Office, 1988), I-D7; Executive Office of the President, "Appendix: The Budget of the United States Government," ed. OMB (US Government Printing Office, 1989), I-D8.

62. Confidential interview, former staff member, US House of Representatives, February 12, 2009.

63. Orr, "Business Associations and Global Financial Governance," 203.

64. Elliot Richardson to Richard Lugar August 30, 1989. Folder "Overseas Development Council," 6. The Papers of Elliot Richardson, Manuscript Division, Library of Congress, Washington, DC.

65. See "The Future of the World Bank," Report of the Conference presented by the Overseas Development Council June 23–24, 1986, Washington, DC, and *Pulling Together: The International Monetary Fund in a Multipolar World,* Catherine Gwin, Richard E. Feinberg, and contributors. US-Third World Policy Perspectives, No. 13, Overseas Development Council, New Brunswick: Transaction Books, 1989.

66. Orr, "Business Associations and Global Financial Governance," 203.

67. The Bretton Woods Fund was a 501(c)4 created by and affiliated with the Bretton Woods Committee. It allowed the committee to do more lobbying than a 501(c)3 is permitted to do. It was decommissioned after about five years because the committee was not doing a great deal of formal lobbying, and it did not want to have to pay the costs of maintaining it. The two organizations had the same members and leadership. When the committee did want to write to Congress, it used Fund letterhead because members wanted to make a distinction for purposes of the Internal Revenue Service. Communication, Bretton Woods Committee.

68. Henry Owen, Paul A. Volcker, Charls E. Walker to Elliot Richardson. August 21, 1989. Box II-2, Folder 5, "Bretton Woods Committee 1989," The Papers of Elliot Richardson, Manuscript Division, Library of Congress, Washington, DC.

69. Positions provided in pamphlet of Bretton Woods Committee-Brookings Institution Conference, "Third World Debt: A New Look," Box II-2, Folder 5, "Bretton Woods Committee 1989." The Papers of Elliot Richardson, Manuscript Division, Library of Congress, Washington, DC.

70. Confidential interview, former Treasury official, October, 2008.

71. See EBM 83176 Executive Board Minutes, 12/19/83, page 15, and EBM 83184 Executive Board Minutes, 12/28/83, page 16, and EBM 83186, Executive Board Minutes, 12/30/83, pages 14 and 15, IMF Archives, Washington, DC.

72. Warren Strobel and Major Garrett, "Jerusalem's Friends, Foes Address Guarantees; Baker, Testifying on Capitol Hill, Hardens Line on Israeli Settlements," *The Washington Times,* World, p. A7, February 7, 1992.

73. EBM 9234 Executive Board Minutes, 3/23/92, page 6, IMF Archives, Washington, DC.

74. Helen Dewar, "Senate Clears Foreign Aid Bill for Final Action Today," *Washington Post,* October 1, 1992.

75. Jacques J. Polak, *The World Bank and the International Monetary Fund: A Changing Relationship* (Washington, DC: The Brookings Institution Occasional Papers, 1994), 21.

76. Griesgraber, "Influencing the IMF."

77. U.S. Congress, House of Representatives, Subcommittee on International Development, Finance, Trade, and Monetary Policy, *Oversight of the International Monetary Fund and the World Bank: A Meeting of a Multinational Group of Parliamentarians Involved in Oversight of the IMF and the World Bank*, 103rd Cong., 2nd sess., November 21, 1994, 3.

78. U.S. Congress, House of Representatives, Committee on Banking, Finance, and Urban Affairs, *Authorizing Contributions to IDA, GEF, and ADF*, 103rd Cong., 1st sess., May 5, 1993.

79. Maartje van Putten, "'Policing the World': Accountability Mechanisms for Multilateral Financial Institutions and Private Financial Institutions" (Ph.D., McGill University, June 2006), 297.

80. Ibid., 298.

81. U.S. Congress, House of Representatives, Committee on Appropriations, *Foreign Operations, Export Financing, and Related Programs Appropriations for 1995, Part 2*, 103rd Cong., 2nd sess., March 1, 8, 10, April 14, 19, 1994, 208.

82. Daniel L. Nielson and Michael J. Tierney, "Delegation to International Organizations: Agency Theory and World Bank Environmental Reform," *International Organization* 57 (2003): 257.

83. Confidential interviews, staff member, US House of Representatives, May 2009, and former Treasury official, June 2009. Confidential memorandum, March 2009.

84. Sebastian Mallaby, *The World's Banker: A Story of Failed States, Financial Crises, and the Wealth and Poverty of Nations* (New York: Penguin Press, 2004), 275.

85. Ibid., 282.

86. U.S. Congress, House of Representatives, Committee on Appropriations, *Foreign Operations, Export Financing, and Related Programs Appropriations for 1997, Part 2*, 104th Cong., 2nd sess., March 27, 28, April 18, 1996; U.S. Congress, House of Representatives, Committee on Banking and Financial Services, *Administration's Authorization Requests for International Financial Institutions*, 104th Cong., 2nd sess., April 25, 1996. The Special Fund was established so that IDA operation would not be disrupted in 1997 when the US was not paying its installment. *Foreign Operations, Export Financing, and Related Programs Appropriations for 1997, Part 2*, 152.

87. Confidential interview, former staff member, US House of Representatives, December 17, 2008.

88. EBM 92132 Executive Board Minutes, 11/5/92, page 47. IMF Archives, Washington, DC.

89. EBM 9334 Executive Board Minutes, 3/12/93, page 32. IMF Archives, Washington, DC.

90. EBM 9582 Executive Board Minutes, 9/6/95, page 54. IMF Archives, Washington, DC.

## Chapter 6

1. U.S. Congress, House of Representatives, Committee on Banking and Financial Services, *East Asian Economic Conditions (Second Segment)*, 105th Cong., 2nd sess., February 3, 1998, 306.

2. John E Owens, "The Return of Party Government in the US House of Representatives: Central Leadership—Committee Relationships in the 104th Congress," *British Journal of Political Science* 27, no. 2 (1997).

3. Diana Evans, "Appropriations in the Republican Era," *Extensions: A Journal of the Carl Albert Congressional Research and Studies Center* Spring (2007): 10.

4. A. Claire Cutler, "Private International Regimes and Interfirm Cooperation," in *The Emergence of Private Authority in Global Governance*, ed. Rodney Bruce Hall and Thomas J. Biersteker (Cambridge: Cambridge University Press, 2002); A. Claire Cutler, Virginia Haufler, and Tony Porter, eds., *Private Authority and International Affairs* (Albany, NY: SUNY Press,1999); Virginia Haufler, "Industry Regulation and Self-regulation: The Case of Labour Standards," in *Enhancing Global Governance: Towards a New Diplomacy?*, ed. Andrew F. Cooper, John English, and Ramesh Thakur (New York: United Nations University Press, 2002).

5. Randall Dodd, "Sovereign Debt Restructuring," *The Financier,* 2002.

6. A company usually seeks a syndicated credit facility when its credit need is greater than an individual bank's ability to meet it. With a syndicated loan, a lead bank structures and markets a credit facility to other providers of credit. The rate is usually lower than that for debt securities, because syndicated debt is senior debt in the event of a bankruptcy. Since the lender has a greater likelihood of repayment, they receive the lower interest rate. They tend to have shorter repayment periods than bonds. In addition, banks can attach more restrictive provisions to the terms that can make them less attractive to borrowers. Figures on expansion taken from BIS Quarterly Review statistics.

7. Anne Krueger, "International Financial Architecture for 2002: A New Approach to Sovereign Debt Restructuring" (paper presented at the National Economists' Club

Annual Members' Dinner, American Enterprise Institute, Washington, DC, November 26, 2001).

8. Owens, "Return of Party Government."

9. Barbara Sinclair, "Transformational Leader or Faithful Agent? Principal-Agent Theory and House Majority Party Leadership," *Legislative Studies Quarterly* 24, no. 3 (1999).

10. Owens, "Return of Party Government."

11. Christopher J. Deering and Paul J. Wahlbeck, "US House Committee Chair Selection: Republicans Play Musican Chairs in the 107th Congress," *American Politics Research* 34, no. 2 (2006).

12. Sinclair, "Transformational Leader?"

13. Evans, "Appropriations in the Republican Era," 11.

14. Ibid., 12.

15. For a comprehensive treatment, see C. Randall Henning, *The Exchange Stabilization Fund: Slush Money or War Chest?* (Washington, DC: Institute for International Economics, 1999).

16. Ibid., 67.

17. Ibid.

18. For some general treatments, see Morris Goldstein, *The Asian Financial Crisis: Causes, Cures, and Systemic Implications* (Washington, DC: The Peterson Institute for International Economics, 1998); ibid.; Joseph E. Stiglitz, *Globalization and Its Discontents* (New York: W. W. Norton, 2002); Robert Wade, "Wheels within Wheels: Rethinking the Asian Crisis and the Asian Model," *Annual Review of Political Science* 3, no. 1 (2000); Bhumika Muchhala, ed., *Ten Years After: Revisiting the Asian Financial Crisis* (Washington, DC: Woodrow Wilson International Center for Scholars, 2007).

19. When the US government provides assistance to the IMF, it does so by issuing medium- to long-term Treasury bonds and acquiring credit balance in its IMF account that the Fund calls a reserve position. Such positions pay a short-term interest rate that may or may not match the amount the Treasury pays on its bonds. When allowing for risk, IMF loans may involve an interest subsidy on the loan that is hidden in the US budget under the general interest cost of the Federal debt, particularly for loans issued under concessional terms. See Adam Lerrick, "Funding the IMF: How Much Does it Really Cost?," in *Quarterly International Economics Report* (Pittsburgh, PA: Carnegie Mellon Gailliot Center for Public Policy, 2003).

20. See "IMF Funding on Hold," *Economic Justice News Online,* Volume 1, No. 2, June 1998. Accessed 11/22/2008 at http://www.50years.org/cms/ejn/story/243.

21. This section relies heavily on the excellent account of the IMF appropriation in James M. Scott and Ralph G. Carter, "The Politics of IMF Reform: The Asian Flu and Abortion Politics," in *Contemporary Cases in US Foreign Policy: From Terrorism to Trade,* ed. Ralph G. Carter (Washington, DC: CQ Press, 2005).

22. Ibid., 395.

23. Ibid., 396.

24. U.S. Congress, House of Representatives, Committee on Banking and Financial Services, *East Asian Economic Conditions*, 105th Cong., 1st sess., November 13, 1997, 18.

25. *Congressional Record,* October 24, 1997, E2075.

26. "Who Needs the IMF?" *Wall Street Journal,* February 3, 1998.

27. Scott and Carter, "The Politics of IMF Reform: The Asian Flu and Abortion Politics," 398.

28. U.S. Congress, House of Representatives, Committee on Banking and Financial Services, *East Asian Economic Conditions (First Segment)*, 105th Cong., 2nd sess., January 30, 1993.

29. *East Asian Economic Conditions (Second Segment)*, 243.

30. Congress set up the Exchange Stabilization Fund in 1933, and it was established in 1934 with $2 billion. That amount had grown to $37 billion in 1997. The secretary of the treasury may use the funds, with the approval of the President, to provide loans and credit to foreign countries.

31. "Voice and vote" restrictions are those that direct the US Executive Directive to use his or her voice and vote on a specific matter. For example, they must vote against loans to Burma/Myanmar.

32. U.S. Congress, House of Representatives, Committee on Banking and Financial Services, Subcommittee on General Oversight and Investigations, *Review of the Operations of the International Monetary Fund*, 105th Cong., 2nd sess., April 21, 1998, 49.

33. Scott and Carter, "The Politics of IMF Reform: The Asian Flu and Abortion Politics," 399.

34. Ibid., 400.

35. See "IMF Funding on Hold," *Economic Justice News Online,* Volume 1, No. 2, June 1998. Accessed 11/22/2008 at http:///www.50years.org/cms/ejn/story/243.

36. See "IMF Funding on Hold," *Economic Justice News Online,* Volume 1, No. 2, June 1998. Accessed 11/22/2008 at http:///www.50years.org/cms/ejn/story/243.

37. Scott and Carter, "The Politics of IMF Reform: The Asian Flu and Abortion Politics," 411.

38. Two confidential interviews with former Meltzer Commission members, January 27, 2009, and February 5, 2009.

39. Confidential interview, former Meltzer Commission member, January 27, 2009.

40. Confidential interview, former Treasury official, October 2008.

41. Note that the G20 financial meeting should be distinguished from the G20 grouping that operates in the WTO on agricultural issues. Lawrence H. Summers, "The Right Kind of IMF for a Stable Global Financial System" (London, England: London School of Business, 1999).

42. For example, see Carla A. Hills and Peter G. Peterson, "Safeguarding Prosperity in a Global Financial System: The Future International Financial Architecture," in *Council on Foreign Relations-Sponsored Project* (New York: Institute for International Economics, 1999). For a report on the World Bank, see Nancy Birdsall, "Rescuing the World Bank: A CGD Working Group Report" (Washington, DC: Center for Global Development, 2006).

43. US Department of the Treasury, "Response to the Report of the International Financial Institution Advisory Commission" (Washington, DC: US Department of the Treasury, 2000).

44. Article IV consultations are the means by which the IMF remains current on the economic conditions of its member countries, even where such countries are not seeking financing. Levinson opposed dismantling the IMF's institutional store of knowledge if one accepts the notion that the IMF is the lender of last resort in a crisis.

45. Confidential interview, former Meltzer Commission member, January 27, 2009, and confidential documentation, Meltzer Commission.

46. United Nations, "Financing for Development: Building on Monterrey" (paper presented at the International Conference on Financing for Development, Monterrey, Mexico, 2002).

47. Barry Herman, "Civil Society and the Financing for Development Initiative at the United Nations," in *Civil Society and Global Finance*, ed. Jan Aart Scholte and Albrecht Schnabel (New York: Routledge, 2002), 173.

48. See "The Future Role of the IMF in Development," ODC Task Force Report, April 2000, and "The IMF Working Group: Analyzing Policy and Influencing Policymakers," August 2000.

49. Herman, "Civil Society and the Financing for Development Initiative at the United Nations," 163.

50. See www.fsforum.org.

51. Thomas M. Callaghy, "Networks and Governance in Africa: Innovation in the Debt Regime," in *Intervention and Transnationalism in Africa: Global—Local Networks of Power*, ed. Ronald Kassimir, Thomas M. Callaghy, Robert Latham (New York: Cambridge University Press, 2001), 125.

52. Sebastian Mallaby, *The World's Banker: A Story of Failed States, Financial Crises, and the Wealth and Poverty of Nations* (New York: Penguin Press, 2004), 10.

53. Eric Helleiner and Geoffrey Cameron, "Another World Order? The Bush Administration and HIPC Debt Cancellation," *New Political Economy* 11, no. 1 (2006).

54. U.S. Congress, House of Representatives, Committee on Appropriations, Subcommittee on Foreign Operations, *Foreign Operations, Export Financing, and Related Programs Appropriations for 2000*, 106th Cong., 1st sess., March 17, 1999.

55. Joshua William Busby, "Bono Made Jesse Helms Cry: Jubilee 2000, Debt Relief, and Moral Action in International Politics," *International Studies Quarterly* 51, no. 2 (2007): 266.

56. Ibid., 267.

57. Helleiner and Cameron, "Another World Order?," 135.

58. Jim Saxton, "IMF Gold Sales in Perspective" (Washington, DC: Joint Economic Committee, US Congress, 1999).

59. In December 1999 and April 2000, Brazil and Mexico had financial obligations falling due to the IMF. In the first step, the IMF sold gold to the member at the prevailing market price and the profits were placed in a special account invested for the benefit of the HIPC initiative. In the second step, the IMF immediately accepted back, at the same market price, the same amount of gold from the member in settlement of that member's financial obligations. In the end, these transactions left the balance of the IMF's holdings of physical gold unchanged but added to the Trust Fund.

60. Helleiner and Cameron, "Another World Order?," 130.

61. Ibid., 131.

62. Ibid., 132.

63. Ibid., 133.

64. Martin A. Weiss, "The World Bank's International Development Association (IDA)," (Washington, DC: Congressional Research Service, 2007), 4.

65. Birdsall, "Rescuing the World Bank: A CGD Working Group Report."

66. John B. Taylor, *Global Financial Warriors: The Untold Story of International Finance in the Post-9/11 World* (New York: W. W. Norton & Co., 2007), 135.

67. Ibid., 145.

68. Susanne Soederberg, "Recasting Neoliberal Dominance in the Global South? A Critique of the Monterrey Consensus," *Alternatives* 30 (2005): 342.

69. U.S. Congress, House of Representatives, Committee on Financial Services, *Reauthorization Requests on U.S. Participation in the International Development Association and the African Development Bank*, 107 Cong., 2nd sess., July 19, 25, 2002, 36.

70. Ibid., 50.

71. Eric Helleiner, "The Strange Story of Bush and the Argentine Debt Crisis," *Third World Quarterly* 26, no. 6 (2005): 955.

72. Ibid., 958.

73. Ibid.

74. Ibid., 963.

75. The "shadow" financial services industry refers to the off-balance-sheet arrangements, derivatives, hedge funds, and other financial intermediaries that generally operate outside the regulated banking sector.

76. When the IMF creates SDRs, it allocates them according to a member's quota share. Since a group of countries joined after 1981, they did not have allocations proportionate to their quotas since none had been issued after they joined. To balance the allocations, some countries needed to receive more SDRs than their quota share would dictate, and this action required congressional approval. The IMF board approved an amendment to the articles in 1997 and it was not submitted to Congress until the financial crisis in 2009.

## Chapter 7

1. Letter from former secretaries on Bretton Woods Committee letterhead, accessed June 15, 2009 at http://www.brettonwoods.org/uploads/pages/224/Former%20Secretaries%20Letter%20on%20IMF%20Approval-5.26.09.pdf.

2. See U.S. Congress, Senate, Report of the Committee on Foreign Relations, *The International Financial Institutions: A Call for Change*, 111st Cong., 2nd sess., March 10, 2010, 13.

3. Ibid., 18.

4. For a discussion of forum shopping, see Daniel W. Drezner, *All Politics Is Global: Explaining International Regulatory Regimes* (Princeton, NJ: Princeton University Press, 2007).

5. See *The Economist,* "It's Mostly Firing: The IMF Downsizes," February 9, 2008, p. 74.

6. Letter accessed June 13, 2003, at http://www.actionaidusa.org/assets/pdfs/imf_gold_letter.pdf.

7. The unfolding of the crisis within the US government has received a good deal of attention. For an account from the Treasury and the Federal Reserve, see Henry M. Paulson, Jr., *On the Brink: Inside the Race to Stop the Collapse of the Global Financial System* (New York: Business Plus, 2010), and David Wessel, *In Fed We Trust: Ben Bernanke's War on the Great Panic* (New York: Crown Business, 2009).

8. James K. Jackson, "Iceland's Financial Crisis" (Washington, DC: The Congressional Research Service, 2008), 3.

9. Ibid., 5.

10. Martin A. Weiss, "The Global Financial Crisis: The Role of the International Monetary Fund (IMF)" (Washington, DC: Congressional Research Service, 2009), 1.

11. For commentary on the matter, see Douglas Rediker, "The Leadership Deficit," *The National Interest,* February 25, 2009, accessed June 22, 2009, at http://www.newamerica.net/publications/articles/2009/leadership_deficit_11249.

12. Jackson, "Iceland's Financial Crisis," 5.

13. Confidential interviews, Capitol Hill, July 17, 2009, and IMF official, July 24, 2009.

14. Confidential interviews, Capitol Hill, July 17, 2009, and IMF official, July 24, 2009.

15. Weiss, "The Global Financial Crisis: The Role of the International Monetary Fund (IMF)," 5. The IMF later replaced this program with a flexible credit line (FCL), which has had two participants, Mexico and Poland. The newer FCL involves prequalification instead of conditionality. A country must be considered to be a "strong performer" before it can sign up. After that, it has no limit on the amount of money the borrower can access for a duration of either six or twelve months, and allows for up to five years of repayment.

16. See James Kirkup and Bruno Waterfield, "Gordon Brown's Bretton Woods Summit Call Risks Spat with Nicholas Sarkozy," *Telegraph.co.uk,* October 16, 2008; accessed 10/16/2008.

17. See Robert B. Zoellick, "Modernizing Multilateralism and Markets," prepared for the Peterson Institute for International Economics, Washington, DC, October 6, 2008.

18. Weiss, "The Global Financial Crisis: The Role of the International Monetary Fund (IMF)," 5.

19. The Country Policy and Institutional Assessment (CPIA) indicator rates countries against a set of sixteen criteria grouped in four clusters: (a) economic management, (b) structural policies, (c) policies for social inclusion and equity, and (d) public sector management and institutions. It is then used as a part of the IDA performance-based allocations.

20. U.S. Congress, House of Representatives, Committee on Financial Services, *The Fight Against Global Poverty and Inequality: The World Bank's Approach to Core Labor Standards and Employment Creation,* 110th Cong., 1st sess., October 3, 2007.

21. See International Trade Union Confederation bulletin "World Bank Publication Promotes Elimination of Worker Protection," accessed June 20, 2009, at http://www.icftu.org/displaydocument.asp?Index=991224962&;Language=EN.

22. See Alex Wilks, "Why Has the World Bank Changed Its Views on Tax and Labour Standards?" Eurodad, published April 30, 2009. Accessed June 12, 2009, at http://www.eurodad.org/blog/index.aspx?id=3607&;LangType=1036.

23. See Finlay Lewis, "World Bank Makes Up with Labor," *CQ Weekly Vantage Point* May 18, 2009, page 1130.

24. Independent Evaluation Group of the World Bank, "Doing Business: An Independent Evaluation" (Washington, DC: The World Bank, 2008).

25. Confidential memorandum, January 22, 2009.

26. Confidential interview, staff member, US House of Representatives, May 2009.

27. See "Revisions to the EWI Indicator," accessed June 20, 2009, at http://www.doingbusiness.org/documents/EWI_revisions.pdf.

28. See H. R. 2346, "SEC. 1626. REFORM OF THE 'DOING BUSINESS' REPORT OF THE WORLD BANK." (a) The Secretary of the Treasury shall instruct the United States Executive Directors at the International Bank for Reconstruction and Development, the International Development Association, and the International Finance Corporation of the following United States policy goals, and to use the voice and vote of the United States to actively promote and work to achieve these goals:

(1) Suspension of the use of the "Employing Workers" Indicator for the purpose of ranking or scoring country performance in the annual Doing Business Report of the World Bank until a set of indicators can be devised that fairly represent the value of internationally recognized workers' rights, including core labor standards, in creating a stable and favorable environment for attracting private investment. The indicators shall bring to bear the experiences of the member governments in dealing with the economic, social and political complexity of labor market issues. The indicators should be developed through collaborative discussions with and between the World Bank, the International Finance Corporation, the International Labor Organization, private companies, and labor unions.

(2) Elimination of the "Labor Tax and Social Contributions" Subindicator from the annual Doing Business Report of the World Bank.

(3) Removal of the "Employing Workers" Indicator as a "guidepost" for calculating the annual Country Policy and Institutional Assessment score for each recipient country.

(b) Within 60 days after the date of the enactment of this section, the Secretary of the Treasury shall provide an instruction to the United States Executive Directors referred to in subsection (a) to take appropriate actions with respect to implementing the policy goals of the United States set forth in subsection (a), and such instruction shall be posted on the website of the Department of the Treasury.

29. Memorandum from Jonathan E. Sanford and Martin A. Weiss, "IMF Reform and Congress," April 7, 2009.

30. Confidential interview, IMF official, July 24, 2009.

31. See Jonathan E. Sanford and Martin A. Weiss, "The Global Financial Crisis: Increasing IMF Resources and the Role of Congress" (Washington, DC: Congressional Research Service, 2009). The funding through the New Arrangements to Borrow (NAB) complicated the matter somewhat because the NAB is a line of credit to be activated when the Fund's resources are drawn down in a crisis. This method of financing was chosen because the Obama administration perceived it would facilitate congressional approval.

32. Ibid., 20–21.

33. See David Rogers, "Orszag's Power Play," April 22, 2009, *Politico,* accessed June 15, 2009, at http:///www.politico.com.

34. See "Statement from the President upon signing HR 2346 on June 24, 2009," accessed July 18, 2009, at www.whitehouse.gov.

35. See Reuters and AP wire stories, July 21, 2009.

36. See Jonathan Weisman, "Obama's Fiats Anger Lawmakers," July 15, 2009, *Wall Street Journal,* accessed July 23, 2009, at http://online.wsj.com/article/SB124761651200542351.html.

37. Confidential interview, IMF official, Washington, DC, July 24, 2009.

38. See, for example, various commentaries offered by Mark Weisbrot, Center for Economic Policy, accessed June 22, 2009, at http://www.cepr.net/index.php/press-releases/press-releases/new-funds-for-imf-approved-by-u.s.-senate-would-worsen-global-economic-downturn,-economists-say/.

39. See Marcus Walker, Charles Forelle, and Brian Blackstone, "On the Secret Committee to Save the Euro, a Dangerous Divide," *Wall Street Journal,* Vol. CCLVI, No. 73, September 25, 2010, 1.

40. Marcus Walker, Charles Forelle, and Brian Blackstone, "On the Secret Committee to Save the Euro, a Dangerous Divide," *Wall Street Journal,* Vol. CCLVI, No. 73, September 25, 2010, 1.

41. See Edwin M. Truman, "The Role of the International Monetary Fund and Federal Reserve in the Stabilization of Europe," testimony before the U.S. House Committee on Financial Services Subcommittee on International Monetary Policy and Subcommittee on Domestic Monetary Policy and Technology, page 4, May 20, 2010. Accessed June 3, 2010, at http:///www.piie.com/publications/papers/print.cfm?researchid =1580&;doc=pub.

42. Rebecca A. Nelson et al., "Frequently Asked Questions about IMF Involvement in the Eurozone Debt Crisis" (Washington, DC: Congressional Research Service, 2010), 2.

43. Ibid., 19.

44. See Stephen Fidler, "Crisis Without Borders: Europe's Contagion Woes Illustrate How a Lack of Market Confidence Spreads," *The Wall Street Journal,* November 26, 2010, p. A14.

45. See Stephen Fidler, "Aid Rules Ease Uncertainty, If Not Pain," *The Wall Street Journal,* November 29, 2010, p. A10.

46. See Jeffrey H. Birnbaum, "Private Funds Prepare to Lobby," *The Washington Post,* December 27, 2006, p. D01.

47. Nelson et al., "IMF Involvement in the Eurozone Debt Crisis," 12.

48. Lawrence Summers, former director of the President's National Economic Council, served as chief economist at the World Bank from 1991 to 1993. Timothy Geithner, secretary of the treasury, worked at the IMF as director of the Policy Development and Review Department from 2001 to 2003.

## Chapter 8

1. Peter M. Haas, "Social Constructivism and the Evolution of Multilateral Environmental Governance," in *Globalization and Governance*, ed. Aseem Prakash and Jeffrey A. Hart (New York: Routledge, 2000); David A. Lake, "Global Governance: A Relational Contracting Approach," in *Globalization and Governance*, ed. Aseem Prakash and Jeffrey A. Hart (New York: Routledge, 2000); Michael D. McGinnis, "Rent-seeking, Redistribution, and Reform in the Governance of Global Markets," in *Globalization and Governance*, ed. Aseem Prakash and Jeffrey A. Hart (New York: Routledge, 2000); Wayne Sandholtz, "Globalization and the Evolution of Rules," in *Globalization and Governance*, ed. Aseem Prakash and Jeffrey A. Hart (New York: Routledge, 2000).

2. Ruth W. Grant and Robert O. Keohane, "Accountability and Abuses of Power in World Politics," *American Political Science Review* 99, no. 1 (2005). See also Maartje van Putten, *Policing the Banks: Accountability Mechanisms for the Financial Sector* (Ithaca, NY: McGill-Queens University Press, 2008); Robert O. Keohane and Joseph S. Nye, Jr., "Redefining Accountability for Global Governance: Political Authority in Transnation," in *Governance in a Global Economy*, ed. Miles Kahler and David Lake (Princeton, NJ: Princeton University Press, 2003).

3. Peter Gourevitch, "Domestic Politics and International Relations," in *Handbook of International Relations*, ed. Walter Carlsnaes, Thomas Risse, and Beth A. Simmons (Thousand Oaks, CA: Sage Publications, 2002), 321. For his initial argument, see Peter A. Gourevitch, "The Second Image Reversed: The International Sources of Domestic Politics," *International Organization* 32 (1978).

4. Frances E. Lee, *Beyond Ideology: Politics, Principles, and Partisanship in the U.S. Senate* (Chicago: University of Chicago Press, 2009), 183.

5. Walter J. Oleszek, *Congressional Procedures and the Policy Process*, 8th ed. (Washington, DC: CQ Press, 2011), 366.

6. Copelovitch's study of the IMF, for example, provides an excellent analysis of the relationship between the policies of the IMF that have evolved in response to changes in the composition of international capital flows. He does not consider the domestic institutional arrangement in the US, although that was not the purpose of his book. See Mark S. Copelovitch, *The International Monetary Fund in the Global Economy: Banks, Bonds, and Bailouts* (New York: Cambridge University Press, 2010).

7. When the IMF lends approves a loan, it makes an administrative decision as to which country's quota will be tapped to fund it. It does not disclose parties on individual loans, but aims to balance the positions among members according to their quotas. See Rebecca A. Nelson et al., "Frequently Asked Questions about IMF Involvement in the Eurozone Debt Crisis" (Washington, DC: Congressional Research Service, 2010), 4.

8. "Senior" leadership levels refers to subcommittee chairs, committee chairs, party whips, majority/minority leaders, and the Speaker of the House.

9. Saskia Scholtes and Francesco Guerrera, "Citi and IFC in Global Trade Funding Alliance," *Financial Times,* June 14, 2009.

10. For commentary on the matter, see Douglas Rediker, "The Leadership Deficit," *The National Interest* February 25, 2009. Accessed June 22, 2009; available at http://www.newamerica.net/publications/articles/2009/leadership_deficit_11249.

11. Nelson W. Polsby, *How Congress Evolves: Social Bases of Institutional Change* (New York: Oxford University Press, 2004).

12. David R. Mayhew, *Parties and Policies: How the American Government Works* (New Haven: Yale University Press, 2008), 291.

13. See, for example, Samuel Loewenberg, "Business Finds Ways to Influence World Bank Projects," *Legal Times.* January 22, 1999. Accessed June 19, 2009, at http://www.samloewenberg.com/articles/99_02_22_worldbank.html.

14. John Zysman, "The French State in the International Economy," in *Between Power and Plenty: Foreign Economic Policies of Advanced Industrial States*, ed. Peter J. Katzenstein (Madison, WI: University of Wisconsin Press, 1978).

15. Joanne Gowa, "Public Goods and Political Institutions: Trade and Monetary Policy Processes in the United States," *International Organization* 42, no. 1 (1988).

16. See Eric Helleiner, *States and the Reemergence of Global Finance: From Bretton Woods to the 1990s* (Ithaca, NY: Cornell University Press, 1994), 196–198.

17. For a comparison of the IMF and WTO, see Nitsan Chorev and Sarah Babb, "A Crisis of Neoliberalism and the Future of International Institutions: A Comparison of the IMF and the WTO," *Theory and Society* 38 (2009).

18. Richard N. Gardner, *Sterling-Dollar Diplomacy in Current Perspective: The Origins and the Prospects of Our International Economic Order* (New York: Columbia University Press, 1980), 379.

19. In 1955, the State Department did attempt to get the purely organizational aspects of the GATT approved in Congress. They worked out an international instrument, called the Organization for Trade Cooperation, whose sole function was to administer the GATT with a regular budget. It passed the Ways and Means Committee 18 to 7. However, the committee chair, Wilbur Mills, would not bring it to the House floor without evidence from President Eisenhower that he would lobby for it. The President did not pursue it and the matter was dropped. See "Oral History Interview with John M. Leddy," pp. 78–80, Harry S. Truman Library and Museum, Independence, MI. Accessed June 6, 2009, at http:///www.trumanlibrary.org/oralhist/leddyj.htm.

20. Terence Stewart, ed., *The GATT Uruguay Round: A Negotiating History (1986–1992)* (Boston: Kluwer Law & Taxation Publications,1993), 1899. See also John Jackson,

*The World Trading System: Law and Policy of International Economic Regulations* (Cambridge, MA: MIT Press, 1989), 33.

21. See "Oral History Interview with John M. Leddy," p. 52, Harry S. Truman Library and Museum, Independence, Missouri. Accessed July 6, 2009, at http:///www.trumanlibrary.org/oralhist/leddyj.htm.

22. Stewart, *The GATT Uruguay Round: A Negotiating History (1986–1992)*, 1906.

23. Incidentially, the ITO most likely would have lacked the same budgetary mechanism, or it would not have had the same force, given the differences between the types of organizations. See Nitsan Chorev and Sarah Babb, "The Crisis of Neoliberalism and the Future of International Institutions: A Comparision of the IMF and WTO," *Theory and Society* 38 (2009).

24. See "Oral History Interview with John M. Leddy," pp. 56–58, Harry S. Truman Library and Museum, Independence, MI. Accessed July 6, 2009, at online at http:///www.trumanlibrary.org/oralhist/leddyj.htm.

25. Chorev and Babb make this point. Chorev and Babb, "A Crisis of Neoliberalism and the Future of International Institutions: A Comparison of the IMF and the WTO," 464.

26. Alan William Wolff, "International Competitiveness of American Industry: The Role of US Trade Policy," in *US Competitiveness in the World Economy*, ed. Bruce R. Scott and George C. Lodge (Boston: Harvard Business School Press, 1985). As cited in Sylvia Ostry, *Governments and Corporations in a Shrinking World* (New York: Council on Foreign Relations, 1990), p. 21.

27. The MTN Coalition's charter members included Citicorp chairman John Reed, AT&T CEO Robert Allen, IBM chairman and CEO John Akers, American Express Co. chairman James Robinson, General Motors CEO Roger Smith, GE Financial Services chairman Lawrence Bossidy, the American Farm Bureau Federation, the National Federation of Independent Business, and the National Association of Manufacturers.

28. As quoted in Miles Weiss, "Business Group to Push for GATT Approval," in UPI financial section, May 15, 1990.

29. Nitsan Chorev, "A Fluid Divide: Domestic and International Factors in US Trade Policy Formation," *Review of International Political Economy* 14, no. 4 (2007): 674.

30. For a discussion of the differences, see Georg Schild, *Bretton Woods and Dumbarton Oaks: American Economic and Political Postwar Planning in the Summer of 1944* (New York: St. Martin's, 1995), 142.

31. Incidentally, the US never completely severed its ties with UNESCO. It retained its observer status during these years and contributed to some UNESCO programs, such as the Intergovernmental Oceanographic Commission and the Man and the Biosphere Programme.

32. David Skidmore, "Who Is at the Helm? The Debate Over U.S. Funding for the United Nations," *Institute for the Study of Diplomacy Case Studies,* Case 227 (2000): 3.

33. Ibid., 4.

34. Ibid., 6.

35. "Senior" leadership levels refers to subcommittee chairs, committee chairs, party whips, majority/minority leaders, and the Speaker of the House.

36. Robert A. Dahl, "Can International Organizations Be Democratic? A Skeptic's View," in *Democracy's Edges*, ed. Ian Shapiro and Casiano Hacker-Cordon (Cambridge: Cambridge University Press, 1999). Alexis de Tocqueville, *Democracy in America*, ed. J. P. Mayer and M. Lerner, trans. G. Lawrence (New York: Harper, 1966); George F. Kennan, *The Cloud of Danger: Current Realities of American Foreign Policy* (Boston: Little, Brown & Co., 1977). Grant and Keohane, "Accountability and Abuses of Power in World Politics."

# BIBLIOGRAPHY


## Newspapers

*Financial Times* (London)
*New York Times*
*Wall Street Journal*
*Washington Post*

## Manuscript Collections

Bretton Woods Conference Files, Bretton Woods Conference Collection, IMF Archives, Washington, DC

Central Files Collection, IMF Archives, Washington, DC

Chamber of Commerce of the US Records, Hagley Museum and Archive, Hagley, DE

Executive Board Documents, IMF Archives, Washington, DC

Institute for Advanced Study, Archives, Princeton, NJ

League of Nations Archives, United Nations, Geneva, Switzerland

Meyer, Eugene. Papers, Manuscript Division, Library of Congress, Washington, DC

National Association of Manufacturers (US) Records 1895-1990, Committee, Records, Hagley Museum and Library, Hagley, DE

National Foreign Trade Council Records, Hagley Museum and Archives, Hagley, DE

Office of the Managing Director Fonds, IMF Archives, Washington, DC

Raskob, John J. Papers, Hagley Museum and Library, Hagley, DE

Richardson, Elliot. Papers, Manuscript Division, Library of Congress, Washington, DC

Rockefeller Foundation Archives, Rockefeller Archive Center, Tarrytown, NY

Sweetser, Arthur. Papers, Manuscript Division, Library of Congress, Washington, DC

Taft, Robert A., Jr. Papers. Manuscript Division, Library of Congress, Washington, DC

Taft, Robert A., Sr. Papers. Manuscript Division, Library of Congress. Washington, DC

## Government Documents

U.S. Congress. House of Representatives. Committee on Banking and Financial Services. *Administration's Authorization Requests for International Financial Institutions*, 104th Cong., 2nd session, April 25, 1996.

———. Senate. Committee on Foreign Relations. *Amendments to the Inter-American Development Bank and International Development Association Acts*, 86th Cong., 1st session, November 15 and December 4, 1963.

———. House of Representatives. Committee on Banking, Finance, and Urban Affairs. *Authorizing Contributions to IDA, GEF, and ADF*, 103rd Cong., 1st session, May 5, 1993.

———. House of Representatives. Committee on Banking and Currency. *Bretton Woods Agreement Act Amendment*, 87th Cong., 2nd session, February 27 and 28, 1962.

———. House of Representatives. Committee on Foreign Affairs. Briefing on Current World Situation, 86th Cong., 1st session, January 28 and 29, 1959.

———. House of Representatives. *Congressional Record*, 96th Cong., 1st session, September 5, 1979.

———. Senate. Volume 122. *Congressional Record*, 94th Cong., 2nd session, February 2, 1976.

———. Senate. *Congressional Record*, 93rd Cong., 2nd session, May 20, 1974.

———. House of Representatives. Committee on Banking and Financial Services. *East Asian Economic Conditions*, 105th Cong., 1st session, November 13, 1997.

———. House of Representatives. Committee on Banking and Financial Services. *East Asian Economic Conditions (First Segment)*, 105th Cong., 2nd session, January 30, 1993.

———. House of Representatives. Committee on Banking and Financial Services. *East Asian Economic Conditions (Second Segment)*, 105th Cong., 2nd session, February 3, 1998.

———. House of Representatives. Committee on Financial Services. *The Fight Against Global Poverty and Inequality: The World Bank's Approach to Core Labor Standards and Employment Creation,* 110th Cong., 1st session, October 3, 2007.

———. House. Committee on Appropriations. *Foreign Assistance and Related Programs Appropriations for 1980. Part 6: International Financial Institutions*, 96th Cong., 1st session, March 14, 27, 28, April 3, 25, 1979.

———. House. Committee on Appropriations. *Foreign Assistance and Related Programs Appropriations for 1982*, Part 4, 97th Cong., 1st session, April 7, 9, 10, June 2, 1981.

———. House. Committee on Appropriations. *Foreign Assistance and Related Programs Appropriations for 1985*, Part 5, 98th Cong., 2nd session, March 14, 15, 29, April 10, 12, 1984.

———. House. Committee on Appropriations. *Foreign Assistance and Related Programs Appropriations for 1987*, Part 3, 99th Cong., 2nd session, March 4–6, 12, 13, 1986.

———. House of Representatives. Committee on Appropriations. *Foreign Operations, Export Financing, and Related Programs Appropriations for 1995, Part 2*, 103rd Cong., 2nd session, March 1, 8, 10, April 14, 19, 1994.

———. House of Representatives. Committee on Appropriations. *Foreign Operations, Export Financing, and Related Programs Appropriations for 1997, Part 2*, 104th Cong., 2nd session, March 27, 28, April 18, 1996.

———. House of Representatives. Committee on Appropriations, Subcommittee on Foreign Operations. *Foreign Operations, Export Financing, and Related Programs Appropriations for 2000*, 106th Cong., 1st session, March 17, 1999.

———. House of Representatives. Committee on Banking, Finance, and Urban Affairs. *General Capital Increase for the World Bank*, 100th Cong., 2nd session, June 15, 1988.

———. Senate. Banking and Currency. *H. R. 3314 An Act to Provide for the Participation of the United States in the International Monetary Fund and the International Bank for Reconstruction and Development*, 79th Cong., 1st session, June 12, 13, 14, 15, 16, 18, 19, 20, 21, 22, 25, and 28, 1945.

———. House of Representatives. Subcommittee on International Development Institutions and Finance. *H. R.* 5262, 95th Cong., 1st session, March 22, 1977.

———. House of Representatives. Banking and Currency. *H. R. 2211 A Bill to Provide for the Participation of the United States in the International Monetary Fund and the International Bank for Reconstruction and Development*, 79th Cong., 1st session, March 7, 8, 9, 12, 13, 14, 15, 16, 19, 20, 21, 22, and 23, 1945.

———. House of Representatives. Committee on Banking and Currency. *HR* 6228, 84th Cong., 1st session, July 11 and 14, 1955.

———. Senate. Committee on Foreign Relations. *HR 6765: An Act to Authorize Acceptance of an Amendement to the Articles of Agreement of the IFC*, 87th Cong., 1st session, July 31, 1961.

———. House of Representatives. Committee on Banking and Currency. *HR* 8816 and S 1742, 89th Cong., 1st session, July 8, 1965.

———. Senate. Committee on Banking, Housing, and Urban Affairs. *IMF Supplementary Financing Facility*, 95th Cong., 1st session, October 13, 1977.

———. Senate. Committee on Foreign Relations. *Increased Resources for International Development Association*, 90th Cong., 2nd session, May 21, 1968.

———. House. Committee on Banking and Currency. *International Development Association Act*, 86th Cong., 2nd session, March 15, 16, and 17, 1960.

———. House. Committee on Banking and Currency. *International Development Association Act Amendment*, 86th Cong., 2nd session, March 23 and 24.

———. Senate. Committee on Foreign Relations. International Financial Institutions, 95th Cong., 1st session, March 9, 10, 1977.

———. Senate. Report of the Committee on Foreign Relations. *The International Financial Institutions: A Call for Change*, 111th Cong., 2nd session, March 10, 2010.

———. House of Representatives. Subcommittee on International Development, Finance, Trade, and Monetary Policy. *Oversight of the International Monetary Fund and the World Bank: A Meeting of a Multinational Group of Parliamentarians Involved in Oversight of the IMF and the World Bank*, 103rd Cong., 2nd session, November 21, 1994.

———. Senate. Committee on Banking, Housing, and Urban Affairs. *Oversight on International Economic Policy as It Affects United States Monetary Affairs, Credit, and Financial Institutions: In Particular on International Debt*, 95th Cong., 1st session, August 29 and 30, 1977.

———. House of Representatives. Committee on Appropriations. *Par Value Modification Appropriations*, 93rd Cong., 1st session, September 14, 1973.

———. Joint Economic Committee. *A Proposal to Link Reserve Creation*, 91st Cong., 2nd session, August 1969.

———. House of Representatives. Committee on Financial Services. *Reauthorization Requests on US Participation in the International Development Association and the African Development Bank*, 107 Cong., 2nd session, July 19, 25, 2002.

———. House of Representatives. Committee on Banking and Financial Services, Subcommittee on General Oversight and Investigations. *Review of the Operations of the International Monetary Fund*, 105th Cong., 2nd session, April 21, 1998.

———. Senate. Subcommittee on International Finance, Committee on Banking and Currency. *S. 1894 A Bill to Provide for the Participation of the United States in the International Finance Corporation*, 84th Cong., 1st session, June 6 and 7, 1955.

———. House. Committee on Banking, Finance, and Urban Affairs. *To Provide for Increased Participation by the US in the International Development Association*, 93rd Cong., 2nd session, June 11, 1974.

———. House. Committee on Banking, Finance, and Urban Affairs. *To Provide for Increased Participation by the US in the International Development Association*, 92nd Cong., 1st session, July 6, 1971.

———. House. Committee on Banking and Currency. *To Provide for Increased Participation by the United States in the International Development Association*, 90th Cong., 2nd session, May 8 and 9, 1968.

———. Senate. Committee on Foreign Relations. *To Provide for the Participation of the United States in the International Development Association*, 86th Cong., 2nd session, March 18 and 21, 1960.

———. House of Representatives. Banking and Currency. *US Quota Increase in the IMF*, 89th Cong., 1st session, March 23 and 24, 1965.

Executive Office of the President. *"Appendix: The Budget of the United States Government,"* edited by OMB: US Government Printing Office, 1988.

———. *"Appendix: The Budget of the United States Government,"* edited by OMB: US Government Printing Office, 1989.

———. *"Appendix: The Budget of the United States Government,"* edited by OMB: US Government Printing Office, 1986.

———. *"The Budget for Fiscal Year 2009,"* edited by OMB: US Government Printing Office, 2008.

Federal Deposit Insurance Corporation. *An Examination of the Banking Crises of the 1980s and Early 1990s*. Washington, DC: FDIC, 1997.

US Department of the Treasury. *"Response to the Report of the International Financial Institution Advisory Commission."* Washington, DC: US Department of the Treasury, 2000.

## Books, Articles, and Chapters

Abdelal, Rawi. *Capital Rules: The Construction of Global Finance*. Cambridge, MA: Harvard University Press, 2007.

Aldrich, John H., and David W. Rohde. "The Consequences of Party Organization in the House: The Role of the Majority and Minority Parties in Conditional Party Government." In *Polarized Politics: Congress and the President in a Partisan Era*, edited by Jon R. Bond and Richard Fleisher, 31–72. Washington, DC: CQ Press, 2000.

Arnold, R. Douglas. *Congress, the Press, and Political Accountability*. New York: Russell Sage Foundation, 2004.

———. *The Logic of Congressional Action*. New Haven, CT: Yale University Press, 1990.

Ascher, William. "The World Bank and US Control." In *The United States and Multilateral Institutions*, edited by Margaret P. Karns and Karen A. Mingst, 115–139. Boston: Unwin Hyman, 1990.

Asher, Robert E., Walter M. Kotschnig, and William Adams Jr. Brown. *The United Nations and Economic and Social Co-Operation*. Washington, DC: Brookings Institution, 1957.

Babb, Sarah. *Behind the Development Banks: Washington Politics, World Poverty, and the Wealth of Nations*. Chicago: University of Chicago Press, 2009.

Barnett, Michael N., and Martha Finnemore. "The Politics, Power, and Pathologies of International Organization." *International Organization* 53, no. 4 (1999): 699–732.

———. *Rules for the World: International Organizations in Global Politics*. Ithaca, NY: Cornell University Press, 2004.

Baruch, Bernard. *Baruch: The Public Years*. New York: Holt, Rinehart and Winston, 1960.

Bauer, Raymond A., Ithiel De Sola Pool, and Lewis Anthony Dexter. *American Business and Public Policy: The Politics of Foreign Trade*. 2nd ed. Chicago: Aldine, Atherton, 1972.

Baumgartner, Frank R., and Bryan D. Jones. *Agendas and Instability in American Politics*. Chicago: University of Chicago Press, 1993.

Baumgartner, Frank R., and Beth L. Leech. *Basic Interests: The Importance of Groups in Politics and Political Science*. Princeton, NJ: Princeton University Press, 1998.

Berry, Jeffrey M. "Interest Groups and Gridlock." In *Interest Group Politics*, edited by Allan J. Cigler and Burdett A. Loomis, 333–354. Washington, DC: CQ Press, 2002.

———. *The New Liberalism: The Changing Power of Citizen Groups*. Washington, DC: Brookings, 1999.

———. "Subgovernments, Issue Networks, and Political Conflict." In *Remaking American Politics*, edited by Richard Harris and Sidney Milkis, 239–260. Boulder, CO: Westview Press, 1989.

Best, Jacqueline. *The Limits of Transparency: Ambiguity and the History of International Finance*. Ithaca, NY: Cornell University Press, 2005.

Bibby, John, and Roger Davidson. *On Capitol Hill: Studies in the Legislative Process*. New York: Holt, Rinehart and Winston, Inc., 1967.

Bird, Kai. *The Chairman: John J. McCloy*. New York: Simon & Schuster, 1992.

Birdsall, Nancy. *Rescuing the World Bank: A CGD Working Group Report*. Washington, DC: Center for Global Development, 2006.

Blustein, Paul. *The Chastening: Inside the Crisis That Rocked the Global Financial System and Humbled the IMF*. New York: Public Affairs, 2002.

Boughton, James. *Silent Revolution: The International Monetary Fund 1979–1989*. Washington, DC: International Monetary Fund, 2001.

Brown, Bartram S. *The United States and the Politicization of the World Bank*. New York: Kegan Paul International, 1992.

Broz, J. Lawrence. "Congressional Voting on Funding the International Financial Institutions." *Review of International Organizations* 3, no. 4 (2008): 351–374.

Broz, J. Lawrence, and Michael Brewster Hawes. "Congressional Politics of Financing the International Monetary Fund." *International Organization* 60, no. 2 (2006): 367–399.

———. "US Domestic Politics and International Monetary Fund Policy." In *Delegation and Agency in International Organizations*, edited by Darren G. Hawkins, David A. Lake, Daniel L. Nielson, and Michael J. Tierney, 77–106. New York: Cambridge University Press, 2006.

Busby, Joshua William. "Bono Made Jesse Helms Cry: Jubilee 2000, Debt Relief, and Moral Action in International Politics." *International Studies Quarterly* 51, no. 2 (2007): 247–275.

Callaghy, Thomas M. "Networks and Governance in Africa: Innovation in the Debt Regime." In *Intervention and Transnationalism in Africa: Global—Local Networks of Power*, edited by Ronald Kassimir, Thomas M. Callaghy, and Robert Latham, 115–148. New York: Cambridge University Press, 2001.

Casey, Kevin M. *Saving International Capitalism During the Early Truman Presidency: The National Advisory Council on International Monetary and Financial Problems*. New York: Routledge, 2001.

Cerny, Philip G. *Rethinking World Politics: A Theory of Transnational Neopluralism*. New York: Oxford University Press, 2010.

Chernow, Ron. *The House of Morgan: An American Banking Dynasty and the Rise of Modern Finance*. New York: Atlantic Monthly Press, 1990.

Chorev, Nitsan. "A Fluid Divide: Domestic and International Factors in US Trade Policy Formation." *Review of International Political Economy* 14, no. 4 (2007): 653–689.

Chorev, Nitsan, and Sarah Babb. "The Crisis of Neoliberalism and the Future of International Institutions: A Comparision of the IMF and WTO." *Theory and Society* 38 (2009): 459–484.

Chwieroth, Jeffrey M. *Capital Ideas: The IMF and the Rise of Financial Liberalization*. Princeton, NJ: Princeton University Press, 2010.

———. "Normative Change from Within: The International Monetary Fund's Approach to Capital Account Liberalization." *International Studies Quarterly* 52, no. 1 (2008): 192–158.

Cigler, Allan J. "Interest Groups: A Subfield in Search of an Identity." In *Political Science: Looking to the Future*, edited by William Crotty, 99–135. Evanston, IL: Northwestern University Press, 1991.

Cigler, Allan J., and Burdett A. Loomis. "Always Involved, Rarely Central: Organized Interests in American Politics." In *Interest Group Politics*, edited by Allan J. Cigler and Burdett A. Loomis, 381–391. Washington, DC: CQ Press, 2002.

Clark, William. "Robert McNamara at the World Bank." *Foreign Affairs* 60, no. 1 (1981): 167–184.

Cleveland, Harold van B., and Thomas F. Huertas. *Citibank: 1812–1970*. Cambridge, MA: Harvard University Press, 1985.

Congressional Budget Office. *"US Participation in the Witteveen Facility: The Need for a New Source of International Finance."* Washington, DC: Congress of the United States, 1978.

Copelovitch, Mark S. *The International Monetary Fund in the Global Economy: Banks, Bonds, and Bailouts*. New York: Cambridge University Press, 2010.

Cox, Gary W., and Mathew D. McCubbins. *Legislative Leviathan: Party Government in the House*. Los Angeles: University of California Press, 1994.

Crabb, Cecil V., Glenn J. Antizzo, and Leila E. Sarieddine. *Congress and the Foreign Policy Process: Modes of Legislative Behavior*. Baton Rouge, LA: Louisiana State University Press, 2000.

Cutler, A. Claire. "Private International Regimes and Interfirm Cooperation." In *The Emergence of Private Authority in Global Governance*, edited by Rodney Bruce Hall and Thomas J. Biersteker, 23–42. Cambridge: Cambridge University Press, 2002.

Cutler, A. Claire, Virginia Haufler, and Tony Porter, eds. *Private Authority and International Affairs*. Albany, NY: SUNY Press, 1999.

Dahl, Robert A. "Can International Organizations Be Democratic? A Skeptic's View." In *Democracy's Edges*, edited by Ian Shapiro and Casiano Hacker-Cordon, 19–36. Cambridge: Cambridge University Press, 1999.

———. *Congress and Foreign Policy*. New York: Harcourt, Brace and Company, 1950.

Davidson, Roger H., and Walter J. Oleszek. *Congress and Its Members*. Seventh ed. Washington, DC: CQ Press, 2000.

de Vries, Margaret Garritsen. *The IMF 1972–1978 Cooperation on Trial*. Vol. I: Narrative and Analysis. Washington, DC: IMF, 1985.

———. *The IMF in a Changing World: 1945–85*. Washington, DC: The IMF, 1986.

Deering, Christopher J. "Congress's Role in Foreign Policymaking." In *Congress Project Seminar on the Role of Congress in Foreign Policymaking*. Woodrow Wilson International Center for Scholars, 2009.

Deering, Christopher J., and Steven S. Smith. *Committees in Congress*. Third ed. Washington, DC: CQ Press, 1997.

Deering, Christopher J., and Paul J. Wahlbeck. "US House Committee Chair Selection: Republicans Play Musican Chairs in the 107th Congress." *American Politics Research* 34, no. 2 (2006): 223–242.

Dell, Sidney. *On Being Grandmotherly: The Evolution of IMF Conditionality*. Vol. 144. Princeton, NJ: Essays in International Finance, Department of Economics, Princeton University, 1981.

Destler, I.M. *American Trade Politics*. Third ed. Washington, DC: Institute for International Economics, 1995.

Dodd, Randall. "Sovereign Debt Restructuring." *The Financier*, 2002, accessed at http//www.the-financier.com April 8, 2005.

Drezner, Daniel W. *All Politics Is Global: Explaining International Regulatory Regimes*. Princeton, NJ: Princeton University Press, 2007.

Duncombe, Bruce F., ed. *Foreign Economic Policy, 1969–1972; International Monetary Policy, 1969–1972*. Edited by David S. Patterson. Vol. III, *Foreign Relations of the United States, 1969–1976*. Washington, DC: US Government Printing Office, 2001.

Epstein, David, and Sharyn O'Halloran. "A Theory of Strategic Oversight: Congress, Lobbyists, and the Bureaucracy." *Jounal of Law, Economics, & Organization* 11, no. 2 (1995): 227–255.

Evans, Diana. "Appropriations in the Republican Era." *Extensions: A Journal of the Carl Albert Congressional Research and Studies Center Spring* (2007): 9–14.

Finnemore, Martha. *National Interests in International Society*. Ithaca, NY: Cornell University Press, 1996.

Fleming, Denna Frank. *The United States and the League of Nations: 1918–1920*. New York: G.P. Putnam's Sons, 1932.

Flexner, Abraham. *Funds and Foundations: The Policies Past and Present*. New York: Harper & Brothers Publishers, 1952.

Fomerand, Jacques. "Mirror, Tool, or Linchpin for Change: The UN and Development." Waterloo, Ontario: The Academic Council on the United Nations System, 2003.

Fosdick, Raymond B. *Letters on the League of Nations from the Files of Raymond B. Fosdick*. Princeton, NJ: Princeton University Press, 1966.

Fox, Harrison W., Jr., and Susan Webb Hammond. *Congressional Staffs: The Invisible Force in American Lawmaking*. New York: The Free Press, 1977.

Frieden, Jeffrey A. *Banking on the World: The Politics of American International Finance*. New York: Harper & Row, 1987.

Friman, H. Richard. "Side-Payments Versus Security Cards: Domestic Bargaining Tactics in International Economic Negotiations." *International Organization* 47, no. 3 (1993): 387–410.

Gardner, Richard N. *Sterling-Dollar Diplomacy in Current Perspective: The Origins and the Prospects of Our International Economic Order*. New York: Columbia University Press, 1980.

Gold, Joseph. "Trust Funds in International Law." In *Legal and Institutional Aspects of the International Monetary System, Selected Essays*, edited by Joseph Gold. Washington, DC: International Monetary Fund, 1984.

Goldman, Michael. *Imperial Nature: The World Bank and Struggles for Social Justice in the Age of Globalization*. New Haven: Yale University Press, 2006.

Goldstein, Morris. *The Asian Financial Crisis: Causes, Cures, and Systemic Implications*. Washington, DC: The Peterson Institute for International Economics, 1998.

Gordenker, Leon, and Thomas G. Weiss. "Pluralizing Global Governance: Analytical Approaches and Dimensions." In *NGOs, the UN, and Global Governance*, edited by Leon Gordenker and Thomas G. Weiss, 17–47. Boulder, CO: Lynne Rienner Publishers, 1996.

Gould, Erica R. "Delegating IMF Conditionality: Understanding Variations in Control and Conformity." In *Delegation and Agency in International Organizations*, edited by Darren G. Hawkins, David A. Lake, Daniel L. Nielson, and Michael J. Tierney, 281–311. New York: Cambridge University Press, 2006.

———. "Money Talks: Supplementary Financiers and International Monetary Fund Conditionality." *International Organization* 57, no. 3 (2003): 551–586.

———. *Money Talks: The International Monetary Fund, Conditionality and Supplementary Financiers*. Stanford: Stanford University Press, 2006.

Gourevitch, Peter. "Domestic Politics and International Relations." In *Handbook of International Relations*, edited by Walter Carlsnaes, Thomas Risse, and Beth A. Simmons, 309–328. Thousand Oaks, CA: Sage Publications, 2002.

Gourevitch, Peter A. "The Second Image Reversed: The International Sources of Domestic Politics." *International Organization* 32 (1978): 881–911.

Gowa, Joanne. "Public Goods and Political Institutions: Trade and Monetary Policy Processes in the United States." *International Organization* 42, no. 1 (1988): 15–32.

Gowa, Joanne S. *Closing the Gold Window: Domestic Politics and the End of Bretton Woods*. Ithaca, NY: Cornell University Press, 1983.

Grant, Ruth W., and Robert O. Keohane. "Accountability and Abuses of Power in World Politics." *American Political Science Review* 99, no. 1 (2005): 29–43.

Greider, William. *Secrets of the Temple: How the Federal Reserve Runs the Country*. New York: Simon and Schuster, 1987.

Grieco, Joseph M. "Anarchy and the Limits of Cooperation: A Realist Critique of the Newest Liberal Institutionalism." *International Organization* 42, no. Summer (1988): 485–507.

———. *Cooperation Among Nations: Europe, America, and Non-Tariff Barriers to Trade*. Ithaca, NY: Cornell University Press, 1990.

Griesgraber, Jo Marie. "Implementation by the Carter Administration of Human Rights Legislation Affecting Latin America." Ph.D. diss., Georgetown University, 1983.

———. "Influencing the IMF." In *Critical Mass: The Emergence of Global Civil Society*, edited by James W. St. G. Walker and Andrew S. Thompson, 153–167. Waterloo, CA: Wilfred Laurier University Press, 2008.

Haas, Peter M. "Social Constructivism and the Evolution of Multilateral Environmental Governance." In *Globalization and Governance*, edited by Aseem Prakash and Jeffrey A. Hart, 103–133. New York: Routledge, 2000.

Hall, Richard L. *Participation in Congress*. New Haven: Yale University Press, 1996.

Hall, Richard L., and Alan V. Deardorff. "Lobbying as Legislative Subsidy." *American Political Science Review* 100, no. 1 (2006): 69–84.

Hamilton, Alexander, James Madison, and John Jay. *The Federalist Papers*. New York: Bantam Books, 1988.

Haralz, Jonas. "The International Finance Corporation." In *The World Bank: Its First Half Century*, edited by Devesh Kapur, John P. Lewis, and Richard Webb, 805–899. Washington, DC: The Brookings Institution Press, 1997.

Hastedt, Glenn P. *American Foreign Policy: Past, Present, Future*. 6th ed. New York: Pearson Prentice Hall, 2006.

Haufler, Virginia. "Industry Regulation and Self-regulation: The Case of Labour Standards." In *Enhancing Global Governance: Towards a New Diplomacy?*, edited by Andrew F. Cooper, John English, and Ramesh Thakur, 162–186. New York: United Nations University Press, 2002.

Helleiner, Eric. "Reinterpreting BrettonWoods: International Development and the Neglected Origins of Embedded Liberalism." *Development and Change* 37, no. 5 (2006): 943–967.

———. *States and the Reemergence of Global Finance: From Bretton Woods to the 1990s*. Ithaca, NY: Cornell University Press, 1994.

———. "The Strange Story of Bush and the Argentine Debt Crisis." *Third World Quarterly* 26, no. 6 (2005): 951–969.

Helleiner, Eric, and Geoffrey Cameron. "Another World Order? The Bush Administration and HIPC Debt Cancellation." *New Political Economy* 11, no. 1 (2006): 125–140.

Henehan, Marie T. *Foreign Policy and Congress: An International Relations Perspective*. Ann Arbor, MI: University of Michigan Press, 2000.

Henning, C. Randall. *The Exchange Stabilization Fund: Slush Money or War Chest?* Washington, DC: Institute for International Economics, 1999.

———. "Political Economy of the Bretton Woods Institutions: Adapting to Financial Change." *The World Economy* 19, no. 2 (1996): 173–189.

Herman, Barry. "Civil Society and the Financing for Development Initiative at the United Nations." In *Civil Society and Global Finance*, edited by Jan Aart Scholte and Albrecht Schnabel, 162–177. New York: Routledge, 2002.

Hills, Carla A., and Peter G. Peterson. "Safeguarding Prosperity in a Global Financial System: The Future International Financial Architecture." In *Council on Foreign Relations–Sponsored Project*. New York: Institute for International Economics, 1999.

Hojnacki, Marie, and David C. Kimball. "The Who and How of Organizations' Lobbying Strategies in Committee." *Journal of Politics* 61, no. 4 (1999): 999–1024.

Hoopes, Townsend, and Douglas Brinkley. *FDR and the Creation of the UN*. New Haven: Yale University Press, 1997.

Hughes, Kent H. *Building the Next American Century: The Past and Future of American Economic Competitiveness*. Washington, DC: Woodrow Wilson Center Press, 2005.

Hughes, Kent Higgon. *Trade, Taxes, and Transnationals: International Economic Decision Making in Congress*. New York: Praeger Publishers, 1979.

Independent Evaluation Group of the World Bank. "Doing Business: An Independent Evaluation." Washington, DC: The World Bank, 2008.

Irwin, Lewis G. "Dancing the Foreign Aid Appropriations Dance: Recurring Themes in the Modern Congresses." *Public Budgeting & Finance,* Summer (2000): 30–48.

Jackson, John. *The World Trading System: Law and Policy of International Economic Regulations*. Cambridge, MA: MIT Press, 1989.

Jackson, James K. "Iceland's Financial Crisis." Washington, DC: The Congressional Research Service, 2008.

Jacobsson, Erin E. *A Life for Sound Money: Per Jacobsson: His Biography*. Oxford: Clarendon Press, 1979.

Jacobsson, Per. "Trade and Financial Relationships Between Countries: The Progress Towards Multilateralism." In *Some Monetary Problems International and National*, edited by Per Jacobsson, 281–317. New York: Oxford University Press, 1958.

James, Harold. *International Monetary Cooperation Since Bretton Woods*. New York: Oxford University Press for the IMF, 1996.

Johnson, Robert David. *Congress and the Cold War.* New York: Cambridge University Press, 2006.

Kahler, Miles, ed. *Networked Politics: Agency, Power, and Governance*. Ithaca, NY: Cornell University Press, 2009.

———. "The United States and the International Monetary Fund: Declining Influence or Declining Interest?" In *The United States and Multilateral Institutions: Patterns of Changing Instrumentality and Influence*, edited by Margaret P. Karnes and Karen A. Mingst, 91–114. Boston: Unwin Hyman, 1990.

Kapur, Devesh. "The Changing Anatomy of Governance of the World Bank." In *Reinventing the World Bank*, edited by Jonathan R. Pincus and Jeffrey A. Winters, 54–75. Ithaca, NY: Cornell University Press, 2002.

Keck, Margaret E., and Kathryn Sikkink. *Activists Beyond Borders: Advocacy Networks in International Politics*. Ithaca, NY: Cornell University Press, 1998.

———. *Activists Beyond Borders: Advocacy Networks in International Politics*. Ithaca, NY: Cornell University Press, 1998.

———. "Transnational Advocacy Networks in the Movement Society." In *The Social Movement Society: Contentious Politics for a New Century*, edited by David S. Meyer and Sidney Tarrow, 217–239. New York: Rowman & Littlefield Publishers, Inc., 1998.

Kennan, George F. *The Cloud of Danger: Current Realities of American Foreign Policy*. Boston: Little, Brown & Co., 1977.

Keohane, Robert O., and Joseph S. Nye, Jr. "Redefining Accountability for Global Governance: Political Authority in Transition." In *Governance in a Global Economy*, edited by Miles Kahler and David Lake, 386–411. Princeton, NJ: Princeton University Press, 2003.

Kingdon, John W. *Agendas, Alternatives, and Public Policies*. Boston: Little, Brown and Company, 1984.

Klingberg, Frank. *Positive Expectations of America's World Role*. Lanham, MD: University Press of America, 1996.

Klotz, Audie. *Norms in International Relations: The Struggle Against Apartheid*. Ithaca, NY: Cornell University Press, 1995.

Krause, Keith, and W. Andy Knight. "Introduction: Evolution and Change in the United Nations System." In *State, Society, and the UN System*, edited by Keith Krause and W. Andy Knight, 1–36. New York: United Nations University Press, 1995.

Krehbiel, Keith, Kenneth A. Shepsle, and Barry R. Weingast. "Why Are Congressional Committees Powerful?" *American Political Science Review* 81, no. 3 (1987): 929–945.

Krueger, Anne. "International Financial Architecture for 2002: A New Approach to Sovereign Debt Restructuring." Paper presented at the National Economists' Club Annual Members' Dinner, American Enterprise Institute, Washington DC, November 26, 2001.

Krutz, Glen S. *Hitching a Ride: Omnibus Legislating in the US Congress*. Columbus, OH: Ohio State University Press, 2001.

Krutz, Glen S., and Peake Jeffrey S. *Treaty Politics and the Rise of Executive Agreements*. Ann Arbor, MI: University of Michigan Press, 2009.

Lake, David A. "Global Governance: A Relational Contracting Approach." In *Globalization and Governance*, edited by Aseem Prakash and Jeffrey A. Hart, 31–53. New York: Routledge, 2000.

Lamont, Thomas W. *Across World Frontiers*. New York: Harcourt Brace, 1951.

Lavelle, Kathryn C. "Exit, Voice, and Loyalty in International Organizations: US Involvement in the League of Nations." *Review of International Organizations* 2 (2007): 371–393.

———. "The International Finance Corporation and the Emerging Markets Funds Industry." *Third World Quarterly* 21, no. 2 (2000): 193–214.

———. "Multilateral Cooperation and Congress: The Legislative Process of Securing Funding for the World Bank." *International Studies Quarterly* 55, no. 1 (2011): 199–222.

———. *The Politics of Equity Finance in Emerging Markets*. New York: Oxford University Press, 2004.

Lee, Frances E. *Beyond Ideology: Politics, Principles, and Partisanship in the US Senate*. Chicago: University of Chicago Press, 2009.

Lee, Frances E., and Bruce I. Oppenheimer. *Sizing Up the Senate: The Unequal Consequences of Equal Representation*. Chicago: University of Chicago Press, 1999.

Lerrick, Adam. "Funding the IMF: How Much Does It Really Cost?" In *Quarterly International Economics Report*. Pittsburgh, PA: Carnegie Mellon Gailliot Center for Public Policy, 2003.

Libby, Ronald T. "International Development Association: A Legal Fiction Designed to Secure an LDC Constituency." *International Organization* 29, no. 4 (1975): 1065–1072.

Lindsay, James M. *Congress and the Politics of US Foreign Policy*. Baltimore: The Johns Hopkins University Press, 1994.

Lipson, Charles. "The International Organization of Third World Debt." In *Toward a Political Economy of Development*, edited by Robert Bates, 12–46. Berkeley, CA: University of California Press, 1988.

Lowi, Theodore J. *The End of Liberalism: The Second Republic of the United States*. New York: W. W. Norton, 1969.

Malbin, Michael J. *Unelected Representatives: Congressional Staff and the Future of Representative Government*. New York: Basic Books, 1979.

Mallaby, Sebastian. *The World's Banker: A Story of Failed States, Financial Crises, and the Wealth and Poverty of Nations*. New York: Penguin Press, 2004.

Mann, Thomas E., and Norman J. Ornstein. *The Broken Branch: How Congress Is Failing America and How to Get It Back on Track*. New York: Oxford University Press, 2006.

Martin, Lisa L. *Democratic Commitments: Legislatures and International Cooperation*. Princeton, NJ: Princeton University Press, 2000.

Mason, Edward S., and Robert E. Asher. *The World Bank Since Bretton Woods*. Washington, DC: The Brookings Institution, 1973.

Matecki, B. E. *Establishment of the International Finance Corporation and United States Policy. New York*: Frederick A. Praeger, 1957.

Mayhew, David R. *Divided We Govern: Party Control, Lawmaking and Investigations, 1946–2002*. New Haven, CT: Yale University Press, 2005.

———. *Parties and Policies: How the American Government Works*. New Haven: Yale University Press, 2008.

McGinnis, Michael D. "Rent-seeking, Redistribution, and Reform in the Governance of Global Markets." In *Globalization and Governance*, edited by Aseem Prakash and Jeffrey A. Hart, 54–76. New York: Routledge, 2000.

Mead, Walter Russell. *Special Providence: American Foreign Policy and How It Changed the World*. New York: Alfred A. Knopf, 2001.

Mearsheimer, John J. "The False Promise of International Institutions." *International Security* 19, no. 3 (1994): 5–49.

Mikesell, Raymond Frech. *The Bretton Woods Debates: A Memoir*. Vol. 192. Princeton, NJ: Princeton Essays in International Finance, 1994.

Milbrath, Lester W. *The Washington Lobbyists*. Chicago: Rand McNally, 1963.

Miller, Richard B. *Citicorp: The Story of a Bank in Crisis*. New York: McGraw-Hill, Inc., 1993.

Miller-Adams, Michelle. *The World Bank: New Agendas in a Changing World*. New York: Routledge, 1999.

Milner, Helen V. *Resisting Protectionism: Global Industries and the Politics of International Trade*. Princeton, NJ: Princeton University Press, 1988.

Milner, Helen V., and B. Peter Rosendorff. "Trade Negotiations, Information and Domestic Politics: The Role of Domestic Groups." *Economics and Politics* 8, no. 2 (1996): 145–189.

Morgan Stanley & Co. *A Summary of Financing: 1935–1953*. New York: Morgan Stanley & Co., 1954.

Morgenthau, Henry Jr. "Bretton Woods and International Cooperation." *Foreign Affairs* 23, no. 2 (1945): 182–194.

Muchhala, Bhumika, ed. *Ten Years After: Revisiting the Asian Financial Crisis*. Washington, DC: Woodrow Wilson International Center for Scholars, 2007.

Muirhead, Bruce. *Against the Odds: The Public Life and Times of Louis Rasminsky*. Toronto: University of Toronto Press, 1999.

Nelson, Rebecca A., Dick K. Nanto, Jonathan E. Sanford, and Martin A. Weiss. "Frequently Asked Questions about IMF Involvement in the Eurozone Debt Crisis." Washington, DC: Congressional Research Service, 2010.

Nielson, Daniel L., and Michael J. Tierney. "Delegation to International Organizations: Agency Theory and World Bank Environmental Reform." *International Organization* 57 (2003): 241–276.

Oleszek, Walter J. *Congressional Procedures and the Policy Process*. 8th ed. Washington, DC: CQ Press, 2011.

Olson, Mancur. *The Logic of Collective Action: Public Goods and the Theory of Groups*. Cambridge, MA: Harvard University Press, 1971.

Orr, James C. "Business Associations and Global Financial Governance." In *Civil Society and Global Finance*, edited by Jan Aart Scholte and Albrecht Schnabel, 199–212. New York: Routledge, 2002.

Ostrower, Gary B. "The United States and the League of Nations, 1919–1939." In *The League of Nations in Retrospect*, edited by United Nations Library, 128–143. New York: Walter de Gruyter, 1983.

Ostry, Sylvia. *Governments and Corporations in a Shrinking World*. New York: Council on Foreign Relations, 1990.

Owens, John E. "The Return of Party Government in the US House of Representatives: Central Leadership—Committee Relationships in the 104th Congress." *British Journal of Political Science* 27, no. 2 (1997): 247–272.

Paulson Jr., Henry M. *On the Brink: Inside the Race to Stop the Collapse of the Global Financial System*. New York: Business Plus, 2010.

Pauly, Louis W. *The League of Nations and the Foreshadowing of the International Monetary Fund*. Vol. 201. Princeton, NJ: Princeton University Essays in International Finance, 1996.

———. *Who Elected the Bankers? Surveillance and Control in the World Economy*. Ithaca, NY: Cornell University Press, 1997.

Payne, Rodger A., and Nayef H. Samhat. *Democratizing Global Politics: Discourse Norms, International Regimes, and Political Community*. Albany, NY: SUNY Press, 2004.

Polak, Jacques J. *The World Bank and the International Monetary Fund: A Changing Relationship*. Washington, DC: The Brookings Institution Occasional Papers, 1994.

Polsby, Nelson W. *How Congress Evolves: Social Bases of Institutional Change*. New York: Oxford University Press, 2004.

Putnam, Robert D. "Diplomacy and Domestic Politics: The Logic of Two-Level Games." *International Organization* 42, no. 3 (1988).

Redman, Eric. *The Dance of Legislation: An Insider's Account of the Working of the United States Senate*. Seattle, WA: University of Washington Press, 2001.

Rockefeller, David. *Memoirs*. New York: Random House, 2002.

Rogers, David. *The Future of American Banking*. New York: McGraw-Hill, Inc., 1993.

Ruggie, John Gerard. "Multilateralism at Century's End." In *Constructing the World's Polity*. New York: Routledge, 1998.

———. "Multilateralism: The Anatomy of an Institution." In *Multilateralism Matters: The Theory and Praxis of an Institutional Form*, edited by John Gerard Ruggie, 3–48. New York: Columbia University Press, 1993.

Salter, Sir Arthur. *Foreign Investment*. Vol. 12. Princeton, NJ: Princeton Essays in International Finance.

Samhat, Nayef H. "International Regimes and the Prospects for Global Democracy." *The Whitehead Journal of Diplomacy and International Relations* 6, no. 1 (2005): 179–192.

Sandholtz, Wayne. "Globalization and the Evolution of Rules." In *Globalization and Governance*, edited by Aseem Prakash and Jeffrey A. Hart, 77–102. New York: Routledge, 2000.

Sanford, Jonathan E. "World Bank: IDA Loans or IDA Grants?" *World Development* 30, no. 5 (2002): 741–762.

Sanford, Jonathan E., and Martin A. Weiss. "The Global Financial Crisis: Increasing IMF Resources and the Role of Congress." Washington, DC: Congressional Research Service, 2009.

Saxton, Jim. "IMF Gold Sales in Perspective." Washington, DC: Joint Economic Committee, US Congress, 1999.

Schattschneider, E. E. *The Semisovereign People: A Realist's View of Democracy in America*. New York: Harcourt Brace Jovanovich College Publishers, 1975.

Schick, Allen. *Congress and Money: Budgeting, Spending and Taxing*. Washington, DC: The Urban Institute, 1980.

Schickler, Eric. *Disjointed Pluralism: Institutional Innovation and the Development of the US Congress*. Princeton, NJ: Princeton University Press, 2001.

Schild, Georg. *Bretton Woods and Dumbarton Oaks: American Economic and Political Postwar Planning in the Summer of 1944*. New York: St. Martin's, 1995.

Schoultz, Lars. "Politics, Economics, and US Participation in Multilateral Development Banks." *International Organization* 36, no. 3 (1982): 537–574.

Schwartz, Anna J. "Reflections on the Gold Commission Report." *Journal of Money, Credit and Banking* 14, no. 4 (1982): 538–551.

Scott, James M., and Ralph G. Carter. "The Politics of IMF Reform: The Asian Flu and Abortion Politics." In *Contemporary Cases in US Foreign Policy: From Terrorism to Trade*, edited by Ralph G. Carter. Washington, DC: CQ Press, 2005.

Sell, Susan K., and Aseem Prakash. "Using Ideas Strategically: The Contest Between Business and NGO Networks in Intellectual Property Rights." *International Studies Quarterly* 48, no. 1 (2004): 143–175.

Shaw, D. John. "Turning Point in the Evolution of Soft Financing: The United Nations and the World Bank." *Canadian Journal of Development Studies* 26, no. 1 (2005): 43–61.

Shepsle, Kenneth A., and Barry R. Weingast. "The Institutional Foundations of Committee Power." *American Political Science Review* 81, no. 1 (1987): 85–104.

Sinclair, Barbara. *Legislators, Leaders, and Lawmaking: The US House of Representatives in the Postreform Era*. Baltimore: The Johns Hopkins University Press, 1995.

———. "Parties and Leadership in the House." In *The Legislative Branch*, edited by Paul J. Quirk and Sarah A. Binder, 224–254. New York: Oxford University Press, 2005.

———. *Party Wars: Polarization and the Politics of National Policy Making*. Norman, OK: University of Oklahoma Press, 2006.

———. "Transformational Leader or Faithful Agent? Principal-Agent Theory and House Majority Party Leadership." *Legislative Studies Quarterly* 24, no. 3 (1999): 421–449.

———. *Unorthodox Lawmaking: New Legislative Processes in the US Congress*. 2d ed., Washington, DC: CQ Press, 2000.

———. *Unorthodox Lawmaking: New Legislative Processes in the US Congress*. Washington, DC: Congressional Quarterly Press, 1997.

Skidelsky, Robert. *John Maynard Keynes: Fighting for Freedom 1937–1946*. 3 vols. Vol. 3. New York: Viking, 2000.

———. *John Maynard Keynes: The Economist as Saviour 1920–1937*. 3 vols. Vol. 2. New York: The Penguin Press, 1986.

Skidmore, David. "Who Is at the Helm? The Debate Over US Funding for the United Nations." *Institute for the Study of Diplomacy Case Studies Case* 227 (2000).

Smith, Fred L., Jr. "The Politics of IMF Lending." *Cato Journal* 4, no. 1 (1984): 211–247.

Smith, Richard A. "Interest Group Influence in the US Congress." *Legislative Studies Quarterly* 20 (1995): 89–139.

Smith, Steven S. "Parties and Leadership in the Senate." In *The Legislative Branch*, edited by Paul J. Quirk and Sarah A. Binder, 255–278. New York: Oxford University Press, 2005.

Soederberg, Susanne. "Recasting Neoliberal Dominance in the Global South? A Critique of the Monterrey Consensus." *Alternatives* 30 (2005): 325–364.

Stewart, Terence, ed. *The GATT Uruguay Round: A Negotiating History (1986–1992)*. Boston: Kluwer Law & Taxation Publications, 1993.

Stid, Daniel D. *The President as Statesman: Woodrow Wilson and the Constitution*. Lawrence, Kansas: University Press of Kansas, 1998.

Stiglitz, Joseph E. *Globalization and Its Discontents*. New York: W.W. Norton, 2002.

Strange, Susan. "The Persistent Myth of Lost Hegemony." *International Organization* 41, no. 4 (1987): 551–574.

———. "Towards a Theory of Transnational Empire, 1989." In *Authority and Markets: Susan Strange's Writings on International Political Economy*, edited by Roger Tooze and Christopher May, 141–156. New York: Palgrave MacMillan, 2002.

Summers, Lawrence H. "The Right Kind of IMF for a Stable Global Financial System." London, England: London School of Business, 1999.

Tarrow, Sydney. *The New Transnational Activism*. New York: Cambridge University Press, 2005.

Taylor, John B. *Global Financial Warriors: The Untold Story of International Finance in the Post-9/11 World*. New York: W.W. Norton & Co., 2007.

Tocqueville, Alexis de. *Democracy in America*. Translated by G. Lawrence. Edited by J. P. Mayer and M. Lerner. New York: Harper, 1966.

Toye, John, and Richard Toye. *The UN and Global Political Economy*. Indianapolis: Indiana University Press, 2004.

Truman, David B. *The Governmental Process: Political Interests and Public Opinion*. New York: Knopf, 1951.

———. *The Governmental Process: Political Interests and Public Opinion*. New York: Alfred A. Knopf, 1968.

United Nations. "Financing for Development: Building on Monterrey." Paper presented at the International Conference on Financing for Development, Monterrey, Mexico, 2002.

van Putten, Maartje. *Policing the Banks: Accountability Mechanisms for the Financial Sector*. Ithaca, NY: McGill-Queens University Press, 2008.

———. "'Policing the World': Accountability Mechanisms for Multilateral Financial Institutions and Private Financial Institutions." Ph.D., McGill University, June 2006.

Vaubel, Roland "The Moral Hazard of IMF Lending." In *International Lending and the IMF*, edited by Allan H. Meltzer, 65–79. Washington, DC: The Heritage Foundation, 1983.

Wade, Robert. "Wheels within Wheels: Rethinking the Asian Crisis and the Asian Model." *Annual Review of Political Science* 3, no. 1 (2000): 85–116.

Weaver, Catherine. *Hypocrisy Trap: The World Bank and the Poverty of Reform*. Princeton, NJ: Princeton University Press, 2008.

Weiss, Martin A. "The Global Financial Crisis: The Role of the International Monetary Fund (IMF)." Washington, DC: Congressional Research Service, 2009.

———. "The World Bank's International Development Association (IDA)." Washington, DC: Congressional Research Service, 2007.

Wendt, Alexander. *Social Theory of International Politics*. Cambridge: Cambridge University Press, 1999.

Wessel, David. *In Fed We Trust: Ben Bernanke's War on the Great Panic*. New York: Crown Business, 2009.

White, Joseph. "Making Connections to the Appropriations Process." In *The Interest Group Connection: Electioneering, Lobbying, and Policymaking in Washington*, edited by Paul S. Herrnson, Ronald G. Shaiko, and Clyde Wilcox, 164–188. Washington, DC: CQ Press, 2005.

Wilson, John Donald. *The Chase: The Chase Manhattan Bank, N.A., 1945–1985*. Boston, Massachusetts: Harvard Business School Press, 1986.

Wilson, Woodrow. *Congressional Government: A Study in American Politics*. 7th ed. Boston: Houghton, Mifflin and Company, 1890.

Wolfensberger, Don "The Founders and Foreign Policy: An Introductory Essay." An Essay for the Congress Project Seminar on Congress' Role in Foreign Policymaking. Washington, DC: Woodrow Wilson International Center for Scholars, 2009.

Wolfensberger, Donald R. *Congress and the People: Deliberative Democracy on Trial*. Washington, DC, and Baltimore, Maryland: Woodrow Wilson Center Press and Johns Hopkins University Press, 1999.

Wolff, Alan William. "International Competitiveness of American Industry: The Role of US Trade Policy." In *US Competitiveness in the World Economy*, edited by Bruce R. Scott and George C. Lodge. Boston: Harvard Business School Press, 1985.

Woods, Ngaire. *The Globalizers: The IMF, World Bank, and Their Borrowers*. Ithaca, New York: Cornell University Press, 2006.

Woods, Randall Bennett. *A Changing of the Guard: Anglo-American Relations 1941–1946*. Chapel Hill: University of North Carolina Press, 1990.

Zetterbaum, Marvin. "Alexis de Tocqueville." In *History of Political Philosophy*, edited by Leo Strauss and Joseph Cropsey, 715–736. Chicago: University of Chicago Press, 1972.

Zysman, John. "The French State in the International Economy." In *Between Power and Plenty: Foreign Economic Policies of Advanced Industrial States*, edited by Peter J. Katzenstein, 255–293. Madison, Wisconsin: University of Wisconsin Press, 1978.

# INDEX

www.ingramcontent.com/pod-product-compliance
Ingram Content Group UK Ltd.
Pitfield, Milton Keynes, MK11 3LW, UK
UKHW020901190926
475595UK00036B/59